The Indispensable Writer's Guide

The Indispensable Writer's Guide

How to successfully build your writing career for maximum financial reward and satisfaction

SCOTT EDELSTEIN

PERENNIAL LIBRARY

Harper & Row, Publishers, New York
Cambridge, Philadelphia, San Francisco, London
Mexico City, São Paulo, Singapore, Sydney

Library of Congress Cataloging-in-Publication Data

Edelstein, Scott.
    The indispensable writer's guide.

    Includes bibliographies and index.
    1. Authorship.   I. Title.
PN147.E25   1989   808'.02   88-45555
ISBN 0-06-055161-5   89 90 91 92 93 CC/FG 10 9 8 7 6 5 4 3 2 1
ISBN 0-06-096137-6 (pbk.) 89 90 91 92 93 CC/FG 10 9 8 7 6 5 4 3 2 1

Contents

3. THE CARE AND FEEDING OF EDITORS 120

4. LIVING WITH REJECTION 161

Acknowledgments

Chapter 13, Taxes for Writers, appeared in somewhat different form in the January 1985 issue of *Writer's Digest,* under the titles "A Writer's Guide to Income Taxes," "Under Special Circumstances," and "Pay As You Go."

"Shelter" by John Edward Sorrell originally appeared, in somewhat different form, in *Sotheby's International Poetry Anthology,* and is Copyright 1984 by the Arvon Foundation. Reprinted by permission of the poet.

The sample contracts and letters of agreement published in Chapter 10 are reprinted by permission of Davis Publications, Inc.; F&W Publications, Inc.; Terry Carr; Jack and Jeanne Van Buren Dann; and Mary Kuhfeld.

The sample letters to agents in Chapter 8 are reprinted by permission of Mary Kuhfeld; and Louis Hatchett, Jr., Frances Gafford, and Rickie Gafford.

The sample collaboration agreement in Chapter 1 appears here by permission of Mary Ellen McGlone and Gloria Gilbert Mayer.

The sample agent-author agreement in Chapter 8 appears by permission of Bobbe Siegel.

The sample royalty statements in Chapter 9 appear by permission of Eunice McClurg and F&W Publications, Inc.

Introduction: Why You Need This Book

The Indispensable Writer's Guide is the one book every writer needs. It is the definitive book for people who want to earn money from writing, or who want to be either part-time or full-time professional writers. If you are a writer, no matter how experienced or inexperienced you may be, this book can help you.

First and foremost, this book is full of inside information, previously well-kept secrets, and other little-known tricks, tips, and shortcuts that can help you achieve more success as a writer with less time, effort, and error. Much of this information will be new to you, and some of it is completely unavailable elsewhere.

If you are already an established professional with a solid record of publications behind you, this book will teach you some important things that you didn't know before, some of which may surprise you, and many of which should help your career.

And if you are a new writer, or are thinking of becoming a writer, this book will give you a clear, accurate, and thorough picture of what the worlds of freelance and professional writing are really like. *The Indispensable Writer's Guide* will separate the facts from the myths, the information from the misinformation, and the romantic dreams from the realities. It will teach you just about everything you will need to know about the business end of writing, from researching markets to dealing with editors to negotiating contracts to finding freelance and salaried writing jobs.

Whole sections of *The Indispensable Writer's Guide* are devoted to subjects rarely or never before discussed in print, or in writing classes and conferences. Chapter 5 explains in detail how to make contact with editors, agents, and other important people in the publishing business, and how to use those contacts to best benefit your writing career. Chapter 7 provides a step-by-step procedure for building a career as a writer. Chapter 13 is a complete guide to writers' taxes, and it will show you how to reduce your federal income taxes, *even if you have made no income from writing in the past year.* This chapter alone could save you several times the price of this book on your taxes each year.

But this book isn't only for freelancers and potential freelancers. Chapter 6 looks closely at most of the job and career options open to writers, of which there are a great many more than people think. This chapter covers salaried and freelance positions, part-time and full-time jobs, and how to sell your services to others. It will help you examine all the options and decide which ones are best for you. Finally, it will provide tips to help you land—or if need be create—the writing job that best suits you.

In the remaining chapters you will find information on such rarely discussed subjects as finding collaborators; securing endorsements; ghostwriting; college and university writing programs; living with rejection; and how to create a writer's resumé that is as convincing and effective as possible.

In addition to all this, *The Indispensable Writer's Guide* is full of tips that will save you months and even years of frustration, failure, and trial and error. For example, it will show you why query letters are often useless, and sometimes worse than useless. It will tell you how to spot the writing "contests" that are little more than scams. It will show you why certain widely touted writers' resources are not all they're cracked up to be. It will inform you of some little-known but very useful resources for writers. And it will teach you the one and only tried-and-true way to get an editor's attention.

This book developed slowly over the past several years, partly as a result of my own experience, partly from a university course in freelance and professional writing that I have taught since 1979. I found, over and over, that much of the important and even crucial information that writers needed simply wasn't available, either through classes on writing and publishing or in books on the subject. I found, also, that some of the information being widely disseminated to writers in some of these books and classes was misleading, inaccurate, or downright false. In fact, I learned that some editors *deliberately* provide false information to newer writers, to keep them separate from the writers those editors know and desire to deal with. This book will make you aware of much of this misinformation, and where it appears.

Chances are good that you want to know who I am and what my credentials are. I've been a professional writer since 1972 and have published over eighty articles and short stories in magazines, book anthologies, and newspapers in the United States and around the world. I've worked as a book, magazine, and newspaper editor, and my freelance editing has included everything from technical articles to advertising copy to political speeches to horror novels. I've been a literary agent, a magazine and newspaper staff writer, a writing consultant, and a ghostwriter. I've published four books besides this one: a book on freshman composition, a streetwise guide for college students, a practical guide for those students' parents, and a science fiction anthology. I've received a writing fellowship and chaired a committee that administers several grants and awards programs for writers. And I've taught writing (creative writing, freelance and professional writing, business and technical writing, and freshman composition) at seven colleges and universities.

This book will be updated every two to three years. If you have any suggestions for additions, emendations, or other improvements in the next edition, I would like to hear from you by mail. Write to me in care of Harper & Row, 10 E. 53rd Street, New York, NY 10022. Any changes that I feel are appropriate will be made in the second edition, and I will gratefully acknowledge by name all the writers who made useful suggestions. I'm also interested in your comments, pro and con.

It is my hope that you'll find *The Indispensable Writer's Guide* to be an invaluable aid to your writing career, and to your future success.

1. ✎

Your Career as a Writer

FREELANCE WRITING VS. SALARIED JOBS

A great many people want to write for a living, or at least think they do. But beyond this, many have only vague or half-formed goals. Some people aren't particularly attracted by the actual process of writing. They just like the thought of getting published, of getting their names in print.

Other people are attracted by the fame, glory, or wealth associated with writing. I don't blame them. I wouldn't mind being rich and famous myself. But the unfortunate truth is that the vast majority of writers aren't rich (many are downright poor), and even fewer are famous. And most writers, no matter how good they are and no matter how hard they work, earn little or no glamor or glory.

When people think about becoming writers, they are usually thinking about becoming *freelance* writers. A freelancer is someone who runs a one-person writing business and sells his or her work—or services as a writer—to other people and organizations.

Freelance writing needs no specific credentials, no particular educational background, and no expensive equipment beyond a typewriter or computer—and these can be rented or borrowed. You can write pretty much anywhere you wish, and you can choose your own goals, subject matter, and hours. Freelancing offers a minimum of supervision and a maximum of freedom. For the most part, you are your own boss.

However, freelance writing offers a minimum of financial security. Unless you have established a regular relationship with an editor, have received a large sum of money up front for a project, or have savings or outside income, you are likely to be frequently concerned about where the next month's rent is going to come from. Every time you send a piece out to an editor, even if it has been officially assigned and contracted for, you have to sweat out whether or not it will be acceptable, and, if so, whether or not the publication will pay you promptly.

Freelancing requires a lot of self-discipline and motivation. You have to be able to sit alone in front of a typewriter, computer keyboard, pad of paper, or tape recorder; to continue working long enough to produce a reasonable body of work; and to persevere at writing and submitting your work even in the face of continued rejection.

Although there are over a hundred thousand people in the United

FREELANCE WRITING

Reward	Likelihood of Being Provided		
	Low	Moderate	High
Easy work		•	
Wealth	•		
Financial security	•		
Glamor	•		
Fame	•		
Control over what you write			•
Steady work	•		
Freedom and independence			•
Self-direction			•
Flexibility of hours			•
Increased personal and sex appeal	•		
Chances for ego gratification		•	
Predictability	•		
Personal contact with others	•		
Paid vacations	•		
Insurance and other perks	•		
Joy of writing			•

SALARIED WRITING JOBS

Reward	Likelihood of Being Provided		
	Low	Moderate	High
Easy work		•	
Wealth	•		
Financial security			•
Glamor	•		
Fame	•		
Control over what you write	•		
Steady work			•
Freedom and independence	•		
Self-direction	•		
Flexibility of hours	•		
Increased personal and sex appeal	•		
Chances for ego gratification		•	
Predictability		•	
Personal contact with others		•	
Paid vacations			•
Insurance and other perks			•
Joy of writing		•	

States who earn their livings at writing, editing, and other writing-related jobs, less than a couple of thousand are full-time freelancers who support themselves entirely through their writing. Most freelancers work at salaried part- or full-time jobs, either in the writing and publishing field or outside of it, earning only a portion of their income from freelance writing.

If you are seriously thinking about being a writer, freelance or otherwise, it is wise to confront beforehand exactly what rewards and drawbacks the profession offers.

The charts here can be helpful.

Both charts are based on generalities, and there are of course exceptions.

Many writers find that some combination of freelance writing and a salaried job in a writing-related field provides the best balance of rewards.

THE BOTTOM LINE AND WHAT IT MEANS TO YOU AS A WRITER

Here is the single most important fact about the publishing industry: *the primary goal of most publishers is to make money.*

Any comprehensive look at the publishing industry and how it operates must return to this central concept again and again, because this is the concept to which people in the industry turn repeatedly to make their decisions. In deciding whether to publish a book, produce a film, change the slant of a magazine, promote an editor to senior editor, or begin a massive advertising campaign, the basic issue is almost always, *will doing this help us make money?* I call this the *bottom-line principle.*

As people in the publishing industry are quick to point out, making money is not the *only* reason publishing goes on. There are some people involved in publishing who genuinely love the field. And there are some who see publishing as an important part not only of our economy, but of our whole culture.

But none of this changes the basic fact that publishing is, first and foremost, a *business.* In order to survive, it must turn a profit, or at least break even. This principle applies equally to publishers of books, magazines, newspapers, and newsletters, and to organizations that produce plays, films, and radio and television programs.

Because of the bottom-line principle, many worthwhile projects never get published or produced, because they are not obvious money-makers. At the same time, because many writers are paid according to how well their writing sells, publishing does offer a very small minority of writers great financial rewards.

The bottom-line principle, however, is by no means universal. Many literary magazines and literary book publishers regularly lose money and often depend on grant support for their survival; neighborhood newspapers and special-interest newsletters are as often as not guided primarily by a spirit of public service; and many ventures are undertaken primarily as hobbies or pastimes. Even organizations that normally embrace the profit motive will sometimes publish or produce projects that they feel are worthy but on which they expect to take a loss. This is quite rare, however, and you are very unlikely to have this happen with your own work.

Some apparent exceptions to the bottom-line principle are in fact not exceptions at all. For example, the editor of a magazine published by a nonprofit organization might be very concerned with the sale of both advertising space and copies of the magazine. *Nonprofit,* after all, doesn't mean "not competitive in the marketplace." Although that magazine might not be a profit-making operation, it may still be required to return its costs to its publisher if it is to survive.

Literary magazines and presses are an unusual case. On the one hand, the vast majority of these are never expected to turn a profit or to have large consumer sales. On the other hand, their directors are often *very* concerned with taking in money—money awarded in the form of grants. Their decisions may be just as oriented toward the bottom line as those of commercial publishers—but the basic question may be, "Will this help us get grant money?" rather than "Will this increase sales?" or "Will this increase advertising revenue?"

Many literary magazines and presses, and many scholarly journals, are concerned with generating not as much money as possible, but as much *prestige* and recognition as possible. In such cases, decisions may often be based in part on the answer to the question, "Will this help us earn awards or prestige?"

The importance of the bottom-line principle to publishing does not mean that the publishing industry as a whole lacks integrity. Most publishers quite willingly obey the law, and most can be trusted to honor any written agreement they enter into. However, it is also true that most publishers, when given the choice between a project that will benefit society but lose money and one that will help no one but be sure to earn a nice profit, will publish only the second project.

What does the bottom-line principle mean to you as a writer? First and foremost, it means that most publishers will be interested in your work *precisely to the degree to which they believe it will help them make money.*

An important distinction must be made here. Your prospects for success as a writer are related less to how much money your work will *actually* help publishers make than they are to how much money publishers *believe* your work will help them make. Even if you have written something that the American public will clamor to buy and read, unless editors *believe* that this will happen, they aren't likely to publish it.

Your work will be evaluated by editors on many different bases—quality of writing, subject matter, style, appropriateness for the publication's audience, and so on. But the *primary* question in an editor's mind—the question on which, for the most part, the decision to accept or reject your work hangs—will be, "Will it help us make money?"

But it is not simply a matter of acceptance or rejection. The more money publishers believe you will help them make, the better they will treat you. Publishers who feel you can make them millions may wine you, dine you, send you on vacations, provide you with a chauffeured limousine, and treat you with great courtesy and respect. (I'm not exaggerating, by the way; publishers have provided all of these items as perks; some of these fringe benefits have even been written into publishing contracts.) Publishers who feel you can help them turn a tidy profit will in most cases treat you courteously and respectfully, though you probably won't receive any special privileges beyond an occasional business lunch. Publishers who feel you cannot help them make money will reject your work—usually quickly and somewhat impersonally.

The reactions of editors and other publishing people to you and your work may change over time. At first, your work will probably receive minimal respect and attention. After you have sold a couple of pieces to an editor, however, he or she will begin giving you a bit more attention, and may become a little friendlier. And if your work becomes a proven money-maker, you might have solicitous publishing people pushing each other out of the way for the privilege of treating you royally and offering you lucrative deals.

MISCONCEPTIONS ABOUT EDITORS

Many of the popular views about editors and publishers, especially those held by new and aspiring writers, are only partly correct, or even outright untrue.

Perhaps the most common misconceptions are that editors wield the most power in publishing firms, and that they have the ultimate decision-making authority. Neither of these is normally true. The person who functions as publisher (or, in the case of TV, film, plays, and radio, the person with the title of producer) is normally the one who makes the biggest and most important decisions, and often many of the minor ones as well. Often the publisher oversees and must approve the decisions of the editor. It is not unusual for an editor to want to publish a particular piece, only to have his or her judgment overruled by the publisher.

In some publishing organizations, the editor and publisher are the same person. In such cases, but normally *only* in such cases, the editor does in fact have final authority.

At large newspapers and national magazines, the publisher tends to make general decisions regarding the publication's finances, slant, and approach, and most of the decision-making power on more specific editorial matters is delegated to the editor-in-chief, who in turn has authority over subeditors. At magazines, these often include article editors, fiction editors, humor editors, managing editors, associate editors, and so on. In the case of newspapers, these may include news editors, feature editors, sports editors, lifestyle editors, and the like. The job titles are different, but the situation for you as a writer is similar: you will be dealing directly with subeditors, who in turn answer to their editors-in-chief—who then must answer to their publishers. The subeditor with whom you work will have some independent authority in selecting material, but on occasion he or she may be overruled by the editor-in-chief. In the case of the largest magazines and newspapers, you may even deal with a sub-subeditor, such as an assistant articles editor or an associate lifestyles editor, who answers to the appropriate subeditor.

In book publishing, the editor is only one cog in the much larger publishing machine. In all but the smallest firms, the editor simply does not have the authority to accept a manuscript for publication. Instead, he or she must meet with the publisher, the subsidiary rights department, the sales department, the promotion department, and often other editors to discuss the book's potential. The editor normally needs approval from all these departments and people before he or she can say to the author or agent, "I'd like to make a deal."

This very book was rejected by one major book publishing firm even though an editor at the firm liked it very much and wanted to publish it. But the sales department expressed doubts about its ability to sell the book, and so it was rejected, over the editor's objections.

Another common misconception is that most editors actively seek and are interested in reading (and publishing) unsolicited freelance material. This is true of some editors; but the majority prefer working with staff writers and/or freelancers with whom they have worked before, or whose work they are familiar with. The reasons for this are pretty obvious: an editor who reads a manuscript from a staff writer or regular contributor knows that the piece is likely to be usable. But an editor who reads an unsolicited manuscript sent in by an unknown writer knows that the chances of that manuscript being usable are less than 10 percent and, in the case of larger publications, less than 1 percent.

This explains in part why breaking into a publication, and breaking into print in general, are so difficult. Not only are the odds against you, but the very expectations of most editors toward unsolicited material are low. Simply because your material comes in unsolicited, editors—consciously or unconsciously—expect that it will probably not be usable. Your work must be good enough to overcome these expectations.

Newer writers also often have the mistaken view that editors and publishers seek the best material they can get their hands on. Of course this is true, but writers often equate "best" with "best-written," whereas for editors "best" almost always means "most closely conforming to our publication's specifications."

Most publications have a set of written or unwritten specifications for material. These specifications can include length, approach, tone, intended audience, subject matter, style, focus, quality of writing, or any of dozens of other items. In some cases, such as Harlequin romances, the specifications are quite rigid. In others, such as *The New Yorker*, they are less rigid and clearcut. Usually the specifications are based quite consciously on the publication's intended audience, and on the habits, interests, and desires of that audience.

Speaking generally, an editor is less concerned with finding great writing than with finding material that fits the publication's "specs." Manuscripts that do not fit those specifications closely will either be rewritten to fit them or, much more likely, rejected outright. The same manuscript, then, might be rejected by one publication with a form rejection slip, then purchased by another—even another publication in the same field.

It is quite common for editors to confuse a piece's quality with the degree to which it fits their publications' specifications. For example, an editor may reject a piece with a note that says, "This piece is much too long for its own good, and its attention to detail is rather wearisome." What the editor may actually mean, but be unwilling or unable to articulate, is, "Your piece is directed at a more intelligent audience than our publication is."

Some writers believe, usually mistakenly, that editors often (and willingly) serve as guides, critics, teachers, and nurturers of talent—or at least that editors *should* assume these roles. In truth, the vast majority of editors provide little or no guidance, criticism, or instruction to writers. Most editors view you as a producer of a commodity; your job is to supply them with usable words. Their concern in most cases is with those words, not with you as a person or a writer. Thus, editors will generally deal with you in a businesslike, slightly formal manner. Friendly chatter is not normally offered, expected, or tolerated. If your work is accepted, you will probably get a short letter saying something like "Dear Linda: Thanks for sending this. We'd like to use it in our March issue and can offer you $300 for it. If this is okay with you, please sign the enclosed form and return it to us. If you have anything else for us, I'd be happy to look at it."

Or, you'll get a specific request for a rewrite, a short rejection letter that says little or nothing, or a form rejection letter. Rarely will you get much of a critique, and even more rarely will you get guidance for your career as a writer. Most editors consider such guidance and criticism to be outside the realm of their responsibilities.

There are two exceptions to this, however—one general and one specific.

First, some editors, if they see something they like in your work, will give you guidance, suggestions, or informal training in *how to write for their particular publications*—that is, how to write material that fits their particular specifications. Sometimes this will be done under the deliberate or inadvertent guise of how to be a better writer in general. Editors who do this obviously feel that you are good enough to write for their publications with a little training. You should take these comments as compliments, whether or not you choose to follow them.

The second exception occurs mainly in book publishing. Some book editors will work with authors to help them think through a project, improve the quality of that particular project, or guide their writing career in general. These editors are gems. As book publishing becomes more corporate, fast-paced, and harshly competitive, this breed of editors is dying out. But there are still some out there, and if you can get one, you are a lucky writer indeed. There are even a very few such editors left in magazine publishing.

There is one other common misconception about not only editors but publishing in general. This is that publishing is a "gentlemen's" (and gentlewomen's) profession, in which everything is done slowly, calmly, carefully, discreetly, with great dignity and attention to detail, and with extreme respect (and even awe) for writers. Quiet, wood-paneled, thick-carpeted offices often come to mind. As partners in the noble effort of publishing, everyone is treated and paid well, but since publishing is above money-grubbing, the topic of money is rarely, if ever, discussed.

It is enough to say here that this view is about 98 percent false. Forty years ago it was only 90 percent false, and some people therefore long for the "good old days." However, this view was never substantially accurate.

YOUR PROSPECTS FOR SUCCESS AS A WRITER

A great many people make their livings—often good livings—as full-time writers. The vast majority of these people are salaried employees working as business and technical writers, advertising writers, publicity and public relations people, journalists, and staff writers for magazines, newsletters, businesses, government, and other organizations.

There are also a great many writers who have full-time, decently paying jobs as editors, writing teachers, and other writing-related professionals. These jobs, while not always easy to get, are normally within reach of intelligent people with good writing skills.

If you simply like to write, or can write well without much effort, and are not terribly concerned about *what* you write or who you work for, then your best bet for a writing career is to shoot for one of these jobs.

If, however, you know exactly what you want to write, or you feel strongly that you want to be your own boss, you will have a much tougher row to hoe. Very few people make their complete livings—even poor livings—as freelance writers. The vast majority of those who do, write primarily or entirely nonfiction. Many of these people used to be full-time journalists, staff writers, or editors and so are able to draw on past contacts in the publishing industry. Many have an ongoing relationship with one or more publications, to which they contribute on a regular basis.

Those freelancers who write primarily or entirely scripts, fiction, or poetry face far more dismal odds for making their entire livings from writing. There are probably no more than five hundred people in the United States who make most or all of their money writing for TV and the movies, and perhaps three hundred who make their livings writing novels. And if you were to add up the numbers of all the poets, playwrights, and short-story writers in the United States who make their livings entirely from their writing, your total would be under one hundred.

Your chances for success as a freelance writer are based on two major factors: the rates of payment and your likelihood of breaking into each particular field. The phrase "breaking in" is quite appropriate, for most publications, genres, and fields of publishing are in-groups that are somewhat to extremely closed to newcomers.

Remember, though, that while it is quite difficult to make all of your living as a freelance writer (especially if you have people other than yourself to support), it is not at all difficult to earn *some* regular income through freelancing, particularly if you have been working at building your career for a few years.

The following chart should prove useful for writers who are contemplating becoming full- or part-time freelancers. (This chart refers to freelance writing only. Salaried writing and editing jobs in some of these areas are often much easier to come by.) The ratings in the chart are generalities. There are and always will be some exceptions to each category.

More than most other fields, freelance writing involves slowly working your way up—writing regularly, submitting your work, researching markets, and making useful contacts. Success—on any scale—as a freelance writer depends on determination, flexibility, patience, and of course writing ability. Let me discuss the first three of these categories in more detail.

Determination

If you are looking for a salaried job, your income is zero until you land that job, at which point you suddenly begin to receive a regular, dependable salary. Freelance income—unless you suddenly sell a book, or a movie or TV script—is likely to rise much more slowly and gradually. The first year or two are usually very hard for freelancers. During this time in your career, you may earn nothing but a stack of rejection slips. You need to be able to keep going in the face of rejection if you are to succeed. After a certain point—usually two to three years—things begin to move much faster.

Flexibility

The more flexible you can be in terms of style, subject matter, and the areas of publishing you are willing to deal with, the more chances for success you create for yourself. If you only want to write mystery novels, that's fine; but this means that those mystery novels will make or break you as a writer. If you can write some articles for your local arts magazine, some short suspense stories for national magazines, some book reviews for your local paper, *and* mystery novels, then your chances of at least some success are much greater. Note that all of these pieces could be mystery-oriented if you wished. If you were to branch out further and also write

Market	Your Chance of Breaking In	Usual Rates of Payment
Television	Very poor to poor	High to very high
Film	Very poor to poor	High to very high
Professional theater	Very poor to poor	Moderate to high
Local, little, and community theater	Fair	None to very low
Radio	Very poor to poor	Very low to low
Major newspapers	Poor to fair	Low to moderate
Smaller newspapers	Fair to good	None to low
Newspaper syndicates	Poor	Low to high[1]
Major magazines[2]	Very poor to poor	Moderate to high
Smaller magazines	Fair to good	None to moderate
Literary magazines	Too erratic to determine	None to low
Books: 150 major trade publishers		
Nonfiction: how-to	Fair	Moderate
Nonfiction: other	Poor to fair	Moderate
Novels: general	Poor	Moderate

Genre novels:		
Science fiction/fantasy	Fair	Low to moderate
Mystery	Fair	Low to moderate
Romance	Fair	Moderate
Western	Fair	Low to moderate
Horror	Poor	Low to moderate
Male adventure	Fair	Low to moderate
Children's/young adult	Fair	Low to moderate
Poetry and short-story collections	Very poor	Very low to low
Books: smaller trade publishers, literary publishers, scholarly publishers[3]		
Nonfiction	Fair to good	Very low to low
Novels	Poor	Very low
Children's/young adult	Fair	Very low to low
Poetry and short-story collections	Poor to fair	None to very low
Books: text and professional publishers		
Nonfiction	Fair to good	Very low to high[4]

[1]Based on number of syndications.
[2]*McCall's, Harper's, Ms., Ladies' Home Journal, Penthouse,* etc.
[3]Scholarly publishers do not normally publish novels or books for children.
[4]Varies widely based on sales.

a proposal for a book on the history of smoking, an article on vacuum-cleaner repair, and a romance novel, your chances of success would be greater still.

But your options don't stop here by any means. You could also market your skills as a freelance editor to local people and publishing companies; you could try doing some part-time advertising or public relations writing; and you could arrange public readings of your work. The list goes on and on, and the more widely you make yourself available, the more chances you have that something will click.

Once some things *do* click, then you can begin *slowly* narrowing your focus down to those areas that have proven most successful for you, eliminating those that appear, after some time, to be dead ends.

You never know what a project might lead to, so think twice before turning something down. A book on vegetable growing could lead to a series of magazine articles on homesteading, which could in turn lead to a novel about a small West Virginia farming town. If you had wanted to be a novelist in the first place, you may have saved yourself ten years of professional struggle by writing that first book on cabbages and cucumbers. Plus, you will have earned yourself some money and the beginnings of a reputation in the process.

Flexibility can also mean working a full- or part-time job, either writing-related or otherwise, and then *slowly* moving out of that job and into full-time freelancing as your freelance income increases.

Patience

The main reason so few people become full-time freelancers is lack of patience. Speaking very generally, it takes one to two years for a new writer to sell his or her first piece (or first few pieces) to a national publication. And even if you write well, try to keep flexible, and work hard and steadily at building a freelance career, it will still probably take you at least six to eight years to reach the point where you are a full-time self-supporting freelancer.

Patience also means learning the art of delayed gratification and response. Once you have put a piece in the mail, you have to wait for the editor's reply. If the editor buys it, you then must wait for a contract, then for a check, then for the piece to be published, then for the reviews or comments to come in. If you have an agent, one more step in the waiting process is added. If you have written a book or a TV or movie script, there is also the waiting for royalties or residuals.

You occasionally read about writers like John Jakes, who supposedly became rich and famous overnight. What you don't hear about quite as often is how long and hard those writers worked at writing, and at career-building, before their "overnight" success. Jakes himself wrote for decades before he had a single best-seller, or anything close to one.

It is a curious fact about the publishing world that success, when it does come, often comes years after all the hardest work is over. Even if you sit down today, write a book, sell it quickly, and eventually become rich and famous from it, you must still wait *one to three years* from the time you finish the manuscript to the time you receive your first royalty check.

EGO GRATIFICATION

For many writers, the psychological rewards of writing and publishing are as important, or nearly as important, as the money they earn. However, new writers should be aware of exactly what ego strokes they are genuinely likely to receive and which ones are no more than improbable dreams.

One of the biggest rewards is seeing your work and your name in print. This is the one psychological reward that virtually every published writer is guaranteed.

Do not expect much in the way of editorial praise, however, as it is given out rarely and sparingly in most cases, even to excellent writers, and even by editors who love what they have read. There are two reasons for this. First, as I explained earlier, editors are likely to view you more as a supplier of goods and services than as a human being. Editorial responses grow out of this attitude, and therefore comments such as "We want to buy it," "I like it," "It looks fine and we'll try to fit it into our June issue" are much more common than "I loved it" or "It's one of the most insightful pieces on this subject that I've read."

There's another, more significant reason why editorial praise is likely to be restrained: editors want to be able to acquire your writing for as little money as possible. The more praise they give you or your work, the more they will appear to value it—and the more money you will therefore tend to expect for it.

Reviews are of course a source of ego gratification if they are favorable, but they can just as easily be sources of pain. Reviews are not necessarily accurate, fair, or reasonable. Virtually no book, movie, TV program, or other publication or production gets unanimously favorable reviews—though a few have gotten unanimously unfavorable ones.

Contrary to popular belief, few writers get many fan letters, and most get none at all. Those who get lots of them are most often the writers of best-selling books. Most readers pay little attention to who wrote what. There are some exceptions, though. If you are writing for a specific audience—readers of espionage thrillers, for example, or science fiction, poetry, literary short stories, or books of history—then you may gain a following among regular readers of that particular subject or genre. It is also possible to gain a following among theater-goers if you have written two or more good Broadway plays. Writers of television and film scripts, no matter how successful they may be, are the *least* likely of all writers to have fans, because virtually nobody notices who writes them.

Other psychological rewards from writing may include doing local or national talk shows, book signings, lectures, readings, and other presentations. The first two of these are normally reserved for writers who have recently published a book.

RULES AND STANDARDS

Every profession has its own basic rules and guidelines. Normally all members of that profession are expected to abide by them. The rules are established by consensus and are more or less arbitrary. All of this also holds true for the publishing industry.

Here are the most basic rules that editors and publishers will expect you to follow as a writer:

1. Submit manuscripts following proper manuscript form (see below).
2. Accompany submissions with proper cover letters (see pages 101–8)
3. Type all correspondence neatly, following an accepted business format.
4. Use standard American written English, except where something else is clearly called for. (Quotations and the use of dialect are common exceptions to this rule. This rule is also often broken for good cause in poetry.) You need not follow any particular set of style guidelines (such as University of Chicago or Modern Language Association) unless a publication or an editor specifically asks you to. Those very few publications that do set strict policies for format or style are almost all scholarly journals. These journals publish clear format and style guidelines at the front of each issue.
5. Do not plagiarize in any way or on any scale.
6. Never make up data or information. Don't lie or twist the truth in anything intended to be truthful or accurate.

7. Appropriately cite and credit all sources of information and all quotes. Writers whose words or ideas you have borrowed or referred to should be acknowledged. If you use the words, photographs, drawings, charts, or graphs of others, you are normally responsible for securing permission and for providing proper copyright information.

8. Never fake or lie about your credentials. However, creative truth-telling, such as saying you've been published in *Reader's Digest* because you sold that magazine a 100-word piece for its "Humor in Uniform" column, is okay, so long as you don't overdo it.

9. Never promise anything you can't deliver.

10. Be civil and businesslike with editors and publishers at all times—in person, on the phone, and in letters—unless the situation clearly warrants otherwise. Generally, you should avoid discussing nonbusiness subjects with your editor or publisher unless you have been given a clear go-ahead to do so. You should remain civil even when you are angry and/or feel you have been wronged. Definitely assert your rights, however.

11. If you do not like the terms that are offered, do not agree to them. You may either refuse them or attempt to negotiate different terms. Accepting terms and then trying to negotiate or argue about them later is extremely bad form.

12. Abide by all the terms you accept and any agreement you sign—unless the other party has already broken that agreement. If you do not intend to comply with an agreement, do not make or sign it.

13. Never threaten a lawsuit except as a next-to-last resort. Actually filing suit is, of course, the final resort.

Editors and publishers, for better or worse, are not so strictly bound by most of the above rules and guidelines, so you should not expect them to follow them all to the letter. However, you should hold them strictly to items 5 through 9 and item 12. Furthermore, you should expect editors and publishers to treat you honestly and fairly at all times, just as you treat them.

ARE PUBLISHERS HONEST?

As far as print publishers go, you can assume that you are being dealt with fairly unless you have some specific reason to believe otherwise. Publishers will normally abide by any contracts they sign and any terms they agree to in writing. Verbal agreements should be taken less seriously, however;

and as a general rule, it is an excellent idea to examine royalty statements very closely and carefully.

From what I know from my colleagues in television and film, *most* of the people in those industries are honest; but as a whole you should be *considerably* more cautious in dealing with them than with print publishers.

There are exceptions to all this, of course. Every industry has some crooks, and you shouldn't be surprised if you run into a few in the course of your career.

ARE MOST PUBLISHERS COMPETENT?

Any industry or business is only as good as the people who work in it. In *any* group of people, some will be expert, some will be competent, some will be marginally competent, and some will be nincompoops. Most writers have at least one horror story about a publisher's errors or incompetence. While some concern (and perhaps even wariness) is justified, both paranoia and hopelessness are not.

Running a publishing firm is a little like launching the space shuttle. There are literally millions of details to oversee, check, and get straight, and the same item or piece of information may pass through a hundred different pairs of hands. Therefore, the sanest attitude you can take as a writer is to be cooperative with your editor and publisher unless the circumstances clearly dictate otherwise, and to assume, unless there is evidence to the contrary, that all is going well. But as soon as there *is* a problem, or a sign that one could easily occur, get in touch with the appropriate person promptly. A phone call is usually best, as it is faster, more direct, and normally more effective than a letter. Explain politely and calmly what the problem seems to be, and if possible offer your assistance in getting things straightened out.

Stick with people and publishing firms that you know do a good job. If you have repeated problems (or a major unresolved problem) with an editor or publisher, your best bet is usually to give that person or firm a polite adieu as soon as you can legally do so, and take your future work elsewhere.

One of the best ways I have found to encourage competence is by providing positive reinforcement. Whenever my editor (or whomever I am working with) does something right, I say, "Thanks, you're doing a great job" or "That was an excellent idea." This lets people know that

I appreciate their efforts and abilities, and it encourages them to continue to help me and to do things right in the future.

It would be unfair to leave this topic without making two things clear. First, you will almost certainly run into at least a few fair-sized problems with publishers and editors in your writing career. Usually these will involve very poor editing (often overediting), though they can involve anything from a lost manuscript to a check that arrives months late. When such developments do occur, grit your teeth and do what you can to set things right—and tell yourself it's all part of paying your dues. Second, castigating publishers behind their backs for their gross negligence and incompetence is a favorite pastime of writers. You should assume that at least some of the stories that you hear from other writers are exaggerated.

TRENDS AND TIMING

In general, the publishing industry reacts to trends rather than sets them. Publishers want to capitalize on already-existing consumer interests more than they want to generate such interest from scratch. Publishers do try to anticipate trends, but in general they tend to be very conservative in doing so, and often they are unwilling to cover a subject unless it has already proven itself to be very popular.

An excellent example involves the rock singer Prince. Prince has been known nationally since 1981, and possibly earlier. But it was not until mid-1984, and the premiere of his movie *Purple Rain,* that book publishers really believed in his potential as a major music figure. That summer, several publishers rushed simultaneously to put together books on Prince. I was asked by one major publisher to find people who could assemble a "cut-and-paste" collection of Prince photos and anecdotes; the publisher wanted a complete manuscript within *ten days.*

Because of the nature of fads and trends, and the suddenness and lateness with which publishers often react to them, selling something you have written often requires near split-second timing. In January or February of 1984, it would have been extremely difficult to sell a book on Prince, since publishers did not as yet have enough confidence in his enduring popularity. That same book would have sold at a very high price a few months later. But by September of 1984, that same book would have been completely unsalable, because by then so many publishers had rushed to do Prince books that the market was flooded.

Sometimes publishers will unwittingly create their own trends. For example, in 1979 and 1980, readers purchased many humor books. Publishers, looking over their sales figures, came to the conclusion that humor sells. Many of them rushed dozens and dozens of humor books (many of them not very funny) into print, hoping to cash in on the humor boom. In doing so, they flooded the market so badly that most of the humor books did not do very well. Those same publishers, looking at the sales figures a couple of years later, came to the conclusion that humor *doesn't* sell! For the next eighteen months, few book publishers would touch humor books. In fact, an editor at one major publisher that had previously done a fair number of humor books rejected a humor book with a letter that said, "I can't see a market for this kind of book." (Note: phrases such as "There isn't a market for this sort of thing" or "This topic is dead" or "I can't see who'd buy this" are editorspeak for "If we published this, I doubt we'd make a profit on it.")

Timing can work for you just as easily as it can work against you, however. You never know when something you've written will happen to hit an editor's desk at just the right time.

Furthermore, timing differs from publisher to publisher and from editor to editor. One book editor may tell writers, "Humor is dead," and sincerely believe it to be true throughout the publishing industry—whereas in fact it is only his own firm that has sworn off publishing humor, because its previous humor titles sold poorly. Another book publisher a few blocks away might insist that humor is alive and doing very well; but, once again, this simply means that particular publisher has made good profits on its humor books. Why does one publisher lose money on a certain kind of book or magazine while another one turns large profits with a similar product? No one really knows.

How do you deal with all this? First and foremost, you have to realize and accept that, to a large degree, matters of timing are out of your control. Success in publishing often involves a good deal of luck. You can make sales, or just as easily lose them, because of forces over which you have no control, and which you have no power to predict. This is one reason why you shouldn't take rejection too seriously.

Once you send something off to an editor, don't lose any sleep over whether it will be bought or rejected. Get on with your life, and with your next writing project. Time your submissions as best you can, but don't worry about whether your timing was right. Leave the fate of your manuscripts in the hands of the gods—which is where their fate will remain no matter what attitude you take.

If you are writing seasonal material, however, be sure to time your submissions appropriately. If you have an Easter piece for a magazine, submit it during the previous summer or (at the very latest) the early fall. Give book publishers a full year of lead time. Newspapers need only a month or two.

It can never hurt to submit your work a little earlier than the times described above, so that if your piece is rejected, you have time to try a second or even third round of markets. It is always better to send in something too soon than too late.

MANUSCRIPT FORM

The publishing industry has specific rules for manuscript preparation, which you will be expected to follow. The more you follow these standards, the more likely you are to be treated as a professional; the less you follow them, the more likely you are to be perceived as an amateur. The standards are of course somewhat arbitrary. Here they are:

Paper

All manuscripts should be on plain, unlined 8½-by-11-inch paper. The paper should be plain white—not buff, ivory, or beige—and it should be thick enough that you cannot easily see through it. Onionskin paper is not acceptable. Avoid erasable paper; it smears easily. The best paper is standard photocopying (xerox) or spirit duplicating (ditto) paper; it looks good and is inexpensive. Currently you can get either kind at any office supply shop for $3 to $7 a ream (500 sheets). Ask for 16- or 20-pound bond. Your paper should have four square corners and should not have holes for binding in notebooks.

Typeface

All manuscripts should be neatly typed, on one side of the page only. Use a standard typeface—one that is clear, readable, and in regular use. Typefaces such as Prestige, Courier, and Delegate are acceptable; Script, Orator, Olde World, Grande, Quadro, Gothic, Cubic, and other decorative typefaces are not. Italic typefaces are unacceptable; bold typefaces are normally acceptable but are best avoided. Letters should be clear and distinct, without ink filling up their enclosed parts; this means you'll need a good, dark ribbon and clean keys. Use black ink only.

Virtually any typewriter in good repair, from an old and inexpensive portable to the most sophisticated electronic job, will produce a clean, clear, readable manuscript if it has an acceptable typeface.

Letter-quality computer printers are acceptable; "near-letter-quality" printers are not. If your printer's type is as clear, distinct, and readable as that of a typewriter, it's acceptable; if it's a step lower, it may not be. Remember that editors read tens of thousands of words a day, so their eyes tire easily. The harder your manuscript is for them to read, the more likely they are to turn it down. Some editors are perfectly willing to read manuscripts printed on the cheapest dot-matrix printers; but I wouldn't take chances.

Both pica (standard size) and elite (slightly smaller) type are acceptable. If your typewriter or printer gives you a choice of pitches, anything from 10 to 12 pitch is acceptable; anything larger or smaller is not.

If you have any doubt about the clarity, readability, or acceptability of a typeface, you are best off switching to one you have no doubts about.

Submission on Computer Disks

Some publishers now accept submissions on computer diskettes as well as those on paper. These submissions, like those on paper, should follow all the rules for manuscript form set forth in this chapter.

In general, it is best to submit a standard paper manuscript rather than a floppy disk unless you *know* for a fact that an editor accepts submissions in disk form. If you like, mention in your cover letter that a diskette version is available. If you *do* submit a floppy disk, be sure to attach to it a hard-copy cover letter.

As time passes, more and more editors will accept disk submissions. The first uniform standards for writing, submitting, and processing manuscripts on computers have just been issued. These standards, and information on them, are available from Ed Kurdyla, OCLC, 6565 Frantz Road, Dublin, OH 43017, (614) 764-6000.

More and more writers are buying personal computers, disk drives, and printers. Are they a necessity for writers? No. They can make writing, rewriting, and editing easier, quicker, less messy, and more convenient. They can help with spelling and page formatting. And more and more publishers are working on ways to typeset manuscripts directly from computer disks. However, the typewritten manuscript remains standard—and is likely to remain so for some time.

No publisher currently *requires* freelance material to be submitted via disk or modem. However, I have heard of one magazine that pays more for manuscripts on disk or modem than for those on paper, on the premise that a typed manuscript is more expensive to set in type. It remains to be seen whether this is an isolated case or will become an accepted practice.

Margins

Margins should be wide enough for editors to write in. One-inch margins on all four sides of the paper are ideal.

Page Headings

The first item on any page of a manuscript (except the cover page and the first page) should be the heading. This consists of the page number and one or more words that identify the piece. Usually the title of the piece, or one or more key words from the title, will work well. If your article is called "How to Make Soap Carvings," the words "Soap Carvings" are fine. You can use your name instead of the title if you like, but this can cause confusion if an editor has two of your pieces, or a piece by someone with a similar name. (Some scholarly and professional journals require that the author's name *not* appear on any page headings.) In general, you are best off identifying your piece by title.

This information should be typed about an inch from the top edge of the paper, either at the left or right margin. If you like, you can put the title in one of these spots and the page number in another. Text should begin a half-inch or so (two to four lines) further down. Use the same format for page headings on every page beyond page one. Cover pages and first pages have no headings.

Photocopying

Make a good-quality photocopy of your original manuscript. Keep the original; submit the photocopy. If a manuscript is lost or damaged by an editor, it is a simple matter to replace it by making a new photocopy. (It is no longer true that editors frown on photocopied submissions. I've never known an editor to raise the faintest objection to a clear photocopied submission.)

The quality and cost of photocopying can vary dramatically from one merchant to another. High price does not guarantee high quality. In general, the best and most inexpensive copying can be found at copy shops and print shops. At this writing the going rate at these shops is 5¢ a page. Telephone around to find the cheapest price. Look under "Printing," "Photocopying," and "Copying and Duplicating Services" in your Yellow Pages. Often the best and cheapest copy stores are located near college campuses.

Whenever you do any photocopying, no matter how little or much, check the following *before* you leave the shop: Are all the pages of your original still there, undamaged, and in the correct order? Is every page of every copy there, copied clearly and in full, free of stains, lines, blurs, and smudges, and in the correct order? (I have found that one time out of four, at least one copy doesn't get made, or comes out damaged.) Checking all this in the store is better than having your manuscript rejected two months later because of a missing page.

Neatness

Each page should be free of tears, wrinkles, creases, large spots, smudges, and any other marks that mar its appearance. A page that looks more than slightly worn should be recopied. Every page should look clean, readable, and attractive. Margins, lines, and letters should generally be even, and the text should be properly aligned with the page—that is, it shouldn't slant. It is acceptable to make corrections in dark pencil or black ink, on either the original or the photocopy. It's fine to use white-out, but be aware that products that white out typewriter ribbon ink will not white out photocopy toner, but cause smudging. You must use a separate product (usually designated "for copies only") for whiting out errors on photocopies. Cutting and pasting or taping your original is fine, so long as it does not show on your photocopies—and it shouldn't if you are careful. Another timesaver is correction tape—thin strips of white sticky tape available at office supply stores. Simply place a strip of tape over an incorrect line, type the correct line on the tape, and photocopy the page.

Corrections

If you wish to correct a word, simply cross it out. Use a ruler. Write or type the new word above it:

```
                       Karen
going to understand," Marla said.   "I missed the
```

If you wish to omit a word, phrase, or sentence, simply put one thick line through it using a ruler:

```
miss her.   I wish I didn't, though.   Every time I
```

If you wish to omit an entire paragraph or group of lines, you may draw lines through the first and last lines of text, then draw a diagonal line from the upper right of the paragraph to the lower left:

```
   This information should be typed about an

inch from the top of the page, either at the left

or right margin, or in the center.   If you like,

you can put the title in one of these spots and

the page number in another.   Text should begin

about a half inch or so (2-4 lines) further down.
```

If you need to add one or more words, use a caret and make the addition as neatly as possible:

```
                                    you
third phase: construction.   If have not already
                                 ^
```

If you have made a spelling or typing error, you may either cross the word out and print or type the proper spelling immediately above; or, in the case of transposed letters, you may use the transposition symbol, which looks like an *S* turned sideways:

```
are designed to operate.   In fact, many academicians
```

Transposed words may be corrected in the same manner:

was wearing an I Ike Like button. When I asked her

If you wish to begin a new paragraph at a point in the text where originally you had not indicated a new paragraph, add a paragraph symbol:

work," Jean said. ¶"You know," Harry said, "I think

If you wish to meld two paragraphs together, use the same symbol and the word *no:*

understand the principle.

No ¶But there are other principles that apply

If you wish to close the gap between two words or letters, use an inverted *U:*

left me standing on the door step. I didn 't know

To delete a letter or punctuation mark, draw a vertical line with a twist through it; if you need to close up the space as well, also add the inverted *U:*

loosent   Smithe   good-bye   papper

If you wish to create a space between two words or letters, insert a vertical or diagonal slash between them:

livingroom   saladdressing   SuAnn Hoskins

If a capital letter should be lowercase, draw a diagonal line through it from eight o'clock to two o'clock. If a lowercase letter should become a capital, underline it three times:

my ⫨father.   There was mr. Creighton from the fbi.

To indicate that a word, phrase, or sentence should be in italics, underline it once:

In William Faulkner's <u>The Sound and the Fury</u>, every

Minor corrections, such as added or changed punctuation or letters, can simply be penned in, either alone or with carets:

the C̆O Canal.   "Bye," I said   typewri†er

If you have made a change but realize that the item was correct as originally typed, you may write "STET" above your change and add a series of dots underneath. This indicates that your "correction" should be ignored:

STET
lo⫻se   said goodbye for good.   Mr. ~~Blish~~ said

Use STET only when your original intention is clear. Otherwise, retype and/or white out items as necessary.

If you have made errors in page numbering, it is not normally necessary to renumber every page. If you have two page 55s, make the second page 55 into 55-A. If you have three 55s, make the third 55-B, and so on. If your manuscript goes from page 31 to page 33, change 31 to 31/32. Renumber all the pages only if you have many such errors.

Make all corrections as neatly and carefully as possible, so that readability is maintained. Make changes in very dark pencil or black ink, to make reading easier and to ensure that the corrections will photocopy clearly. The number of corrections you may make on a page will be determined primarily by readability. As long as a page is still readable, you have not made too many corrections. But if there is *any* problem with readability, or if a part of the page looks unattractive, you should either retype the page, or cover up and retype the appropriate section.

Poetry manuscripts, since they are single-spaced, and since they are likely to receive careful word-by-word scrutiny, are exceptions to the above rules. Poetry manuscripts should be free of all visible corrections.

Editing

The same attention to detail that you pay to your manuscript's physical appearance should be paid to its clarity, conciseness, grammar, diction, spelling, sentence structure, and style. Edit and proofread each page carefully. Check spelling as necessary. If you aren't sure about a point of grammar, punctuation, or diction, check it.

Binding

Prose and poetry manuscripts should be submitted without plastic covers, staples, notebooks, or other bindings of any kind. Manuscripts of eighty pages or less should be held together with a paper clip in the upper left-hand corner; the larger the manuscript, the larger the clip. Office supply stores sell large butterfly clamps, which are simply extra-large paper clips. Size #2 clamps will hold up to forty pages; #1 clamps will hold nearly a hundred. Manuscripts longer than eighty or so pages should be placed, unbound, in manuscript mailing boxes or two-part cardboard boxes large enough to hold a ream of paper. These are available from some print shops, copy shops, and office supply stores. (Be sure to buy blank boxes; don't use boxes with advertising, designs, or the print shop's name on them.) Manuscript boxes are also available by mail from Papyrus Place, 2210 Goldsmith Lane, Louisville, KY 40218. Or, manuscripts can be placed between sheets of stiff cardboard, and the whole thing can be held together with rubber bands.

Book proposals should be placed inside two-pocket folders; see pages 269–70 for details.

Scripts for television, radio, film, and drama *should* normally be bound. See the books listed on page 52 for more details.

Social Security Number, Rights for Sale, Copyright Notice

The advice I am about to give you on all three of these topics reflects standard practices, rules, and expectations within the publishing industry. Nevertheless, it will directly contradict advice published in some other books on writing. I can only say that the other books are in error, and that if you follow their advice, you run the risk of being considered an amateur by editors.

Social Security Number   Don't mention it, either on a manuscript or in a cover letter. When your publisher needs it, you will be asked for it. Do of course provide it once it has been requested.

Rights for Sale   Don't mention what rights you wish to sell, either in your cover letter or anywhere on the manuscript itself. Either the publication will buy only one-time use, or it will offer you a contract, which you can either accept or negotiate. The only exception to this rule is if the piece you are offering for sale has already been (or is scheduled to be) published elsewhere. Then you simply mention the previous or forthcoming publication(s) in your cover letter.

Copyright Notice   Don't place a copyright notice anywhere on your manuscript; this is neither necessary nor helpful, and to some editors it shows you to be an amateur. Your unpublished manuscript is fully protected under U.S. copyright law whether or not a copyright notice appears on it.

There are two exceptions here, however:

• If the piece has been previously published, or if it will be published shortly, you should provide a proper copyright notice on the first page (or the cover page, if there is one) of the manuscript; for example, "Copyright 1986 Artlines, Inc."

• Special rules apply to scripts for television and film. See the books recommended on page 52 for details.

Page Format

Formats differ from genre to genre. An example will illustrate each of the following descriptions.

Articles, Essays, Short Stories, and Other Short Prose Pieces   There should be no cover page. The title of the piece, either in all capitals or

FIRST PAGE OF PROSE MANUSCRIPT

Scott Edelstein
179 Berkeley Street, Apt. 1
Rochester, NY 14607
244-0645

About 1200 words

The Mister Phenomenon

by Scott Edelstein

When I was small, there were lots of misters in my life. The bank manager was
Mr. Mayer. The man who pumped gas at the corner station was Mr. Philipedes. Even
the sweaty, alcoholic barber who held my head roughly and asked in a thick accent,
"Hey, handsome boy, you got any girlfriends?" was named, not Harry, but Mr. Reynolds.

As the years passed, I came to call fewer and fewer people mister. Partly I was
just growing up, and adults no longer required--or, in many cases, deserved--this
overt sign of respect and deference. But other things were happening as well: the
culture was becoming steadily more informal, less class-conscious, and more mechan-
ically cheery. Today I call my hair stylist Bev, the man at the gas station (whom I
pay after pumping gas myself) Tom, and the vice president at the bank Carol.

But the words Mr. and Mrs. (and, to a lesser extent, Miss and Ms.) have not
fallen into disuse. We have simply transferred their use--along with our respect,
trust, and concern--from human beings to retail establishments.

In Rochester, if I need some tile work done, I can call Mr. Grout. If I need
my driveway paved, Mr. Blacktop can handle the job. If my hydraulic jack is on the

Edelstein/2

fritz, Mr. Pneumatic Tool Repair will take care of it. If I'm thirsty, I can have
a drink at Mr. Ed's, Mr. K's, Mr. T's, or Mr. Dominick's. And if for some reason I
grow dissatisfied with Bev, I can have my hair cut by my choice of Mr. B, Mr. C,
Mr. D, Mr. Farina, Mr. Frank, Mr. Thomas, or one of the folks at Mr. and Miz Hair
Bazaar.

In all, Rochester has no less than 44 businesses that begin with the word Mister,
from Mr. Appliance to Mr. Warehouse. Stops in between include, among others, Mr.
Cool-Tool Sales, Mr. Drywall, Mr. Mender, Mr. Real Estate, and Mr. Mobile Wash.
Three mister establishments--Mssrs. Collision, Mechanic, and Tow--have the same owner.
Not surprisingly, virtually all of these businesses were founded, and are owned and
managed, by men.

Forty-four is actually a pretty paltry number of mister organizations for a major
North American city (see chart). Buffalo has 84 mister enterprises. The borough of
Manhattan has 129. And Toronto wins a Mister Mister album for having no less than
352 Mister something-or-others actively doing business. In fact, if you wanted to or,
God forbid, had to, you could comfortably seat the entire population of Brighton
inside Toronto's mister establishments.

In a single morning on your next trip to Toronto, you could patronize Mssrs.
Business Card, Ground Beef, Garbage Bag, Shower Door, and Portion Control. After lunch
at Mr. Shishkebob you could spend the afternoon bargain-hunting at Mr. Milk, Mr.
Front-End, Mr. Countertop, Mr. Outdoors, Mr. Gas Tank, Mr. Big Screen TV, Mr. Lucky's
House Furnishings, Mr. Halibut, and Mr. Jerk. After dinner at Mr. Eaters you would
likely be more than ready to book swift passage out of town through Mr. Travel (on
Danforth Ave.).

Manhattan is another good spot for mister aficionados. Boasting 129 mister
organizations (plus 92 beginning with Miss, 30 with Ms., and 22 with Mrs., including
Miss Pert Lingerie, Miss Oops, Mrs. J's Sacred Cow Steak House, and Mrs. Weinberg's

in upper- and lowercase, should appear in the exact center of the page, or slightly above. Two spaces directly beneath the title should be your byline—the name to which you wish the piece credited in print. Normally, this will be your own name, but if you use a pseudonym, it goes here. The word *by* should precede your name. The text of the piece should begin three to eight lines below your byline—roughly three-fifths of the way down the page.

An inch from the top and the left edge of the page, type your *real* name. Directly under this, flush left, type your street address and apartment number (or your P.O. box number); directly under this, also flush left, your city, state, and zip code, either five or nine digits. Directly under this, again flush left, type your phone number. If you have both home and work phones, type them both, and indicate which is which. Including your phone numbers, especially the number (or numbers) where you can be reached during business hours, is very important, as an editor may need to reach you with an urgent question. All of this information should be single-spaced in upper- and lowercase type.

Next, drop down two spaces, and, once again flush left, indicate your membership in any *appropriate* professional writer's organization, such as the Authors Guild or Science Fiction Writers of America. Use common sense in deciding which professional affiliations to list. The editors of *Scientific American* won't be impressed that you're a member of Western Writers of America. The purpose of listing an association membership is to establish that you are a working professional in that field or genre.

Local writers' organizations, academic organizations, and any other groups that are not composed primarily or entirely of practicing professional writers should not be listed. Don't mention that you're a member of the National Writers Club, the Sierra Club, or the North Shore Women Writers' Alliance.

In the upper right-hand corner of the page, indicate the approximate length of your piece. To determine the number of words in the whole piece, count up the number on two or three typical pages. Average these out so that you know how many words are on a typical page. Multiply this figure by the number of pages, and make appropriate allowances for any pages that are not filled with text. Round this number to the nearest hundred words if the piece is fifteen hundred words or less; to the nearest five hundred words if the piece is fifteen hundred to ten thousand words; and to the nearest thousand words if the piece is over ten thousand words.

If there are two or more authors for a particular piece, use your common sense in deciding how to list names, addresses, phone numbers, and professional affiliations (though you should conform pretty much to the standard form described above). You can list all the pertinent information for each writer; or, if you prefer, you can choose one mailing address and/or phone number for the group.

All text in a prose manuscript, from the first line to the last, should be double-spaced, except for lengthy quotations from other sources, which are normally single-spaced and have half-inch wider margins.

Articles for scholarly and professional journals should follow slightly different guidelines: (1) there *should* be a cover page, which should follow the format for book cover pages except that no word length should be indicated; (2) your name, address, and phone number should appear only on the cover page, not on page one; and (3) you should not indicate a pseudonym. As with poetry, if you wish to use a pen name, you should bring up the matter with the editor only after your piece has been accepted for publication.

Books and Book Proposals   For these you will need a cover page. The rules for the cover page are the same as those for the first page of a short prose manuscript, with the following exceptions.

• No text appears on the cover page.

• The word length may appear either in the upper right, or centered, six to fourteen lines below your byline. If you are preparing a book proposal, indicate the *proposed* length of the completed manuscript rather than the actual length of the proposal—for example, "Projected length: 100,000 words." Round the length off to the nearest thousand words if the length is (or will be) under twenty thousand words; to the nearest five thousand words if the manuscript is (or will be) twenty to a hundred thousand words; and to the nearest ten thousand words if the book is (or will be) over a hundred thousand words. If your book will consist largely or primarily of visual materials, also list the number or proposed number and type of illustrations—for example, "160 line drawings."

• If your book is being represented by an agent, omit your address and phone number. Instead, under your name, indicate your agent's name,

COVER PAGE FOR A BOOK MANUSCRIPT OR PROPOSAL

Scott Edelstein
179 Berkeley St., Apt. 1
Rochester, NY 14607
716-244-0645

Agent:
Bobbe Siegel
41 W. 83 Street
New York, NY 10024
212-877-4985

THE INDISPENSABLE WRITER'S GUIDE

How to Get the Most Money, Success,
and Satisfaction from Your Writing

by Scott Edelstein

About 150,000 words

address, and phone number. Or if you prefer, put your address and phone number(s) in the upper left and agent information in the upper right.

All text for books and book proposals should be double-spaced, just as it would be in short prose manuscripts. New chapters should begin on new pages, anywhere from a quarter to halfway down the page. The very first page of text normally should not contain any of the information on the cover page, although some writers like to type the title and byline near the top of it. If your manuscript is a collection of articles, short stories, poems, or other short pieces, your name, address, phone number, and institutional affiliations should not appear on any of the individual pieces.

Use your common sense in preparing your table of contents, acknowledgments, index, and other such items.

Chapter 9 will discuss preparing book proposals in detail.

Poetry   You do not need a cover page unless you have written a book-length work (in which case, follow all the instructions immediately above for preparing a cover page, with one exception: do not indicate the length of the project).

Each poem should begin on a separate page, no matter how short it might be. Type your name and address, but not your phone number, near the top of the first page of each poem, just as you would on the first page of a short prose manuscript. However, on a poetry manuscript, this information may go in either the upper left or upper right of the page. Do not list any institutional or organizational affiliations, any word or page counts for the poem, or any pseudonym. (Once a poem has been accepted you may write the editor requesting a pseudonymous byline.)

Drop down an inch or so, then type the title of the poem, in uppercase letters, flush against the left margin. Drop down three or four lines, then begin the poem. If a poem is very short, you may begin it further down the page, so that it looks more vertically centered. A 1-inch margin at the bottom should be considered a minimum; it may be enlarged up to 2 inches to enable you to end a page without splitting a stanza.

You may single-space your poem, double-spacing between stanzas; or if you prefer, you may type your lines 1 ½ spaces apart, leaving 2 ½ spaces between stanzas.

Prose poems follow the rules for poetry, though of course they are typed in paragraphs rather than stanzas.

John Edward Sorrell
3328 W. 2nd, Suite 5
Vancouver, British Columbia   V6R 1H9

SHELTER

The sun falls all afternoon, to earth;
Lands behind these spring elms; but can't hold
Earth's precarious edge where they root,
Draws the elms with it, down into dark.

   In the bright dark Beth and I'd hold hands tight,
   Sweaty--suck, suck, and crack great big red-hots
   Called Atomic Fireballs--as, onscreen, Sarge
   Flashed and swept whole nests of Japs, no sweat.

   Cross-stepping back home to her house, we'd stop
   Short--testing each other--quick, skip the crack:
   To fix her dad's back. He'd be standing watch
   Against the window with his bottle.

   Forever the red-checked tablecloth, stained.
   He'd say just wipe spills off, never make us
   Eat our greens, never make us anything
   Much, but hamburgers, hot dogs, and beans.

   In class, at the bomb drill's clang, we'd all jump
   Under our desks--but Beth. She'd jump in
   With me, us giggling--till, late in May, Miss Raines
   Yanked us out, called down Beth's dad. Who just stared.

   At last muttered what difference did it make
   If we held hands at the final flash--
   That week, backed their station wagon up,
   Stacked two by fours, lugged big rough gray blocks.

   Murmured over his scraped knuckles, bad back,
   Told Miss Raines to go scream bloody murder
   At Beth's mother, not him, they could both scream
   Their heads off at a little girl who's scared.

He kicked the spade. We climbed from the elms. Hands
Scooped dirt, scooped, till eyes met earth's edge. He said
Here we were, planting ourselves, roof of stars
Sprouting up from us, deep, our shelter.

We dug our own hole back by the woods,
Built our shelter walls deep with his scraps.
We'd pull his old study door, our roof, tight.
One day, peeled her blouse, my shirt, and tested.

Late, tiptoed in: By the night light's faint glow,
He still stood watch, rubbing his back, bottle
In one arm, half cradled, bare undershirt
Soaked black with sweat. In the window mirrored
Pale and dark, he softly rocked; hoarse, murmured
How stars now sheltered towns, they'd never drop
The bomb, never bomb our street thick with elms--
Where they dropped it, the earth waved with tall palms--
So far down, that if they just had let him
Fly by the stars, he'd have flown on, on by
The huddled, pinned lights of towns and dropped
Nothing, not the first light flashing out
So far down, no screams from those tiny fires
So far down, no one could have caught him--
His own wife didn't know him anymore.

Beth's palm soothes my knuckles. We stand watch.
Our elms will rise again with dawn, sun
Flash the earth's edge, climb to lose that edge
And shelter us with calm morning light.

She winces; then smiles. She lays and presses
My hand on her warm, round swell: I feel our child
            Deep within, kick,
                Testing.

Scripts for Television, Film, Radio, and Stage   The formats for work in these genres are fairly complex, and quite different from all those discussed above. Detailed descriptions of these manuscript formats appear in *The Writer's Digest Guide to Manuscript Formats* by Dian Dincin Buchman and Seli Groves (Writer's Digest Books) and in the books on the appropriate genres listed on page 52.

Ending Your Manuscript

When your piece ends, simply stop typing. There is no need to type *end* or *30*.

ILLUSTRATIONS

If illustrations and/or photographs accompany your manuscript, follow these guidelines:

• Each illustration or photograph should appear on a separate 8½-by-11-inch page. A caption, photo credit, or illustration credit should appear on the same page. If this is difficult or impossible, type captions and credits on blank labels and stick them on the backs of the pages.

• Illustrations and photographs smaller than 8½ by 11 are acceptable, so long as they are attached to 8½-by-11-inch pages. Photos and illustrations smaller than 5 by 7 inches should be enlarged, if possible.

• Number illustrations consecutively: illustration 1, illustration 2, and so on.

• Illustrations should normally be integrated with text. That is, if a paragraph on page 92 refers to two photos of a parrot, those photos should appear on the next two pages, which should be numbered 92a and 92b. The next page of text should be page 93. Naturally, if your visual material is not intended to be integrated with text in the published version, you need not integrate it in manuscript. Simply place the visual material at the end.

• You may, if you wish, send slides instead of color photographs. These should be placed in plastic sheets (usually holding twenty slides each), which can then be placed at the end of your manuscript. If you have captions, a separate sheet of captions should immediately follow the slides. A separate page of photo or illustration credits may also be appended. If you are submitting a book proposal, the slides and your caption and credit sheets may go in the left-hand pocket of the proposal folder. Number all slides, captions, and credits.

• When initially submitting hand-drawn illustrations, keep the originals and send clear photocopies.

• Keep a duplicate set of transparencies and the negatives to all prints.

• Although cardboard backing is not usually necessary when submitting manuscripts, you should probably include sheets of cardboard on the top and bottom of an illustrated manuscript to protect photos, drawings, and slides. Also write "Please Do Not Bend" on the outside of your mailing envelope, and on your return envelope (if one is enclosed).

WRITER'S BLOCK

The term *writer's block* has been used to refer to a variety of conditions: the inability to finish a particular project; the inability to finish any writing project; the general inability to write decently; and even the inability to confront a blank page at all.

There is no single cause of what we call writer's block. Physical or emotional stress, overwork, excessive distraction, personal problems unrelated to writing, a looming deadline, physical illness, poor diet, poor or too little sleep, and changes or disruptions in your routine can all lead to a temporary inability to write what you want when you want. Writer's block can also be the result of asking or expecting too much of yourself, either in your writing or in your life in general. Then there is simple laziness masquerading as writer's block. If you're honest with yourself you should be able to distinguish between the two.

The block may be partly or entirely a result of the particular piece you are writing. For instance, you might have written yourself into a corner; or you might be thinking repeatedly along the same unproductive line, unwilling or unable to take a different tack; or you might simply be so bored or weary of working on that project that you've dried up and need a break. In such a case, you may want to figure out how to make your current project as painless, or as close to painless, as possible. Or consider ways to finish that project and get it out of the way as quickly as you can. If absolutely necessary, perhaps you should consider abandoning the project. (This should normally be a last resort—but sometimes writer's block can simply be an intuitive awareness that a particular project isn't going to work out.)

Then there are natural cycles. Many writers have creative cycles that include periods in which material simply doesn't flow. They may be able to (often subconsciously) process and create ideas and images, but they can't produce the steady stream of words that they would like to. Or they may simply need time away from creative activity to rejuvenate themselves and catch their breaths. It pays to know your own cycles and habits (creative and otherwise) so that you can flow with them rather than try to work against them. In fact, you might want to keep a journal of your work habits and productivity for a couple of months to see if any natural cycles emerge.

Often the cause of writer's block is so obvious that writers overlook it. One writer I know couldn't write for a week after the death of one of his friends—but it never occurred to him that the death was the cause of the block. Another had trouble writing during hay fever season; she didn't realize that the antihistamines she was taking were dulling her brain.

If you do come down with writer's block in any form, the first thing you should realize is that it's probably not serious. For all the talk and worry about writer's block, it usually doesn't last long—normally no more than a few days. In fact, most writers make far more out of writer's block than they should. Usually if you don't worry about it, it'll go away. But sometimes if you try to conquer it, your anxiety will only exacerbate the condition.

If writer's block occurs to you frequently, you might also examine your life as a whole, to see if the block is connected to anything specific in it (for example, drinking or drug use, certain foods, a particular person's presence, your menstrual cycle, or the weather). You may also want to consider whether you should be a writer at all. Maybe at heart writing isn't satisfying to you, or you're really more interested in money and publication than you are in actually writing.

However, searching for causes isn't always the best way to get rid of writer's block. Many writers deal very successfully with blocks simply by trying different things and seeing which ones work. Here are some things that have worked for other writers; one or more may work for you.

- Physical exercise
- Meditation
- Put the page, chapter, or project aside for a while. Ignore it for a day, week, or month while you do something else: another writing project, another part of that same project, or something entirely unrelated to writing. If necessary, put all of your writing aside for a while.

• Work on another project (writing or otherwise) simultaneously, or alternate between the two projects.

• Distract yourself. Go to a movie, take a walk, or read a book. Get your mind *off* the problem and let your subconscious reorient itself.

• Retype your last page, then keep going. Or type or retype something else.

• Sit down at your desk. Then write a letter or something else that you *can* easily write. Then return to your project.

• Change how, where, or when you write. Trade in your typewriter for a pen and pad, or try writing as soon as you get up instead of late in the afternoon. Or move your computer from your basement to your attic.

• Try to make your circumstances for writing as comfortable as possible. Get yourself a comfortable chair, or hook up a stereo in your office. Keep a pot of hot coffee, or a cooler with a few cold beers, by your desk. (I do at least half my own writing with new wave rock blaring in both ears.)

• Make a list of all possible directions your piece can go next. Don't exclude any ideas, even if they seem absurd—if you come up with something, write it down, no matter what it is. Then try out one or more of these ideas, until something clicks.

• Sit quietly for a few minutes, either concentrating on your own breathing or letting your mind wander. Then, gently return your attention to the spot in your piece where you are stuck. *Don't* try to come up with an answer; instead, simply see whatever bubbles up out of your subconscious. Whatever it is, write it down and try it—even if it seems silly. It may make more sense than you realize at first. I once solved a big dilemma this way.

• Talk over your piece (or your situation) with one or more other writers (or nonwriters). Invite and consider fresh ideas, suggestions, and perspectives. Brainstorm together.

• Plan to reward yourself when you finish the project you're stuck on.

Poet Louise Gluck has perhaps the wisest comment of all on writer's block: "I question the assumption behind writer's block, which is that one should be writing all the time . . . at times we simply have nothing to say. Then we need to get back in the world and put more life into ourselves."

SEXUAL EQUALITY IN LANGUAGE

For all its richness of expression, the English language is curiously inflexible when it comes to writing about imaginary or hypothetical people.

There is no word in English that means *his or her* or *he or she,* though there certainly should be. *They, them,* and *their* have come into more and more frequent use in recent years, and will eventually become standard. Using *he* to refer to *he or she* and *his* to refer to *his or her* is no longer generally acceptable. But *he or she* and *his or her* are often awkward.

There is no standard, simple, or satisfying solution to this dilemma. In general, I recommend either of the following: (1) using *they, them,* and *their;* or (2) using *he or she, his or her,* etc., whenever possible and your choice of *he* or *they* whenever context renders *he or she* awkward.

A few writers have chosen to use the feminine alone—that is, to use *she* to mean *he or she,* and so on. Other writers alternate, using *he* to mean *he or she* at times and *she* at other times. This is usually acceptable.

Whatever option you choose, keep in mind that each publication has its own particular solution to this problem, and your work will normally be edited to conform to that publication's guidelines concerning gender.

TYPEWRITER AND COMPUTER RENTAL

If you don't own a typewriter or computer, or if you need one in an emergency, it is usually possible to rent one. Typewriters can be rented by the day, week, or month through office supply dealers and typewriter rental firms. Look under "Typewriters" in your Yellow Pages. It pays to get quotes and compare prices: the cost can vary a good deal. IBM Selectrics, for example, can be much more expensive than standard portables, and a standard portable may be all you need.

Typewriters can also be rented by the hour or portion thereof. Some office supply stores and photocopying firms, and a few print shops, offer inexpensive hourly typewriter rentals. Many public libraries, and virtually all college libraries, have coin-operated typewriters that can be rented at 25¢ a crack, usually for about ten or fifteen minutes. Some public and college libraries have typewriters available at no charge. Often the typewriters are hidden away in some remote corner, so ask a librarian where they are. In small libraries you may simply be shown into the back room and permitted to use a staff member's typewriter. If you wish to use one of the typewriters in a college library, don't volunteer the information that you are not a student or employee at that institution. Most college libraries, and all the facilities therein, are open to everyone—but some aren't. Most colleges and universities also have microcomputer labs containing a dozen or more personal computers and printers. Some of these are open to the general public at no charge.

Personal computers, accessories, and entire personal computer systems are usually available for lease, and often for short-term rental, from computer dealers. Check both "Computers" and "Word Processors" in your Yellow Pages. Rentals typically last at least a month, but some firms will rent by the week, and a few by the weekend or even by the day. (If a dealer tells you, "I've never heard of daily rentals" or "I'm sure nobody in this town rents computers by the day," don't take that as gospel.)

A few enterprising people run word processing centers that rent computer systems by the hour, day, and half-hour. Occasionally these services offer take-home rentals, but normally customers must use the computers on the premises. Computer rentals are often available on a walk-in basis, but some establishments require or prefer that you reserve computer time in advance. Some centers will permit customers to use their computers via modems. Software rentals are also sometimes available, and some centers offer laser printing as well. These firms are usually listed under "Word Processing" in the Yellow Pages, but also check under "Computers." Some copy shops now offer computer and laser printer rentals as well.

The biggest benefit of these hourly rental services is that you can do all the letter-quality printing you like without having to purchase a letter-quality (or any) printer. You can also duplicate disks, make use of color monitors, and so on.

If you do not own either a typewriter or a computer, I strongly urge you to invest in a typewriter of your own. A good manual portable—which will do very well—costs only $45 to $75 new, and around $30 used. New electronic ones are going for as little as $125 to $175.

PSEUDONYMS

Here are some good (and common) reasons for using a pen name:

• You don't want to be associated with something you've written (for example, pornography, pieces attacking the Catholic church, an exposé of the Mafia, or a trashy fantasy novel).
• You want to avoid publicity or public attention.
• You have a reputation (as a minister, insurance saleswoman, or Lion's Club member) that might be damaged by publication of your work under your own name.
• Your own name is ugly, hard to remember or spell or pronounce, too common, or too similar (or even identical) to someone else's. If your name

is Garth Titt, Vladimir Taterczynski, Mary Jones, or Ronald Reagan, you would be wise to adopt a pseudonym.

• Your name looks or sounds inappropriate for your material. If you write sword and sorcery novels (like *Conan the Barbarian*) and your name is Arnold Feinstein, you should become Odin Walsh instead. Or if you've written a serious study on male homosexuality and your name happens to be Bruce Fagg, you'd better find a pen name like Lawrence Goldman. (By the way, editors don't care what sex you are. The editors at Harlequin are perfectly happy to buy romance novels from men, and the editors at pornography publishers are glad to buy stuff written by women. However, they may insist that you use a pen name of the appropriate sex for the sake of their readers. They may also request or insist on a pen name with the proper "feel," as discussed above.)

• You want to develop a separate literary persona. Some writers create not only pseudonyms but whole new personalities to go along with them; they exhibit those personalities on talk shows and in interviews to help promote their writing careers.

• You want to build careers in two or more different fields of writing. If, for example, you want to write both academic treatises on Dickens and male adventure novels, you are better off writing under two different names so that there's no danger of not being taken seriously as a Dickens scholar because you write "trash."

Many of these purposes can be achieved without pseudonyms at all, simply by picking an appropriate variant of your real name. For example, Rebecca King can disguise her identity as a woman by becoming R. L. King. Peg Barker (born Margaret Ellsworth Barker) can disguise her identity completely by becoming M. Ellsworth Barker. (Ms. Barker will be perfectly able to cash publishers' checks made out to M. Ellsworth Barker, so long as she has proper identification.)

It's also perfectly legitimate to use one or more pen names just because it's fun, because you like a certain name, or because you've always wanted to be called something else. You may choose just about any pen name you want, for just about any reason.

Some rules of common sense apply. You may not use the name of someone else who is already well known; for example, you can't choose the pen name Richard Nixon, though R. L. Nixon would be fine (Richard L. Nixon would *not* be Kosher, however, since people might still mistake you for Richard M. Nixon). You also may not use the same pen name as another well-known author (for example, Blanche Knott or Piers Anthony).

Incidentally, if your name happens to *be* Richard Nixon—or Alice Walker, or George Eliot—you are perfectly free to use it on everything you write.

Your pen name may be the name of a real person; for example, Edward Martin or Susan Norris. However, you shouldn't use the name of someone you know without his or her written permission.

Pseudonyms should be easy to spell and remember, so that people can easily request your work in bookstores and libraries.

It is perfectly legitimate to use your own name on some of your work and one or more pseudonyms on others. However, remember the value of name recognition; the more you use the same name on your work (at least within any one genre), the more likely people are to remember that name, and the more likely you are to build a following.

If you're a man and want to use a feminine pen name (or vice versa), that's perfectly fine. It's also fine to use a single pen name for the collaborative work of two or more writers.

You do not need to register, copyright, or patent a pseudonym. If you use a pseudonym, you may copyright your work in either your own name or your pseudonym. See pages 358–63 for details.

If you do use one or more pen names, you should of course use your own name in all your dealings with publishers and editors. Sign your own name to letters and contracts. The only place you should use your pseudonym is on your manuscripts. However, you have the option of using that pseudonym when giving interviews, appearing on talk shows, and so on.

If you use a pen name, editors and publishers will automatically keep your true identity from readers. However, if you wish your identity kept *entirely* secret—from everyone except a few people at your publisher— you must specifically request it; otherwise, word will get around through the publishing grapevine. If you have an agent, it is possible to keep your true identity from *everyone* except your agent. Simply instruct him or her to keep your identity a complete secret, and on your manuscripts put only your agent's name and address and your pseudonym.

Publishers will make out checks to your real name rather than your pseudonym unless you specifically request otherwise. There is normally no reason why you wouldn't want checks to be issued in your own name; but, if you like, you may set up a bank account under your pseudonym, or arrange to have checks that are made out to your pseudonym deposited to (or cashed against) your account. Check with your bank. Banks are also usually willing to open AKA (also known as) accounts.

One final note on pseudonyms: sometimes you will see a series of books (often romance or adventure novels) all written by the same pseudonymous author. In many cases this pseudonym is a "house name," or "house author," and the books are actually written by several different writers. This is not uncommon in paperback publishing and is the one case where several different noncollaborating writers may share the same pseudonym.

COLLABORATIONS

A collaboration is like a marriage (and a three-way collaboration is like a ménage-à-trois): each person brings his own strengths, weaknesses, beliefs, feelings, and biases to it; and the process involves regular discussion, negotiation, compromise, and cooperation.

Here are some tips for writers who are contemplating working together on a project—or for writers in search of collaborators:

• Each project is unique. Two writers might work together beautifully on one project but be unable to cooperate on another.

• There is an infinite number of ways in which a collaboration can be arranged. You and your collaborator can work together on every sentence; you can alternate scenes or chapters; one of you can do a first draft, the other a second draft, and so on; one can do the research and the other the writing; or you can combine some or all of these to suit the material and your work habits.

• As a project evolves, you may find that you and/or your collaborator may need to change your plans, your work habits, or your working relationship. *Don't* consider this a problem but, rather, a natural occurrence.

• Writers usually expect that a two-way collaboration will require roughly half as much work per writer as a similar solo project would. This is not always true. Sometimes—depending on the number of drafts, how well the collaborators work together, and the particular project—each writer may put in considerably more (or less) effort than he or she expected.

• Don't forget that as you multiply the number of writers, you divide the amount of money. A $15,000 advance may sound like a lot of money, but if an agent takes 15 percent and the book is a collaboration between two writers, each writer winds up with only $6375 minus expenses and taxes.

• If you run into problems—whatever they may be—try not to blame your collaborator. Instead, put your energy into positive action. See if there's a way things can be worked out and the project completed. Negotiation and compromise are usually better than fighting or scuttling a project. Put your heads together and see if some new workable (though not necessarily happy or ideal) arrangement can be set up. Remember that collaboration is primarily a business relationship. Though tempers may flare and egos may get hurt, these are really just annoying side effects; the main point of your collaboration is to complete the writing project.

• Even in the best of collaborations, there will probably be times when the two (or three) of you will disagree.

• Sometimes you may simply have to admit that the collaboration isn't working, or isn't going to work. If you and/or your collaborator reach this stage, the wise thing to do is to discuss the matter directly, calmly, and nonjudgmentally. Then cut your losses. Work out a way for one of you to back out of the arrangement, or to bring in a replacement writer, or for both of you to scuttle the project. Be very clear about the terms of your breakup. If you originally signed a written agreement to cover your collaboration, it is a good idea to draw up and sign a new agreement covering the breakup. Usually a statement saying "Our agreement dated ———— is hereby and henceforth void, by our mutual agreement" will do.

If your project is a small one—for example, a jointly written feature article for your city paper—then an informal oral agreement with your collaborator is all that is necessary. But for anything much longer, and for anything likely to earn more than about $300, it is extremely important that you and your coauthor draw up and sign a document setting forth the terms of your collaborative efforts. This eliminates (or at least reduces the chances of) future tensions, arguments, ambiguities, misunderstandings, and lawsuits.

You and your collaborator(s) should consider the following issues and come to some agreement on each of them before any significant work on your joint project begins. Most or all of these items should be addressed in your written agreement:

• How will the project's earnings be divided? (Usually money is divided equally among all collaborators, but it doesn't have to be.)

• How will earnings from spin-off projects, licenses for products (T-shirts, lunchboxes, etc.) developed as a result of the project, and any other such income be divided?

• Who will make author appearances on talk shows, give interviews, give lectures, give readings, and otherwise promote the work? How will such efforts, and the money derived directly from them, be divided? What other efforts to promote the work (such as the preparation and sending out of news releases) will be undertaken? How will this effort be shared?

• How will expenses incurred in the research and writing of the project be shared? How will expenses for promotion (advertising, the hiring of a publicist) be shared? If the project is being self-published or self-produced, how will the responsibilities and costs involved in publishing or producing the project be shared? How will other costs (like legal costs, or the cost of preparing an index) be shared? Who will be responsible for the cost and effort of submitting the project?

• If both (or all) collaborators have agents, which agent will handle the project?

• How will the byline read? Which name goes first?

• Who will be responsible for signing any agreements concerning the project? All collaborators? One in particular?

• Who will bear the responsibility of handling correspondence and other details (correcting galleys, preparing an index) for the project?

• Who will receive payments? Will one collaborator receive all payments, then promptly pay other collaborators, or will publishers and agents be directed to write a separate check to each collaborator? (If one writer is to accept payment on behalf of all the collaborators, the agreement should state that payment will be made by that writer to the other collaborators within a specific period of time—certainly no later than thirty days after receipt of money from publishers and/or agents.)

• Who will be responsible for what sorts and amounts of effort in completing the project? (Usually agreements simply state "We will share equally in the writing of the manuscript." This is fine.)

• What will be done in the case of a disagreement? (One common option here is to name an arbitrator in your agreement, whose decision will be binding on all coauthors in the event that you cannot otherwise reach an agreement.)

The above considerations also apply if you are writing the text to a book and your collaborator is providing illustrations or photographs. Most of them apply, too, if your collaborator is really a pseudocollaborator—that is, if your collaborator's contribution consists largely or entirely of his or her byline, which you are adding to your project to make it more attractive to editors or producers. (See pages 291–93 for more on this topic.)

No such agreement is necessary when you are simply purchasing the services of another person—for example, when you're hiring an illustrator to do line drawings for your book or article, or when you're hiring an editorial service or freelance writer to rewrite your manuscript for an hourly fee. In such cases, a simple written agreement covering the services to be rendered and the fee to be paid is sufficient.

An excellent example of an agreement between contributors appears on pages 50–51. The form of this agreement—a letter written jointly from each collaborator to the other—works very nicely. (The book discussed in this agreement was published by Evans in 1984 under the title *Kids' Chic.*)

If you are collaborating with one or more other people on a book, be especially wary of the option clause in your book contract. Ideally this clause should be struck from the contract altogether; but if the publisher insists on keeping it, it should be changed to give the publisher as narrow an option as possible. For example, if you have sold your publisher a jointly written romance novel, the option clause should give the publisher the first shot at "the next romance novel or proposal therefor written jointly by both authors." You should carefully guard against an option clause that gives the publisher the first look at the next book or proposal written by *either* of the collaborators *or* their next collaborative work. You should at most grant only an option on your next *collaborative* book or proposal.

If your contract with a publisher for a book you have written on your own gives it the first option on your next book, this does *not* apply to any book in which you share a byline with one or more other authors. (For more information on option clauses, see pages 354–55.)

The guidelines above also apply to author-agent agreements that give your agent the option to represent your next work; see pages 247–51 for details.

Suppose you don't yet have a collaborator but want one. Where can you find the right person? Here are some resources to consult: friends, relatives, and other people (especially influential or wealthy people) you know (see pages 177–80 for details); your agent; people in local and national writers' groups, clubs, centers, and other organizations, or at writers' conferences; a literary attorney; one or more of your editors; one or more of the reference books and resources (Writer Data Bank, Dial-a-Writer, etc.) on pages 223–25; or editorial services (for a list of these, see *Literary Market Place;* also see pages 411–12).

If you are in need of an illustrator, photographer, or translator for your

January 26, 1983

Gloria Gilbert Mayer

     and

Mary Ellen McGlone

Dear Gloria and Mary Ellen:

Each of us writes this letter to the other to confirm a number of matters ancillary to our agreement of December 20, 1982 with M. Evans and Company, Inc. with respect to a non-fiction work tentatively entitled How to Dress Your Kids Happily, Successfully, and Inexpensively. That agreement is as follows:

1. Each of us commits to the other that she will use her best efforts to fully perform her respective responsibilities in the creation of How to Dress Your Kids Happily, Successfully and Inexpensively in order that the work may be completed in a full and timely manner.

2. All income of every kind and nature generated from or as a consequence of the December 20, 1982 agreement with M. Evans and Company, Inc. shall be equally shared by us in all respects.

3. Should any income be generated as a consequence of the publication of How to Dress Your Kids Happily, Successfully and Inexpensively, but such income shall be derived from sources not controlled by the December 20, 1982 agreement with M. Evans and Company, Inc., such income shall be nonetheless shared by us.

4. To the extent that decisions are to be made concerning the development of additional income sources as a result of publication of How to Dress Your Kids Happily, Successfully and Inexpensively, and such decisions shall be ours to make, we agree to be guided by the following parameters:

(a) All that shall be done must be consistent with and
    not violative of the terms and conditions of the
    December 20, 1982 agreement with M. Evans and Com-
    pany, Inc.

(b) Where alternative courses of action are available,
    we agree to pursue the alternative which is most
    apt to increase the income stream available to us.
    Where we may differ on the appropriate alternative
    to be pursued, we agree to negotiate with one anoth-
    er in good faith in order to resolve our differences
    without trauma and expense. If, notwithstanding
    such efforts, we shall be unable to agree upon an
    appropriate course of action, we then agree to
    submit the matter to Samuel L. Kaplan, or some
    other arbitrator deemed mutually acceptable, and
    his decision shall be deemed final and binding upon
    us. (In acting as arbitrator, Samuel L. Kaplan, or
    any other party selected by us, shall not be obliged
    to proceed with formality and in accordance with
    rules of evidence; rather, he may make his decision
    based upon such information as he deems necessary
    and shall receive that information in such manner
    as he deems appropriate.)

                    Sincerely,

                    _____
                    Gloria Gilbert Mayer

                    _____
                    Mary Ellen McGlone

work, either to serve as a collaborator or simply to hire on a freelance basis, you can find lists of all these professionals in *Literary Market Place*.

More information on collaboration appears on pages 291–93.

OTHER BASIC BOOKS

Although this book is quite thorough on some points and utterly definitive on others, no single book on writing can discuss absolutely every topic. Below is a list of recommended books that cover quite thoroughly those topics only touched upon in this volume:

Writing for Film

The Screenwriter's Handbook by Constance Nash and Virginia Oakey (Barnes & Noble) is the best guide for prospective screenwriters.

Writing for Television

Television Writer's Handbook by Constance Nash and Virginia Oakey (Barnes & Noble) is quite good. Also very good is *Television Writing— From Concept to Contract* by Richard A. Blum (Focal Press). This volume covers writing documentaries as well as dramatic scripts, and focuses on public and cable TV as well as the major networks.

Writing for the Stage

How to Write a Play by Raymond Hull (Writer's Digest Books) and *The Playwright's Handbook* by Frank Pike and Thomas G. Dunn (Plume Books) deal with both playwriting technique and the business end of playwriting, including getting your plays produced. Also see *Three Genres*, two paragraphs below.

Writing for Radio

Not much is available on this topic. However, J. Michael Straczynski's *The Complete Book of Scriptwriting* (Writer's Digest Books) has some useful information on writing radio scripts, as well as information on writing for TV, film, and stage.

Fiction and Poetry Writing

Three Genres by Stephen Minot (Prentice-Hall) is an excellent and thorough book on the techniques of writing fiction, poetry, and drama. Also inspiring, and very unusual, is Natalie Goldberg's *Writing Down the Bones* (Shambhala), which treats writing as an unfolding of both creative and spiritual impulses.

Nonfiction Writing

There is no better book than William Zinsser's *On Writing Well* (Harper & Row); it is clear and to the point—and a joy to read.

General Writing, Usage, and Style

The Elements of Style by William Strunk and E. B. White (Macmillan) has been a standard writer's companion for decades. This excellent reference book is inexpensive, useful, and easy to read. You will probably not need any of the larger style manuals, such as the Modern Language Association or University of Chicago guides, unless you write for scholarly journals.

Word Processing

The Word Processing Book by Peter McWilliams (Ballantine) and *Writing with a Word Processor* by William Zinsser (Harper & Row) are both excellent. The two books complement rather than duplicate each other, and if you are new to word processing, both are worthy investments.

Basic References

Every writer should have a good, thick dictionary and a good thesaurus. Your dictionary should be large enough to contain 95 percent of the words you are likely to look up. It need not be unabridged, but the thicker it is, the better. Unabridged dictionaries run as inexpensive as $25 in hardcover. Slightly less complete dictionaries go for as little as $10 in hardcover and $3 or $4 in paperback. You may be able to find a good used hardcover version at a fraction of the cost of a new one. Don't get a dictionary that you won't use—that is, one so large and heavy that you're unwilling to pick it up, or one with print so small that you need a magnifying glass. As for a thesaurus, get one that proceeds alphabetically, as it will be much easier to use.

If you are a poor or mediocre speller, purchase a dictionary of commonly misspelled words, listed alphabetically by their proper spelling. I also recommend *The Bad Speller's Dictionary* (Random House), which lists commonly misspelled words alphabetically by their most common *incorrect* spellings. Correct spellings appear next to the misspellings.

There are, of course, other good books on these subjects, as well as on dozens of more specialized areas of writing such as romance writing, fillers, science fiction, cookbook writing, and so on. Throughout this book, as I discuss a topic, I will recommend useful books that supplement my own discussion.

GENERAL TIPS AND RECOMMENDATIONS

• Everyone's experience in writing and publishing is unique. What works for one writer may fail for another. Fred may find a particular editor a complete joy to work with, while Ethel may find that same editor uncooperative and closed-minded.

• Some writers get lucky breaks, and others get unlucky ones. Circumstances beyond your control will undoubtedly play a significant part in your career. Put in your best efforts and let the chips fall where they may. The more you are willing to put in regular, concerted effort toward writing, marketing, and general career-building, and the longer you keep at all these tasks, the better your chances of success become.

• It is quite true that good work often goes unpublished and that a great deal of schlock sees print. Every one of us, at one time or another, has read a perfectly dreadful piece, often by a famous or well-to-do writer, and said, "Hell, I can write better than that." However, it remains generally true that good writing gets published more often than bad writing.

• No editor or publication is perfect. Each will have his or her (or its) own limitations and drawbacks. One publication will treat you courteously and will pay careful attention to detail, but will pay slowly or in small amounts. Another will pay well but will overedit your work. A third will pay well and quickly and will provide good editing, but will reject half your work with little or no comment.

• Keep careful records of all your submissions: what was sent; the editor, publisher, and address to which it was sent; the date on which it was sent; and the date on which you received a reply.

• For writers who are slow, poor, or incompetent typists, or who hate to type, I strongly recommend professional typists and typing services. If you can get a typist who has a top-quality typewriter—or, better yet, a computer—you can get great-looking results.

If you think you may want to revise your manuscript, or if you suspect your editor will ask you to, it pays to have it put on a computer disk. You can do this one of two ways: have it typed by someone with word processing equipment, or have the typed manuscript transferred to a disk with an optical scanner, a piece of equipment that some large word processing services own. Once a manuscript is on a disk, making changes is quick, easy, and inexpensive.

The cost of manuscript typing varies widely. Some typists charge from $1 to $2 a double-spaced page. Some typists charge by the hour, and I've seen rates ranging from $8 to $28 an hour. Call around to get quotes and compare prices. You should be able to get quality work for $1 to $1.25 a page, $1.50 to $1.70 for work put on a computer disk. If you are being charged by the hour (most manuscript typists can do six to ten pages an hour), $10 an hour is reasonable ($12 if the manuscript is being put on a disk). Prices in Canada run about 25% higher. Some typists will give discounts for long projects (those over fifty or a hundred pages). If you are being charged by the page, ask for elite or 12-pitch type; this gives you about fifty more words a page than the standard pica, or 10-pitch, type.

To locate manuscript typists, check the "We Type Manuscripts" section of *Writer's Digest* magazine or the reference book *Literary Market Place.* But the very best sources of ads for inexpensive typists are the newspaper of your nearest college and any prominent bulletin boards at that college. You can also check your Yellow Pages under "Typing Services," "Word Processing," and "Secretarial Services," but these services are often more expensive (sometimes much more) than independent typists and manuscript specialists. Typing services offered by copy and print shops also tend to be expensive.

If you do hire a typist, be sure he or she understands manuscript form completely. Explain it thoroughly; better yet, give the typist samples, such as the examples in this book.

Be sure to proofread every word in every manuscript *carefully* once it has been typed. Typists make errors, and sometimes major ones, even if they have the most sophisticated equipment.

Typists will correct any of their own errors at no charge. If you make revisions of your own, and want these changes made on a computer disk, you will normally be charged by the hour ($12 to $20 an hour is fair).

When you send your work out to be typed, always keep a photocopy, so that you are safe if your work gets lost.

• The word "manuscript" is often abbreviated "ms." by editors and writers. The plural of ms. is mss.

• If you've written a piece that tells a true story but that can be meaningful and/or entertaining if read as fiction, feel free to submit it to fiction markets as a short story or novel, as well as to nonfiction markets as an article or nonfiction book. No editor will object to publishing a true story as fiction.

• If you need to telephone an editor, do it on a Tuesday, Wednesday, or Thursday if possible. Mondays and Fridays are typically very hectic. You may call literary agents any day of the working week, however. The best hours to call anyone in publishing are 10 to 12 AM and 2:15 to 4:15 PM.

• Much of the publishing world slows to a near-standstill between December 20 and January 25. Don't expect much to happen during this time.

• If your editor or publisher suggests that you meet for lunch, say yes. The publishing firm will pick up the tab, and the food will usually be good.

2. ✎

Marketing Your Work

WHEN IS A PIECE READY TO SEND OUT?

This important question confronts every freelancer every time he or she comes close to completing a project. The more of a perfectionist you are, the more difficult answering this question becomes. There is a tendency to want to keep working on a piece indefinitely, fine-tuning it here and there, each time getting it a little closer to perfection. But this can go on forever, and the piece never leaves your desk.

On the other hand, it is also tempting for some writers (particularly newer ones eager for publication) to get a piece out to editors as soon as possible, and sometimes they get it out *too* soon, before it has been thoroughly thought through or rewritten. A piece that goes out too soon is likely to come right back.

Here are some tips that should help resolve this dilemma:

• Usually a piece is not done until you have read it over, both aloud and silently, and it looks, sounds, and feels right. Trust your feelings here: if something about the piece feels wrong, but you can't put your finger on it, you are probably better off not sending it out yet. Put it aside for a few days, then come back to it and see if you can pinpoint the problem. If on this later reading you feel fine about the piece, go ahead and send it out.

• Don't be afraid to rewrite, revise, and edit as much as you need to. And don't skip the final step of editing for proper grammar, punctuation, syntax, and diction, and for typographical errors.

• Remember that some pieces will need a lot more work than others. Sometimes an edited first draft will be in excellent shape; other times extensive rewrites are necessary.

• As you go through a piece, the amount of rewriting and editing you will need to do will normally shrink each time. Once you have reached the point where you are simply tinkering with occasional words and phrases, finish that round of editing and then stop. While further rounds of editing might improve the piece marginally, it won't be worth the effort you'd put into it. The only exception to this rule is poetry, which by its nature requires close attention to small details.

• You can always change your mind. If you decide a piece is finished and send it out, then later realize it can use some more work, you can always make those changes. If the piece sells, you can usually submit a revised manuscript or make changes on your galleys. And if it doesn't sell on the first round, you can make the changes before sending it out again.

SHOULD YOU SLANT EACH PIECE
TOWARD A PARTICULAR MARKET?

Most books on freelance writing, and most people who teach classes in writing and publishing, stress the importance of writing each piece for a particular market—of doing your best to make each piece conform to one particular publication's style, format, and other specifications.

However, a strong case can be made for doing precisely the opposite: for ignoring a publication's specifications and writing exactly what it is you want to write—then trying to find the most likely markets for it. This is how I work, and it's the strategy I recommend to most writers.

If you are the kind of writer for whom creativity and the rewards of writing what you want to write come first and foremost, then you should write what you damn well please, and only when it is completed to your satisfaction should you think about marketing it. But if you are a writer for whom making money is most important—and particularly if you want to earn the most money for the least labor—you may lean toward the first approach.

The main ideas behind slanting your work toward one particular market are: (1) the more you zero in on the specifications of that publication, the more likely you are to produce something its editor will want to buy; and (2) no matter what happens, you know that you have at least *one* market for what you are writing.

By slanting a piece toward a particular market, however, you may severely limit your other options for that piece. For example, if you slant your article on puffins exclusively toward *Smithsonian* magazine, and *Smithsonian* rejects it, what can you do with it next? You can of course send it to other magazines, but you may wind up getting rejection letters that say, "This is too much of a *Smithsonian* piece for us." You can also rewrite the piece; but if you hadn't written it so clearly for *Smithsonian* in the first place, a rewrite would be unnecessary. Every time you slant a piece toward a particular publication, you are to some degree slanting it away from its competitors.

Slanting your work in one *general* direction often works well, though. By slanting a piece toward a *group of readers*—housewives, or back-to-the-land types, or amateur inventors—you target a particular *group* of publications, rather than only one.

Naturally, if you are writing a piece *on assignment,* or on spec (see page 129 for a definition) for a particular publication, you *should* gear it closely to that publication's needs.

A CLOSE LOOK AT THE MARKETS

There are thousands of places (or "markets") in the United States and Canada in which to publish your work, plus thousands more elsewhere. Many of these markets are invisible to the general public. These hidden markets include in-house publications, scholarly journals, government publications, resource and reference publishers, textbook publishers, medical and technical publications, journals for the various industries and professions (sometimes called trade journals), video and film scripts for business and industry, and so on and on. A quick look through almost any of the resources on pages 75–82 of this book will reveal dozens, even hundreds of markets you probably never considered before.

Even many consumer publications never make their way into libraries, bookstores, or newsstands. Insurance companies, banks, airlines, auto clubs, and countless other businesses regularly publish magazines only for their customers. Literary magazines and books often get minimal distribution through stores and libraries, but are nevertheless read by an enthusiastic (though small) group of readers. Publications directed at readers who share a common interest may be unheard of by most people, but may be read avidly by members of that audience.

What follows is a look at many of the major markets. Because I am dealing with whole categories of publications, I must speak in generalities. Follow the guidelines later in this chapter to learn exactly what markets are right for your projects.

MAGAZINES, JOURNALS, AND NEWSLETTERS

Magazines are where most beginning writers get their start, and the small and medium-sized ones are some of the easiest places to break into print.

The vast majority of magazines have a narrow focus and a very specific audience. *Motor Trend, Organic Gardening, Ellery Queen's Mystery Magazine, Yachting, Dance, The New England Journal of Medicine, Antaeus, The Nation, Easy Rider, Chicago, Yankee, Scientific American, Campus Voice,* and *College Composition and Communication* are each directed at a particular readership, and each publishes only material that is likely to appeal to that audience. The trick is to find the magazine whose audience, approach, or both closely match your own.

In general, the smaller a magazine's readership, the less it pays and the easier it is to break into. However, most of the middle-sized magazines are very open to new writers, and are excellent places to get started.

Fiction and Nonfiction

The great majority of magazines publish primarily or entirely nonfiction, though a few of these will also publish some fiction or poetry of interest to their readers, especially if it is humorous or satirical.

The following magazines publish fiction on a regular basis: *The New Yorker, Harper's, The Atlantic, Saturday Evening Post,* and a very few other prestigious general-interest magazines; the largest men's magazines; most women's magazines; many (though not all) literary magazines; and genre magazines (mystery, science fiction, horror, etc.).

Few other magazines publish much fiction regularly or at all, and in general the market for short fiction is limited. Each type of magazine—men's, women's, literary, science fiction, mystery, and so on—publishes its own particular kind of fiction. So, to a strong degree, does each magazine within each of these categories.

Payment for both fiction and nonfiction may be made by the word, by the column inch, by the page, or by the piece. Rates for previously unpublished material can range from a few contributor's copies to a few thousand dollars. Here is a general breakdown:

• The largest and most prestigious consumer magazines pay between 25¢ and $1 a word, even more in some cases. Magazines in this category include *Architectural Digest, The Atlantic, Cosmopolitan, Esquire, Family Circle, Good Housekeeping, Harper's, Ladies' Home Journal, Macleans, McCall's, Modern Maturity, Ms., The New Yorker, Omni, Parents, Penthouse, Playboy, Reader's Digest, Rolling Stone, Saturday Evening Post, Seventeen, Vogue, Woman's Day,* and a couple of dozen others. These magazines are generally quite difficult to break into.

• The great majority of magazines are special-interest publications, the larger of which pay between 10¢ and 25¢ a word. The hundreds of magazines in this category include *The Artist's Magazine, Astronomy, Cricket, Dance, Field and Stream, High Times, Medical Economics, The New Republic, Outside, Popular Mechanics, Prevention, Sail, Self, Swank, Twin Cities, Washingtonian, The Writer,* and *Yankee.*

• Some of the smaller special-interest magazines, many trade and professional journals, and the larger literary magazines tend to pay 5¢ to 10¢ a word. Magazines largely or solely devoted to fiction also tend to pay these rates. Examples here include *Artspace, Asimov's Science Fiction Magazine, City Miner, Ellery Queen's Mystery Magazine, The Iowa Review,* and *Prism International.*

• The smallest magazines and newsletters pay nothing at all except for a few free copies and/or a free subscription. Some pay a pittance of 1¢ to 5¢ a word. Publications in this category include the lesser-known literary magazines, most newsletters, most scholarly and medical journals, some technical magazines, some professional and trade journals, and most in-house periodicals. Magazines with very small or specialized readerships often fall into this category.

Reprint sales normally earn half to two-thirds a publication's regular rate for new material, though in some cases rates can go as high as 100 percent or as low as 30 percent.

Poetry

The vast majority of published poems appear in literary magazines. (Not all literary magazines publish poetry, however.) This poetry is geared toward a highly literate audience.

The small amount of poetry published in commercial magazines (with the exception of *The New Yorker, Harper's, The Atlantic,* and two or three others) is *not* written for a highly literate audience, but for an unsophisticated one. Most of the poetry in these magazines would be described as sophomoric or even subliterate by literary magazine editors. Don't confuse the commercial with the literary market for poetry, as they publish very different sorts of things. Read the magazines and you'll see.

The smaller literary magazines pay for material in free copies and/or subscriptions. The larger and better-known ones pay $5 to $40 a printed page, or $15 to $75 a poem. The commercial magazines pay $20 to $100 a poem, occasionally a bit more. The top magazines (like *The New Yorker*) pay a good deal more. However, your chances of breaking into one of these top magazines with a poem (unless you have already been widely published in literary magazines) are very close to zero.

There are many commercial and literary magazines in Canada and the British Commonwealth that publish poetry.

NEWSPAPERS

You are limited almost exclusively to nonfiction in these markets, though once in a while you might be able to sneak a short story or poem into print somewhere, especially in a Sunday magazine supplement.

Rates of payment vary greatly from paper to paper. Generally, the larger the circulation, the more the paper pays. Small town and neighborhood papers often pay nothing at all, or perhaps a pittance of $10 to $25 for a freelance article or review. Papers of circulations between 20,000 and 100,000 (serving either middle-sized cities or the suburbs of big ones) usually pay between $25 and $100 for an article and $15 to $40 for a review or very short piece (under a thousand words). Big-city papers pay anywhere from $100 to $400 for a full-length article (over fifteen hundred words), $75 to $200 for a shorter piece, and $25 to $100 for a review. A few of the biggest papers sometimes pay more.

Keep in mind that, with the exception of a small handful of big-city papers, you can keep selling the same piece to paper after paper, provided that the piece has not previously appeared in print in that city or region. Newspapers usually pay the same (or close to the same) rates for reprinted material as for new pieces.

Small-town and neighborhood newspapers are usually quite easy to break into; sometimes it's simply a matter of calling the editor and saying, "I'd like to write for you." The bigger the paper, the harder it is to break in, but even many big-city papers are quite receptive to features and reviews from newer writers.

SYNDICATES

If you have a regular feature, column, or comic strip that you wish to syndicate, you may try to syndicate it yourself, publication by publication. This is a lot of work. Most writers prefer to approach the syndicates. These organizations sell their clients' work to newspapers and magazines throughout the United States and often outside it as well. The more publications that publish an item, the more money both the syndicate and the writer make.

Most people are familiar with the five or six biggest syndicates, but there are over a hundred smaller ones. Some of these specialize in features for religious publications, college newspapers, and other specialized markets. A good listing of syndicates and the names of their editors can be found in the annual volume *Editor and Publisher Syndicate Directory.*

Before you approach a syndicate, you will first need to complete quite a few samples of your column or feature. You can begin with as few as six to eight, but chances are that before any syndicate editor says yes, he or she will want to see a good many more, often as many as twenty-five to fifty—maybe even more than that. (If you are asked to write a large number of samples—say, more than twenty-five—you have the right to ask for some development money to pay for your time. Don't expect to always get it, however.)

To approach a syndicate, write its editor a short letter explaining what readers your work is intended for, what focus it has, and what makes it different, special, or unique. Be concise and businesslike, however; don't give the editor a sales pitch. Inform the editor of your publications and other writing achievements, and of any other appropriate background, expertise, or training you may have. Enclose several (or more than several) samples of the column or feature you are offering for syndication.

If your work gets syndicated in only a few publications, you'll earn peanuts. But if it catches on at some point and becomes widely syndicated, you may find yourself quite well-to-do, perhaps even wealthy. Payment for syndicated publication is usually lower per newspaper or magazine than for sales you might make yourself. However, a syndicate is far more likely to place your work in a large number of publications, and your total earnings may thus be greater—perhaps much greater.

The largest syndicates are extremely difficult to break into. If you have material you wish to syndicate, don't be discouraged by rejection. Six months later, submit new work (either a new idea or new samples of the same idea or both) to the same syndicate (and the same editor, if he or she still works there). If this material gets rejected, too, try a third time six months later. Most of the people who are represented by major syndicates were rejected at least twice by those very same syndicates before being taken on.

Some book agents will represent material for syndication. This representation is helpful but not strictly necessary.

TELEVISION AND FILM

Breaking in here is quite difficult, and *much* more difficult if you don't have an agent. Living in the Los Angeles area can help a good deal, at least in terms of making contacts and learning industry scuttlebutt. But this is a very tough row to hoe no matter how talented you may be.

The money is excellent, however. A half-hour script for a TV show ordinarily earns its writer several thousand dollars. Original scripts for full-length films earn their writers over $10,000, and frequently a great deal more. Film treatments often go for five-figure sums. The sale of movie or TV rights to a play or book can go for as little as a few thousand dollars or as much as a few hundred thousand. The sky is the upper limit, and the lower limits are also pretty high.

The risk is commensurate with the money. The TV and film industries are nowhere near as friendly or open as print publishing, and for writers they can sometimes be downright cruel. It is roughly as difficult for a new writer to make it in Hollywood as it is for an unknown actor or actress. In fact, it is sometimes easier to write or rewrite a TV or film script into a novel, sell the novel, and then (with luck) sell the TV or film rights to it. (You *might* also be able to get the job of turning the novel into—or back into—a script. Or, if the script is already finished, you might be able to sell that to the producer who bought the TV or movie rights.)

BOOKS

Tens of thousands of books are published in the United States every year; even more are published elsewhere. The chart that follows looks at the many different book markets. All the estimates of salability are for projects that are decently written and either useful or entertaining (or both). In cases of professional, text, scholarly, and nonfiction trade books, the presumption is that projects are unique or unusual in content or approach. Projects that are poorly written or that offer readers little in the way of

Trade Books

Type of Book	Salability to a Major Publisher through an Agent	Salability to a Major Publisher without an Agent	Range of Advances—Major Publishers	Salability to a Smaller Publisher with or without an Agent	Range of Advances—Smaller Publishers	Range for U.S. Royalties[1]
Self-help and how-to—task orientation	Fair to good	Poor to fair	$3000–$100,000; usually $5000–$25,000	Fair to good	0–$15,000	**Adult Trade Books** Hardcover: 10–20% of cover price; usually 10% on the first 5000 copies sold, 12½% on the next 5000 copies, and 15% thereafter. Trade paperback: 6–8% of cover price; usually 7½–8%.
Self-help and how-to—psychological orientation	Poor to fair	Poor	$3000–$25,000; usually $5000–$15,000	Poor to fair	0–$10,000	
Other nonfiction (reference, collected essays, humor and satire, cookbooks, history, etc.)	Fair	Poor	$3000–$75,000; usually $5000–$20,000	Fair to good	0–$15,000	
General novels	Fair[2]	Poor[2]	$3000–$400,000; usually $5000–$15,000	Poor to fair[2]	0–$15,000; usually 0–$7500	

Type of Book	Salability to a Major Publisher through an Agent	Salability to a Major Publisher without an Agent	Range of Advances—Major Publishers	Salability to a Smaller Publisher with or without an Agent	Range of Advances—Smaller Publishers	Range for U.S. Royalties[1]
Mystery novels	Fair to good	Poor to fair	$3000–$25,000; usually $5000–$10,000	Fair	0–$10,000	Mass-market paperback: 6–10% of cover price; usually 8%.
Romance novels	Fair to good	Fair	$3000–$25,000; usually $5000–$15,000	Fair	0–$10,000	
Western novels	Fair to good	Fair	$3000–$15,000; usually $3000–$10,000	Poor to fair	0–$5000	
Horror novels	Fair	Poor	$3000–$50,000; usually $3000–$15,000	Poor to fair	0–$10,000	
Male adventure novels	Fair	Fair	$3000–$15,000	Fair	0–$10,000	
Science fiction novels	Fair	Fair	$3000–$50,000; usually $3000–$15,000	Poor to fair	0–$10,000; usually 0–$5000	

Category						Trade Books for Children and Young Adults
Short-story collections[3]	Poor (rarely handled by agents)	None to very poor	$2000–$15,000; usually $2000–$6000	Poor to fair[4]	0–$7500; usually 0–$2500	
Poetry collections	Very poor to poor (extremely rarely handled by agents)	None to very poor	$1000–$5000	Poor to fair[4]	0–$5000; usually 0	
Anthologies	Fair	Poor	$7500–$50,000[5]	Fair	0–$15,000[5]	
Fiction for children and young adults	Fair to good	Fair	$2500–$15,000	Poor to fair	0–$7500	
Nonfiction for children and young adults	Fair to good	Fair	$2500–$15,000	Fair	0–$7500	Hardcover: 10–15% of cover price; usually 10%.
Picture books for children	Fair	Poor to fair	$2000–$15,000	Fair	0–$3000	Trade paperback: 5–7% of cover price. Mass-market paperback: 6–8% of cover price.

Type of Book	Salability to a Major Publisher through an Agent	Salability to a Major Publisher without an Agent	Range of Advances—Major Publishers	Salability to a Smaller Publisher with or without an Agent	Range of Advances—Smaller Publishers	Range for U.S. Royalties[1]
Other Books						
Textbooks	Good	Fair to good	0–$25,000; usually $2500–$10,000	Fair to good	0–$15,000	Hardcover and paperback: 8–20% of amount received by publisher; usually 10–15%.[6]
Professional, technical, and medical books	Good	Fair to good	0–$15,000; usually $3000–$10,000	Good	0–$10,000	Hardcover and paperback: usually 10–15% of amount received by publisher; sometimes 10–15% of cover price.

| Scholarly[7] books | Good | Good | 0–$10,000; usually 0–$3000 | Good | 0–$5000; usually 0 | Hardcover: 10–15% of amount received by publisher or cover price. Paperback: 5–10% of amount received by publisher or cover price. No royalties may be paid on first 1000–2500 copies or on 1st printing. |

[1] Royalties for copies sold in the United States via regular retail outlets at discounts of less than 50 percent. Lower royalties apply to sales made under other circumstances.

[2] Ratings are for completed books. Novels are usually more difficult to sell on the basis of proposals. First novels, except romance, science fiction, horror, and western novels, are even harder to sell on a proposal basis.

[3] Includes both general and genre (mystery, science fiction, etc.) collections.

[4] The major markets here are literary and university presses.

[5] Includes the cost of all permissions, which must be purchased from contributors.

[6] These rates apply to college textbooks. Royalties for high school and elementary texts may be lower, perhaps much lower.

[7] Refers to books for a scholarly audience, *not* to any book published by a scholarly or university press. Some publishers that specialize in scholarly works also publish some trade books, or books that appeal to both markets at once. Usually trade royalties are paid on such books. Some houses that publish primarily trade books also publish scholarly titles, or some titles for both audiences. Examples include Harper & Row and St. Martin's Press. Royalties paid are based on the type of book.

entertainment, guidance, information, or new approaches to a topic are of course considerably less salable, and probably unsalable. The chart also applies to writers who are new or not terribly well known. Writers with widely recognized names, and famous people in any field, can often command higher advances and royalties, and they of course have a much easier time selling their work. My figures and ratings are, of necessity, generalities, and there will be exceptions to each of them. They do, however, accurately reflect the current realities of book publishing.

Collections of short stories and poems are almost always difficult to sell. However, if some or many of the pieces in your collection have previously appeared in magazines or anthologies, this will make the book more attractive to editors and publishers. The more such publications you have, and the more prestigious those publications are, the better. Other previous publications of fiction or poetry also help.

A book's actual earnings are the result of copies sold, which generate royalties, and of the sale of subsidiary publication rights to other publishers, both domestic and foreign. A book may receive only a small advance, or none at all, yet ultimately earn its author a great deal of money.

A note on advances: some publishers sometimes offer huge advances; others never offer any advances at all. A book worth only $5000 to one publisher may be worth $25,000 to another. Though a widely-published writer is, generally speaking, likely to earn higher advances than a new one, I have heard of first novels selling for several hundred thousand dollars and books by well-known writers receiving advances of only two or three thousand dollars—and sometimes no advances at all. The same publisher might offer $300,000 for one book and $3000 for another.

THE IMPORTANCE OF MARKET RESEARCH

Before any company introduces a new product, it researches the potential market for that product. Your writing is also a salable product; to successfully market it, you too will need to do careful and thorough market research.

Suppose you have written a parody of travel articles. Do you send it to the major travel magazines, such as *Travel-Holiday* and *Travel and Leisure?* Or should you first try the in-flight magazines put out by the various airlines? Do any of these publications publish humor? Of the ones that do, would any of them stand for a parody of the very articles they most often publish? Would *National Lampoon* perhaps be your best bet?

What are the addresses of these publications, and what are the names of their editors? Which editor at each publication is the right one to send your manuscript to? Are there any other magazines that might be interested in your piece?

Your market research will (and must) answer these questions. Without this research, you can waste your time, energy, and money submitting your work to unlikely or inappropriate markets, or to the wrong editors at the right publications. Without it, you may overlook the publications that are your best bets for a particular piece.

Because each publication has its own particular style, approach, readership, and specific requirements for material, it is usually not sufficient to know merely a publication's general focus. *Ms., Playgirl,* and *Good Housekeeping* are all women's magazines, but they print very different kinds of material. *Asimov's Science Fiction Magazine* and *Amazing Stories* are both science fiction publications, but they print different sorts of stories and are targeted at somewhat different readerships.

The best way to conduct market research is to seek out and read recent and current issues of the publications that may be potential markets. In the case of TV shows, this means watching the shows. In the case of play and movie producers, it means learning what other projects they have produced in the past couple of years and, if possible, seeing one or more of those productions. In the case of book publishing, it means being familiar with the titles currently being published by the presses you have in mind. Second-hand sources, such as *Writer's Market* and the writers' magazines, are *not* adequate substitutes for your own first-hand research. The only exceptions to this rule are newspaper and syndicate markets.

Even if you write regularly in a particular field, I recommend doing a survey of the markets in that field every four to six months, to see if there have been any changes in publications' styles, formats, slants, areas of coverage, addresses, or editors, and to see if any new publications have been founded or old ones closed down. If you write for a publication occasionally but do not read it regularly, be sure to read an issue every few months to keep abreast of any changes.

WRITER'S MARKET *AND* OTHER STANDARD RESOURCES

Writer's Market is an annual reference work listing a wide variety of markets for writers in many fields, including popular magazines, trade journals, book publishers, syndicates, play producers, producers of business and industrial films, cartoonists who buy gags, greeting card markets, and so on. It normally publishes, for each publication: name and address; a paragraph or more of description on what it publishes; information on rates of payment, time required to respond to manuscripts, rights purchased, and when payment is made; the names of one or more editors; and other useful information for writers. It has spawned such annual progeny as *Novel & Short Story Writer's Market, Inspirational Writer's Market, Photographer's Market, Poet's Market, Songwriter's Market, Artist's Market,* and *Children's Writer's and Illustrator's Market,* as well as related titles from other publishers such as *Audio-Visual Market Place, Religious Writer's Marketplace,* and *Microcomputer Market Place.*

Writer's Market's main competitor, the annual *Writer's Handbook,* also contains a list of many markets. Here the information on each market is considerably more limited, but it always includes names, addresses, and rates of payment for each publication. *The Writer's Handbook* also includes several hundred pages of articles on the craft of writing and the business aspects of the profession.

These are the best-known, and perhaps the best-selling, reference books for writers. They are not, however, the most useful.

There are also magazines and newsletters for writers. The most popular general magazines are *Poets & Writers, The Writer, Writer's Digest,* and *Writer's Yearbook.* Each of these regularly publishes a good deal of useful information for writers on many different subjects, including markets.

All of these reference books and magazines faithfully pass on to readers the market information they receive from publishers. However, the information they provide is limited, and sometimes inaccurate or unreliable. In part this is simply because no publication's slant, approach, or style can be accurately conveyed in a few words or sentences. For example, although both Zebra Books and North Point Press publish "adult fiction," Zebra is unlikely to publish a collection of literary short stories, whereas North Point publishes such collections on a regular basis.

Furthermore, editors do not always take the time or care to write good descriptions of their wants and needs, and a great many publishers in all fields fail to supply these magazines and reference volumes with any information at all and thus receive no coverage in them. Sometimes this failure is deliberate: the editors already have all the contacts with writers they desire, and they do not wish to be inundated with manuscripts from writers with whom they are not familiar.

A few editors deliberately provide misleading information to writers' magazines and reference books as a way to keep amateurs and writers they don't know personally from breaking into their publications. The main way they do this is by asking writers to send their work to "The Editors" or "Editorial Department." Any manuscripts that come in so addressed are automatically put in the "slush pile"—the stack of submissions earmarked to receive the least consideration. Some publications will specify an editor by name—but the intended effect is the same. For instance, "Jane Smith, Assistant Editor" may actually be a secretary who has been told to put all manuscripts addressed to her in the slush pile.

The New Yorker, and a few other publications, have used the opposite tack, but with similar intent. For many years, *The New Yorker* listed its editor as William Shawn in *Writer's Market.* Shawn was in fact its editor-in-chief for those years, but he normally worked only with those writers whom he knew personally, by reputation, or by recommendation. If *you* had sent a manuscript to Shawn, it would normally have gone directly into the slush pile. (Shawn has since left *The New Yorker.*) *The New Yorker* is one of the very few magazines that does not publish a list of its editors, or any of its staff, in each issue. Writers who wish to be published in *The New Yorker* are expected to work their way up in the literary scene so that they can learn the name of a *New Yorker* editor from a publisher, agent, writer, or other editor.

If all this seems crass or deceitful, remember that editors are seeking some way of making a preliminary judgment as to which manuscripts are worth the most serious consideration. If *The New Yorker* were to reveal the names of its editors, each of those editors would immediately be deluged with hundreds, perhaps thousands, of manuscripts. The way around all this is to find out who the appropriate editor of a publication is, and then to address your work to him or her *by name.* The importance of this, and the means for locating the right editors, will be discussed later in this chapter.

Lag-time is another reason why reference sources sometimes provide less-than-accurate information. Months can pass between the time an editor sends information to a reference publication and the time that information sees print. By the time you read it and send your manuscript out, the publication may have changed its focus, format, policies, address, editors, and/or owners.

Editors also sometimes provide misleading or untrue information concerning rates of payment, time required to respond to manuscripts, circulation, when payment is made, rights purchased, frequency of publication, and other such details. Sometimes editors will go so far as to state in one or more of the standard writers' resources that they consider unsolicited manuscripts, when in fact they do not. What is more common, however, is for publications that *do* consider unsolicited material to claim publicly that they don't. See pages 124–26 for details.

Also keep in mind that editors don't always know what it is they want to publish—and even if they do, they are not always able to articulate it clearly. Information in reference publications can be *unwittingly* misleading to writers for this reason. (For the same reason, official guidelines for writers provided by any publication should also be taken with a grain of salt.)

After all this, you may be surprised to learn that I consider most writers' magazines, and most reference books for writers, to be valuable resources. But they should be used properly: they are *places to begin* researching your potential markets, not places to do *all* your research. By using these resources, and others that I will describe shortly, you can establish a pool of *possible* markets for a manuscript. Further research will establish which of these markets are viable and which are not.

Incidentally, there is one form of writers' publication that does *not* normally suffer from any of the problems described above: the professional journal or newsletter. This is a publication put out by a professional writers' organization, such as Western Writers of America or the American Society of Journalists and Authors. Usually these publications are provided free to members only, though in some cases outsiders can order subscriptions for a fee. These magazines and newsletters usually have reliable and up-to-date market information.

USEFUL RESOURCES

To begin your market research, start with one or more of the reference sources listed below. No writer will need all of these resources; pick the ones that are most useful for the kind(s) of writing you do.

Most of the information sources below are quite expensive to purchase, but many or most of them can be found in any large urban or college library. The reference volumes can most often be found in the reference section, sometimes on "ready reserve" directly behind the reference desk. In the list that follows, magazines are marked with asterisks; reference books have no such mark. The listing is alphabetical. Addresses are provided for resources not commonly available in public libraries.

Artist Update* Published monthly by the Foundation for the Community of Artists, 280 Broadway, Suite 412, New York, NY 10007. Carries information on markets, grants, and contests for writers, as well as for artists in other fields.

AWP Newsletter* Published four times a year by the Associated Writing Programs, Old Dominion University, Norfolk, VA 23508. Primarily devoted to college writing programs and the teaching of writing. Publishes some useful information for writers of literary fiction, poems, and essays.

The Bloomsbury Review* Published bimonthly at 1028 Bannock Street, Denver, CO 80204. Each issue of this very interesting magazine contains numerous reviews of books of nearly all types—trade books (including children's books), scholarly books, books from university and literary presses, and a good many other books that most other magazines overlook. *Bloomsbury* can help you determine what publishing houses are publishing what kinds of books.

Directory of Literary Magazines Published every other year by the Coordinating Council of Literary Magazines. Publishes a good deal of information on a limited number of literary magazines and presses. Because this volume is not published annually, some of its information may be out of date.

Directory of Poetry Publishers Published every other year. A very good resource for poets. Publishes thorough, detailed, and extensive listings of over 1500 markets for poetry.

Directory of Publishing Published annually. A good list of book publishers in England and most other foreign countries, with fairly thorough data on each publisher. Also includes a list of foreign literary agents.

The Dramatist's Bible Published annually by the International Society of Dramatists, Box 1310, Miami, FL 33153. Provides a comprehensive list of theaters throughout the English-speaking world. A paragraph on each theater explains script requirements, size of cast, length of season, and so on. Provides the names of contact people and/or artistic directors in many, though not most, cases. Includes market information on play publishers and producers of radio scripts. Other lists include: agents who handle plays; writers' organizations; fellowships, grants, and awards for playwrights; college and university playwriting programs; playwriting contests; and writers' colonies that are open to playwrights. Also provides market information for composers and librettists.

Dramatists Sourcebook   Published annually by Theatre Communications Group, 355 Lexington Avenue, New York, NY 10017. This comprehensive volume contains a good deal of useful information for playwrights, including a list of producers who look at unsolicited manuscripts; fellowships; grants, contests, and residencies for playwrights; play publishers; and agents who represent playwrights.

Editor and Publisher International Yearbook   Published annually. A good listing of many—though by no means all—newspapers in the United States and other countries. Includes both basic data (such as name, address, and circulation) and the names of editors and department editors. Also lists some syndicates.

Editor and Publisher Syndicate Directory   Published annually. A very good, very thorough listing of virtually every syndicate in the United States, as well as the proper editor or contact at each. Listings are grouped both alphabetically and by subject area. There is also a list of most syndicated items (comic strips, columns, etc.) available in the United States, together with the names of their sponsoring syndicates. This is the very best resource for writers seeking syndication.

*Forthcoming Books**   Published six times a year. The subject-guide section of this volume lists by subject most recently published and soon-to-be-published books in the United States. Useful for learning which presses publish books on a particular topic and what books will soon be available on that topic.

*Freelance Watch**   Published monthly by Joseph Overman, Box 1191, Meade, MD 20755. Publishes information on markets, contests, and grants for writers. Also reprints writers' guidelines from a variety of publications.

*Freelance Writer**   Published monthly at Box 65798, St. Paul, MN 55165. This newsletter carries market information that is current, thorough, accurate, wide-ranging, and quite useful.

*Freelance Writer's Report**   Published monthly by Cassell Communications, Inc., Box 9844, Ft. Lauderdale, FL 33310. An extremely good source of market information. Also includes job listings and general information for writers.

Gale Directory of Publications   Published annually. Lists the names, addresses, and editors-in-chief and/or publishers of a great many magazines and newspapers. *The Working Press of the Nation* (see below) is a far more informative and useful guide, but the Gale directory is better than nothing if *The Working Press* is not available.

The Globe* Published monthly by the International Society of Dramatists, Box 1310, Miami, FL 33153. This is a newsletter of information on markets, contests, and other opportunities for playwrights.

International Directory of Little Magazines and Small Presses Published annually. Includes information on a great many literary magazines and literary book presses in the United States and elsewhere, with their editors' names and some descriptions of the wants and needs of each. It's quite comprehensive. However, be aware that a good many of the publishers listed will be defunct by the time you send them your work, simply because literary magazines and presses have a very high mortality rate. Also note that many of these publications will have readerships of under 500 people, and some will have readerships of 100 or less. Many literary magazines are published irregularly, regardless of the frequency of publication specified in this volume.

International Literary Market Place Published annually. Similar to *Literary Market Place* but covering countries outside the United States and Canada. See *Literary Market Place* below.

International Writers' and Artists' Yearbook Published annually. Provides information on book, magazine, newspaper, and other markets in English-speaking countries outside North America. Also provides some information on foreign agents.

Library Journal* Published biweekly (monthly in summer). Follows the book publishing industry closely, though not as closely as *Publishers Weekly* (see below). Its emphasis is on reference and scholarly books and on nonfiction in general. Not usually found on library shelves, but just about every library gets it. Ask a librarian to get you issues from the back room.

Literary Market Place Published annually in December (for the following year). A very good source of information on book publishing, *LMP* lists most of the book publishers in the United States as well as many of those in Canada. For each publisher, it lists the address, phone number, and names of most staff members, including most or all editors. Listings include book publishers of every type. There is also a partial listing of syndicates; a listing of newspaper magazine supplements; a good list of literary agents; lists of major newspapers, book publicists, employment agencies, literary prizes, and publishing courses and workshops; a good list of editorial services and consultants; a national list of manuscript typists; and quite a few other lists of people and firms related to book publishing. Does not carry a list of periodicals.

Literary Markets *   Published bimonthly by Bill Marles, P.O. Drawer 1310, Point Roberts, WA 98281; in Canada, 4340 Coldfall Road, Richmond, BC V7C 1P8. Publishes information on markets and contests.

Magazine Industry Market Place   Published annually. A thorough compilation of most magazines published in the United States (but not Canada). Listings include basic data (address, frequency of publication, circulation) and the names of many principal employees. Its lists of editors for each publication are generally less comprehensive than those of *The Working Press of the Nation, Volume 2* (see below). This volume also includes many of the same supplementary lists as *Literary Market Place.*

Markets Abroad *   Published by Michael Sedge and Associates, 2460 Lexington Drive, Owasso, MI 48867. Provides excellent, detailed, and up-to-date information on markets outside the United States and Canada, as well as general information for writers wishing to submit their work abroad.

Member List   Alliance of Resident Theatres, Room 315, 325 Spring Street, New York, NY 10013. This is a list of about eighty theaters in New York City and the names of their artistic directors. Useful for playwrights.

National Directory of Weekly Newspapers   Published annually. A good list of the nation's weeklies, including most of the tinier papers. Lists addresses, circulations, and the names of editors, publishers, and/or owners.

New Writer's Magazette *   Published bimonthly at Box 15126, Sarasota, FL 34277. Publishes a good market column each issue.

Poets & Writers Magazine (formerly *Coda*)*   Published bimonthly at 201 W. 54th Street, New York, NY 10019. An interesting magazine that prints articles and information on a wide variety of writing topics, including the business end of writing. Publishes some information on markets, grants, and contests.

Poet's Handbook Written by Lincoln B. Young and published by Fine Arts Press, Box 3491, Knoxville, TN 37927. Includes long lists of magazine and book publishers that publish poetry, as well as a list of greeting card publishers. Lists payment rates, address, and a one-sentence description for each magazine; lists only addresses for book and greeting card publishers. Does not provide any editors' names. Not to be confused with the general handbook on poetry writing of the same title written by Judson Jerome and published by Writer's Digest Books.

The Poet's Marketplace This volume is published by Running Press, and is not to be confused with the annual *Poet's Market,* published by Writer's Digest Books. As of this writing, *The Poet's Marketplace* contains a good deal of useful information on magazines that publish poetry and on presses that publish poetry books, posters, broadsides, postcards, and so on. It also contains some information on grants, contests, and the like. If regularly updated, it should be quite useful.

Publishers' Catalogs Annual Published annually. This is a fairly comprehensive collection of catalogs on microfiche cards. Many publishers of all sizes are represented, but many others are not. Some libraries that carry this may not keep it on the shelves; ask a librarian for it.

Publisher's Directory Published annually. An excellent list of over 9000 lesser-known book publishers, including trade, text, scholarly, professional, nonprofit, scientific, alternative, association, and government publishers. Also lists producers of classroom materials, reports, and data bases. Has lots of useful information, but often provides only the names of publishers' most important editors. Does not list some major publishing houses.

Publishers' Trade List Annual Published annually. This multivolume work includes catalogs and listings of published titles from many U.S. publishers. A good many major publishers are not represented here, but a great many small and little-known ones are. Most libraries carry this, but many do not keep it out on the shelves. Ask a librarian for it.

*Publishers Weekly** Published weekly. The professional journal of book publishing. Indispensable for writers seeking to keep up with book publishing. Even the ads are useful. Includes news, features, and lots of book reviews. *PW* is not always available on library shelves, but the vast majority of libraries get it. Ask a librarian for it.

School Library Journal* Published monthly. Similar to *Library Journal,* but for school libraries. It's found in many public libraries as well, though you must usually ask a librarian for it. Reviews new books published for children and young adults (ages 3 to 17). Provides strong (though not comprehensive) coverage of children's and young adult trade book publishing. Most useful in tandem with the "Children's Books" issues of *Publishers Weekly.*

Small Press* Published monthly at Box 3000, Denville, NJ 07834. The *Publishers Weekly* of small and independent book publishers, this magazine can help you keep on top of what many smaller publishers are doing. Especially helpful are the spring and fall "Announcement" issues, published in April and October. Not to be confused with *Small Press Review* (see below).

The Small Press Review* Published monthly by Dustbooks, Box 100, Paradise, CA 95969. Carries excellent market information on literary magazines and presses. Not to be confused with *Small Press* magazine.

Standard Periodical Directory Published annually. A thorough list of most of the country's magazines, grouped by subject. Includes all of the basic facts (addresses, circulation, frequency of publication) but omits all but the most powerful editors at many publications.

Subject Guide to Books in Print Published annually; an annual supplement is published six months later. Lists by subject most books in print in the United States. Very useful for learning what books are available on a particular topic, and what presses publish books on that topic. The following related guides will also prove useful: *Paperbound Books in Print (Subject Guide),* published twice yearly, and the annual volumes *Subject Guide to Children's Books in Print, El-Hi Textbooks and Serials in Print, Religious and Inspirational Books and Serials in Print, Scientific and Technical Books and Serials in Print, Medical and Health Care Books and Serials in Print, The Small Press Record of Books in Print, Canadian Books in Print, British Books in Print, International Books in Print,* and *A to Zoo: Subject Access to Children's Picture Books.*

Theatre Directory Published annually by Theatre Communications Group, 355 Lexington Avenue, New York, NY 10017. This is a list of nonprofit professional theaters and their artistic directors. Helpful to playwrights.

Ulrich's International Periodicals Directory Published annually; a supplement is published quarterly. Lists names and addresses of a great many magazines throughout the world.

The Working Press of the Nation Published annually. By far the best resource available for writers seeking information on magazine and newspaper markets in the United States. Volume 1 lists virtually every newspaper in the country, from the largest to the smallest, including special-interest and college newspapers. Each entry lists basic information (address, phone number, circulation, frequency of publication) for each paper, as well as a complete or near-complete list of editors. Volume 2 lists similar information for an extremely large number of magazines. For the writer of shorter material, this resource is invaluable.

The Writer* Published monthly. Publishes articles on many different writing topics, plus some market information. Each issue provides a listing of the markets in one or more particular fields—travel, books, humor, short fiction, and so on. These listings are roughly as useful as those in *Writer's Market.*

Writer's Digest* Published monthly. Each issue contains articles on the art, craft, and business of writing, as well as a long column listing markets. One issue a year looks at the "top 50" fiction markets; another looks at the "top 50" poetry markets.

The Writer's Handbook Published annually. Discussed earlier.

Writer's Market and its many spin-offs. Each published annually, late in the year, for the following year. Discussed earlier.

Writer's Nook News* Published quarterly by Eugene Ortiz, 10957 Chardon Road, Chardon, OH 44024. Provides useful market information and information on other writing topics (conferences, contests, etc.).

Writer's Yearbook* An annual magazine published in January and usually available on newsstands through March, though it can be ordered from the publisher through the end of the year. Published by the people at *Writer's Digest,* it is quite similar to that magazine in format and content. Each issue contains an overview of the leading magazine and book markets, as well as a look back at the previous year's happenings in writing and publishing. May be shelved in libraries either with magazines or books. Sometimes found behind the reference desk.

Use the resources listed above to establish a preliminary pool of market possibilities for each piece you have written. Then follow the steps below.

RESEARCHING MAGAZINE, JOURNAL, AND NEWSLETTER MARKETS

Once you have established a preliminary list of possible markets, head for the nearest *large* library. Try to get to the central library in a major city or to the main library at a large college or university. This is usually worth the trip, even if the library is some distance away.

Ask the librarian for the library's guide to its serial holdings. This is a listing of every periodical to which that library subscribes. Usually the magazines are listed in alphabetical order only, though some libraries may also have a subject listing. Note which publications on your preliminary list are available in the library, and note where you can find a current or recent issue of each. Then check through the list for other magazines that might be good markets. This is easy if the library has a subject list available. If it doesn't, you may simply want to look for certain key words in the alphabetical index. For example, if you are looking for a magazine that would publish a piece about breeding dachshunds, you would look for all the periodicals that begin with the words *dog, pet,* and *canine*— and, just to be safe, *dachshund.*

Then actually look at each of these magazines. Get the most recent issues you can. Look through the latest issue carefully and one or two other issues briefly.

Check the magazine's current editorial address. This may be different from its advertising and/or subscription address. Also look at the list of staff. With *very* few exceptions, all magazines and newsletters list the names of most of their editors in what is called the masthead or staff box, usually near the front of the magazine. How to decide who you should send your manuscript to will be discussed later in this chapter.

Look at the material in the magazine carefully, and ask yourself some questions. What subjects get covered? How long do the pieces run? To what readers does the material seem to be directed: young or old, intelligent or not particularly intelligent, wealthy or poor? Is the material upbeat or downbeat, light or serious? What slant does much of the material seem to take? What biases, preferences, or inclinations do the editors appear to have? The trick here is to infer from published material what editors' likes, dislikes, and preferences are.

In your observations, keep in mind that the more famous a writer is, the less he or she is expected to follow a publication's normal guidelines. If the market you are considering happens to have a piece by Brooke Shields, Carl Sagan, Pat Boone, Norman Mailer, Gloria Steinem, or some other celebrity in it, don't try to infer the publication's focus from that celebrity's work.

Before you put the magazine down, look at its table of contents. Into what areas or departments are the contents divided? Which areas receive the most coverage, and which receive comparatively little? Check to see which features or columns appear to be written by regular contributors and which are open to freelancers. Some magazines may have a regular column written by a different freelancer each month, such as *Omni*'s "Last Word."

While you are in the library, it is a good idea to browse among the magazines, especially those shelved in the same sections as the particular magazines you are researching. I have come across good markets that I'd previously been unaware of just by letting my eyes wander from shelf to shelf.

The next step in your research is to check out one or more large newsstands and/or bookstores with large selections of magazines. Visiting these dealers can be very valuable, as a good newsstand or bookstore should carry a much wider variety of commercial magazines than even the best library. Many also carry a few scholarly and professional journals and a surprisingly large array of little-known special-interest publications.

At newsstands and bookstores, magazines are normally grouped by subject matter. You can thus quickly learn of any new or previously undiscovered magazines that might be good markets for your work by simply scanning the proper shelf. Because new periodicals spring up every week, you may well find something new each time you visit.

Unfortunately, it is difficult to give any publication more than a quick skim while standing in the store. If all I need from a magazine is the address and an editor's name, I can usually jot this information down while browsing. (Don't forget to bring a pen and paper with you!) However, if I need to look through a publication fairly carefully, I buy it. (It's a tax-deductible business expense.)

As a rule of thumb, if you cannot find a magazine in a major urban or university library *or* at a major urban newsstand or bookstore, chances are that it is not a magazine worth sending your work to. Most likely either it has ceased publication (magazines and newsletters have a high mortality rate) or its circulation is miniscule. Exceptions: certain in-house, scholarly, technical, and professional journals; most foreign publications; journals distributed by clubs and associations to their members and by schools to their alumni; and magazines and newsletters given out free by businesses to their clients and customers (in-flight magazines are good examples of this last category). These publications may be alive and well, yet still unavailable at newsstands, libraries, and bookstores.

If you cannot find a magazine at either a large library or a major newsstand or bookstore, you can, of course, always order a current issue from the publisher. A few publications will send writers free sample copies on request; but in most cases, you'll have to buy them. Also, most libraries can get issues of most magazines for you through interlibrary loan. This can take anywhere from a few days to six weeks; two weeks is about average.

RESEARCHING NEWSPAPER AND SYNDICATE MARKETS

This is much easier than researching magazine markets, primarily because most newspapers have more or less the same format and the same requirements for material. With a newspaper, it is usually enough to find out the address and the proper editor's name. This can be done by using the reference sources listed earlier in this chapter, particularly *The Working Press of the Nation: Volume 1.*

One of the areas in which newspapers do differ is in the number and kinds of magazine supplements they publish. For example, most large papers publish their own Sunday magazines, but only a few publish separate book supplements. *Literary Market Place* provides a list of magazine supplements and their editors for many U.S. papers. *The Working Press of the Nation: Volume 1* provides the same information in its regular entries.

Your primary resource for syndicates is the *Editor and Publisher Syndicate Directory.* A partial list also appears in *Literary Market Place.*

RESEARCHING BOOK MARKETS

There are thousands of books publishers (or "houses") in the United States, and each one is different. Some publish over a thousand books a year; some publish one or two. Some are family businesses; some are owned by huge conglomerates. Some will publish almost anything that seems commercially viable; others have very narrow orientations.

Consumer-oriented publishing is known as *trade* publishing. Trade books are sold largely through bookstores, although a good many trade books, particularly reference books, are sold primarily or entirely to libraries and mail-order customers. Other products of book publishing include textbooks, books for the professional market, books for the scholarly market, calendars, computer software, and audio and video cassettes. *Jane Fonda's Workout Book* is a trade book. So is *Programming Your Apple II.* But *Listing Real Estate Successfully* is a professional book. So is *Techniques for Teaching the Learning Disabled. Prose Styles of Nineteenth Century Newspapers* and *Values and Voting in the Fifties* are scholarly books. Text, trade, professional, scholarly, audio, video, calendar, and software publishing are considered separate fields, though a publisher may be active in two or more of these areas.

Trade publishing is broken down into two major areas: general books, and books for children and young adults. These are also considered separate fields of publishing; many publishers do books in both areas, but most have a separate division, and separate editors, for each.

Before you can do any kind of serious market research into book publishers, you will need to determine which area or areas of publishing your book falls into. If it falls into more than one area (for example, a history of draft resistance might be both a trade and a scholarly book), there is nothing wrong with submitting it to editors in both areas.

If you have a trade book or book proposal, you may need to do research into *agents* rather than publishers. The majority of trade books sold to major publishers are sold through agents, and many major book publishers simply will not look at unagented manuscripts. Chapter 8 discusses agents and how to get one in detail.

If you wish to deal with a smaller or more specialized trade publisher, or if your book has a limited consumer audience (for example, if you have written a guide to building your own harpsichord), you will probably need to sell your book without an agent's assistance. Scholarly, text, and professional books are also normally (though not necessarily) marketed without an agent's help.

Begin your research by going to some large libraries and bookstores (preferably more than one of each) and browsing through the appropriate sections. Write down the names of the presses that publish books in the field. Remember to differentiate between text, trade, scholarly, and professional books, and between books for children and books for adults. If your book on computers is a professional book, note which publishers do *professional* books dealing with computers and ignore those that publish only consumer-oriented computer books. If you've written a *text* on computers, check out the texts available in a large university bookstore and that university's library. If you've written a book called *Computers in China,* check both the section containing computer books and the section containing books on Asia or the Far East.

Your best research can be done in bookstores that specialize in a certain field, area, or topic. If you've written a book on meditation, visit a "new age" bookstore. If you've written a scholarly book on Agatha Christie's work, visit a mystery bookstore; also check out the literary criticism section in a large bookstore on or near a college campus.

Check out your own private book collection, too, and those of your friends. Sometimes footnotes, references, and bibliographies from books on similar topics will lead you to possible publishers.

The following resources will also help you develop a list of market possibilities: *Literary Market Place, Publisher's Directory, Subject Guide to Books in Print* (and/or, as appropriate, one or more of the spin-offs listed on page 80), *Forthcoming Books, Publishers' Trade List Annual, Writer's Market, The Writer's Handbook, Writer's Yearbook, Novel and Short Story Writer's Market,* and the annual "book market" issue of *The Writer.* If you have a manuscript with a literary bent, these works may prove useful: *Directory of Literary Magazines, International Directory of Little Magazines and Small Presses, Poet's Handbook, Poet's Market, The Poet's Marketplace,* and the *Small Press Record of Books in Print.* If you are seeking a publisher outside of North America, look in the *International Literary Market Place, International Writers' and Artists' Yearbook,* and/ or the *Directory of Publishing.* To see if each publisher you are considering still publishes books in your subject area (and is still in business)—and to learn of other markets as well—check the industry magazines: *Publishers Weekly, The Bloomsbury Review, Library Journal, Small Press, The Small Press Review,* and/or *School Library Journal.* Also check recent or current book catalogs from publishers and distributors.

Go to a library and ask the librarian for the two most recent "Announcements" issues of *Publishers Weekly*. "Announcements" issues are published twice a year, for spring and fall, in January or February and in August or September, respectively. These two issues are easy to identify because they are much thicker than other issues—four to five hundred pages, as opposed to the usual fifty to a hundred. These "Announcements" issues can also be ordered directly from the publisher, R. R. Bowker. The annual ABA (American Booksellers Association) issue, published each April or May, is also very helpful. Issues other than the "Announcements" and ABA numbers can be useful as well, as these also carry reviews of new books and advertisements from publishers. *Publishers Weekly* is of course also available by subscription, and on a few newsstands.

Library Journal publishes a "New Spring Books" issue in January or February and a "New Fall Books" issue in August or September. These will be the most help, although other issues can also be useful.

Look through issues of either or both magazines from cover to cover. They will be filled with publishers' advertisements, and a major part of each magazine's text will be devoted to listing, describing, and reviewing new and forthcoming books from hundreds of publishers. Read the ads as well as the text carefully. Make note of which presses publish books in the subject area (and in the same general publishing area—text, trade, scholarly, or professional) of your own project.

If you have written a book for children or young adults, you should look not at the "Announcements" issues of *Publishers Weekly*, but at the "Children's Books" issues. These, too, are published twice a year, normally in February and sometime during the summer. *School Library Journal*, particularly its "Spring Books" and "Fall Books" issues, can also be very helpful. If you have written a book with a religious orientation, look at *PW*'s most recent "Religious Books" issues, published semiannually in March and September or October. (*Library Journal* does not have special children's or religious issues.) *Children's Writer's and Illustrator's Market* can also be very helpful.

In all cases, be sure you are looking at the most recent issues. Anything older than a year may give you a less accurate picture of what the various presses are publishing *now*.

Publishers Weekly and *Library Journal* both cover trade book publishing quite thoroughly; *PW* does a better job with books for the consumer, but *LJ* is better with reference works. Both magazines cover scholarly and professional publishing to some degree, though *LJ* is generally more thorough. Both cover textbooks scarcely at all. If you have written a textbook, you will probably need to rely largely on *Publishers' Trade List Annual. School Library Journal* covers children's trade publishing fairly well, but it, too, has very little coverage of textbooks.

As for publishers' catalogs, these are never on display, but many libraries and bookstores will let you look through their collections if you ask. Simply explain that you are a writer seeking information on publishers. These catalogs will tell you in detail *exactly* what each firm publishes. Be sure to look through catalogs that are no more than one year old—the more recent the better. (Some libraries may also have *Publishers' Catalogs Annual,* which makes many publishers' catalogs available on microfiche. Ask your librarian for this.)

If your library and bookstore cannot supply you with all the catalogs you need, you can always write or call publishers directly to request them; most will be happy to send current catalogs at no charge. Publishers' addresses can be found in *Literary Market Place, Publisher's Directory, Books in Print, Paperbound Books in Print,* and *Forthcoming Books.* Be sure to note the publisher's editorial address; it may be different from the address for ordering books.

MARKET RESEARCH FOR SCRIPTS

If you're a writer of stage plays or radio scripts, your market research will be largely limited to using the reference materials listed earlier in this chapter. However, it remains important to learn the name of the artistic director or other proper contact at any theater or organization you wish to send your manuscript to. Simply call up during business hours and ask for that name.

If you write material for film and/or TV, you cannot function alone. Your marketing efforts will need to focus on finding a good agent; see Chapter 8 for details. The only scripts that can be effectively marketed without an agent are those intended for industrial, business, or educational purposes, and those marketed to local producers.

LOCATING THE PROPER EDITOR

Before you can send a manuscript out, you need to know who to send it to. *Never* send a manuscript to "Editor" or "Editorial Department"; these are fancy names for the slush pile. *Always*—and this is a rule never to be broken—send your work to editors *by name*. This is the single best way to get an editor's attention.

Once you know the names of the editors at a publishing firm, you still need to decide which editor is the right one to send your manuscript to. It is *not* sufficient to pick an editor at random. It is a mistake to think, "Well, I'll just send my manuscript to the editor-in-chief." At many publications, this is one way to guarantee that your manuscript winds up in the slush pile. And shooting too low can be just as much of a problem as aiming too high.

The rules for scoping out the right editor change from one area of publishing to another and from one publication to the next. But those rules are not impossible to follow or understand.

Magazine, Journal, and Newsletter Editors

Check the list of staff people, usually near the front of each issue. If the magazine or newsletter has a small editorial staff—say, one editor and one or two assistant editors—then you should send your work to the editor. If, however, the publication has several departments—say, food, drink, music, and visual art—and an editor for each department, then you should send your manuscript to the editor of the appropriate department, even if there is also an editor-in-chief and one or several other general editors (managing editors, assistant editors, associate editors, and so on). If the magazine has a large staff—say, an editor and four or more managing, assistant, and/or associate editors—but no specific department editors, then you are best off sending your manuscript to one of the lower-ranking editors. But don't get lower than assistant or associate editor.

Major national magazines such as *McCall's* and *Penthouse* have dozens of editors. If you are dealing with a magazine of this size, you are usually best off addressing your manuscript to the assistant or associate editor of a particular department—for example, the assistant articles editor or the associate food editor. Going higher could dump you into the slush pile.

Contributing editors should be ignored in all your editorial calculations. This title is usually honorary. Likewise, if a magazine lists an editorial board consisting of several people, as well as the regular positions of editor, assistant editor, and so forth, chances are good that members of this editorial board do no actual editing.

In general, the smaller a magazine is, the higher you can aim in choosing an editor. The larger and better-known a publication is, the lower you should aim.

If (and only if) you simply *cannot* get your hands on a recent issue of a particular magazine, you may wish to refer to the list of editors in *The Working Press of the Nation: Volume 2,* which is the most comprehensive and reliable list available. If you are looking at literary and "little" magazines, use the *International Directory of Little Magazines and Small Presses* or the *Directory of Literary Magazines.*

Newspaper Editors

Major newspapers will usually have an editor-in-chief, one or more managing editors, and one to several other editors who have general tasks and titles. There will also be specific editors for different sections and topics. Typically, these might include travel, food, entertainment, TV, sports, news, books, lifestyle/fashion, the Sunday magazine, business, real estate, and so on. If you are submitting your work to a major newspaper, always send it to the editor of the appropriate department.

Major newspapers do not usually publish the names of their department editors, although often the name of the Sunday magazine editor will be published in issues of that magazine.

If your piece is appropriate for more than one department—often, for example, a piece would do well in either the lifestyle section or the Sunday magazine—it is perfectly Kosher to send it to editors in both departments, though not at the same time. If one department editor bounces it, *then* try the other.

In the case of smaller dailies and weeklies, check the appropriate reference source below to see if the newspaper you are considering has a department editor in the subject area of your piece. If so, send your piece to him or her. If no such editor is listed, send your manuscript to the managing editor—or, if there is no managing editor, to the associate or assistant editor. In the case of the tiniest papers—those with editorial staffs of one, two, or three people—you may send your work directly to the editor-in-chief. If your reference source lists no editor-in-chief, send it to the publisher; if no publisher is listed, send it to the owner.

The Working Press of the Nation: Volume 1 is the book to use to learn the names of editors at most newspapers. *The National Directory of Weekly Newspapers* will give you all the information you need for little papers not listed in *The Working Press of the Nation*. *Literary Market Place* contains a fairly good list of Sunday supplements and their editors.

Editors at syndicates appear in the *Editor and Publisher Syndicate Directory*.

Book Editors

The names of U.S. and Canadian book editors are listed in the annual reference volume *Literary Market Place*. Because of the care its editors take to be thorough and up-to-date, *LMP* contains information that is accurate as of the Thanksgiving prior to the year on its cover.

If a publisher is not listed in *LMP*, then look it up in the *Publisher's Directory*. This reference work lists a number of small and specialized publishers *LMP* doesn't. If the publisher in question is a literary press, use the *International Directory of Little Magazines and Small Presses* and/or the *Directory of Literary Magazines*. If you are looking for editors at book publishers outside of North America, use *International Literary Market Place*.

As with magazines, be careful not to pick an editor who is too high up. Avoid sending your work to editors-in-chief and senior editors. In general, you will do best sending your work to someone who is simply designated an editor, without any modifying adjective. If no one in the firm has such a title, send your work to the *lowest* person in the following pecking order who *is* listed. From the top down, they are: publisher, editor-in-chief, managing editor, senior editor, associate editor, assistant editor.

Some publishers have department editors—editors who handle only nonfiction, only health books, only mysteries, and so on. If such designations are given, you should of course send your manuscript to an editor in the proper department.

Many publishers who publish children's books as well as adult books will have a separate heading or subheading in *LMP* for their juvenile divisions. Those that publish in one or more general areas of publishing (trade, text, scholarly, professional books, etc.) usually have a separate heading or subheading for each area.

Although editors in all areas of publishing tend to move from one organization to another quite frequently, in book publishing the pace of job changes is dizzying. It is not too unusual for an editor to move from one press to another every six to ten months. Keeping up with the "musical editors" game in book publishing is therefore both important and difficult.

If you really want to keep up with the trends and changes in the book publishing industry, reading *Publishers Weekly* is invaluable. Its "People" column will tell you of recent staff changes in book publishing, and its other features will give you a clear idea of what is happening elsewhere in the industry. If you regularly update the listings in *LMP* with the information in *PW*'s "People" column, you will have a pretty accurate picture of which editors work where and of how high up they are.

TELEPHONING

There is one other way to learn the names of editors at all kinds of publications: call and ask. In the case of a small publisher, ask the person who answers, "What's the name of the editor in your ―――― department?" or "Who's editing your books in the ―――― field?" If the firm has published a particular book that you admire, or that is similar to your own, you may want to ask for the name of the editor responsible for that book.

If the publisher is large or medium-sized, ask the person who answers to connect you with the editorial department. Then ask the person who answers in the editorial department one of the questions in the previous paragraph.

In most cases, the people you speak with will be happy to give out this information. The worst that can happen is that you don't get it. If you're asked why you want it, answer frankly, "I've written something that your editor might want to see. I'd like to send it in, but I don't have his or her name." Only give this information if you are asked for it; don't volunteer it.

RESEARCH TIPS

• Whenever you make note of an editor's name, double-check its spelling. If you have been given the name over the phone, spell the name back to the person who gives it to you to make sure you've gotten it right. And whenever you type a letter to an editor, double-check that you've spelled the name correctly. Nobody likes to have his or her name misspelled.

• If, after all your market research, you doubt whether a piece you have written would be appropriate for a particular market, but still feel it just *might* be right, give that market a try. At least a quarter of the times I have sent work out on hunches or long shots, I've sold it.

• If, in doing your market research on a particular publisher, you come across a published piece *very* similar to your own, remember that its publisher is *not* likely to publish yours—unless you can rewrite your piece to make it noticeably different.

• Keep in mind that a particular subject or approach does not have to appear frequently in a publication (or in a list of a book publisher's titles) to be viable. If a publication focuses mostly on health but does an occasional fashion item, then it may well be a viable market for your fashion manuscript. In fact, because fashion is not the publication's central focus, you may find that you have considerably less competition from other freelance fashion writers.

• Often publications will specify a minimum or maximum length for submissions. But many publishers are much more flexible about word lengths than they claim to be. Research the particular market to find out what lengths it actually does publish, not what it claims to publish.

• The writing and publishing industry, more than most others, is subject to change, luck, karma, and acts of God. Thoroughly researching your markets will greatly improve your chances of success—but freelance writing is still very much a game of chance.

VANITY PUBLISHING

If you research book markets, you will come across ads in magazines that begin with phrases like "Writers wanted," "Become a published author," and "To the author in search of a publisher." These ads have usually been placed by vanity publishers. These presses will publish virtually anything that comes their way, provided that the writers (or other interested parties) will put up all the money for the project plus enough to guarantee the firm a reasonable profit. Vanity publishers also place display ads in the Yellow Pages under "Publishers." Vanity publishing is perfectly legal; it is just not always perfectly moral.

Typically, when you make an inquiry to a vanity press, you will receive some promotional material, which may describe some of the commercially successful books it has published in the past. Be aware that it will *not* mention the vast majority of the press's books, which have been commercial failures for their authors. You will also probably receive a request to submit your manuscript for evaluation. If you do send in a book or book proposal, it will normally be accepted for publication unless it is libelous or pornographic. The editor may be quite enthusiastic about your book, and may even say something like, "We see strong sales potential for this book." However, no guarantees of sales or profits will be made. The publishing firm will then offer you a contract to sign. The company will typeset, design, publish, and promote your book; you in turn will pay for all this. Although the charge can vary greatly depending on the size and nature of the book, $10,000 is not unusual for a three-hundred page prose book.

A vanity press will generally do a professional job of designing, printing, and binding your book. There will normally be some minimal promotion and advertising for it. The book will be included in the publisher's catalog, and it will be made readily available to bookstores and libraries. However, book dealers and librarians know full well which publishers are vanity presses, and they rarely order from those publishers because they know that the quality of the books is, to put it politely, quite uneven. So the chances of selling many copies of any vanity press book are small, unless you can somehow drum up interest and orders yourself. Vanity presses pay royalties on copies sold, just as regular book publishers do. But the great majority of vanity press books never come close to paying back the authors' initial investment. In general, most of the sales you are likely to make will be those based on your own efforts at self-promotion.

There have been clear exceptions, of course, and there have been cases of writers who began with vanity publishers and later made names for themselves in mainstream publishing. Veterinarian Louis Vine, for example, published his first book with a vanity press. But his most recent book, which has been well received and widely read, was published by a major commercial publisher.

Don't go to a vanity press in the hopes of establishing a record of publication and thereby making a name for yourself. Editors in mainstream publishing look down on virtually all vanity press books. To them, you are more of an amateur if you have published a book with a vanity press than if you have published nothing at all.

If you feel strongly that your work deserves publication but have been unable to place it with a mainstream publisher, your best bet is usually self-publishing rather than vanity publishing. Self-publishing is also the best option for many writers who want to exercise careful control over the design, production, promotion, sale, and distribution of their work. Furthermore, editors do not attach the same stigma to self-publishing that they do to vanity publication. For a detailed discussion of self-publishing, see pages 116–19.

SUBSIDY PUBLISHING

A variation on vanity publishing is subsidy publishing, in which a press that normally publishes work at its own expense offers to publish, sell, and distribute an author's book as part of its regular line—provided the author (or someone else) will put up the money to do so. Subsidy publishing occurs on a small scale among book publishers of all types and sizes.

Normally the publisher is the one to suggest a subsidy arrangement. *Never* make this suggestion yourself to a publisher, unless you are friends with its owner; if you do, your work may be rejected unread.

Subsidy publication is a much better arrangement than vanity publication, since in most cases the publishers involved have decent reputations among booksellers and librarians, and competent staffs of sales and promotion people. However, subsidy publication can be every bit as costly as vanity publication; though it is not as financially risky, there is still no guarantee that you will make a profit on your investment, or even earn it back. Subsidy publishing is of course clearly inferior to mainstream publishing, in which publication costs you nothing, and may earn you some money.

PUBLISHING COOPERATIVES

Writers have traditionally had four basic options available for getting their work into print: commercial publishing, literary and small press publishing, vanity and subsidy publishing, and self-publishing. But there also exists a fifth, and considerably lesser-known, option: publishing cooperatives, also called coops or collectives.

Publishing coops are generally devoted to publishing work of high literary quality. Print runs and sales are small, and distribution is limited, just as with most other literary publications. Most coops sell a major portion of their publications in the metropolitan areas in which they are based. Publishing coops can operate in a variety of ways, but they differ from other publishing ventures in these important respects:

• Most decisions, including what to publish and what not to publish, are made by coop members.

• Writers whose work is published by the coop are usually members of the coop. They normally share in the tasks of running the organization and preparing and distributing its publications.

• Coop members, and the writers a coop publishes, are usually drawn from the metropolitan area or general region in which the coop is based.

• Publishing coops are nonprofit. In some cases writers do not earn royalties on books sold; in no case do they earn advances. Writers may be required to contribute to the cost of publishing their work, though usually they are not.

There are now four major publishing cooperatives in the United States, though there are many lesser-known ones as well. The major coops are:

The Berkeley Poets Workshop and Press, Box 459, Berkeley, CA 94701, (415) 843-8793. Publishes fiction and poetry books.

Fiction Collective, c/o English Dept., Box 226, University of Colorado, Boulder, CO 80309, (303) 492-8938. Publishes novels, collections of short stories, and occasionally anthologies. Unlike other coops, the Fiction Collective accepts submissions from nonmembers, who must, however, become members if their work is accepted for publication.

Alice James Books, 33 Richdale Avenue, Cambridge, MA 02140, (617) 354-1408. Publishes poetry books.

Washington Writers' Publishing House, Box 15271, Washington, DC 20003, (202) 363-8036 or (202) 543-1905. Publishes poetry books. Has also published one anthology.

Most publishing coops are open to new members. However, publishing coops look for people who are genuinely interested in cooperative efforts in editing and publishing. If you join, you'll be asked and expected to contribute some of your time and talent to the organization and its ventures. So if all you're looking for is a publisher that will publish your work, don't approach a cooperative.

POETRY ANTHOLOGIES

In your market research you've probably come across ads in writers' magazines that begin "Poems Wanted" or "Attention Poets." These ads solicit poems for inclusion in magazines and anthologies; some also mention poetry contests with cash prizes. Some of these ads are for quite legitimate publications. But be careful. Here's why.

One excellent way to make money is to assemble large, expensive anthologies of previously unpublished poems, then to sell copies of the anthology to its contributors. The more poems (and contributors) you have, the more money you can make. If the book costs you $10 a copy to print, and you sell one copy to each of five hundred contributors at $35 a copy, you've made yourself a quick $12,500 profit. Because many contributors buy more than one copy, and because their friends and relatives may also purchase copies, the profits can be even larger.

To be financially successful in such a venture, a publisher needs to exercise minimal discretion in selecting poems for publication; usually anything not libelous, obscene, or advocating an illegal act will make it into such an anthology. To maximize profits, the publisher wants contributions from as many different people as possible and so will limit each contributor to one poem per book.

This is exactly how most poetry anthologies that advertise for poems in writers' magazines work. The writer sends in a poem, has it accepted, and is offered the chance to purchase, well in advance of publication, a copy of the impressive, well-made hardcover anthology in which it will appear—usually at a discount. Not surprisingly, free author's copies of the book are not provided.

As an added incentive, all submissions may be automatically entered in a poetry contest, with a hefty first prize ($1000 in a couple of cases). These contests are real, and to my knowledge winners are selected legitimately and all prizes are awarded.

However, since the publisher makes no money from a poem unless its author purchases at least one copy of the book in which it appears, it may *require* each contributor to buy a copy. Typically, the writer receives a prepublication order form with a letter (usually a form letter) accepting his or her poem for publication. Those poets who do not place an order are informed that their work may be dropped from the anthology unless they order at least one copy. In other words, unless the publisher gets the contributor's money months prior to publication, the poem may not be published.

If you read the ads for some of the anthologies closely, you'll see that they warn contributors about this. For example, the small print may say, "Accepted poets may be required to purchase a copy in order to ensure inclusion."

None of this sounds bad at all to many poets, who see it as a good way to break into print. However, editors of almost all legitimate literary and commercial magazines and presses consider such publications nothing more than vanity press appearances.

There are two other things to consider. First, these anthologies generally have few readers outside of their contributors, and the contributors' families and friends. Try to find one of these anthologies in a bookstore. In fact, many of these anthologies—and their publishers—aren't even listed in *Books in Print* or *Forthcoming Books,* so a bookstore would have great difficulty ordering these books even if it wanted to.

Second, the poems in these anthologies are, at best, of extremely variable quality. Some poets who are pleased when they learn that their work has been accepted are considerably less pleased when they learn what kind of company they are keeping.

None of this means that every poetry anthology fits the above mold. In fact, the great majority of poetry anthologies are not at all like those described above: they do not require that their contributors purchase copies, they give those contributors free copies, they are sold primarily through bookstores rather than mail order, and they are published by well-known publishing firms. A good rule of thumb is this: if a poetry anthology advertises for submissions, be on your guard; but if it is listed in the markets column of a reputable writers' magazine, you needn't worry.

MANUSCRIPT SUBMISSION

Once you've determined which editors and publications to send a manuscript to, you need to know the rules for submitting it. Generally, the more closely you follow these rules, the more likely an editor is to consider you a professional writer; the more you ignore them, the more likely you are to be seen as an amateur who hasn't yet learned the ropes of freelance writing.

Normally submissions should be sent flat in a standard 9-by-12-inch or 10-by-13-inch envelope, either white or manila. Clasp envelopes are preferable because they are less likely to pop open in transit. A full-length book or script, or anything else too large to fit into a 10-by-13-inch envelope, should be sent in a padded mailing bag, sometimes called a jiffy bag. These are available in office supply stores. Mailing bags that are not self-sealing should be firmly stapled shut. Strong packaging tape also works well.

You may print or type your editor's name and address and your name and return address directly on the package, but typed mailing labels look more professional. On the front of the package, write in large letters, in ink, how the manuscript is to be sent—usually first class. If you choose to weigh items yourself, make sure you have an accurate scale and a *current* chart of postal rates; they can and do change with little notice.

Each submission should include your manuscript, a cover letter, and a self-addressed stamped return envelope (SASE). If you are submitting a book manuscript or proposal, you may, if you like, omit the return envelope and enclose return postage in a small envelope on which you have typed the words "Return Postage." If you are submitting a computer diskette, attach a hard-copy cover letter to it.

Your cover letter should be the first piece of writing an editor sees upon opening your package. It should therefore be placed on top of your manuscript (or on top of your first manuscript, if you are sending more than one). If the manuscript is held together with a paper clip, simply slide the cover letter under the clip. If you have a bound script, clip the letter to the cover of the script, either face up or in a #10 envelope on which you have typed the editor's name. If you are submitting a book proposal, clip the letter to the front of the proposal folder in the same manner. If you are submitting a book in a manuscript or typing paper box, place the cover letter in the box, on top of your cover page.

Your return envelope or mailing bag (large enough for your manuscript to easily slip inside) belongs at the end of the manuscript(s). If your manuscript is boxed or bound, place the return packaging underneath. If your piece is paper-clipped, slip the envelope under the clip behind the last page of your manuscript. Include your name and address on the return envelope, both in the center and in the upper-left-hand corner, to be safe. Here again, typed labels are better than hand-printing in ink. If you are enclosing return postage, clip this to the front of your cover letter.

If you are sending your work outside of the United States and its possessions (Guam, U.S. Virgin Islands, Puerto Rico, etc.), you may not use U.S. domestic postage stamps. These are stamps that bear a letter (as of this writing, either A, B, C, D, or E). You may, however, use any other regular U.S. stamps or postage meter tapes. For return postage, include International Reply Coupons of roughly equal value. These coupons, exchangeable for their value in postage in just about every country in the world, are available at most—but not all—U.S. post offices.

Canada is an exception to the equivalent-value rule. When sending a manuscript to Canada, enclose one International Reply Coupon for every 2½ ounces your return package will weigh.

One alternative to sending return postage (or reply coupons) and a return envelope is to enclose a regular business envelope with a first-class stamp on it (or with one International Reply Coupon clipped to it, if you are making a submission to a foreign market). In your cover letter, say something like this: "If you decide to pass up this piece, there's no need to return it to me. Simply write me using the enclosed business envelope." This may save you money, depending on the current postal rates and the cost of photocopying in your area.

If a manuscript has been requested ("solicited") by an editor, or if you have written a piece on speculation or on assignment (these terms are defined on pages 126–29), you need not enclose return postage, reply coupons, or a return envelope.

Submissions going to markets in the United States and its possessions should normally be sent first class—or, if they weigh over 12 ounces, by priority mail. It is neither helpful nor necessary in most cases to insure your package, to purchase a return receipt, to send submissions via registered mail, certified mail, special delivery, or express mail, or to use Federal Express, UPS, or some other private carrier. If you like, you may send large manuscripts by the post office's special fourth-class manuscript rate. This is usually cheaper than first class, but it's also slower, and your manuscript can take five to fifteen days or longer to reach its destination. Some editors also think there's something vaguely sleazy about manuscripts sent fourth class. Personally, I always use first class or priority mail.

Sending manuscripts to foreign countries can be a little tricky. Anything going to Canada or Mexico should go by first-class or priority mail (though the rates to Canada are slightly higher than for domestic mail). There are also special rates for "printed matter" sent to these countries, and in most cases unpublished manuscripts qualify as "printed matter." However, manuscripts sent by this method can take a very long time to reach their destinations. Manuscripts may *not* be sent to Canada or Mexico by fourth-class mail.

For sending manuscripts to other foreign countries, I recommend overseas airmail. This gets manuscripts to their destinations quickly—usually within a week or so—although it is very expensive. Airmail rates to Central America and the Caribbean are a bit cheaper, but not much. You can send manuscripts abroad by surface mail, which is far cheaper, but I advise against it. Manuscripts can take months to arrive, if they ever arrive at all.

The post office does have special rates for manuscripts sent airmail to certain countries. Check with your post office clerk for details. To make your inquiry, you'll need to know where the manuscript is going, how much it weighs, and how many pages it contains.

In general, editors and publishers will not automatically acknowledge receipt of your manuscript, though some book publishers do provide this courtesy. You may enclose a postcard with your manuscript for this purpose if you like, but don't be surprised if the postcard is overlooked in the crush of other demands.

A special note for authors of film or television material: TV or film scripts, treatments, and concepts should normally be registered with the Writers Guild before they are submitted to producers—and probably before they are submitted to agents. Radio scripts may also be registered. For details on registration, see page 363.

COVER LETTERS

A cover letter is a letter from a writer to an editor introducing a particular piece of writing—and, if appropriate, introducing the writer.

A good cover letter should be concise, businesslike, and informative. It should give an editor all the pertinent facts—and nothing more. It should be typed, single-spaced, in standard business form, on plain white 8½-by-11-inch paper or your own business or personal stationery. Generally, it should be no longer than one page, but it may go to two if absolutely necessary.

A cover letter should begin by explaining what is being submitted and, in some cases, why it's interesting, why it's being submitted, and why it's appropriate for that particular publication. Make your case in three paragraphs or less.

A cover letter is a form of business-to-business communication. It is *not* an advertisement or a piece of public relations. Don't tell the editor what a genius you are or how wonderful your manuscript is. Unmitigated self-promotion makes editors gag. Editors also aren't impressed, and some will be negatively impressed, if you give them a hard sell. A friendly but businesslike tone usually works best.

It *is* permissible, or even recommended, to explain how your piece is unusual, unique, special, or of particular interest to the editor. For instance, if your article on college fraternities is the first one ever written for the parents of fraternity members, say so in your cover letter. If your novel is written from the point of view of a native Grenadan during the

U.S. invasion, let the editor know. But be brief, matter-of-fact, and straightforward.

In many cases, especially with fiction, there may be no such points to make. Fine. Don't make any. If one or two sentences about your manuscript are all you need, don't try to say more.

If your manuscript has been written on assignment or on speculation (see page 129) or if it has been specially requested by the editor, be sure to remind the editor of this in your cover letter.

Once you've discussed your piece as much as you need to in your cover letter, you should talk a little about yourself. Here again, include only information that is pertinent. Previous publications, pieces accepted but not yet published, writing awards, and other writing achievements are usually worth mentioning. Use some common sense here. Don't tell an editor at *Scientific American* of your sales to *True Confessions.* And don't tell the editor of *The Georgia Review* about your publication in *Prevention.* In general, editors of literary magazines and presses are favorably impressed only by other literary journals, major magazines and newspapers, and major and literary book presses. Don't mention any achievements that are trivial—such as winning fourth prize in the Sacramento Romance Writers' Contest.

If you've earned a graduate degree in writing, this is worth mentioning to editors of publications with a literary bent—but generally not to editors of commercial magazines, except those that publish serious fiction or poetry. If, while earning that degree, you worked with a well-known writer, it's fine to mention that, too, to the right editors.

If you've got academic or professional training in a field that pertains to your piece, by all means mention that. And if you've got particular expertise or experience that seems appropriate, say so. For instance, if you're submitting an article on the joys of solitude, mention in your cover letter that you spent three years living alone in the wilderness. If you've written a book called *How to Make $25,000 a Year as a Waiter or Waitress,* your cover letter should explain that you've been a waitress for over seven years at four different restaurants.

Make what achievements you have sound as good as possible. For example, if you've published two very short articles in two neighborhood newspapers, you might write, "I've published nonfiction in local publications." Or let's say you're submitting your first novel. You've never written fiction before, but you did have some poems published in *Antaeus* and *The Hudson Review,* and articles on dog breeding in *Dog Fancy* and *Dog*

World. Your biographical paragraph might read like this: "Although this is my first novel, I've published short work in *Antaeus, The Hudson Review,* and other national magazines."

If you've got a large number of credentials, don't list them all. Just list the most notable and appropriate ones, as in the sample cover letter on pages 104–5. If you've got no publications, writing achievements, or other appropriate credentials or background, then there's nothing to say. Don't bring up the topic at all. And if you have any shortcomings or handicaps, or if your piece does, *don't* mention them.

What *not* to say in a cover letter, and why:

• "My novel is full of sex, violence, and all the other things that make people buy books." Editors can find plenty of material full of sex and violence. You haven't explained what makes *your* piece special and worthy of an editor's attention. Furthermore, you're trying to tell editors their business. They know full well that sex and violence sell books and magazines.

• "This article has what it takes to knock the world on its behind." This sounds arrogant as well as unbusinesslike. An editor's likely response will be, "Oh, yeah?" He or she may even look for reasons to reject the piece.

• "I know it's not perfect but I did the best I could with what resources I had." This makes the editor *expect* your manuscript to be poor. If your piece isn't good enough to send out, don't send it; if it is, then it needs no apologies.

• "I just know this book is destined for best-seller status." You know no such thing; you're only guessing and hoping.

• "I've worked many long, hard hours on this manuscript and feel it is in excellent shape. My wife also labored long and hard typing it." Editors aren't moved by how long you or anybody else worked. All they care about is whether or not your manuscript is publishable.

• "I and my whole family would be thrilled to have this piece published in your journal." The editor doesn't give a hoot what thrills you or your family.

• "All the members of my writer's group loved this piece, and so did three professors at the University of Kansas." Editors want to make up their own minds about your piece and generally aren't interested in knowing that other people liked it. However, if someone well known liked the piece and is willing to recommend it to the editor, that can help you a great deal. But don't just tell the editor, "Stephen King read and loved this

SCOTT EDELSTEIN
Literary Services
179 Berkeley St., Suite 1
Rochester, NY 14607
Telephone: 716-244-0645

April 4, 1988

Wendy Wenner
Meadowbrook Press
18318 Minnetonka Blvd.
Deephaven, MN   55391

Dear Wendy:

I wanted you to have a chance to see this proposal,
HOW TO HAVE MORE SEX THAN YOU CAN STAND OR IMAGINE, my
parody of how-to-find-a-mate (or one night stand)
books in particular and self-help books in general.

The book shows readers how to have the most orgasms on
their block by eliminating secondary activities such
as errands, conversation, and personal hygiene from
their schedules and replacing them with incessant sex.
An entire chapter is devoted to having sex more efficiently; another explains how to combine sex with other
activities. There is even a section of special tips
for Ohio residents.

The proposal includes an introduction by Blanche
Knott, author of the seven bestselling collections of
TRULY TASTELESS JOKES, written especially for this
volume.

My parody question-and-answer columns, "Ask Arty" and
"Question Mark," have appeared regularly in The
Artist's Magazine and Writer's Digest, respectively.
I've published about eighty other short pieces, many
of them humorous, in a wide variety of magazines, and
I have six serious non-fiction books out or due out
in the near future: COLLEGE: A USER'S MANUAL (Bantam,
1985); SURVIVING FRESHMAN COMPOSITION (Lyle Stuart,
Spring 1988); THE NO-EXPERIENCE-NECESSARY WRITER'S
COURSE (Stein and Day, Fall 1988); PUTTING YOUR KIDS

THROUGH COLLEGE (Consumer Reports Books, Fall 1988);
THE INDISPENSABLE WRITER'S GUIDE (Harper & Row,
Winter 1989); and NOVEL APPROACHES (Writer's Digest
Books, Spring 1989). Excerpts from any of these
books, and/or samples of my magazine columns or
other short pieces, are available on request.

Write or call if you have any questions. Meanwhile,
welcome to spring.

Sincerely,

Scott Edelstein

Enc.
HOW TO HAVE MORE SEX
THAN YOU CAN STAND OR IMAGINE

92 Annapolis Lane
Minneapolis, MN 55404
(612) 555-4140

March 2, 1989

Ms. Eileen Clement
The Hypothetical Review
2248 Wendell Road
Portland, ME 01775

Dear Eileen Clement:

   I've been writing short fiction for the past three
years, and reading and enjoying The Hypothetical Review for
the past five. I thought one of my most recent stories,
"Partridges," might be right for your magazine, so I'm enclosing it now. I'll also enclose a return envelope and
return postage.

   My earlier work has appeared, or is scheduled to appear,
in The Example, The Imaginary Quarterly, and Assumption.
I have an M.F.A. in Creative Writing from the University of
Columbus, and I'm currently at work on a novel.

   I look forward to your reply.

                              Sincerely,

                              Mary Ann Jacobs

horror novel." Unless the editor hears directly from Stephen King, he or she is not going to believe you—even if King *did* love the book.

• "I'd be willing to accept a reduced rate of payment (or no payment at all) to get this published." This makes you sound like not only an amateur but a desperate amateur, and you will have the editor expecting your manuscript to be semiliterate. Offering work at bargain rates or for free almost never helps people get published and usually helps prevent it.

On pages 104–5 is a sample cover letter I used to market a proposal for a humor book. On page 106 is a basic cover letter, one that can be used in cases where there is little to say about yourself or your submission.

What about cases where there is nothing at all to explain about either your piece or yourself? Is a cover letter still necessary? Well, I'd probably try to find something—even a sentence or two—to say. But if that were impossible, I'd still enclose a brief cover letter, simply as a courtesy. Adding a cover letter to your submission establishes a person-to-person contact, however minimal, between you and your editor. This makes the editor feel a bit more like a human being and less like an editing machine, which puts you at a slight psychological advantage with that editor.

Some writers have difficulty deciding how to address an editor in a cover letter (and in correspondence in general). Generally, you should feel free to use first names if any of the following have occurred:

• You have spoken with the editor (either on the phone or in person) and were addressed by your first name.

• You have had previous correspondence from that editor in which he or she addressed you by your first name.

• You have had a direct ongoing relationship with the editor for some time. Normally this means that the editor has either published some of your work or rejected at least a few of your pieces with personal letters.

• The editor has given you a clear indication that he or she finds informality acceptable. Usually this is evident from the editor's correspondence. For example, if an editor signs his name "Bill Green," you can begin your next letter to him, "Dear Bill," even if "William Green" is typed beneath his signature. If the editor types out his full name and signs only "William" above it, begin your next letter to him, "Dear William."

If none of these conditions apply, you are best off addressing editors by their full names: "Dear Glenda Korn," "Dear H. J. Guerra," "Dear Rodney Foxworth," and so on. I try to avoid use of the terms *Mr.*, *Ms.*,

Mrs., and *Miss* as much as possible, not only because some women have a distinct preference for one particular title, but because it is often difficult to tell a person's sex from his or her name. Anyone named Lynn, Marion, Pat, Daryl, Lee, Chris, Bobbie, Sal, or Maury might be either a man or a woman. And once in a while you will run across a woman named Jeffrey or a man called Carol.

Usually people will indicate whether they wish to be called by a nickname. If no such indication is given, stick to full names. For example, address an editor as Patricia Schick unless she has indicated that she likes to be called Pat or Patty.

Each cover letter should be freshly typed; never use photocopied form letters, even if you're sending identical letters to a dozen different editors.

HOW MANY PIECES CAN YOU SEND TO ONE EDITOR AT A TIME?

Short poems of one to three pages each should be submitted to magazines in groups of five to seven poems, with the total package running no more than ten or eleven pages. If your submission includes longer poems, the total should still not exceed ten to twelve pages. If any one poem is ten pages or longer, it should be submitted on its own. Don't submit only one or two short poems at a time; this implies that you aren't producing poetry on a regular basis. If this is true, you want to hide this fact from poetry editors.

Submit only one book manuscript to any one editor at a time. Getting two or more books from the same author at once can be overwhelming. The same advice applies to book proposals and to manuscripts of chapbooks (short books running sixteen to eighty pages). The only exception to this rule is short manuscripts for children's picture books—say, those running less than twenty manuscript pages each. If you are submitting only the text for such books, you may send two or three books at a time, up to a total of about fifty pages. If you are submitting all the artwork for such a book, however, it is best to send only one book at a time. (If you are sending the complete text but only *samples* of artwork, you may send two or three books at once.)

Scripts for television, movies, radio, and stage should normally be submitted one at a time. The same goes for treatments and outlines. Very short material such as TV concepts may be submitted in batches. *Very* short one-act plays running thirty pages or less may sometimes be submitted two at a time. Use common sense here; don't give any producer or director so much that he or she will feel put upon.

Short stories, articles, and essays are best sent to editors one piece at a time. However, short items (under two thousand words each) can be sent in groups of two, and extremely short pieces (fifteen hundred words and under) can be sent in groups of three. Short reviews can be sent singly or in groups of up to four.

If you are approaching a syndicate with a column or other regular feature, you should send at least half a dozen samples. If an editor at a syndicate likes what you have sent, chances are you will be asked to submit a great many more sample columns before you are offered a contract. But six to ten samples are an ideal number to start with.

One writer I know insists that short stories and articles should always be sent to editors two at a time. "That way," she says, "you give editors the choice of one piece or the other instead of yes or no." My own experience, however, has been that editors react more favorably to prose pieces sent one at a time, unless those pieces are quite short.

It's considered Kosher to send a manuscript to an editor, then to send a second piece to that same editor after a decent interval (say, three weeks or so), even if the editor hasn't responded to the first piece. You can do this again with a third piece a few weeks later; but three pieces under consideration by the same editor is generally the upper limit. If you've sent a batch of two or three very short pieces at once, you should wait until you've gotten a response to at least one of them before you send the editor anything else. The same advice applies to groups of short poems.

If you do send more than one piece to an editor at one time, it is sufficient to enclose a single return envelope. However, the editor may not respond to all the pieces as a group. If an editor returns one or more pieces and hangs on to one or more of the others, don't get excited or worried. In itself, this means nothing, good or bad. Chances are the editor will respond to your other pieces shortly.

It is perfectly fine to send two different manuscripts to two different editors at the same publication or firm so long as the two editors work in different departments or on different publications. For example, you can simultaneously send an article on allergies to the food editor of *Glamour* and a separate piece on train travel to the travel editor. However, it would *not* be proper to simultaneously send a food article to *Glamour*'s food editor and a different food article (or another copy of the same article) to its assistant food editor.

SIMULTANEOUS SUBMISSIONS

A simultaneous submission—also called a multiple submission—is the submission of the same piece (or pieces) to two or more different editors simultaneously. Fifteen years ago, this practice was strictly forbidden. Nowadays, it is acceptable nearly everywhere.

Obviously it is to your benefit to make multiple submissions of most of what you write. By getting the same piece out to many editors at once, you save yourself waiting time and greatly increase your chances of publication.

Most editors condone the practice of making multiple submissions, but a few do not. Unless an editor specifically states otherwise—either in person, in a phone conversation, or in a market notice printed in a writer's magazine or resource book—you can assume that simultaneous submissions are acceptable.

If you don't know an editor's policy regarding multiple submissions, the best course is not to worry about it. Submit the manuscript, and *don't* mention that other editors are also looking at it. The only problem that can result from such a strategy is that two or more different editors may want to publish the same piece. This is rare; but if it happens, it is easily dealt with.

Let's say you send out copies of a piece to ten different editors. After a few weeks and two rejections, one editor offers to buy it. The offer seems reasonable, so you accept it. Are you in any trouble? No, because all you have to do is write polite letters to each of the seven other editors, asking to withdraw your manuscript. A sample of such a letter follows. Note that you don't need to say that your manuscript's been sold elsewhere, and you don't need to give any reasons for your withdrawal. Simply send the letters out by first-class mail, and you are fully covered.

Will editors mind that you've withdrawn your manuscript? Not usually, unless you wind up having to withdraw several manuscripts from the same editor within a short period of time.

What if, before your withdrawal letters reach their destinations, another editor asks to use the same piece? In this *extremely* unlikely circumstance, you should be honest. Write or call the editor and say, "I'm sorry, but I've accepted another offer to publish the piece; a letter of withdrawal went out to you a couple of days ago." The editor may be disappointed but is unlikely to be angry at you. Since the editor likes your work enough to want to publish it, you can even turn this situation to your advantage.

SCOTT EDELSTEIN
Literary Services
179 Berkeley St., Suite 1
Rochester, NY 14607
Telephone: 716-244-0645

April 19, 1988

Ms. Gina Fuqua
<u>Mad Hatter</u>
88 Public Road
Salina, KS 77556

Dear Gina Fuqua:

On March 11 I sent you a copy of my article, "How to Turn Old Hats Into Tote-Bags." Unfortunately, I must withdraw this piece from your consideration and ask that you return it to me in the return envelope I provided.

I do have other articles on hats in the works, however, and I will send you a new piece as soon as one is ready. I hope I haven't caused you any inconvenience.

Thanks. All best wishes.

Sincerely

Scott Edelstein

Say to the editor, "I'm sorry we couldn't get together on this piece, but I'd love to write more for you in the future. Is there something in particular you'd like to see?" Or, if you've got one or more other pieces that might be appropriate for that editor, you can say, "I'm sorry about this piece, but I do have something else that I think might be up your alley, and I'd be happy to send it along immediately."

If a publication publishes reprints as well as original material, you need not even send its editor a letter of withdrawal. Instead, send a short, polite note explaining that first rights to the piece have been sold but that the piece is available for reprinting.

Incidentally, if you do withdraw a manuscript, you may either ask to have it returned to you or instruct the editor to destroy it. If you request its return, don't be concerned or surprised if it never arrives. Busy editors sometimes opt to ignore withdrawn manuscripts rather than return them. And you needn't worry that your manuscript, or an idea from it, will be stolen.

I'm well aware that some other writers and books recommend (sometimes quite strongly) against making simultaneous submissions. They are simply behind the times; simultaneous submissions are now the rule rather than the exception. There *are* four circumstances in which simultaneous submissions should never be made, however. First, don't send the same piece to two or more citywide newspapers in the same city at once. Newspapers often rush pieces into print, sometimes before notifying authors that their work has been accepted. You don't want the same piece appearing in two competing newspapers—and neither do either of those papers. However, it is okay to send the same piece to two different neighborhood newspapers in the same city at once, provided they cover two different neighborhoods, or to two or more newspapers in different cities.

Second, if you have written a piece on assignment for a publication, you are obliged to send it first *only* to the editor who assigned it (or, if the editor has left the firm, to his or her successor). If for some reason a decision is made not to publish the piece, you can then—and only then—send it elsewhere. Pieces written on speculation (see page 129) and completed pieces editors have asked to see can be submitted elsewhere simultaneously unless you have been specifically asked not to do so.

Third, if a contract you sign with a publisher includes an option clause (see pages 354–55) requiring you to give that firm the first option to publish a subsequent manuscript, you must of course submit that new manuscript first only to that particular publisher.

Fourth, there is one area of publishing in which multiple submissions are not considered Kosher: professional journals. These include scholarly, technical, scientific, medical, and trade journals. Multiple submissions *are* permitted, however, among book publishers in the same fields.

Two final, and very important, points about simultaneous submissions. First, if you get an offer to publish a piece, do *not* try to play one editor against the other. Don't say to one editor, "Well, four other editors have this piece; let me check with the others first to see if they can offer more." And don't call up any of those other editors and say, "I've got an offer of $300 on that cooking piece I sent you. Would you care to top it?" In either case, the editors are likely to say, "I'm not interested in an auction. Go peddle your manuscript somewhere else."

If you get an offer to publish your manuscript, judge that offer entirely on its own merits. If it seems acceptable, take it; if it's not good enough, either turn it down or attempt to negotiate better terms. But *don't* use the fact that the manuscript is still out elsewhere as a bargaining chip. Don't even mention the fact that the manuscript is in other editors' hands. It won't help you, and it can hurt, perhaps badly. Literary agents and David Stockman can get away with this kind of bargaining; you and I cannot.

Second, if you accept, either verbally or in writing, an offer from an editor to publish something you've written, and shortly thereafter you get a better offer from someone else, it is sleazy—and in most cases illegal—to accept the second offer and back out of the first one. Editors expect you to keep your word, just as you expect them to keep theirs. If a better offer comes along, you are obliged to turn it down with your regrets. However, you can always offer to write something else for the editor who makes the second offer. Or, if the second editor is willing to use the piece as a reprint, accepting the offer is perfectly fine.

Sometimes I'm asked, "Okay, if I can send out as many copies as I want, how many is the right amount? Three? Fifty?" It all depends on how much you're willing to invest in postage and photocopying, and how timely the particular piece is. If it's going to get dated quickly, it is to your advantage to get ten or more copies out to editors simultaneously. I also send out eight to fifteen copies of a piece if I think its chances of selling are comparatively slim, or if reply times are apt to be slow—as they are, for example, with play producers. Sending out three to five copies of a short piece or book proposal at once is pretty standard. However, if you'd like to send out more, you're free to do so.

Completed manuscripts for books (unless they are very short—say, sixty pages or less) typically go out to no more than three editors at a time. There is no rule against sending out more, however.

CONTESTS AND AWARDS

In the past few years, the number of literary contests in North America has grown enormously. But entering these contests is generally a poor use of your time and energy. While there's nothing wrong with entering a few literary contests each year, the great majority of your career-building time should be spent on other efforts—particularly on submitting your work to editors.

The simple fact is that any contest has no more than a few winners; your own entry will be judged against all the other entries, and only the very best will receive prizes. But when you make a regular submission, your work isn't being judged against anything; if the editor thinks it's well done and appropriate, he or she will buy it. In fact, it's quite possible that a manuscript you submit for a contest that fails to win might have been published if you'd sent it in as a normal submission. Of course, you can always cover your bets and submit the same manuscript both ways.

While most writing contests and awards are exactly what they seem, many are not. Here are some examples:

• A good many awards cannot be applied for. For example, you can't apply for a William Carlos Williams poetry prize with either a published or unpublished poetry book; instead, your publisher must send copies of your published poetry book to the contest judges. And you can't enter the "contest" for the Emily Clark Balch Prize awarded by the *Virginia Quarterly Review*. Many writers do try to enter because they see announcements of the award in writers' publications. But in fact there is no contest to enter; the prize is given for the best poem and short story published in the *Virginia Quarterly Review* during the previous year, and all the poems and short fiction pieces published in that magazine are automatically entered in the competition.

• Publication is not necessarily part of a literary award. It is possible, for example, to win second place (and goodly sums of money, such as $500) in quite a few literary contests, but not to be published as part of your prize.

• Many contests require the payment of a "reading fee" or "entry fee." Typically this is $1 to $5 for short pieces, $5 to $10 for a book-length work. All of these fees, when added together, are used to pay the contest winners their prize money. If there is money left over (and usually there is), it goes to support the publication of books or magazines by the sponsoring organization—or it goes into the pockets of the sponsors. Entering such a contest is just like entering a lottery: you bet your money (and your work), and if you win you take home many times your investment. In some cases, however, the odds are heavily stacked against you; I know of contests that charge $3 an entry and award prizes totaling under $300 (in one case only $150). If these contest organizers get five hundred entries, they are making a lot more money than they are paying out in awards.

Since the practice of charging entry fees began a few years ago, these contests have proliferated greatly—for obvious reasons. The whole notion of an entry fee irks me, but such fees are here to stay, in large part because prestigious literary and academic organizations require them regularly. Indeed, the practice of charging fees has already spread beyond contests: a number of literary magazines and presses now charge writers *submission* fees. In some cases writers must now pay for the privilege of having their work considered for publication—up to $10 for a single book-length manuscript.

If you enter a contest and do not win, you can normally enter again without prejudice on the next round. If you *win* a contest, however, you may not be permitted to enter it again in the future. Whether you win or not, you will almost never get the slightest bit of critical reaction to your piece. Unless you win, you will normally receive nothing more than a form letter expressing regret.

If you wish to investigate literary contests in general, you can find lists of some of them in the following:

Literary Market Place (see the heading Prize Contests, *not* Literary Awards)

Writer's Market (see pages 71–72 for details on this volume)

Grants and Awards Available to American Writers (PEN, 568 Broadway, New York, NY 10012)

The Dramatist's Bible and *Dramatists Sourcebook* (see pages 75–76 for details on these volumes) list contests for playwrights, librettists, composers, and lyricists.

Poet's Market and *The Poet's Marketplace* (see page 79 for details) list literary competitions for poets.

Virtually all writers' magazines and newsletters carry notices of literary awards and contests. A few of these also carry ads promoting various competitions.

SELF-PUBLISHING

If you *self-publish* your book, you are arranging and paying for its publication solely through your own efforts, and you are responsible for selling and distributing it however you can. You have complete control over every aspect of its publication and marketing, and you foot the entire bill for all of this yourself. All the copies printed belong to you and all the profits go into your pocket. You may, if you like, establish an imprint for your book(s)—for example, Blackbird Books, Hartwell House, or Scott Edelstein Press; this is not necessary, however.

The biggest difference between vanity publishing and self-publishing is that editors usually have no respect for authors of vanity press books— but they *do* respect authors whose self-published books have sold well. Some well-known authors who have self-published their work include Anais Nin, Peter McWilliams, Avram Davidson, Lynda Barry, and Herman Melville.

Self-publishing can be expensive. It usually takes a good-sized wad of cash up front. More important, self-publishing takes lots of energy and a fair amount of chutzpah, because if you expect to sell your book you're going to have to promote it vigorously—or pay someone else to do it for you.

Writers who contemplate self-publishing often underestimate (or fail to consider) the sheer amount of work required. Simply filling orders from bookstores can be very time-consuming, and properly promoting a single book can be almost a full-time job in itself.

As a rule of thumb, those authors who have made a profit by publishing their own books have written good books targeted at specific audiences; produced well-made, professional-looking volumes; and promoted and publicized those books carefully and steadily. Books that are poorly conceived, written, designed, produced, or promoted usually lose money— often a lot of money.

How does self-publishing compare with traditional commercial publishing? If your book is published by a commercial press, you won't have to invest a single penny up front. You'll earn royalties, and possibly an advance, and usually your book will be professionally edited, designed, and produced. However, you'll have virtually no say in, and certainly no control over, *how* your book is designed, promoted, or sold.

If you publish your own book, you'll be able to control all aspects of designing, printing, illustrating, binding, and hustling the volume; on the other hand, you'll have to pay for it all yourself, and you'll have to personally shoulder all the appropriate tasks and responsibilities.

Which route should you go? It depends. If you have money and lots of time (or, alternatively, *lots* of money) to invest, self-publishing may be a viable option for you. Otherwise, you are usually better off entrusting your book to a traditional commercial or literary publisher. This entails something of a risk, since the publisher may do a less-than-ideal job of publishing and promoting it; but at worst the book will sell poorly and go out of print, and you can then republish it yourself.

Another reason to self-publish is if the people you are writing for can best be reached through means other than bookstores (for example, through hospitals, toy stores, shoe stores, museum gift shops, or mail order). Traditional publishers almost invariably concentrate on bookstore sales and pay relatively little attention to unusual outlets; some ignore nonstandard outlets entirely, no matter how many copies those outlets may be able to sell.

A good many writers turn to self-publishing only when their books are unanimously rejected by commercial or literary presses. There's nothing wrong with this—after all, publishers have been known to make the same mistake *en masse.* And sometimes a book that may not be profitable enough to interest traditional publishers may still turn a good profit for an author through self-publication and self-promotion. (In fact, sometimes *only* the author will give a book the promotion it deserves; the same book, even if it were published by a major press, might receive only token promotion and publicity, because it's not by someone already famous.)

If you are seriously considering self-publishing your book, keep these things in mind:

• Don't publish anything unless you genuinely feel it's worth publishing. Don't publish a poor or mediocre book just to see your words in print.

• Do a professional job of typesetting, designing, and printing the volume. A shoddy-looking book is difficult to sell, no matter how good it may be.

• You must have faith in your book. Otherwise you'll never be able to muster the energy necessary to promote, sell, and distribute it.

• Self-publishing almost certainly won't make you rich. A few people have managed to make good livings through carefully publishing and promoting their own work. A good many others have made small profits, which supplement their incomes from other sources. But I know of only two writers who have struck it rich through self-publishing.

• It is possible to self-publish a book, then sell the rights (or in some cases actual copies of the book itself) to a major publisher. This has been done with increasing frequency in the past few years. Cartoonist Harvey Pekar built a career for himself in just this way. Self-published books may be submitted to editors just as you would submit an unpublished manuscript. You may submit either a finished copy of the book or a manuscript. Naturally, no major press will be interested in a self-published book unless it has already sold well; but the more copies it *has* sold, the more interested publishers will be, and the larger an advance they will probably pay for it. Be sure to include sales figures in your cover letter. For more details on this topic, see page 286.

• It is possible in some cases to have a self-published book distributed through a national book distributor—especially if the book is in a genre or field in which that distributor specializes (for example, literary publications or health books). A good list of book distributors appears in *Literary Market Place*. Some distributors specialize in small-press and self-published books and handle titles from dozens of different tiny presses. Check the spring and fall "Announcement" issues of *Publishers Weekly* for display ads from these distributors; also read *Small Press* magazine.

• Publisher's Marketing Association (2401 Pacific Coast Highway, Suite 206, Hermosa Beach, CA 90254, 213-372-2732) can provide cooperative marketing services (including exposure at book fairs, publicity to reviewers and librarians, inclusion in a regular catalog, and direct-mail promotion) for self-publishing writers.

There are several good books on self-publishing that will tell you just about everything you need to know:

> *The Complete Guide to Self-Publishing,* by Tom and Marilyn Ross (Writer's Digest Books)

How to Publish, Promote, and Sell Your Own Book, by Robert L. Holt (St. Martin's Press)

The Self-Publishing Manual: How to Write, Print, and Sell Your Own Book, by Dan Poynter (Para Publishing)

101 Ways to Market Your Books, by John Kremer (Ad-Lib Publications, 51 N. 5th Street, Fairfield, IA 52556)

The Publish-It-Yourself Handbook, by Bill Henderson (Harper & Row)

How to Get Happily Published, third edition, by Judith Appelbaum (Harper & Row). About a third of this volume is devoted to self-publishing.

Publishing, Promoting and Selling Your Book for Self-Publishers and Impatient Writers, by John C. Bartone (ABBE Publishers' Association, 4111 Gallows Road, Annandale, VA 22003)

Peggy Glenn's *Publicity for Books and Authors* (Aames-Allen Publishing Company) contains much useful information for publicizing yourself and your book.

For a good list of printers that handle small jobs such as self-published books, see the *Directory of Short-Run Book Manufacturers* (Ad-Lib Publications, 51 N. 5th Street, Fairfield, IA 52556).

These periodicals can also be helpful:

Small Press (see page 80 for description and address)

IPN Marketing News (Publishers Media, Box 546, El Cajon, CA 92022). This newsletter is devoted partly to book marketing.

Many other useful tips on promoting your work appear on pages 227–28 and 298–304.

3. ✎ _____

The Care and Feeding of Editors

THE EDITOR'S ROLE

Editors have difficult jobs. Not only must they be proficient—if not expert—at many different tasks, they must play at least a dozen different roles, sometimes all at once.

In most cases, editors are employees of publishing firms and must answer to owners, publishers, chief executive officers, or other editors at those firms. Editors have a major responsibility to adhere to and carry out the wishes of those higher up. The only exceptions are editors who are themselves publishers or owners of the publications they work for. Editors must also work smoothly and efficiently with art directors, advertising people, layout and design staff, typesetters, secretaries, other editors, and a slew of other publishing employees. They need to meet deadlines, handle endless details, and keep track of a thousand different things at once, all while keeping their tempers and getting along with others.

However, editors have an equally strong responsibility to their writers. They must be reasonably available to writers, read and respond to manuscripts fairly promptly, provide competent editing of manuscripts, and treat their writers courteously and fairly.

One of an editor's biggest jobs is to act as liaison between the publishing firm and writers. It is the editor's job to act as the publisher's representative in dealings with you _and_ to act as your representative in dealings with the publisher.

Good editors realize that if they can't keep both sides reasonably happy, they aren't doing a good job. They are therefore careful to treat their writers well, to see that they are paid reasonably and on time, and to stick up for them in dealings with management. However, they also know just how far they can go in this regard, and they're careful not to jeopardize their writers or themselves by pushing their bosses too far or too hard. Wise *writers* therefore expect support and cooperation from their editors, but not miracles.

A good editor knows the English language inside out, can work well both alone and with others, can quickly find and correct flaws in written work, can negotiate well, can balance the needs and interests of opposing parties, and can converse pleasantly and efficiently on business matters. Not surprisingly, most editors don't do all of these things well every day. Editors range in ability from splendid to quite incompetent—just like members of all other professions.

Although editors can and do come from a wide variety of backgrounds, they typically have strong backgrounds in literature and/or writing. Many editors have bachelor's degrees in English or a related field, and a good many also have advanced degrees. Many editors got their starts in low-level publishing jobs, as secretaries, editorial assistants, design people, advertising or book salespeople, research assistants, proofreaders, copy clerks, or copy editors. Editors are typically underpaid and severely overworked.

The publishing business, by and large, is quite fast-paced, and some editors change jobs frequently, usually to accept a promotion or higher pay. It is possible for someone with savvy to advance very quickly; secretaries can become editors within a year and senior editors in two or three years more.

There are many different editorial jobs, and many different titles. A title won't always reveal an editor's responsibilities or level of authority, nor does it necessarily correspond to any particular task or group of tasks. Not all editors evaluate manuscripts. A copy editor, for example, normally is responsible only for reading through previously accepted manuscripts carefully, checking for factual errors, libel, clarity, conciseness, and proper usage. A copy editor may also change a manuscript to conform to a publication's standard style.

An editor who actually makes decisions on submissions is called an acquisitions editor, and is said to "be acquiring" for his or her publishing firm. An acquisitions editor may have virtually any title, from assistant editor to editor-in-chief.

A person with the title of publisher is normally in charge of everything that goes on at a publishing firm or publication, including all editorial functions, art direction, layout and design, payroll, accounting, advertising, distribution, sales, and so on. He or she may simultaneously hold the title of editor or editor-in-chief, and may perform some or many editing functions. At very large firms, the publisher may answer to a chief executive officer, a president, or a board of directors.

Some publishing firms (the Hearst Corporation, for example) have literally hundreds of editors; others have a total of one. The number of editors a firm has may mean very little, however. The tiny book publishing firm of Evans and Company, with just a couple of editors, has published best-sellers on a fairly regular basis.

At some publishers, many or all of the editors are on staff—that is, they are salaried employees with regular hours. Other publishers make wide (and in some cases exclusive) use of freelance editors, who are paid by the hour, the page, or the project.

EDITORS' RESPONSES

Once you've sent work out to editors, when should you expect replies? When should you start getting impatient? And what should you do when you haven't heard?

There's no absolute standard for reporting times. Some editors read and respond to manuscripts almost immediately; others can take months, even a year or more.

Sometimes editors will hold onto a piece because they're interested in it but cannot make up their minds, or because they need to convince their colleagues or superiors of its merit. Either of these processes can take months. Convincing one's boss of a piece's quality can be especially tricky and time-consuming. The editor has to wait for the right moment to bring the piece to the boss's attention, give the boss plenty of time to read it (and gently prod if nothing seems to be happening), and try to get the boss excited about it. And then there's the boss's boss . . . This process can be especially slow in book publishing, where firms can sometimes take as long as a year to decide on projects that interest them.

When editors take an unusually long time to respond to a manuscript, however, don't automatically assume they're interested in it. They might just be very busy or very lazy.

If possible, it is best not to wait by the mailbox or telephone for editors' responses. This will only drive you crazy, or at least make you very nervous. The most well-adjusted writers are those who send their work out and then forget about it, letting the chips fall where they may. Once a month or so they check their records and get in touch with those editors who are late in responding; but otherwise they spend their time writing new material rather than worrying and fantasizing about the pieces that are currently in editors' hands.

Here's how long you should wait before inquiring about a manuscript:

• Articles, essays, reviews, and short stories: ten weeks
• Poetry: three months
• Books and book proposals: three months
• TV, film, radio, and stage scripts: six months

The publishing world slows down considerably in late December and January. If the waiting period listed above expires between December 20 and January 31, it is usually best to hold your inquiry until early February.

If you haven't heard in the appropriate length of time, it is both wise and proper to write or call the editor and politely inquire about your manuscript's whereabouts. I much prefer to make a phone call. A call can be handled quickly and immediately, and if you're polite and businesslike most editors (or their assistants) will be happy to answer your inquiry. A letter, on the other hand, requires another letter in response. This takes time—time an editor often does not have. All too often, editors who have been too busy to read manuscripts promptly are also too busy to respond to written inquiries. However, if you do choose to write, enclose a stamped, self-addressed business (#10) envelope for the editor's reply.

Years ago I used to send inquiry letters that included a checklist of options: "still under consideration," "returned previously," "never arrived," "whereabouts unknown," and so on. The editor could simply check the appropriate box and send the letter back to me. This yielded slightly better results than regular letters.

All things considered, however, the phone is your best bet. If the response to your phone call is, "I haven't gotten to it yet. May I have some more time?" I suggest you say, "Certainly, but I'd appreciate your getting to it within the next week or two." If you're told, "I'll try to track it down and get back to you," simply say, "Fine." Either way, give the editor one more month to respond to your manuscript. If you haven't heard by then, simply write the submission off—assume it has been lost or is being ignored. Get it out to someone else.

You may or may not want to try another manuscript on that same editor. Sometimes it's worth giving him or her the benefit of the doubt; after all, the postal service or a sloppy mailroom clerk may have lost your piece. (Manuscripts do vanish mysteriously quite often—roughly 5 to 10 percent of the time, more often for submissions to literary publications.) But if two manuscripts sent to the same editor mysteriously disappear, I'd simply avoid that editor in the future.

This doesn't always mean that you should write off that firm or *publication,* however. Perhaps there is another editor you can deal with. You might even resubmit to that editor the manuscript the first editor failed to respond to.

If a manuscript receives no response, it is not necessary to withdraw the piece from consideration—nor is it helpful. If your manuscript has been lost or is being ignored, withdrawing it serves no purpose. If the piece is still under consideration, or if it will get considered eventually, withdrawing it scotches all possibility of selling it. Though it's rare, I've heard of cases where editors have accepted pieces after sitting on them for a year—and after refusing to respond to mail inquiries.

Keep in mind that when you submit a manuscript, you are submitting it to a person, not a position. If an editor at *Rolling Stone* rejects your manuscript, then later takes another job elsewhere (or even moves to a noneditorial job at that same firm), feel free to send that same manuscript to his or her successor. I've sold work in this manner. One agent I know sold a piece to the editor of *Swank* after it had been rejected by that magazine's three previous editors.

Incidentally, it is *not* considered proper or professional to insist (or even request) in a cover letter that an editor respond to a manuscript by a certain date. Only agents may set such deadlines.

UNSOLICITED MANUSCRIPTS

Unsolicited means "unasked for." An unsolicited manuscript—sometimes called an "over the transom" submission—is one that has been sent to an editor without being specifically requested.

Most magazine and newspaper editors read unsolicited manuscripts. However, the larger or more prestigious a publication is, the less likely it is to consider unsolicited pieces, or at least to consider them very carefully or seriously. Hundreds of publications of all sizes and orientations rely entirely on staff-written material and don't consider unsolicited material at all. In general, though, you may assume that an editor considers unsolicited manuscripts unless he or she has published a notice to the contrary in a writers' magazine.

Just because a publication or editor has a policy against unsolicited manuscripts, however, doesn't mean the door is completely closed. A good many editors are perfectly willing to listen to ideas or look at proposals for pieces; they just don't want complete pieces sent to them unrequested.

Let's say Hilda Nesmith, editor of *Florida Life* magazine, doesn't read unsolicited manuscripts. You can still write her a letter telling her about an article you've written and asking if she'd like to see it. Or you can call her on the phone with the same information and request. If she says, "Sure, send it on," your piece has been officially solicited. More information on this form of inquiry, called querying, appears on pages 142–43. Another approach is to contact the editor and ask to write one or more pieces on assignment, or "on speculation." These terms are discussed and described on pages 126–36.

The fact is, too, that many of the editors who publicly say "no unsolicited manuscripts" don't always mean it. If you can get someone who knows the editor—one of the editor's business associates, writers, friends, or relatives—to recommend your writing, chances are that when your manuscript arrives, the editor will read and consider it. A recommendation from nearly anyone famous, or from someone well known in your field, should also do the trick.

Then there are the editors, and there are more of them than you might think, who are perfectly willing to read unsolicited material, but are *not* willing to wade through the mountains of material they would get if they proclaimed to the world, "Yes, we read unsolicited manuscripts." These editors will tell writers' magazines and the editors of market guides, "Sorry, we don't accept unsolicited work." This is an outright lie, but it weeds out 95 percent of all potential submissions. Of those editors who claim not to read unsolicited material, perhaps a quarter of them are using this ploy. There's certainly no harm in ignoring an editor's "no unsolicited work" policy; in fact, ignoring it may well get you published. The worst that can happen is that your manuscript will be returned unread.

If you do ignore official policy, *don't* write in your cover letter, "I know you don't usually look at unsolicited work but thought you might make an exception in my case," or worse, "I know you don't consider unsolicited material, but my piece is so damn good that you ought to look at it anyway." Don't mention anything about the policy at all.

You'll recall from Chapter 2 how important it is to write to editors by name, not by position. Often doing this is all it takes to have your unsolicited piece considered. Some publications have an official policy against unsolicited material, but that policy only applies to manuscripts addressed to "Editor" or "Editorial Department." Those addressed to specific people go right to those persons' desks, and as often as not they get read and considered.

Furthermore, even if a publication has an official policy against unsolicited pieces, any editor is free to ignore that policy if he or she wishes. So if you send your manuscript to a particular editor by name, it is up to that editor, rather than someone in the mailroom, to decide whether or not that piece gets considered.

Finally, sometimes you just get lucky. An editor is about to bounce your manuscript unread, but something about your cover letter, your credentials, or your stationery catches her eye. Or he's looking for a piece on raising chinchillas, and your unsolicited piece on that subject hits his desk at just the right moment.

What if you don't know whether an editor reads unsolicited material? Take the chance and send your piece.

Once you have broken into a particular publication, any rules forbidding unsolicited manuscripts will no longer apply to you. You can send that editor anything you like, unsolicited.

ASSIGNMENTS AND HOW TO GET THEM

A great deal of published material is written on assignment—that is, contracted for in advance and written to a set of specifications agreed upon by the writer and editor. The idea for the assignment can come from the editor, the writer, or a third party.

Much of the short nonfiction published in this country is written on assignment. TV shows, films and videos for corporations, and advertising and public relations copy are all usually written on assignment. Most nonfiction books and a good many novels are written on assignment, too: a publishing agreement is signed based on a book proposal, which consists of an outline of the project and additional material, usually an introduction and one or more sample chapters. The writer is obliged to complete the book according to the terms of that agreement. It is rare for plays, short stories, or poems to be written on assignment.

Many editors prefer making assignments to buying unsolicited material, because assignments are more reliable: in each case the editor knows who will be writing the piece, when the piece will be turned in, how long it will run, what approach it will take, and exactly how much it will cost. This makes the editor's planning and budgeting much easier. Some writers prefer working on an assignment basis for most of the same reasons.

The biggest benefit to the writer of working on assignment is that publication and payment are virtually guaranteed. Another benefit is that if an editor likes your work, he or she is likely to give you one assignment after another. Not only does this provide you with a steady income, but being a regular contributor can often lead to other, bigger things—becoming a staff writer at that publication, becoming an editor, or landing assignments from other publications. Editors may also recommend you to their colleagues as someone who's competent and reliable.

But there are drawbacks to working on assignment, too. You will be required to meet a deadline; if you miss it, you may never get an assignment from that editor again. You will have to write your piece the way you and your editor agreed it should be written, even if you later feel that a different approach is best—unless you can convince your editor to allow that new approach.

When an editor assigns a piece to a writer, this does *not* legally obligate the editor to publish and pay for the piece once it is completed and turned in. It *does*, however, obligate the publication to do one of three things: publish the piece and pay the agreed-upon fee for it; not publish the piece but pay the full fee; or not publish the piece, return the piece and all its rights to its author, and pay a "kill fee" of an amount acceptable to the author. The "kill fee" is a sort of consolation prize; it protects the editor from having to publish something he or she considers substandard and protects the writer from having to work without pay. Smart writers who take on assignments will negotiate a kill fee at the time an agreement is made. This way there is no question of what fee is proper or appropriate later on, should the assignment not be acceptable to the editor. Kill fees are discussed in detail on page 169.

In many cases, editors and writers may agree on a fourth option in the event a piece is unusable as submitted: the editor may give the author specific suggestions on how to make the piece publishable and a specific (and reasonable) amount of time to make such revisions. The author then has the option of rewriting the piece to the editor's specifications in the hope of making it usable. If the rewrite is unacceptable, the writer will get the piece back and the full amount of the kill fee.

For newer writers, the biggest problem is getting an assignment in the first place. Most editors shy away from giving assignments to writers whose work they are not familiar with, or who have few or no previous publications. Anyone can write an editor to ask to be given an assignment, but editors are going to give assignments only to those writers they feel can write the sort of material they need. The one exception might be editors of publications that pay nothing for material; these editors can't afford to be choosy.

Many writers wait until they have sold a freelance submission to an editor before asking for an assignment. But there's another option: if you can show an editor that you are able to write the kind of piece he or she publishes, you have a good chance of being given an assignment, even if that editor never heard of you before, and in some cases, even if you've published little or nothing before. To do this, write the editor a letter introducing yourself and your work. In the letter, list your previous relevant publications; let the editor know of any appropriate background or training you may have; enclose published and/or unpublished samples of your writing that resemble the kind of material the editor seeks to publish; and make your letter as clear, concise, and professional as possible.

If you're trying to get an assignment from *Sail* magazine, for example, your best bet is to send the editor photocopies of your previously published sailing pieces. (Samples of published work are sometimes called *clippings* or *clips*.) If you haven't published anything on sailing, then photocopies of articles on other forms of recreation will do. Next best would be samples of published nonfiction (either articles or book excerpts) on any topic. Samples of poetry, fiction (unless it is sailing-oriented), or technical or scholarly articles will not be helpful. You may send unpublished material if it is all you have, or if it seems more appropriate, but published work is more convincing. If you've had work accepted for publication but not yet published, send the pieces in manuscript and tell the editor when and where the pieces will appear. If you don't know exact publication dates, simply say the pieces are "forthcoming." In your cover letter, explain your background and interest in sailing in sufficient detail to sound knowledgeable and reliable.

How much sample material is enough? However much it takes to show that you can write the kind of material the editor needs. Two or three short articles (or book excerpts) of one to three thousand words each are ideal. Don't overwhelm the editor; a good rule of thumb is to provide material that will take, in all, about fifteen minutes or less to read.

There are two general approaches to asking for assignments. The first is to convince an editor of your abilities and say, "I'm available to write whatever you'd like on assignment." Another way is to present an idea for a specific piece; if the editor likes it and believes you can write it competently, you'll get the go-ahead. If the editor likes your writing but not the particular idea for a piece, submit other ideas until something clicks; or offer to write an assigned piece of the editor's choosing.

You may if you wish suggest to an editor two different ideas for assignments, but not more than two at once. And be reasonable; don't write every week or two with a couple of new ideas for articles. This makes you a nuisance, not a potential contributor.

A sample letter presenting a specific idea for an assignment appears on pages 130–31. A sample letter offering to do pieces of an editor's choice on assignment appears on pages 132–33.

These letters should be kept to one page, two if absolutely necessary. Each letter should of course be freshly typed; editors don't react well to photocopied form letters. Enclose a stamped return envelope for the editor's reply. If you wish to have your writing samples returned, say so in your letter and enclose a return envelope of appropriate size bearing sufficient return postage.

If you receive no response to your request for an assignment after four to six weeks, you may wish to follow up with a polite phone call or letter. A phone call is far more likely to bring good results. The editor who is too busy to answer your initial letter may also be too busy to answer your follow-up missive.

Another way to work your way into writing assignments is to write one or more pieces "on speculation" for an editor. This is the ambiguous middle ground between an assignment and an unsolicited submission. When editors ask you to write something "on spec," it means they are interested in your topic and will publish your finished piece *if* it's good enough. It also means that they have every right to reject the finished piece for any reason—and if they do reject it, they owe you no money and no apology. In essence, then, an "on spec" piece is an assignment without any editorial commitment—or, if you prefer, a solicited freelance submission. No written agreement is necessary or appropriate when writing a piece on spec, although a formal agreement is of course necessary once the piece is accepted.

There's nothing wrong with writing a piece on speculation. When you're asked to write a piece on spec, it usually means the editor doesn't

8 Harper Road
Omega, VA 22333
703-555-8660

April 29, 1989

Clara Hardwick
Employer Review
450 Product Court
Service, FL 33990

Dear Clara Hardwick:

Each working day, American workers spend over 240,000
person-hours using water coolers. A recent study has
shown that the average office worker spends seven
minutes a day quenching his or her thirst at the
cooler. These "water breaks" can make a real difference in productivity for corporations employing more
than 1000 people.

Concern about this among management has sparked the
development of a new product: the personal water
cooler. Similar in design to an overlarge thermos,
this inexpensive device keeps one gallon of water
cold for up to ten hours. Placed near an employee's
desk or work station, it can increase his or her productivity by reducing his or her number of trips down
the hall.

Six manufacturers now produce and sell personal water
coolers. Prices range from just under twenty dollars
to just under fifty. Design, efficiency, and durability vary greatly. Some models are free-standing;
some must be placed on shelves, desks, or tables.

I'd like to write an article (tentatively titled "The
Personal Oasis") of roughly 3000 words for Employer
Review which will introduce these products, explain
why they are useful, describe the features of each
model, and rate each product for efficiency, conven-
ience, safety, durability, and overall value.

My previous work has appeared in a dozen magazines
ranging from Glamour and Cosmopolitan to National

Business Review and Office Products Monthly. In several of these magazines I've published pieces rating office products, including electric staplers, personal lighting, and telephone systems. My first book, The World's Best Office Products, is forthcoming from McGraw-Hill. Clippings are enclosed.

If you're interested in assigning me "The Personal Oasis," please write or call. Feel free to get in touch if you have any questions.

Sincerely,

Grace W. Ticknor

Enc.
Writing samples

233 Armitage Lane
Albuquerque, NM 87108
(505) 555-9221

May 3, 1989

Bertram Carroll
Albuquerque Magazine
23 El Cholo Blvd.
Albuquerque, NM 87101

Dear Bertram Carroll:

I've been following Albuquerque Magazine since its
first issue two years ago, and am pleased that it has
achieved wide readership and success throughout northern
and central New Mexico.

For the past four years, I've been writing freelance
articles on assignment for magazines and newspapers which
include Parents, the Albuquerque Journal, the Denver Post,
Organic Gardening, New Mexico, Southwest Profile, and
Private Colleges. Many of these articles concern people,
places, and events in Albuquerque.

Enclosed are photocopies of three recently published
pieces which deal with some of Albuquerque's most unusual
business and artistic ventures.

I'd like to do some freelance work for Albuquerque
Magazine on assignment, and am open to most any topic
dealing with Albuquerque or New Mexico. I work fast, am
scrupulous about meeting deadlines, and can modify my
style to suit virtually any topic or readership. I've
lived in Albuquerque for the last eleven years, and would-
n't want to live anywhere else.

If this prospect interests you, please get in touch
by mail or phone. I'm enclosing a stamped return envel-

ope; whatever you decide, I would appreciate the return
of my writing samples.

     With best wishes.

                                   Sincerely,

                                   Nan McWilson

want to take a chance on giving you an assignment. But once you have written two or three publishable pieces for an editor on spec, you can usually make the jump to writing on assignment. If the editor doesn't suggest making this jump, propose it yourself.

Even if you've written dozens of pieces on assignment for several different publications, don't expect to get an assignment from every new editor you approach. The editor of *Skiing* may not feel comfortable giving you an assignment if you've never written a skiing article before, so don't be surprised or offended if you're asked to do your first piece on spec.

There's one other good way for a new writer to get assignments, and that's to start out small. By small, I mean publications that pay little or nothing at all. If you live in a large city, try a neighborhood newspaper; if you live in a small town, try the local paper. Make an appointment to meet the editor, explaining that you'd like to write for the publication. At your meeting, show the editor some samples of your writing, and either suggest some ideas for articles or ask to be given a story to cover—or both. Keep writing for that paper until you've published ten or more pieces; this will give you a good selection of samples to use to get assignments from other, larger publications.

The one problem with writing on assignment for publications that pay nothing is that if an editor decides not to use your piece, you're not entitled to a kill fee. The editor owes you an explanation, but nothing more.

Once you have established a relationship with an editor—either by selling the editor a couple of pieces or by getting to know him or her well personally—your requests for specific assignments can be more informal. Always give the editor a clear idea of what you intend to write, what approach and tone your piece will take, and how long it will be; but you can now write a more informal letter, and you needn't include a stamped return envelope. If you prefer, you can request assignments over the phone or in person.

While you should feel free to solicit assignments from editors at any point in your career, keep in mind that newer writers can generally build their careers faster by putting most of their efforts into sending completed pieces to editors. Once you have a few publications under your belt, you can go the assignment route more and more often.

Many writers prefer working on assignment because they don't want to write anything unless they have first secured an editorial commitment. This means there's little chance that something they write won't earn them money, which is a definite plus. But it also means these writers don't publish anywhere except those places where they can land assignments. Worse, it means that some potentially good pieces never get written, simply because no editor will agree to commission them in advance. Furthermore, if you limit yourself to writing only on assignment, you can limit your writing income. If you can get assignments from *Twin Cities* but not from *Cosmopolitan*, then you are never going to see anything you write in *Cosmo*. But if you write some pieces first and *then* send them around, you might place one with *Cosmopolitan*, earning yourself $800 or more in the process.

In certain cases it *is* far better to write a piece on assignment, or even on spec, than to write it first and submit it second. Suppose, for example, you wish to interview someone famous or difficult to reach, or to gain access to some facility or area that is closed to the public. Under these circumstances, a commitment from an editor—even an on spec commitment—can provide the credentials you need to get past the guard or secretary who turns everyone else away. If you've got such an editorial commitment, you can legitimately say, for example, "I'm Oliver Small-wood, and I'm doing a piece on the governor for *Parade* magazine. Could she give me thirty minutes of her time later this month for an interview?" The freelancer without a commitment from an editor is likely to be turned away; because you have an agreement with an editor, however, you're more likely to be granted the interview. Someone may call your editor to make sure you really do have such a commitment; but even if you've got only a spec arrangement, your editor will tell whoever's checking, "Yes, that's right, he's doing that piece for us."

In general, you will be expected to pay all your own expenses (travel, research, typing, etc.) when writing on assignment. If you will have more than minor expenses, it is to your benefit to estimate them in advance. This enables you to request, or insist on, a fee that is large enough to pay these expenses and still leave you with a reasonable fee for your services.

If your expenses will be fairly large—say, $100 or more—you may want to negotiate to have them paid separately from your author's fee. Some publications, particularly the larger and better-paying ones, will go along with this. Make sure that your written agreement specifies what expenses your publisher will pay. Standard practice is for the writer to pay all the expenses out of pocket, to save receipts (this is essential), to submit them to the publisher, and to be reimbursed with one check for the total. If you wish to have your publisher pay for certain expenses, this point must be negotiated *before* a written agreement is signed, and preferably before it is drawn up.

If editors want you to provide illustrations or photographs to accompany your assigned manuscript, the following guidelines apply:

• Photographs or illustrations should be provided for by an additional fee (which may need to be separately negotiated).

• Your written assignment agreement should specify the kind of illustrations or photographs (line drawings, black and white prints, etc.) to be turned in, the number to be turned in, which rights to those photos or illustrations you are selling, and the fee for those items.

• If you are unable to supply photos or illustrations that will meet your editor's standards or specifications, simply say so. Except in very unusual cases, this won't cause you to lose the assignment. The editor will simply assign the photos or illustrations to someone else.

• If you are unwilling or unable to provide photos or illustrations but know someone else who can, feel free to make a recommendation to the editor.

• In some cases you may wish to supply photos or illustrations, but the editor will insist on assigning them to someone else or using a staff person. This is the editor's right.

ASSIGNMENT AGREEMENTS

Assignments may be made by editors in letters, phone calls, or face-to-face conversations. However, it is important that the terms of any assignment be spelled out in writing and signed by both parties—or at least by the editor—before you begin the project.

Some publications have standard printed agreements that cover assignments. Others simply send out formal or informal letters of agreement. Books written on assignment—that is, contracted for on the basis of proposals—are usually covered by long and complex written contracts. All of these are fine, providing their terms are reasonable. (The terms of any assignment agreement *are* negotiable, by the way. Just because something has been typed out, or even printed as a standard form, doesn't mean it can't be discussed or changed.)

What is *not* generally acceptable is a simple oral agreement between you and the editor. You are far safer with a written agreement that clearly spells out the terms of the assignment.

This doesn't mean that an editor who offers you only an oral agreement is crooked. In fact, sometimes the most scrupulously honest ones won't offer written agreements *because* they always keep their word. However, you should usually insist on some form of written agreement; if you have to write it up yourself, fine. This will cover you in case your editor quits or gets fired, in case there is any question or disagreement later on, or in case your editor develops amnesia.

A written agreement should include the following:

- A brief description of the piece to be written. This may specify the topic, style, slant, contents, tone, and anything else you or your editor consider important.
- The date by which the piece must be completed and turned in to the editor.
- The amount of payment to be made to you.
- When the payment will be made.
- The rights the publication is buying.
- The amount of the kill fee to be paid in the event the manuscript is rejected, and when that fee is to be paid. Don't overlook this very important provision. Insist that it be a part of your agreement.

These items appear frequently in assignment agreements, but are optional:

- Conditions for rejection of the completed assignment. These may specify what reasons are acceptable and/or by what date a decision to reject the piece must be made.
- Provisions for revision. These allow the writer to revise the manuscript if it is unsatisfactory. Provisions might include the amount of time permitted for a rewrite, the editor's obligations to specify what needs to be rewritten and how it can best be improved, and the date by which a revision, if necessary, must be requested.
- Provisions concerning accompanying illustrations and/or photographs: who is to provide them; their style, content, and format; when they are due; the rights being purchased; and the fee to be paid.
- Provisions concerning the payment of expenses by the publisher.

The assignment agreement must be signed by the editor or publisher; it should *not* have been signed by a secretary or assistant in the editor's absence. Even though your editor is usually the one who will sign a letter of agreement, that agreement remains in force if the editor leaves, in

SCOTT EDELSTEIN
Literary Services
179 Berkeley St., Suite 1
Rochester, NY 14607
Telephone: 716-244-0645

January 3, 1989

Kathryn Reed
The Imaginary Review
88 Dayton Road
Cincinnati, OH 45220

Dear Kathryn:

I'm pleased that you like my idea for an article entitled, tentatively, "Learning Made Cheap and Easy," and that you plan to publish the finished piece in The Imaginary Review.

I agree to provide you with a copy of this article in finished form, neatly typed in accordance with professional standards, on or before February 28, 1989. The article will be between 2500-3000 words long, and will introduce and explain the work of Dr. Marilyn Snyder, director of the Center for the Study of Cognition and Memory, to a general readership. The tone will be upbeat and the language will be easily understandable to the average reader.

In return, The Imaginary Review agrees to pay me $600 within sixty days of delivery and acceptance of the final completed manuscript. This entitles The Imaginary Review to first world publication rights to the piece.

If you find my completed article unsatisfactory, you shall so notify me within thirty days of your receipt of the manuscript, and you shall at that time provide suggestions for revision. I shall then have thirty days to deliver a revised manuscript to you. Should this version also prove unsatisfactory, all rights to "Learning Made Cheap and

Easy" shall revert to me and, within sixty days of
your receipt of the revised manuscript, <u>The Imaginary
Review</u> shall pay me a kill fee of $200, at which time
both parties shall each have no further obligation to
the other under this agreement.

    Two copies of this letter are enclosed. If these
terms are acceptable to you, please sign and date both
copies; return one to me and keep the other for your
files.

                             Sincerely,

                             Scott Edelstein

I agree to the above terms:

_____
Kathryn Reed, THE IMAGINARY REVIEW

Date:_____

which case his or her successor inherits all the obligations of the agreement.

It is not uncommon for editors to make an assignment orally, then to send a written agreement covering that assignment a week or two later. This is fine. However, don't sign anything you're not happy with, and feel free to negotiate the terms of that agreement. If a written agreement leaves anything important, such as the amount of kill time, unspecified, insist that it be specified.

If an editor makes an assignment orally but doesn't add, "I'll be sending you a letter of agreement next week," be sure to say, "I presume you'll be sending a contract or letter of agreement shortly. Is that correct?" If the editor says no, don't panic. Simply say, "Well, I need something in writing. Why don't I send you a letter of agreement, which you can sign and return to me?" A good many editors are pleased to be offered this option, as it saves them the trouble of writing up agreements themselves. An assignment agreement written by an author appears on pages 138–39.

There are only two cases in which a written agreement covering an assignment is not necessary or useful: (1) if you are a salaried employee and are writing the assignment as a part of your job; and (2) if the publication is offering you no remuneration for your piece, in which case you have no rights that need protecting by a written agreement.

Payment for an assignment may be in one or more parts. For book proposals, the standard arrangement is half the advance on signing of the contract, half upon acceptance of a complete acceptable manuscript. Articles are usually paid for only after they have been completed, although sometimes a portion of the fee can be paid up front if the author is well known and/or if the piece involves moderate or large travel or research expenses.

INVOICES

Once an assignment has been turned in and deemed acceptable, it is the editor's obligation to arrange for payment to be sent to you. Many authors have found that submitting an invoice along with a finished piece speeds up the payment process. An invoice can be quite simple, and can be typed on either your printed stationery or plain white paper.

The invoice should be dated and include the following items: the title of the piece; the date it was turned in; a brief description of the piece (this may include subject matter, slant, word length, or anything else that

SCOTT EDELSTEIN
Literary Services
179 Berkeley St., Suite 1
Rochester, NY 14607
Telephone: 716-244-0645

March 2, 1989

INVOICE

Re: The Karma Principle

Description: 2500-word article on plotting fiction

Terms: Written on assignment for <u>Writer's
               Monthly</u>. See agreement dated
               10/17/88.

Payment: $500, to be paid on acceptance of
               completed piece. <u>Now due</u>.

The above assignment was turned in to Greg Danneman
on March 2, 1989.

Scott Edelstein

can briefly and easily identify it); a reference to the legal agreement that accompanied the assignment—for example, "See our agreement of 8/14/88"; and the amount due. A sample invoice appears on page 141.

It is also useful to send an invoice for a piece written on spec once it has been accepted by an editor. However, it is neither useful nor proper to submit an invoice for an unsolicited manuscript that has been accepted.

If you are not paid for *any* piece, including an unsolicited one, within forty-five days, it is an excellent idea to send out a "past due" invoice to the publisher's accounts payable department and to make a polite phone or mail inquiry to your editor.

QUERIES

A query, or query letter, is a letter in which you ask if an editor would be interested in a particular project. It introduces you and your work and/or your idea for a piece.

You have already seen how a query letter can be used to request an assignment. A query letter can also be used if you wish to submit a manuscript but know that the editor or publication will not accept unsolicited material. Thus query letters are useful and often necessary if you wish to submit a book proposal to a major publishing house. It is also useful (and entirely Kosher) to write a query letter to an editor about a piece immediately after it has been returned unread by that same editor or publication because of a "no unsolicited material" policy. It is *not* useful to write a query letter asking permission to submit a manuscript *unless* you know for a fact that an editor will not read unsolicited submissions.

Some writers always send query letters on the theory that they save postage and trouble. Their rationale is that if an editor doesn't like the idea behind a piece, there's little point in sending in the piece. The problem with this reasoning is that query letters—even the best ones— can only give a partial perspective on the pieces they describe. An editor may reject an idea presented in a query simply because the idea doesn't lend itself well to a three-paragraph description. But the same editor might fall in love with that piece were she to read it.

Furthermore, a good many editors, including some who read unsolicited manuscripts, don't respond to queries at all because they're too busy. If you send one of these editors a manuscript, he or she might like it, buy it, and publish it; if you send the same editor a query, you might never get a response. This happens often.

The general rule for query letters, then, is to use them only when you have to.

Look back at the query letter on pages 130–31. If you wish to ask an editor to assign you a specific piece, you should write a letter similar to this one. But if you want to ask the editor to look at a piece you've already completed, paragraph four should be altered to reflect the fact that the article has already been written. Paragraph six should be replaced with something like this: "If this piece sounds as if it might be up your particular alley, let me know. I'd be happy to send you the manuscript." Writing samples can be omitted, since you are only trying to get the editor to look at your work, not commit to a deal.

If you want to ask an editor to look at a particular manuscript, there's nothing wrong with making your request by phone.

If you receive no response to your query after four to six weeks, follow it up with a polite phone call.

LETTERHEAD STATIONERY

Do you need printed stationery to be a freelance writer? No. Plain white 8½-by-11-inch paper will do perfectly well.

But printed stationery will make a good initial impression on some editors. I have found that my printed stationery and mailing labels often get my work read by editors who normally refuse to read unsolicited manuscripts.

Printed stationery probably makes the biggest difference when you're sending work to book publishers. At many book houses, mailroom clerks are instructed to return authors' unsolicited manuscripts unread rather than deliver them to editors. But tasteful printed stationery with the words *Literary Services (not Writer* or *Freelance Writer)* will get your manuscript past the mailroom clerk and onto editors' desks, presumably because the clerks mistake you for a literary agent. (This will work, of course, only if you send your manuscripts to editors by name, not by title.)

Spending $100 on some good letterhead and envelopes and

printed address labels may thus be one of the best business investments you can make.

The most effective stationery is simple, understated, and straightforward. The printing should be in black, dark blue, or dark brown ink. The paper should be of good quality, in white, ivory, buff, or some other soft color. The standard size is 8½ by 11 inches, but 8 by 10 is also acceptable. Avoid onionskin or other unusually thin paper. Also be sure to choose a paper style that enables your typewriter or printer to produce dark, clear letters; test out paper samples before placing your printing order. Use the same paper and the same color ink for stationery and envelopes, and definitely get both. Also order some blank sheets to be used for the second pages of letters. These go for 2¢ to 3¢ a sheet.

Type should be easily readable, clear, and even a bit elegant-looking. Avoid oddball or obscure typefaces. Your stationery should have nothing on it except your name, address, and phone number(s). (If you have more than one phone number, indicate which is for business and which is your home. Do include both, so that editors can reach you easily.) Add the words *Literary Services* on a separate line. Avoid logos, illustrations, cutesy descriptions such as *Purveyor of Words and Phrases,* and the trite phrase *From the desk of.* Use the word *suite* instead of *apartment;* this sounds more professional. Your envelopes should be imprinted with the same style of type, though you may wish to reduce the size.

I also recommend ordering gummed labels, roughly 2 inches high by 4 inches wide, with your name and address printed on the top half. These can be used as address labels and on the covers of scripts, manuscript boxes, and folders containing book proposals; the title of the manuscript and your byline can be typed in the blank area. Gummed labels—the kind you lick—are not expensive. Pressure-sensitive—"peel off"—labels are much more expensive and usually not worth the extra money.

If you like, you may write to editors using the stationery of your employer, provided it is fairly innocuous looking, not absurdly inappropriate, and not against company policy. Use common sense here. If you work for Dow Chemical, don't use company stationery when sending your work to *Organic Gardening*.

WRITERS' GUIDELINES

Many publications print sheets of guidelines and specifications for free-lance writers. Usually referred to as "editorial guidelines," "tip sheets," or "spec sheets," these materials explain what kinds of pieces a publication is looking for; what focus, slant, tone, or themes those pieces should have; how long they should be; what audience the publication seeks to reach; rates of payment; when payment is made; rights usually purchased; and other basic information. Although you should take spec sheets seriously, understand that they are not the Ten Commandments. Some exceptions are usually possible. If a spec sheet asks for material of 2000–7500 words, for example, this doesn't mean your 1600-word piece won't be seriously considered (though your 15,000-word article probably would be returned unread).

Editorial guidelines are available upon request from editors. If you mail your request, enclosed a stamped, self-addressed business envelope. If you don't receive a reply, don't assume the editor doesn't want to hear from you. That publication may simply have no official sheet of guidelines to send out.

You do *not* need to request a spec sheet before you make a submission to a particular editor or publication.

DEADLINES

It is very important that you meet your deadlines. Editors often plan well in advance, and a manuscript that does not arrive in time can force them to change publishing schedules, and even entire issues or editions.

If you consistently meet or beat deadlines, this will establish you as a reliable writer. This encourages editors to continue to work with you. If you miss an editor's deadline, he or she may choose never to work with you again.

Newspapers, particularly dailies, have the tightest deadlines. A piece turned in even ten minutes late can wreak havoc on a page or section. If you're writing a piece for a newspaper, take your deadline very seriously. Deadlines for films, television shows, and plays are usually equally urgent—sometimes more so, because there may be whole production companies waiting to go to work the moment your manuscript arrives. Magazines are usually, though not always, a bit more flexible about deadlines.

Books are the one area of publishing where deadlines are not *always* so important. Book authors often ask for extensions of deadlines, and publishers usually, though by no means always, grant them.

If, at any point in the writing of a piece, you realize that you're not going to meet a deadline, stop and rethink the project. What can you do to restructure it, shorten it, or approach it differently so that the deadline *can* be met? This might result in a piece that is less thorough or well written than you'd hoped; but usually you're better off turning in a passable but unspectacular piece on time than missing the deadline altogether. If you realize that you're not going to meet a deadline under any circumstances, let your editor know immediately. This enables him or her to reschedule the piece, to suggest new ways to approach your material so that the deadline *can* be met, to grant you an extension, or to scuttle the project before you put any more effort into it.

If you accept an assignment and then turn the piece in after your deadline, the editor is not obligated to publish or pay for it, no matter how good it may be. Nor are you entitled to a kill fee. You have legally voided your agreement by missing your deadline, although the editor may choose to pay for and publish the piece anyway.

A big part of meeting deadlines is setting reasonable ones in the first place—or, if they are set by your editor, refusing to accept unreasonable ones. If an editor suggests a deadline that seems unreasonable, you can say, "No, that's too soon. But I can do it by ————." If an editor insists that a piece must be done by a certain date, and you sincerely doubt you can finish it by that date, you are probably best off saying, "I'm sorry. I simply can't do the job in that amount of time." If you *do* let yourself be talked into accepting an unreasonable deadline, be assured that *you* will be the one held solely responsible if you miss it. (When editorial pressure on this has been unrelenting, I've found myself saying, "Would you prefer we agree to this deadline and I fail to meet it, or that we agree to a later one I can promise to meet?" This usually works.) If you are the one setting the deadline, as is often the case in book contracts, think the project through carefully and be sure to give yourself sufficient time to complete it. Add a little extra time to be safe.

What if you finish a piece early? By all means turn it in early. Editors love writers who beat deadlines.

REWRITING

Sooner or later an editor is going to ask you to rewrite one of your pieces. Should you do it? Here are some tips to help you decide:

• Don't automatically reject or accept the idea of a rewrite. Listen to the editor's reactions carefully, and judge them on their own merits. If you need to, ask questions. Find out exactly what the editor feels needs improvement and what you can do to improve it. Keep in mind that an editor may be less concerned with literary quality than with making the piece conform to a standard style or approach, or with making it more attractive to a specific readership.

• You do not have to slavishly accept every suggestion for rewrite that an editor makes. Few editors expect you to do everything they suggest, and most are quite willing to compromise. If an editor makes five suggestions for rewriting a piece, and you agree with three of them, feel free to incorporate those three changes and ignore the other two. In fact, both editors and writers agree on the following rule of thumb: when a good writer and a good editor work together, the writer usually accepts two-thirds of the editor's suggestions and rejects the rest.

• There is nothing wrong with bargaining over revisions. For instance, if an editor wants you to rewrite scenes two, three, and four of a short story, and you feel that only scene four needs work, it is fine to say, "I'll rewrite the third and fourth scenes as you've requested if you'll let the second scene stand."

• You will have to decide for yourself exactly how much you are willing to compromise to get your piece published. Compromise itself is neither a virtue nor a sin; it all depends on the particular situation. Sometimes compromise is useful or necessary; other times it can be inappropriate or damaging to your piece.

• If an editor asks for a rewrite, you always have the option of saying, "I'm sorry, but either you'll have to take the piece as is or reject it." In such a case, the editor in turn has the right to say, "Okay, then, I'm rejecting it."

• If you genuinely disagree with an editor about something, stand your ground, at least at first. Explain as cogently as you can why you feel the way you do. Many editors will let you have your way at this point, whether or not they actually agree with you.

• Some editors may ask you flat out, "Why did you write this in this way?" or "Why do you feel that my suggestions will harm rather than help your piece?" Don't let such questions fluster you; they are usually asked quite sincerely. Answer them straightforwardly and honestly. Most editors don't mind being argued with, and many will change their minds if your explanations are reasonable.

• An editor who requests a rewrite is normally under no obligation to buy or publish that rewrite, even if you rewrite it precisely to his or her specifications. As one editor at *The New Yorker* told me, "Rewriting is always a gamble." If the piece is rejected after being written on assignment, however, you are entitled to a kill fee and all rights to your piece.

• If you are writing for television, *you should expect everything you write to be drastically rewritten* by producers, directors, story editors, staff writers, consultants, and even actors. Very little of what you write will ever make it onto the screen intact. This is one of the most basic facts of life for television writers, and if you're unwilling to accept it, you should forget about writing for TV.

• Scripts for film, stage, and radio are also usually tampered with a good deal by directors and other people.

THE EDITING PROCESS

Between the time your work is accepted and the time it is published, it will be edited at least once, typeset, and proofread. Writers frequently worry about whether their work will emerge from these steps intact, or even in recognizable form.

Every manuscript an editor plans to use needs copyediting—to correct errors in grammar, punctuation, spelling, syntax, and diction; to ensure that the piece conforms to publication or house style; to make sure that the entire piece reads clearly and smoothly; and to eliminate material that is repetitious or unnecessary.

Copyediting may be done by the editor who accepts your work, by another in-house editor, by an editorial assistant, or by a freelance copy editor. Some publications might also have a fact checker look the manuscript over to make sure that every claim it makes is true. Some might also have a lawyer read certain manuscripts to make sure they provide no grounds for lawsuits.

You are going to have to learn through painful, and sometimes pleasurable, experience which publications provide appropriate editing and which ones do not.

A good rule of thumb is to trust an editor the first time around. If the editing of a manuscript is botched, *politely* say so. Be specific about what was less than satisfactory, and ask the editor to be more careful next time around. If your second piece isn't edited much better than the first, then it's probably time to move on to another editor or publication—or else to accept poor editing at that publication as a fact of life. This last option is often the smartest one if you write for newspapers, for reasons which I'll explain shortly.

The editor who bought your piece may or not be the person who actually copyedits it. However, he or she is the one to write or call if the editing on that piece is less than satisfactory. He or she also is the one responsible for seeing to it that your next piece is edited properly.

Never expect or insist that every one of your golden words remain unchanged. Let editors do their job—which is to improve your manuscript by doing exactly as much editing as necessary.

If you write for a newspaper, you will not usually have any say in the editing of your piece, nor should you expect any. This situation is unfortunate, but it's usually the result of tight deadlines rather than any lack of consideration on editors' parts.

If you sell material to a magazine, your right to approve the editing depends on the magazine. If you are not automatically given this right, there's nothing wrong with asking for it, but don't always expect to get it. If you do ask for it, do so as soon as your piece has been accepted, and try to make your right to approve editing a part of your legal agreement with that publication.

Many magazine contracts include a "right to edit" clause, which gives editors the right to edit your material as they see fit. I normally let such a clause stand the first time around. If my piece is then edited acceptably, I continue to allow that provision to stand in future contracts with that publication. But if the editing is poor, then I may insist (or at least ask) that I be given the right to approve editing in the future. Sometimes I get this, and sometimes I don't.

If your written or oral agreement contains nothing at all about editing, then you are by default giving editors the right to edit as they please, provided they don't do anything utterly outrageous. Again, there's nothing wrong with granting editors this right; but if your piece is badly edited, you may want to ask for the right to approve the editing in the future.

Nearly every book publisher automatically grants writers the right to examine and approve all editing, and the right to change or veto any editing that is unsatisfactory. If this right is not a part of your book contract, insist that it be added. If you have been given the right to approve all editing, you will eventually receive your original copyedited manuscript (or a photocopy) and/or galleys (also called galley proofs). Galleys are strips or pages of typeset material that has not yet been proofread. Your job is to make any changes or corrections that are necessary. If you disagree with any item of editing, change that item back to its original form.

Before type has been set, you may make changes in a copyedited manuscript directly on the manuscript. Follow the guidelines for making copyediting corrections on pages 25–27. To make changes in typeset material, you should use standard proofreader's marks, both in the text itself and in the margins. Pages 151–52 provide a complete guide to these marks and their use.

If you have written a book, you may also get a third chance to make corrections: many book publishers routinely send their authors prepublication copies of their books. Others send page proofs—typeset material that has been pasted up onto unbound, numbered pages. Illustrations, charts, graphs, and/or indexes may be omitted. This material is also sent to reviewers in advance of publication. Copies may also be sent to well-known writers and other personalities in the hope that they'll respond with endorsements of the book. A very few publishers skip the galley stage and send their authors page proofs only.

When you receive a copy yourself, read it over promptly and carefully. If any changes need to be made at this stage, let your editor know; you may either list them on a separate sheet, or mark up the pages as if they were galleys and return them to your editor.

It is essential that you go through copyedited manuscripts, galleys, page proofs and prepublication copies *very carefully*—line by line, word by word, and letter by letter. You can easily overlook a good many errors unless you spend the time and effort to check *everything*. Don't assume that editors will catch all the problems, because they won't. To be sure, check everything against your original manuscript. All of this careful checking is both tedious and time-consuming, I know. But the effort is worth it, as it ensures that your piece will be published in the very best possible shape.

When you go over your copyedited work, try not to be too protective of your original. If a change has been made, try to figure out why rather than objecting to it automatically. Don't be picky. Let small changes go,

PROOFREADER'S MARKS
FOR USE IN CORRECTING GALLEYS AND PAGE PROOFS

Correction	How to Mark Text	What to Put in the Margin
insert a letter or number	lose, if he	O
insert a comma	with me but I	↑
insert a period	goes Still, he	⊙
insert a space	livingroom. I would	#
insert a semicolon	me then she	;
insert a colon	ways you can	:
insert a hyphen	say goodbye to	=
insert an apostrophe	Sams order was	∜
insert quotation marks	said, Hello, then	∜ / ∜
insert a word	biggest, offer	*best*
insert superscript number	$e = mc$	2
delete a letter or punctuation mark	the written/word	ℓ
delete a word	really really hard	ℓ
close space	pair of book ends	⌒
delete and close space	lionness looking at	ℰ
spell out number	at least 7 different	seven
change word to number	at least seven different	7
change to lowercase	the Mailman brought us	lc
change to uppercase	men from mars	cap
transpose letters	cool, clear watre	tr
transpose words	I like like	tr
move lines	line 2 line 1	tr
set in italics	read The Writer's Bible?	ital
set in regular typeface	an example of	roman
set in boldface type	another example of	bf

Proofreader's Marks *(Continued)*

Correction	How to Mark Text	What to Put in the Margin
set in small capitals	still another example	(sc)
begin new paragraph here	end.¶Then you would	¶
no new paragraph; run lines together	end, he knew. no¶ Then he thought	(no¶)
do not make indicated correction; leave as printed	This is the ~~way~~ we	(stet)
move left	⌐ said he would be going	(move left)
move right	said he would be going ⌐	(move right)
move down	trying to ⌐be⌐ cool	⊔
move up	really ⌐would be⌐ best	⌐
move elsewhere	So I said to him, "Why not?" "That's a good idea; should we try it?" he answered. So we grabbed the shovel and	(tr)
two or more corrections on the same line	understood why he lost the	(tr)/(#)/ê

and concentrate on the major ones. If a bit of editing changes your work but neither improves nor harms it, let it stand. You'll earn some psychological brownie points with your editor, and this will make him or her more willing to compromise on issues that really matter to you. If there's some editing you simply don't understand, feel free to write or call your editor to discuss it. Calling is usually best, as it takes up less of everybody's time.

If an editor has a question about something or feels the need to explain a certain bit of editing, he or she will either write you a note in the margin or, more likely, write it on a "flag"—a small piece of gummed paper stuck to the page. Read all flags carefully and respond to them thoroughly. This is one of your obligations to your editor. And don't tear them off, or your editor will never know what point you responded to.

EDITORIAL ETIQUETTE

Follow these simple guidelines and the publishing process will be smoother for everyone involved:

• Never allow yourself to be mistreated. Insist on reasonable terms, fees, and deadlines; expect your editors to be reasonably available and responsive; and require them to keep all agreements and promises they make. But do not expect editors to be perfect. They make mistakes, just like everybody else, and sometimes those mistakes will involve you or your work. When editors do err, point out the error promptly and nonjudgmentally, without getting angry or upset. Encourage them to fix the error, if it's fixable, and to avoid repeating it in the future. Feel free to offer your assistance if you think it will help.

• If editors make *repeated* errors or mistreat you, advise their superiors. You may be best off not dealing with those editors in the future, if that's possible.

• If editors seem willing to chat or make small talk, feel free to share in this. But if they're strictly business, you should be, too.

• If editors are curt or abrupt, or even a little disgruntled, don't take it personally. Chances are they're very busy or under a great deal of pressure. Or this may simply be their personal style. Respond in a terse, nononsense manner yourself, and don't assume that anything is wrong—unless you spot other evidence to that effect.

• Editors have biases, quirks, and pet peeves—after all, they're human. Don't be surprised if you inadvertently step on some editors' toes—and don't be so naive as to think that editors are "above all that."

• Some writers worry about being blacklisted by an editor, a publication, a publishing firm, or the entire publishing world. These writers often take care to be extra polite, even obsequious, to editors. This is unnecessary, and even counterproductive. While it is true that some editors do have private "shit lists"—that is, lists of people who have offended them and with whom they therefore refuse to work—it is rare that people make it onto these lists arbitrarily or by accident. Even if you do make it onto one editor's blacklist, this isn't going to affect your status with other publications, or (in most cases) with other editors at that same publication.

• Remember that dealing with writers is only one small part of an editor's job and that, in most cases, editors answer first to their employers and second to their writers. So don't feel abused if an editor takes a couple of days to return your phone call, or otherwise treats you as less than a top priority.

• If an editor does a good job for you, does a favor for you, or otherwise earns your appreciation, express your thanks in a letter. Editors like getting praise at least as much as writers do.

• Don't be afraid to use the phone to contact an editor. Most editors are happy to answer questions and discuss projects over the telephone, and a few even prefer it. However, some editors *don't* like using the phone, so don't be offended if you have to talk to a secretary, or if you get told, "Send me a letter about it and I'll get back to you."

• When should you phone an editor or publisher collect? This is a touchy question with no simple answer. I never call editors or publishers collect because it's simpler, and because, like almost all writers, I can write off the cost of the calls on my taxes. *Generally,* though, you can make collect calls to editors and other people in publishing under the following circumstances: when you are returning someone else's call; when you are calling to negotiate a contract you have been offered, or to ask a question about that contract; when you are calling an editor who publishes your work regularly to speak about a specific item of business; or when you have been asked by someone at the publishing firm to make the call—for example, your editor says, "Call Marlene Graham in the Royalties Department on Monday morning." Other calls to editors and publishers should *not* normally be made collect. Collect calls should of course be made person-to-person.

• For a thorough overview of etiquette in dealing with editors, read William Brohaugh's excellent *Professional Etiquette for Writers* (Writer's Digest Books).

BUSINESS ADVICE

The following tips will help you thrive, as well as survive, as a writer:

• Never assume that a deal has been made with an editor until you have both agreed to the terms, by reaching a firm and final oral agreement, by signing a written agreement, or by your editor's stating the terms in a signed letter. Deals can and do fall through at the last minute.

One fairly common occurrence of this sort is the 90 percent acceptance, when an editor says, "I like your piece and want to use it. Unfortunately, I can't *promise* that I'll be able to; but there's a 90 percent chance that I will." Or you might get this variation: "I like your piece but can't commit myself to it right now. Can I have a few more weeks to consider it?" There could be any of a dozen reasons for this: the publication is overstocked with material; the editor needs the approval of someone higher up; the next issue might not have room if the ad people close the deal they've been working on; the editor wants to see if interest in your subject remains strong two months from now; and so on.

When this happens, the editor has three options: buy your piece and risk wasting the money if it isn't used; reject it and lose the chance to publish it; or hang onto it, sometimes for up to a year, until a final decision can be made. Many editors choose this last option and hope you will cooperate. Some editors attempt to elicit this cooperation by saying that there is a 90 percent—or even a 99 percent—chance that they'll be able to use the piece.

However, anything less than a firm agreement to publish a piece means the same thing: the editor has the right to reject the piece for any reason at any time, without obligation. The actual rate of eventual acceptance under these circumstances is probably more like 40 percent.

If you find yourself in this situation, it is usually best to give the editor more time. You have the right to say, "I'm sorry, but I need a commitment. I have to ask you to either buy the piece or return it to me." If you do, 90 percent of the time the piece will be returned to you. I recommend against this strategy in most cases.

You *can* ask the editor to make a decision within a specific period of time. Three additional months is usually fair to both sides. Or you can ask, "How much more time do you think you need to decide?" and give the editor that amount of time, but add, "I'll expect a final decision from you by that date." If the editor doesn't decide by then, or asks for still more time, you can then decide whether to force the issue or continue to sit tight.

• Just as a deal is never certain until both sides have clearly and unambiguously agreed to it, never assume that money from a publisher is yours until the check is in your hands, you have deposited it in the bank, *and it has cleared.* Just about any writer can tell you horror stories about publishers' late or bounced checks. Don't think this won't happen to you; it *will,* sooner or later. Don't spend a penny of money from *any* (that's right, *any*) publisher until the actual funds are in your account. Things can and often do go wrong when it comes to getting paid.

• Keep copies of all correspondence with editors—both letters you've written and those you've received. These letters can be useful if you ever have to take a publisher to court—and you may, someday.

• If you are mailing something valuable, important, or timely—for example, corrected galleys, or a completed manuscript that will just barely be making its deadline, or a package of expensive photographs or illustrations—purchase the legal protection of a return receipt. Write a description of the item you're sending on the receipt, so there can be no question later about what you sent. Insist that the receipt include the signature of the person accepting delivery and the date delivery is made. When your package is delivered, the receipt will be signed, dated, and mailed back to you. Your receipt of it provides legal documentation that your package was, in fact, delivered to its proper address. Save these receipts as long as necessary.

If you have written a piece on assignment or under contract to a publisher, and you have *any* (repeat, *any*) reason to doubt the publisher's honesty, purchase a return receipt when you send in your manuscript. This protects you in the event the publisher claims that the manuscript was never received.

• Keep a copy of every contract or letter of agreement you receive. It is just as important to keep a copy of every item of correspondence—both letters you send and those you receive—relating to the creation or sale of your work.

• Whenever you discuss the slant, approach, or other specifications of a piece with an editor, in person or on the phone, make careful notes of the points of your discussion. Hang onto those notes for later reference. It is also an excellent idea to type up those points of discussion and promptly send them in a letter to your editor, so that he or she, too, has the information on file. This heads off potential disagreements later over what was discussed or agreed to.

AUTHOR'S COPIES

Book contracts almost always have a specific provision for free author's copies. Ten copies is the minimum; with some pushing you can often get twenty-five. Additional copies are usually available at a discount of 40 percent or more; ask for this provision if it is not already in your contract.

Most publishers of magazines, newspapers, and anthologies provide contributors with one or two free copies automatically, as a courtesy. In the case of newspapers, though, you'll usually have to pick up copies at the newspaper's office; they won't be sent to you automatically. Rarely is a provision for free author's copies included in a magazine or newspaper publishing contract.

Some publishers do not automatically supply author's copies, but will be happy to send you some on request. Virtually no publisher has a policy *against* sending authors free copies.

When I sell a piece to a magazine, I write my editor a short note as soon as we've struck a deal. The note says, "I'd appreciate receiving two or three author's copies on publication." If the copies haven't arrived within two weeks after the piece's publication (and often they don't, since editors often forget to send out authors' copies in the crush of deadlines and details), I give the editor a call or send another short note. Almost always this does the trick. If it doesn't, though, I shrug my shoulders, buy a couple of copies of the magazine, and forget about the matter. It's not important enough to badger the editor about any further.

ASKING FOR MORE MONEY

When you first begin writing for a publication, you should expect to receive its lowest, or close to its lowest, rate of pay. The longer you have written for a publication, the more pieces you have produced, and/or the more published work you already have under your belt, the more money you are likely to be paid.

There are exceptions here, though. The advance for a book, for example, is based on the projected sales of that book, not on previous publications or credentials. If your fourth book has a smaller projected audience than your first, it may earn a much smaller advance than the first. Other exceptions are some publications (many literary magazines, for example) that pay a set rate per word, page, or piece, regardless of an author's fame or lack of it. But most publishers and producers reward seniority with higher pay. However, they will not all do so automatically. Some editors will keep paying you the same rate until you ask for more.

You always have the right to ask for more money for something you have written, or have agreed to write on assignment, including your first sale to a publication. You also have the right to refuse an offer. However, the publisher or editor has the right to refuse to go any higher. No halfway reasonable editor will ever penalize you or reject your piece because you asked for more money. The worst he or she will do is say, "Sorry, but that's as high as I can go."

If you have been writing a column or regular feature for a publication, you should expect a hike in the rate of payment every year or so. If one is not granted automatically, feel free to ask for one.

If a magazine, newspaper, or newsletter has purchased four of your freelance pieces and paid you the same rate for each, it is not unreasonable to ask for a slightly higher rate beginning with the fifth or sixth piece. After about your dozenth sale to that publication, you are within your rights to ask for another small rate hike. If you keep selling to that publication on a regular basis, you should expect (and if necessary ask for) additional rate hikes every year or so.

A 25 percent rate hike is a reasonable expectation and request. (If you are already being paid four-figure sums, only ask for or expect 20 percent.) However, if your editor offers slightly less, don't quibble.

If an editor refuses to give you a rate hike, suggest a compromise. You might suggest that you continue to receive the same rate per word but be given more or longer assignments. Or that you be paid the same flat fee per piece but be permitted to turn in shorter pieces. Or, if you are turning in a regular feature that tends to run fifteen hundred to two thousand words and are being paid $300 for each piece, you might arrange to be paid 20¢ a word in the future, based on actual length.

Don't ask for a rate hike if the publication doesn't have variable rates, or if it never pays any of its contributors at all. (Though if it pays some of them and hasn't been paying you, by all means ask to start getting paid after you've published several pieces in it.) And once you are receiving a publication's highest rate, don't push for more money. Don't ask a publication to violate its own policies for you.

If an editor has been upping your payment rate occasionally without your having to ask, don't ask for still more money (unless the increases have been miniscule). In fact, since your editor has been thoughtful enough to give you rate increases without prompting, it's a good idea to send him or her a brief letter of thanks.

WHEN YOUR EDITOR LEAVES

One of the most disconcerting things about being a freelance writer is that editors tend to come and go. You may spend years building a relationship with an editor, only to have that relationship suddenly severed when he or she quits to take a job elsewhere—or to become a musician, a freelance editor, or even a freelance writer.

However, there are ways to soften the shock of an editor leaving—and even ways to turn this to your advantage.

When an editor you have worked with leaves a publication, the first thing to do is call up his or her secretary, assistant, or co-editor. Find out the name and telephone number of the person who has taken your old editor's place. In the case of book publishers, this will mean finding out which editor already employed at that firm has taken over your book. Also find out where your old editor is currently working, and ask for the address and phone number of that firm.

Wait a week or two so that both people can get used to their new jobs. Then call up your old editor. Offer congratulations on the new job, and ask for some information on the new publication. What kind of material is he or she looking for now? What are the new rates of payment? Talk about some possible ideas for pieces, and see if you can get an assignment or two.

Then write or (preferably) call the person who took over your old editor's job (or who inherited your book). Introduce yourself, and explain what you've written before for that publication and when it was published. Tell the new editor where else your work has appeared and describe your credentials, training, or background, as appropriate. Say you look forward to working with him or her in the future, and leave your address, home and work phone numbers, and the correct spelling of your name.

If you're currently writing a piece on assignment or on spec for that publication, inform the new editor of the arrangements (with reference to the written agreement you and your old editor signed, if any); explain what the piece is about, when it is due, and what the agreed-upon payment is to be.

If any of your work was accepted by the previous editor but has not yet been published, inform the new editor of this. Give the title and a brief description of each piece, and bring the editor up to date on what has and has not been done to each: for example, whether a piece has been typeset, whether you've received galleys, whether you've returned those galleys, and so on. Also ask if the editor has any news for you about your work—for example, if a publication date has been set or if a piece has been copyedited yet.

Finally, let the new editor know that you are available to write pieces on assignment. If you like, suggest some ideas of your own for assignments—including ideas his or her predecessor rejected. If you are dealing with a magazine or newspaper editor, see if you can swing a deal on an assignment right then.

Once you've established contact with this new editor, it's a good idea to submit a manuscript within the next month or two, if possible, so that the connection doesn't fade. Be sure to say something in your cover letter to connect you with the call or with your earlier letter, such as, "I enjoyed talking with you on the phone last month, and hope that you're enjoying working for Acme Publications." Enclose a business card if you like.

The problem of editors leaving is especially acute in book publishing. It is common for a writer to sell a book to one editor, only to have that editor leave the firm before the book is published, and sometimes before it is completed. It is possible for a single book to go through three or four editors. When your editor leaves, your book is considered an "orphan."

If your book is orphaned, grit your teeth but don't panic. It's important to establish a good relationship with your new editor and get him or her excited about your book. Besides doing all the things I recommend in the previous paragraphs, spend a few minutes describing your book to your new editor. Explain what your book is about, what audience(s) it is written for, why those people will be interested in it, and, most importantly, what makes your book original, special, or unique. You might want to send a copy of your original book proposal. Don't assume that it is readily available; your new editor may not even know where to look for it. In addition, explain what you and/or the publisher have done so far to promote the book, design its cover, prepare press releases, and so on.

Then, as the months pass, keep in touch. Don't constantly nag, but drop a note or call every month or two if you don't hear from your editor. Offer to help however you can; if the editor requests your help, give it freely and willingly. All of this is essential to keeping the editor interested in your book.

Finally, if your editor leaves, remember that any agreements you've entered into have been made with the firm, not with the editor. If you sell a book to Karen Winter at Macmillan and she takes a job at Viking the day after you sign a contract, she cannot take your book with her to Viking. You've got to write it for Macmillan, and you'll have to work with whoever Macmillan decides will take over the project. However, unless your contract stipulates otherwise, you can take your *next* book to Winter at Viking—or wherever she happens to be working at the time.

4. ✐ _____

Living with Rejection

REJECTION AS AN OCCUPATIONAL HAZARD

Rejection is an unavoidable part of being a freelance writer. And it stays part of being a freelance writer no matter how wealthy or well known you may become. No less a literary figure than John Updike recently confessed on a TV talk show that he still has work rejected on occasion.

There is only one sure way to avoid having your work rejected: never submit it. The trick is not to avoid rejection, but not to let it get to you. This is not always easy, especially when something you've worked hard on, been proud of, and had high hopes for gets bounced instantaneously—or worse, after six months—with a form rejection slip.

The first thing you should keep in mind is that your *writing* has been rejected, not you. An editor who rejects something you have written is making a judgment (which may or may not be valid) *only* about that piece of writing, not about any other piece of writing, your worth as a human being, or your overall ability or potential as a writer. *Never* take rejection personally.

If something you have written gets bounced by an editor, the best thing you can do is shrug your shoulders and send the piece right back out again. If the editor makes some comments about the piece, think those comments over. Consider each one separately, on its own merits. If after reading them, you believe the piece should be revised, do so before sending it back out. If you disagree with the editor, ignore the comments and submit the piece elsewhere as is.

Never write, call, or visit an editor to argue the merits of a rejected piece. Keep silent even if your piece about Broadway theater is rejected with a note that says, "Sorry, but we just published a piece on Cabbage Patch Dolls and we don't want to do another one this soon." Arguments, no matter how well justified, will get you nowhere, and may well anger and alienate the editor, thereby eliminating a potential buyer. Accept rejection when it comes, just as you would bad weather.

Of course, you'll never be able to make yourself completely immune to rejection. Each time a piece comes back, you'll probably feel a small pang of disappointment. So allow yourself to feel that pang. Balance it out by treating yourself to something you enjoy—a long walk, a glass of wine, or perhaps a Chinese dinner. Then get back to the business of writing, submitting your work, and building your writing career.

Learning not to become too discouraged is the most important part of accepting rejection. *Some* discouragement is inevitable, especially in the early phases of your career, when rejection is frequent (or even constant), and when the money and ego rewards are few or nonexistent. But keep telling yourself that persistence will probably pay off, and keep writing and submitting your work.

I know of several writers who focus on sending material to editors for a period of two or three months; then, for another two or three months, they'll take a break from marketing their work and focus entirely on writing. If recurrent rejection gets you down, this is one excellent way to give yourself a respite from it.

In most cases you will simply not know why a piece has been rejected. A form rejection letter certainly will not tell you; explanations like "It doesn't suit our needs at this time" or "Unfortunately, we do not feel it is appropriate for our publication" are merely elaborate ways of saying no.

Even if you get a personal letter from an editor rejecting a piece, don't expect a reason—and if you *get* a reason, don't take it too seriously. Some editors write sane, sensible, and helpful rejection letters. But a good many editors fire off letters without much thought. Sometimes these letters are written to sound professional and knowledgeable but not actually to mean anything. A few editors will go so far as to lie about the reason for a rejection, simply because it's easier or more convenient than telling the truth. Few editors have the time to reflect on submissions at any length, let alone respond with informed and intelligent critiques. Often they only skim pieces quickly to see whether they might be appropriate for their publications.

Some editors play it safe and never discuss their reasons for rejection. These editors just say something like, "Sorry, this one isn't right for us" or "This one didn't really grab me" or "This isn't quite the sort of thing we're looking for." Two common phrases are "There's no room for it on our list" and "We can't fit it into our magazine." These phrases translate to nothing more than "We don't want to publish it."

Not only is some rejection likely at every stage of your career, but you will probably receive an occasional (or more than occasional) form rejection slip until you become a writing superstar. In part this is because the largest and most prestigious publications receive so many submissions that they can give very few writers thorough consideration. (In general, the larger or more prestigious the publication you submit your work to, the more likely you are to receive a form rejection letter in response.)

Often editors are so pressed for time that they find themselves slapping form rejection slips on everything, or nearly everything, they turn down. Sometimes pieces that come very close to publication are rejected by the same impersonal form letters as those that are subliterate. This is particularly true of literary magazines and literary book publishers. Several of my pieces that received form rejection slips later sold to well-known and well-paying publications.

If you write for a publication on a regular basis and your editor at that publication suddenly begins rejecting much, most, or all of your work, give him or her a call and say something like this: "I'm getting concerned about the writing I've been doing for you lately. A lot of it hasn't seemed right to you. Can you give me some suggestions for my next few pieces for you?"

Is rejection inevitable? *Yes*—at least, some rejection is. I've never met a writer who has published everything he or she has written. Keep this in mind the next time an editor says no.

KEEPING FAITH

No career in any field is built quickly and easily. Why expect a writing career to be different? If you sincerely wish to make all or part of your living as a freelance writer, persistence in the face of rejection is as important as writing ability. A great deal of good work gets rejected repeatedly, and sometimes snottily. Whenever you grow despondent and feel like giving up, remember these examples:

• One writer sold *three* nonfiction books after five years of complete and unremitting rejection during which he received over one hundred rejections, including many form rejection slips, *on each book.* One book received over one hundred and fifty rejections (including twenty-five on submissions made by an agent) before it sold.

• A well-respected poet had a collection of his poems accepted by a major poetry press after receiving exactly ninety-nine rejections.

• One short-story writer sent no fewer than twenty-one stories to *The New Yorker* over a period of several years. On the twenty-first rejection, the *New Yorker* editor wrote to her and said (I'm paraphrasing), "We appreciate seeing your work, but it's clear that the sort of story you write just isn't right for *The New Yorker.*" The writer ignored the letter and sent her next story to the same *New Yorker* editor. The editor bought it.

• *Gone With the Wind* and *To Think That I Saw It on Mulberry Street,* Dr. Seuss's first book, were both rejected over fifteen times before being published and becoming best-sellers.

• Ronald Anthony Cross, a science fiction writer who has published widely in the field, simply could not sell anything to one particular editor. He sent twenty stories and two novels to that editor over a period of twelve years; all were rejected. Finally, after a delay of nine months between submission and reply, the editor bought Cross's twenty-third submission.

• A novelist submitted a proposal to an editor at a major hardcover house. The editor rejected it. Several years and many rejections later, the same author submitted the same proposal to the same editor. This time the editor bought it. This same author submitted a proposal to another editor, who wanted to buy it but was overruled by his superior. Two months later the superior took a job elsewhere; the editor pulled the proposal from his file, got it approved by his new supervisor, and made an offer to the author.

• Some years ago I sent a short story to the editor of a leading science fiction magazine. He returned it with a very brief letter that said, "Dear Scott: Why are you wasting my time—and your own—with this crap?" I immediately sent the story to the other leading science fiction magazine, which bought and published it.

• This very book was rejected several times before Harper & Row bought it. Another of my books went to no fewer than thirty-four publishers, of which only two made offers of publication. Yet another book received over twenty-five rejections before a publisher said yes.

REJECTION SLIPS

What do form rejection letters mean? The one thing you *know* they mean is no. Beyond this it is generally impossible, and useless, to speculate.

There are two exceptions to this, however. First, a few large publications—*The New Yorker,* for example—have two, three, or even four different form rejection letters. These represent different levels of booby prizes. The highest level is for pieces that have merit of one sort or another but that nevertheless do not make the grade. These letters might say something like, "Despite the obvious merits of your work, this submission isn't quite right for us." If you receive a form letter of this sort, you probably at least captured an editor's attention. Keep offering this editor your work.

The other exception is when an editor has penned some comments on the bottom of the rejection form. If an editor sees a glimmer (or more than a glimmer) of talent in a piece, he or she might write "Try us again" or "Keep trying" on the bottom. Do just that if you get such a message. An editor who feels that a piece has some clear merit might write a slightly longer message; for example, "Good writing, good control—just not a very interesting subject. We'd be happy to see more." And if a piece came reasonably close to being accepted, you might get a couple of sentences: "Close to what we want, but a bit wordy. I like your characters and style. Feel free to send more." This is the equivalent of getting a personal rejection letter.

Do not assume, however, that if no such comment appears on the form letter, the editor hated the piece. Not all editors take the time to write such encouraging messages on rejection slips, even when the pieces they are rejecting come quite close to being accepted.

Some rejection slips lie. Certainly a great many lie when they say, "We have read the enclosed material carefully" or "We have given your work careful consideration," since in many cases only the most cursory perusal was actually given. A few large publications send writers rejection slips that say, "We have read the enclosed carefully," when in truth the manuscripts were not even glanced at, but removed from their envelopes, placed in return envelopes with form rejection letters, and put right back in the mail. If your manuscript comes back quite quickly with a form rejection slip and no personal comments appended to it, it's possible that the piece went unread. If you get two successive manuscripts back from a large publication in this manner, then I suggest forgetting about that publication, at least for a year or so (at which point personnel or policies may have changed). Instead, concentrate on getting your work into the hands of editors who'll at least give you a reading.

OTHER FORMS OF REJECTION

A personal letter of rejection is usually an encouraging sign; chances are good that the editor saw some positive qualities in your writing. Your piece may even have come quite close to being accepted, and if an editor tells you this, you can be sure it's true. Send this editor more of your work.

There is one exception here: occasionally a publication will choose to type form rejection letters on a memory typewriter rather than photocopy them. If you get a personal letter of rejection, but the body of the letter reads much like a standard form rejection and makes no specific reference to your piece, you have probably gotten nothing but a high-class form rejection slip.

If you get your piece back with no reply at all—no letter and no form rejection slip—this may not be an editor worth dealing with in the future. Next time try a different editor at that publication. If this isn't possible, either give the first editor one more chance or write him or her off entirely. This advice also applies to editors who neither return your manuscript nor respond to it.

REJECTION AFTER ACCEPTANCE

Most editors and publishers will do what they promise to do. However, sooner or later you will probably encounter, first-hand, the phenomenon of postacceptance rejection. This occurs when a piece is formally accepted by an editor—verbally, through a letter, or through a signed agreement— and then rejected some weeks or months later. It also occurs when an editor officially gives you an assignment, then either chooses not to publish the finished piece after accepting it or cancels the assignment before you have turned it in.

There are dozens of reasons why this can happen. Here are a few common ones:

• Your editor leaves, and one or more of the new editors dislike your work.
• The publication changes its policies after accepting your work.
• The publication encounters space or format problems.

• Your piece gets used as a weapon in an office power struggle.
• The publication is trying to save money by publishing less freelance material, or less material in general.
• A competing publication gets a similar piece into print first.
• A recently published piece on the same theme as your piece received negative reader response.
• Your editor's judgment is vetoed by someone higher up.
• The publication is going out of business, or being merged with another one.

Postacceptance rejection will usually come quite unexpectedly. When it does, there is probably nothing you can do to reverse the decision, so it is not a good idea to plead with or yell at your editor, or accuse him or her of moral bankruptcy.

If you have already been paid for a piece, partially or entirely, before it is rejected, you are entitled to keep this money. If a publication wants to back out of a deal and asks for some of its money back, you do *not* have to return a penny, nor should you unless your original agreement specifically requires you to.

But what about money that was to be paid to you in the future?

Unless your agreement specifically stipulates otherwise (as in a kill fee arrangement), the publisher legally must still pay you in full for your piece, even though it has chosen not to publish it.

However, any sums to be paid to you *on publication*, or within a specified time after publication, are no longer due you, since publication will no longer occur. It is for precisely this reason that publishers often prefer to pay writers partly or entirely on or after publication—and why you should try to be paid on acceptance whenever possible.

While in many cases it may be best to stand your ground and hold out for everything to which you are entitled, sometimes it may be wiser to compromise with the publication. Here are some things to consider in making your decision:

• Don't let your editor (or anyone else at the publication) ignore the issue of money. When you first learn of the rejection, let the editor know promptly, firmly, and politely that you still expect to be paid everything you have been promised in your agreement. When the time for any payment nears, remind the editor again that the payment is due. Unless the editor says something to the contrary, you should assume that payment(s) will be made on time.

• If you are offered a reasonable kill fee (see the section below), you are probably best off taking it. This will ensure that you are paid something for your trouble, while at the same time keeping you and your editor on good terms. If the kill fee you are offered seems too small, however, ask for, or insist upon, a larger one. If no kill fee is offered, suggest it yourself.

• If your editor offers some other reasonable form of compromise, such as publishing a different one of your pieces in place of your rejected piece, you should probably go along with it.

• If the rejection is not your editor's fault—for example, if some higher-up issued a decree banning all articles on political issues, including yours— let the editor know that you're aware of this and that you'd still like to keep working with him or her. This builds goodwill, and it will help keep the editor receptive to your work—presuming you're still willing to have anything to do with that publication.

• If at all possible, try to do all your negotiating with the editor who originally accepted your piece, as he or she will be likely to feel some obligation to you. If you allow yourself to get referred to someone else, or if your editor has left the firm, you will be in a much poorer bargaining position.

• Be polite and businesslike at all times, even if you wind up having to say, "I suppose I'll have to refer this matter to my attorney."

• If straightforward bargaining doesn't work, and/or you know the publication is on shaky financial ground, try making a personal appeal that will place your editor on your side. For instance, you might say, "Tom, I appreciate your position, and I can tell you're in something of a bind yourself. I'm willing to settle for half of the money we originally agreed upon. Would you do me a personal favor and see if you can get that much for me?" This approach often works when editors claim their hands are tied, or that they'd like to help but someone higher up is making the money decisions.

• If you know the publication is having serious financial problems, you may be best off compromising more than you would like. If a publication is in danger of going under, you are going to be lucky to get anything at all. In such circumstances, take what money you can and run.

• If you have had a piece accepted for publication but are to receive no compensation for it, and that piece is subsequently rejected, you are not entitled to a kill fee. Unfortunately, your only recourse is to submit the piece elsewhere.

• If an editor accepts your piece orally or by letter, says that a formal written contract or letter of agreement will follow, and backs out of the deal before the letter is sent or the contract signed by both parties, then legally no deal was ever made or broken. You can try asking for a kill fee under these circumstances, but you're unlikely to get it.

Throughout this section I have discussed the question of money. But what about publication? Most contracts state flatly, "The Publisher agrees to publish the Author's Work," usually by a particular date. Isn't there anything you can do to compel a publication to publish your work once it has agreed in writing to do so?

Unfortunately, the answer is no. A publication has the right to choose not to publish your material, even if it has specifically agreed to do so in writing, so long as it adheres strictly to the contract in terms of *payment.*

KILL FEES

Kill fees are commonly offered on three occasions: when a publication chooses not to publish a piece it previously accepted; when an editor decides to cancel an assignment previously made to a writer; or when a writer turns in an assigned piece that is less than publishable.

Kill fees are useful and intelligent. They protect publishers and writers from doing much damage to each other, and they help keep both sides reasonably content.

Kill fees range from 15 to 50 percent of the purchase price of a piece. Most writers consider one-third to be appropriate, and 25 percent to be the acceptable minimum.

Sometimes a payment already made can function as a kill fee. For instance, if a publication agrees to pay you $600 for a short story, half on acceptance and half ninety days thereafter, and after paying you the first $300 the editor decides not to publish your story after all, he or she may say, "Let's forget the whole deal. Keep the $300 we've given you so far, and we'll give you all your rights back." This is one more reason why it is always best to be paid on acceptance rather than afterward.

POSTPONEMENT

Postponement of publication is a fact of writing life, and it shouldn't be taken personally. Generally, I wouldn't get annoyed if a magazine or newspaper delayed publication of a piece up to three months beyond its originally scheduled publication, or if a book publisher postponed publication by as much as six months. However, if postponement went on longer than this, I would express some dissatisfaction to my editor; and if it continued for *much* longer, I'd strongly urge my editor to do everything possible to get the piece into print.

The best way to limit postponement is to put a deadline for publication into your publishing contract. If your piece is not published by this date, then the publisher loses its right to publish the piece at all, and a new agreement (and an additional payment) must then be negotiated. If a publication deadline nears and your piece still has not been scheduled or published, it is a good idea to remind your editor of the impending deadline. Three months' warning is appropriate.

If your piece is postponed more than once and if all or part of your payment is to be made on or after publication, you can ask to be paid before publication. You've certainly got a good rationale for it: if the piece had been published according to the editor's original plan, you would have been paid already. Three times out of four the editor will simply say, "Sorry, I can't do that." But sometimes a sympathetic editor will bend the rules a bit to get you paid before publication actually occurs.

JUDGING EDITORS' COMMENTS

It is quite common for different editors to reject the same piece for precisely opposite reasons. For example, a short story might be rejected by one editor for having strong characters but a weak plot, and by the next for having a great plot but unbelievable characters. The next editor may like both the plot *and* characters, but find fault with your writing style.

Weighing editors' comments will be easier if you keep the following principles in mind:

• The choice of what to do with a piece is ultimately your own. This is both a right and a responsibility. You must make the final decision about whether a piece is finished and about what additional work, if any, to do on it.

• Consider each editor's comments separately. Don't seek some sort of editorial consensus. It is very possible that one editor will be quite right, another quite wrong. However, if two or more editors make similar comments, there is a good chance that what they have to say is at least partly valid. (But if, after considering their comments carefully, you still think your piece should remain as is, don't change a word of it. It *is* possible for several people to come to the same erroneous conclusion.)

• It is possible for an editor to be right about one aspect of a piece and dead wrong about another. Consider each comment individually.

• It is tempting to accept editors' praise and reject their criticism, or at least to examine negative comments critically and to accept praise without judgment. But the fact is that praise can be just as wrongheaded, misguided, or self-serving as criticism. The wise writer will take both praise and criticism from all sources with two grains of salt, and will carefully examine both positive and negative comments. The most intelligent writers remain careful and tough critics of their own work, no matter how wealthy, widely published, or widely praised they become.

• If an editor who has consistently published your work decides to reject a piece, you *must not* automatically assume that something is wrong with that piece, or that you've lost your touch. Instead, examine the editor's comments, and your own piece, with the best critical eye you can muster.

REVIEWS

Most writers think of rejection as something only editors do to writers. But the fact is that once your work is published, it is open to both intelligent criticism and blind attack by reviewers and literary critics. Some of these people may (and eventually will) say negative things about your work, or even about you, in print. This form of rejection can be especially devastating to new writers.

The most important things to keep in mind here are: (1) no matter what you write, not everyone is going to like it, and (2) we're all entitled to express our own opinion, no matter how odd. Wise writers let reviewers' comments—both criticism and praise—roll off their backs.

Some reviews will be quite biased and unfair. *By far* the sanest reaction is to ignore their tone and look for their content, then examine that content with as much objectivity as you can. Does the reviewer make some good points, even though they may be couched in offensive rhetoric? If so, take these points to heart; if not, ignore them.

The same advice applies to praise from critics. Accept what praise seems legitimate, and reject any that seems ill-informed or inappropriate.

Regardless of what a reviewer or critic has to say, avoid stewing in anger over his or her blindness, or withering in shame for having written something that you now realize is flawed. Don't waste your time attacking your critic or reviewer, trying to defend or explain yourself or your work, contacting the offending critic personally, or writing a letter to the publication in which the review or critical essay appeared. These tactics will do absolutely no good and will make you look petty and childish.

There are only three circumstances when you *should* reply to a published review or essay which examines your work. The first is when you wish to thank a reviewer or critic personally for a perceptive or useful discussion of your work. The second is when a reviewer gets the title, publisher's name or address, price, spelling of your name, or publication date of your work wrong. In such a case, you should write the publication which published that review or essay to correct the error. However, do no more than correct this factual information, even if you have been called "scum of the earth" by the reviewer.

The other circumstance in which a reply may be appropriate is when you wish to deliberately create (or increase) attention for your work. Your response (written to the publication that published the review or essay) might take the form of attacking your critic, or of responding to his or her key points, or of clarifying your intentions in writing the book. The point, however, is trying to increase sales of your work, not exacting revenge or cleansing your name.

Be careful how you do this. If you have written a serious journalistic work, you are likely to do more harm than good if you respond angrily and stridently; a calm, reasoned reply is probably more appropriate. However, if someone has written a review claiming that your humor book is juvenile and insulting, a reply that is deliberately juvenile and insulting, and obviously meant to be so, might be just the ticket—provided, of course, that it's also funny.

OTHER IMPORTANT TIPS

Here is some other useful advice on rejection:

• Send out a rejected manuscript to another editor as soon as possible after it comes back to you.

• Whenever you get a manuscript back, immediately check through it to make sure that all of its pages are there, in correct order, and free of folds, tears, stains, smudges, and penned-in comments. (I have had editors not only reject pieces, but write snotty comments on certain pages in ink, so that the pages had to be retyped. I have also had editors and secretaries stamp the first page of some manuscripts with the word "Received" and a date.) Checking for this reduces your chances of having the piece rejected in the next round.

• If an editor rejects something you have written without an explanation, it is generally not helpful to call and ask why. There are two exceptions here, however: (1) if the editor publishes your work fairly regularly and (2) if a piece has been rejected after being accepted.

• Don't tell an editor, either in a cover letter or a conversation, that a piece has been rejected elsewhere. This can't possibly help you, and it could hurt. Similarly, if an editor buys or expresses interest in something you have written, *never* respond with something like, "Thank you, Ms. Williamson! You are the first editor to see merit in my work." This is not only amateurish, but also tends to make editors mistrust their own judgment. Instead, respond in a concise, businesslike way—as if acceptance and editorial interest are not new to you.

• Suppose you get a rejection letter on a book or book proposal from an editor that reads, "This is a good book, and one I'd like to do. But the last few books we did on this topic didn't sell well, so I'm afraid I'll never convince anyone else here to take a chance on yours." Or, perhaps, "This is a terrific project, but none of our salespeople could figure out how to sell it." Get the book out quickly to another house, but keep a close eye on the editor who wrote you that note. (This means reading the "People" column of *Publishers Weekly* each week.) If and when he moves to another house, send him that book again, if you haven't sold it already. Remind him in your cover letter of how much he liked it; you might even enclose a photocopy of his earlier letter to you. He may be able to convince the people at his new firm that your book is worth publishing.

• Never give up completely on something you have written, and *never* throw it away. Something unsalable today may be quite salable a year, or a decade or two, from now, especially if you have built a reputation in the meantime.

5. ✐

Making and Using Contacts

THE IMPORTANCE OF CONTACTS

Are contacts important to a freelance writer? Definitely. Are they absolutely necessary? No, not quite. But who you know is almost as important as how well you write.

My friend Nancy, who has published in several of the largest and most prestigious magazines in the United States, is a good example. When I asked her, "How'd you break into those publications?" she said, "Oh, I knew someone at each of those magazines." "Did that really make much of a difference?" I asked. She looked at me with a confused expression. "Of course it did. If I didn't know those people, I'd never have published in any of those magazines at all. In fact, if it weren't for my contacts, I'd never have published anywhere but in the local newspaper, and maybe not even there."

Nancy is a good writer. All of her work is certainly good enough to be published. If it weren't, all the contacts in the world wouldn't have done much for her. But in Nancy's case, as in the case of many writers, personal contacts made the difference between publication and rejection.

Editors, like most of us, tend to place a value on familiarity. If a manuscript arrives on an editor's desk from an unknown name, it's just paper to be read and evaluated. But an editor who knows you from a face-to-face meeting, a phone conversation, correspondence, or a recommendation from a trusted source is going to take a slightly more favorable view of your manuscript. And the more the editor enjoyed meeting or talking with you, the more favorably disposed he or she is likely to be toward your piece.

Besides helping to get you serious editorial consideration, contacts will supply you with advice, information, and favors—and often a great deal more. Knowing the right people can help you find and hook up with a good agent; learn of a publication just getting off the ground; hear about a publication's need for a particular kind of piece; learn of editorial or policy changes at a publication; hear about a job opening; get a job interview, or even a job; find out who's to be trusted and who's not to be; get recommendations for fellowships, scholarships, awards, or admission to college writing programs; get admitted to writers' workshops or conferences; learn the scuttlebutt about a particular publisher's financial position or plans for the future; get referrals to other useful contacts; and so on and on. Sometimes contacts can provide moral support, pep talks, or shoulders to cry on when the professional chips are down. Occasionally a contact may even become a friend or lover.

Although editors are among the best and most obvious contacts, they are not the only people who can be helpful to you. Getting to know publishers, art directors, agents, sales representatives, publicity people, secretaries, bookstore owners and managers, and virtually anyone else in publishing can be potentially helpful—if not directly, at least in referring you to other contacts.

Getting to know other writers—especially well-known and well-published ones—can also be very beneficial. Writers can introduce you and/or your work to their agents, editors, or publishers; to other publishing people; and to other writers who, in turn, can make connections for you.

In fact, almost anyone who knows someone in publishing can be a useful contact. If your barber also happens to cut the hair of an editor at Dell, he can be a big help to you if he'll introduce you to that editor. So ask him to.

Contacts are most helpful in making personal introductions to agents and editors, and in getting your work onto their desks. But contacts can also be enormously helpful in virtually every phase of the publishing process. If you've written and sold a book and know a well-known actor, politician, or other personality, perhaps he or she will write a good quote for the book's cover, or at least sign his or her name to an endorsement you've written. If you know a book reviewer, you can probably convince him or her to review your book. If you know a sales rep for your publisher, you can ask the rep to give your book a slightly bigger push. If you know a bookstore owner or buyer, you can ask him or her to buy a larger number of copies and perhaps arrange a book signing and/or publication party for you.

Some people feel—quite incorrectly—that making and using contacts is somehow cheating, that talented writers should be able to make it on the quality of their writing alone. But, like it or not, the publishing world doesn't always work this way. Contacts help put you a step or two ahead of most of the competition. They can make the difference between acceptance and rejection of a decently written manuscript, and between large and small success.

Contacts will rarely, if ever, make a success out of a bad writer. Contacts are not a magic lamp; they cannot help you publish a piece that is not worth publishing. But they can get you a more serious or sympathetic reading, and more attention in general.

You do not have to compromise one ounce of your personal or professional integrity to make and use contacts well. If you publish occasionally in *The Artist's Magazine,* for example, and write a piece for its sister publication, *Writer's Digest,* there's nothing wrong with asking your editor at *The Artist's Magazine* to tell the editor at *Writer's Digest* how much he or she likes your writing. If you're submitting a book to an art book publisher, it's also perfectly reasonable to ask your editor at *The Artist's Magazine* to write or call the book editor with a plug for your work, or to write an endorsement for your book (see pages 288–91 for details).

The more difficult it is to break into a particular market or area of publishing (see the chart on pages 12–13), the more important having contacts becomes. However, this doesn't mean that you need to toady to influential people; that you are out of luck if you were not born with important contacts; that you need to move from Las Cruces, New Mexico, to New York; or that you have to sleep with editors to get anywhere. You do not need to leave your home town to make contacts, though an occasional trip to New York, Los Angeles, or some other publishing center can certainly help.

To some degree, making contacts occurs naturally, without your even trying. Once an editor buys one of your pieces, or at least writes you a letter saying that he or she likes something you've written, you've established the beginnings of a relationship with that editor. If you begin to publish in that publication regularly, you automatically build on your relationship with that editor. You may also get to know a few other people at that publication. When one of the staff people you know at that publication moves on to a job with another firm, you then have a contact at that firm. Use it.

Some writers find the whole game of making contacts repugnant. They can't bear glad-handing and socializing, or even making polite phone calls, and are often attracted to freelance writing precisely because it allows them to avoid such things. If you're such a person, don't despair. It *is* possible to make it on your talent alone, though it means being especially persistent in both writing and submitting your work.

Many writers have done very well by making contact with only one very important person: a good literary agent. If you write nothing but books, films, TV scripts, plays, or some combination of these, an agent may be able to handle all the contact-making, market research, and manuscript submission for you—for roughly 15 percent of your gross receipts. However, many writers with agents—myself, for one—still regularly make and use contacts in magazine and newspaper publishing to help get their short work published and in book publishing to give their books and book proposals that extra push.

LOCATING AND MAKING CONTACTS

Writers' conferences are excellent sources of contacts, as are other writers' gatherings such as public readings, lectures, classes, workshops, and so on. At all of these, it's simply a matter of approaching the right person at the right time.

At a writers' conference, for example, there is likely to be a "meet-the-lecturers" session—usually a cocktail party. Here it is easy to approach someone directly. Similarly, it is perfectly Kosher to approach a writer after he or she has given a reading, though it is important to follow the etiquette set forth below.

It's also possible for just about anyone to make useful contacts through local writers' clubs, centers, and organizations, as well as through national writers' organizations and associations in particular fields of writing. If you are a science fiction writer, for example, you can make some contacts by joining Science Fiction Writers of America and by reading its publications regularly.

You never know who else might be helpful. Ask your friends, relatives, and acquaintances for the names and phone numbers of anyone they know who's in publishing, or who is a published writer. Chances are good that at least one or two of them have a friend or relative who can help you. Your likeliest prospects will be people who live in or near publishing centers such as New York City or Toronto, or, in the case of film and TV, Los Angeles. Think of all the people you know who live in or near any of these cities. Other good prospects, regardless of where they live, are wealthy or well-to-do people, lawyers, doctors, college professors, and owners of good-sized businesses, all of whom are likely to have influential friends and acquaintances. However, don't overlook the people who might seem less helpful at first glance. The starving musician down the street may turn out to be Alfred Knopf's nephew.

People who are famous or well known in almost any field can often be enormously helpful. If you know a popular actor, scientist, architect, or philosopher, chances are he or she knows at least one person connected with publishing. Politicians, lobbyists, and high-ranking government officials also often have writing or publishing contacts.

Some of the most useful—and most overlooked—contacts are secretaries. If you know an editor's secretary or assistant, you are in good shape: assistants can not only introduce you and/or your work to editors, but can do this at a time when they know the editors will be receptive.

There are plenty of other ways to make contacts, and plenty of other people to make contact with. All it takes is a little ingenuity—and a little chutzpah. Say you write children's books and would like to get to know some children's book editors and writers. You can write or call the Society of Children's Book Writers and ask for the names and addresses of any children's writers in your area. Then you can invite some of those people to lunch. You can also get names and addresses from your local writers' center, from the reference book *Something About the Author,* or from the manager of a good bookstore with a large children's section. (You will generally have better luck if you try a privately owned bookstore rather than a chain store.) If you know the manager personally, see if he or she will introduce you to an editor or writer directly. You might also check with the children's librarian at a nearby library (the larger the better) to see whom he or she knows.

Another good place to start is a college or university. Make an appointment with the head of the English department, or the creative writing department, if the college has one. Ask for the names and phone numbers of any writers or publishing people he or she knows. In particular find out who in the department has had work published, and ask for their phone numbers and office hours. It's not a bad idea to ask the secretary of the department the same questions; he or she may know more about such things than the department head. Then make an appointment with each of these people. You need not be a student to do this, but don't admit that you're not unless you're asked. Most professors should be willing to give you ten or twenty minutes of their time, and chances are good that one or more of them can provide you with useful names, addresses, or suggestions. In general, the larger or more prestigious the college is, the better results you will have.

Often one contact can lead to another in a chain that ultimately brings success. Christina Baldwin sold her book *One to One* in such a manner. When she learned of a conference on women in writing, she wrote the director and told her of her unpublished book, and of her work teaching. She was invited to be a panelist at the conference. At the conference she was introduced to agent Meredith Bernstein. Baldwin gave Bernstein her manuscript. The next day Bernstein called Baldwin, told her she loved the book, and a few hours later took it to an editor at Evans and Company. Ten days later, Bernstein had made a deal with Evans.

Not every chain of contacts brings success, of course. Some will ultimately lead nowhere, or in circles. The longer the chain gets, and the less well you know the people in it, the more fragile it is.

Follow-up is a very important step in making and using contacts wisely. Suppose, for example, you meet the editor of *Smithsonian* magazine at a party or writer's workshop. At this meeting, you mention a short piece you've written on the phenomenon of *déja vu,* and the editor asks to see it. When you send the piece in, *be sure* to begin your letter with, "Thank you for speaking with me last week. I'm pleased that you're interested in 'Remembering the Present,' my piece on *déja vu,* and I'm sending it along now, as you requested." If people have agreed to read a manuscript, provide some information, or otherwise be of help, be sure to tactfully remind them of exactly what they offered to do.

The same rules apply when the follow-up comes months or even years later, or when you are renewing a contact you made a long time ago and have not kept up with. For example, you might begin a letter like this: "If my name sounds familiar, it's because we met at the John Irving reading in Minneapolis a couple of years ago. Shortly thereafter, you supplied me with the names of two editors at *The New Yorker,* which turned out to be very helpful and for which I continue to be grateful."

Follow-up is especially important in cases where your contact has agreed to contact other people on your behalf. For example, if someone has agreed to write you a recommendation, or to call an editor or agent to praise your work, call after a reasonable amount of time to see whether they have done so. If not, gently remind them of the importance of their help, and of your gratitude for it. Then follow up again later.

ETIQUETTE FOR MAKING AND USING CONTACTS

People aren't going to help you unless they want to. Your job, therefore, is to make people *want* to help you. In using contacts, you are asking other people for favors—not demanding your rights. When you first make a contact with an editor, writer, or other publishing person, he or she owes you nothing, no matter how terrific your writing is, and no matter how badly you need a break.

The most important rule of etiquette is to be friendly, polite, and considerate of other people's needs and pressures. Don't grovel, whine, wheedle, plead, or demand. Avoid expressions of awe, even if they're sincere. Don't lie, attempt to bribe, or offer false compliments. However, there's nothing wrong with treating someone to a meal or doing someone a favor.

For writers who are not yet skilled in the social graces, I strongly recommend reading Dale Carnegie's *How to Win Friends and Influence People* (Pocket Books). How you interact with others partly determines your ability to get them to help you; so if you are by nature nervous, shy, or frightened of people, this book can help enormously. So can some coaching from someone with good social skills.

You will usually have to initiate contacts yourself; this means getting used to walking up to people, or calling them, and introducing yourself. Tact and timing are important here; so are watching and listening for subtle signals. For example, if you want to meet a writer who has just given a reading, don't rush up to her immediately. Give her a few minutes to pay her respects to close friends and the reading organizers. But don't wait until the writer is trying to leave, either.

Probably the biggest mistake aspiring writers make in seeking help from others is asking for the impossible or the very difficult. Keep your requests reasonable. Try to ask people only for things they can provide without much effort. The less time or energy it takes to honor your request, the more likely it is to be honored.

Knowing what to ask for is closely related to the influence your contact has. Don't expect writers to get you job interviews with their publishers.

But if you know a publisher, you can ask him for an interview at his firm. The better you know someone or the closer you are to him or her, the more you can ask for.

Always remember that your contact has the right to say no. Never force an issue. Don't make your contacts feel that they have an obligation to help you. Never insult or get angry at anyone for declining to help. When the answer is no, for whatever reason, let the matter go at that.

If someone *postpones* helping you, take that postponement at face value unless you clearly have reason to take it otherwise. When someone says to you, "Well, now's not a good time for me. Can you call me back in a couple of weeks?" do just that. Chances are he or she is being sincere, not just trying to get rid of you.

Here are some other tips on etiquette that can help:

• Be a good listener. Let your contact speak. If your background or one of your manuscripts is pertinent to the discussion, say everything that's appropriate, but no more.

• Keep calm and act natural. Don't be hurried or anxious, even if your time is very limited. Make the most of what time you have.

• Dress appropriately for all meetings and occasions. When in doubt, dress up a bit.

• If your contact is informal and friendly, respond in similar fashion. If your contact is curt and businesslike, be businesslike yourself. Without mimicking the other person, modify your own natural style enough to make the other person comfortable.

• When your contact wants to end the discussion, don't try to prolong it. Thank him or her for speaking with you, and say goodbye. If you have an absolutely urgent question, you may say, "May I ask one last question?" But if the person says no, consider the conversation at an end.

• If you are referred to a contact by a mutual acquaintance, mention his or her name as you introduce yourself. For example, "Hi, Ms. Seltman. My name is Marsha Tansey; Howard Mann suggested I call you."

• If you are trying to reach someone by phone but can only get through to a secretary, spouse, boyfriend, etc., leave a message that includes your name, phone number, *and reason for calling.* It is often helpful to add, "Calling collect is fine." Never belittle secretaries or try to bully your way past them. If your call is not returned within three business days, call again. Repeat the process as necessary. If, after making three calls and leaving three messages, your call has not been returned, and you've been reasonably available to answer your own phone, you can assume that the person does not wish or intend to speak to you.

• If you are trying to reach someone and a secretary or operator asks you, "What do you wish to speak to them about?," don't get nervous or defensive. This is just part of the secretary's job. Answer honestly and straightforwardly.

• Don't interrupt other people's conversations. Likewise, if you are talking with people at a party or other gathering, don't try to keep their attention all to yourself for more than a few minutes. They will probably want to mingle with others, and may even have an obligation to do so. At a gathering, you've usually got no more than five to ten minutes to speak with someone. Use that time wisely. If you've got six questions to ask, only ask the most important ones.

• If you want to meet someone in person, especially for the first time, invite them to lunch at a restaurant near their home or office. This enables busy people to meet with you without giving up any of their valuable time, since they have to eat lunch anyway. Pick a spot that has good food and service, serves alcohol, and provides pleasant and relaxing surroundings. Lunch takes at least 45 minutes, usually longer; you'll have that person all to yourself during this time. You should of course foot the entire bill and leave a decent tip.

• Don't fake friendship or romantic interest in an attempt to get someone to help you. It rarely works, and usually causes problems. And it's sleazy.

• If someone is rude or obnoxious to you, don't be rude or obnoxious back. Simply leave or hang up. If you think the person may be drunk or otherwise intoxicated, try contacting them again when they are sober.

• There will be times when you get the message "go away" loud and clear, either directly or through indirect but no less indisputable signals. When you get this message, don't fight it. Politely say good-bye, and leave or hang up.

• A telephone answering machine will be enormously helpful in enabling people to reach you. Inexpensive models start at $40. This is an extremely worthwhile (and tax-deductible) investment.

BUSINESS CARDS

Business cards are one of the best investments a writer can make. They give an air of professionalism and reliability to whoever has them: some people really do look upon writers who have business cards with more respect and trust.

When you make contact with someone in person, you can help maintain that contact by giving him or her your card. A scrap of paper with your name, address, and phone number on it not only looks grungy and takes time to write, but is far more likely to get lost or thrown away. Most people hang on to the business cards they are given; many automatically add them to their Rolodexes, or make new listings in their address books. These people then have your name, address, and phone number available on file, should there ever come a time when they can do something for you—or you can do something for them.

Spreading business cards around to editors, other publishing people, and other writers can be one of the best and cheapest sources of breaks. Let's say you have a short chat with an editor at a writers' conference. You happen to mention that your husband is a jockey. You give her your card. Nine months later, the editor is told by her superior, "See if you can get a piece on what it's like to be a jockey." She remembers her conversation with you. If you hadn't given her your card, she wouldn't know how to contact you. But you *did* give her your card, which she locates, and a few minutes later you've got yourself an assignment.

It is neither necessary nor appropriate to enclose a business card when making a submission to an editor. However, it is not a bad idea to include one with an assignment query, or when returning your first signed contract with that editor.

Business cards are almost ridiculously inexpensive. A box of 500 costs about $12—about 2¢ a card. I have found that the cards that get the best results, and that look most professional and impressive, are raised-letter cards printed in black ink on white card stock. These cards are usually the *cheapest* ones available. Colored stock, colored inks, and offset printing normally look less professional—almost a bit flighty.

Avoid logos, designs, photographs, or decorations on your card; they detract from the card's impact. Get cards that are simple and straightforward. They should state your name, profession, address, and phone number(s). Include both home and work numbers so that you are easy to reach by phone. Use the word *suite* instead of *apartment.*

For your profession, you might list *Writer,* or *Freelance Writing and Editing* or *Literary Services.*

It doesn't hurt to give your card to virtually everyone you meet, even people you think are unlikely to be helpful to you—your mechanic, for example. But you never know—maybe the mechanic's cousin is an editor, and maybe one day he will say to your mechanic, "Boy, I wish I could find a decent writer out where you live."

Keep your cards in a convenient, easy-to-reach location, and always carry some with you. When you attend a writers' conference, workshop, reading, or other writers' function, bring plenty of cards. I always keep a few business cards in my wallet. At first you may forget to hand out your card to people you meet, but with practice it will become automatic.

SOME FINAL WORDS ABOUT CONTACTS

One of the central principles of making and using contacts is goodwill. If you are simply hustling people to get everything you can out of them, they are unlikely to be very cooperative. A saner and more successful approach is one of mutual aid and friendliness. From the start, offer your goodwill in exchange for the help of others. When appropriate, offer your assistance in return; you might say, for instance, "If I can return the favor sometime in the future, feel free to ask." And once someone has helped you out, send a brief thank-you note. This not only makes the contact person feel good, it makes them more likely to help you, and others, in the future.

It's not only important to offer your future aid, but to give it when it's asked for. In a sense, the whole publishing business runs on cooperation. By helping others, you are not only doing them a service, you are serving the entire publishing community, and, ultimately, yourself as well.

Once you've made it to the point where you've got knowledge or influence that can help other writers, don't be miserly. Return the favors that others did for you. This will encourage other aspiring writers, in turn, to offer aid and goodwill to the generation of writers that follows—and so on into the future.

6. ✎

Marketing Your Talents and Services .

CAREER OPTIONS

There are hundreds of ways to make money as a writer. Here is a list of *some* of the freelance and salaried jobs open and appropriate to writers:

Editor (including assistant editor, managing editor, department editor, copy editor, production editor)

Technical writer/editor

Medical writer/editor

Proofreader

Manuscript reader/evaluator (usually for a book publisher)

Editorial assistant/editorial secretary

Staff writer (for a magazine, newspaper, or book publisher, a newsletter publisher, a manufacturer, a service organization, a branch of government, a retail firm, or other firm or agency)

Copy writer (for catalogs, instruction manuals, etc.)

Newsletter writer/editor

Audio writer (writing audio scripts for business, industry, nonprofit organizations)

Literary agent

Agent's assistant

Business writer

Journalist

Columnist (on any subject, for any periodical)

Reviewer (of books, art, dance, film, music, restaurants, etc.)

Audiovisual writer

TV/radio reporter or news writer

Gag writer (for cartoonists)

Comedy writer (for comedians or comedy troupes)

Greeting card writer

Resumé writer

Speechwriter (for politicians, business executives, high-level government employees)

Public relations/public information writer

Advertising writer

Writer of instructional materials (for schools and other organizations)

Industrial scriptwriter (of films and videotapes for business and industry)

Video scriptwriter (for videotapes sold to consumers)

Annual report writer (for corporations and nonprofit organizations)

Family history writer

Grant writer

Ghostwriter

Collaborator

Researcher

Translator

Indexer

Writing consultant

Fund-raiser

Publicist

Writer-in-residence (see pages 194–95 for details)

Writing tutor (either working privately or for an educational institution or corporation)

English-as-a-second-language instructor (through public or private educational institutions, or through a private language school such as Berlitz)

English-as-a-foreign-language instructor (teaching English through a school or private agency in a foreign country)

English and/or journalism teacher

Reading teacher

Reading tutor (at a school, through a private or public agency, or on your own; includes tutoring illiterate and semiliterate adults, and tutoring children and adults with learning/reading disabilities)

Substitute teacher

College writing teacher (at academic institutions, business schools, technical schools, and secretarial schools)

Freelance teacher (teaching writing or writing-related workshops and seminars through community organizations, colleges, writers' centers, high schools)

Employee of a writers' club, organization, or center

Publishing employee (in subsidiary rights, promotion, sales, layout and design, etc.)

Arts administrator/employee of an arts organization

Anthology editor

Lecturer/speaker

Librarian

Storyteller

Performer (reading from or performing your work or others')

Copy aide (also known as copy clerk, copy boy, copy girl, editorial aide—in essence a gofer and assistant at a newspaper or magazine)

In most of these areas, both full-time and part-time salaried positions *and* freelance work are available.

Writers looking for work tend to gravitate toward the fields of publishing and education. But these two fields together offer only a small fraction of the opportunities available to writers. If you want to be a public relations writer, for example, you might be able to find a job at virtually any large or medium-sized business, nonprofit organization, or government agency—as well as at specialized public relations firms. Most organizations with five hundred or more employees, and many smaller ones, hire writers, editors, and other people with writing and writing-related skills.

Any organization that needs to communicate in writing—either to people outside the organization or to people within it—needs writers and editors. These organizations include federal, state, county, city, and other government agencies and offices; colleges and schools; national and professional associations; hospitals; consulting firms; manufacturing firms; unions; public-service organizations; and other large corporations and nonprofit organizations.

Even within the publishing industry, most of the opportunities for both freelance and salaried jobs exist where most writers don't think to look. Publishers of catalogs, instruction manuals, brochures, textbooks, and technical and trade journals—to give only a few examples—regularly hire writers, editors, and other professionals on both a salaried and a freelance basis.

The first and most important decision you need to make regarding writing and writing-related jobs is whether you want to work on a salaried basis, a freelance basis, or both. Refer to the charts on pages 2 and 3 to help you decide. Some writers combine three, four, or more different writing-related activities to earn their livings.

FIVE LIKELY OPTIONS

Five accessible writing-related areas that offer the most opportunities for writers are freelance editing, teaching college-level writing, teaching writing workshops, working in publishing, and being a writer-in-residence.

Freelance Editing

You can sell your services as a freelance editor to other writers, to publishing firms, and to organizations in other fields that produce written materials for either internal or external distribution.

Many publishing companies, particularly book publishers, regularly hire freelance editors on an hourly or project-by-project basis. Average pay runs from $15 to $25 an hour, although some publishers prefer to negotiate a flat fee for each project, and a few prefer to pay by the page. Rates of payment are often negotiable. Most publishers prefer (or insist on) hiring local editors to do freelance work, although some hire out-of-town editors. Local publishers will be listed in your Yellow Pages.

To approach a publisher, find out the name of its editor-in-chief or editorial director using *Literary Market Place, Publisher's Directory,* or *The Working Press of the Nation.* If the press is quite small, get the name of its publisher, director, or general manager. Write a short letter to this person by name, expressing interest in doing freelance editing. Enclose a copy of a resumé geared toward editing jobs. Follow up with a phone call two to three weeks later, and try to set up an appointment. If the publisher is interested, you will probably be given an editing test lasting from one to four hours.

A great many other kinds of organizations also hire freelance editors. To be seriously considered by one of these organizations, however, you must first determine what people or divisions will need your services; then you'll have to locate and contact the specific person who has the authority and the budget to hire you. This may take some calling around. If the person you reach can't help you, ask him or her for the name and position of someone who can. Remember that in large organizations there may be several different people or divisions that need editors. If you are turned down by one arm of such an organization, perhaps another division or department is still a possibility. Do *not* approach personnel offices; go directly to the person(s) you would report to if you were hired. See pages 209–11 for details.

It is perfectly okay to approach as many organizations at a time for freelance editing assignments as you wish. It is also acceptable (indeed, sometimes necessary) to do editing projects for several different organizations at once.

Once you have satisfactorily completed one editing job for an organization, your chances of getting additional work from that organization are good. Let your contact know that you are interested in new projects.

Organizations that can be helpful to freelance editors and copy editors are the Editorial Freelancers Association (Box 2050, Madison Square Station, New York, NY 10159, 212-677-3357), the Association of Editorial Businesses (c/o SSR, Inc., 2120 L Street NW, Washington, DC 20037, 202-543-1800), and the Freelance Editors Association of Canada (34 Ross Street, Suite 200, Toronto, Ontario, Canada M5T 1Z9, 416-593-4692).

Teaching College-Level Writing

The competition for full-time, tenure-track jobs teaching writing and English is very stiff. By far the most openings are in freshman composition and in technical writing, though openings can be found in most other areas of writing, literature, and linguistics. You'll need at least an M.A. to teach full time at a junior or community college. Most full-time teaching jobs at four-year schools require an M.F.A. or Ph.D., though in some cases an M.A. is sufficient.

Teaching freshman composition on a course-by-course basis is another kettle of fish entirely. Most universities with enrollments of 10,000 students or more, and many smaller colleges and universities, including community colleges, regularly hire nontenure-track composition instructors. These instructors receive few or no benefits and are paid a flat fee for each course taught. The pay is terrible; it usually ranges from $800 to $3200 a course, with $1600 being average. Some community colleges, and some business and technical schools, may pay as little as $500 to $1000 a course. The primary credential for teaching freshman composition is an M.A. or M.S. in English, writing, or journalism. Writing ability is of course also expected and required.

It is normally quite acceptable to teach at two or more colleges or universities at the same time.

Most full-time and many part-time college teaching jobs in writing are advertised in the *Associated Writing Programs Job List,* available from Associated Writing Programs, Old Dominion University, Norfolk, VA 23508. This list is published about ten times a year. Advertisements for full-time (and some part-time) openings teaching writing, literature, and linguistics on the college level appear in the *Modern Language Association Job List* (Modern Language Association, 10 Astor Place, New York, NY 10003), published four times a year, and *The Chronicle of Higher Education* (1255 23rd Street NW, Washington, DC 20037), published weekly.

Tenure-track freshman composition positions are frequently advertised in the *AWP Job List,* but the nontenure-track openings often are not. However, most universities and community colleges are interested in hiring more composition teachers. Simply get the name and phone number of the director of freshman composition from the English department, call the director, and explain that you'd like to join the part-time composition faculty. Follow up this call with a short letter and a curriculum vitae (a resumé for a teaching position); then phone two to four weeks later to set up an interview.

Many colleges and universities also have writing laboratories that hire tutors, usually by the hour. Pay runs from $10 to $15 an hour. When you contact the director of freshman composition, also ask about the possibility of working in such a lab. In some schools the composition director oversees the lab; in others, the writing lab will have its own director, whom you must approach separately.

If you are thinking of teaching or tutoring writing, don't overlook business colleges, art and design colleges, technical colleges, or secretarial colleges. Often these schools offer writing classes or writing tutoring—and if they don't, you can propose that they start. At these schools, all you need by way of academic degrees is a B.A., preferably in English, writing, or journalism. You of course need demonstrated writing ability as well.

Writers interested in college teaching will want to keep a complete academic dossier (with their curricula vitae and recommendations) on file with a placement service. The service can then send a photocopy of the dossier to anyone who requests it (including people and organizations outside of academia). Although most colleges offer placement services to their alumni, a better, more prestigious, and more effective bet is the job placement service offered by Associated Writing Programs (Old Dominion University, Norfolk, VA 23508) to its members. Membership is open to anyone, and the placement service is available for a small additional fee.

Teaching Writing Workshops

If you are already proficient in one or more areas of writing, you can generate extra income by teaching writing workshops in that field. A huge variety of organizations now offer short writing workshops to their members or employees or to the general public. These include corporations, libraries, art centers, community groups and centers, writers' organizations and centers, senior citizens' organizations and centers, high schools, YMCAs and YWCAs, bookstores, literary cafés and bars, women's centers, and of course colleges, community colleges, and universities. (Most colleges, community colleges, and universities offer a wide variety of such workshops, usually on a noncredit basis, through programs with titles like Adult Education, Community Education, Community Services, Noncredit Classes, Lifelong Learning, Continuing Education, New College, Elderhostel, and so on.) Workshops can run an evening, a day, or a weekend, or they can meet once or twice a week for four to ten weeks. One two-hour session a week for six to eight weeks is typical.

Many of these organizations already offer a regular series of courses and workshops. Simply call the director of the series and set up an appointment. At the appointment, give him or her a verbal sales pitch, a written proposal for your writing course, and your resumé. Don't worry if the organization has never offered a writing workshop or course before; the director may be intrigued by the idea of expanding into a new area. Novelty is more often a plus than a minus in these cases. A course is likely to be turned down if it partly or entirely duplicates another course already being offered by that program; so be able to explain exactly what makes your course different or special.

If the organization hasn't offered *any* courses or workshops of any kind before, don't let that stop you, either. Draw up a brief written proposal explaining why the course would be beneficial to the organization and its constituents. Call the director, briefly describe your credentials, and explain your idea in a few sentences. Offer to send your written proposal and your resumé. If the director agrees to look at them, send them on, and call a couple of weeks later to make an appointment to discuss your idea.

Short courses and workshops have been offered on virtually every writing topic, from the most general to the most specific. Course titles have included Journal Writing for Women, Writing Magazine Articles, Science Fiction and Fantasy Writing, How to Make Money from Your Writing, Write for Your Life, Romance Writing, Business Writing for Executives, How to Write Better Letters, Writing for the Health Care Industry, A Brief Introduction to Creative Writing, Writing for Children, and Writing Family Histories.

The pay for these workshops and courses is usually pretty low (around $25–$35 per classroom hour, with no pay for preparation time), but it's often negotiable. Workshop instructors may also be paid by the session or the student (say, $35 for each student enrolled in the workshop).

If you're suggesting a course or workshop to an organization that hasn't offered such things before, you should clearly state in your proposal how much you expect to be paid and where you expect the money to come from. (In most cases, suggest that your fee be paid from the tuition charged for the workshop, with a little money left over for the sponsoring organization to pocket. This negates in advance any arguments of "we like your idea but can't afford to do it.")

Some organizations have two or more such programs, which operate independently; it is usually quite acceptable to approach more than one program within the same college or organization with workshop ideas.

Instructors of noncredit writing courses and workshops do not need to possess any academic degrees, even if their courses are offered through colleges—provided they are otherwise qualified to teach a particular area of writing.

Poets & Writers, Inc. (201 E. 54th Street, New York, NY 10019) publishes *Author and Audience,* a list of some of the organizations across the United States that sponsor writing workshops. Jeffrey Lant has published an interesting volume called *Money Talks: The Complete Guide to Creating a Profitable Workshop or Seminar in any Field* (JLA Publications, 50 Follen Street, Suite 507, Cambridge, MA 02138).

Working in Publishing

The publishing industry offers a wide variety of jobs besides those involving editing, copyediting, and proofreading. Publishers also employ graphic designers, layout and pasteup people, researchers and fact checkers, promotion people, publicity people, sales reps, artists and art directors, typesetters, accountants and bookkeepers, secretaries, mail clerks, circulation people, and so on. If the field of publishing in general interests you, and you don't yet have the training or skills to be an editor, you should seriously consider working in publishing in a nonediting capacity. You might also consider first attending one of the publishing workshops or courses discussed on pages 395–400.

If you are interested in an editing job, especially in book publishing, there is no better introduction to the field, and no better way to break in, than to take a job as an editorial assistant or secretary for an editor. You will learn a great deal about an editor's responsibilities very quickly, and if you're sharp you will be given editing and proofreading projects very soon. Editorial assistants and secretaries regularly get promoted to editors, often within 2–3 years, and secretarial jobs in publishing are not hard to come by, at least in New York City.

If you're interested in a job in publishing, you may want to pay a visit to one or more of the employment agencies that specialize in the publishing field. Most of these agencies are based in New York City, and the great majority (though not all) of the jobs they handle are in the New York area. Both *Literary Market Place* and *Magazine Industry Market Place* publish comprehensive lists of these agencies. The three best-known agencies are the Lynne Palmer Agency, the Helen Akullian Agency, and Remer-Ribolow.

Most jobs in U.S. publishing are in New York City. In Canada, most such jobs are in Toronto. However, some publishing jobs exist in all major cities and many small towns throughout the continent.

Writers' Residencies

The terms *writer-in-residence* and *writer's residency* can mean many different things. In general there are four types of writers' residencies:

1. Nonservice or low-service residencies, in which writers work primarily on their own projects and devote either a small amount of time or no time at all to working with students or other writers. Writers' colonies invariably offer such residencies (see pages 406–10 for details), as do some fellowship programs (see pages 400–406).

2. Community-service residencies. In these, writers spend twenty or more hours a week offering classes, lectures, workshops, manuscript criticism, readings, and other services to residents of a particular city or area. Sometimes writers may be in residence at particular organizations, such as prisons, homes for the elderly, hospitals, writers' centers, and so on.

3. Residencies at colleges or universities. Here a "residency" may simply be a teaching appointment lasting from one term to two years. Or it may be a modified appointment in which the resident writer need only teach one or two courses each term and give a couple of readings or talks. Some college residencies bring writers to campus for as little as a week or two to teach, lecture, work with students individually, and read their own work.

4. Residencies in elementary, middle, junior high, and high schools. At these residencies writers act primarily as educators, working with several different classes each day. They may also assemble anthologies of student work, organize student readings, or head up other student-oriented literary projects. Sometimes they may be given some time to work on their own writing, and occasionally they may be asked to give readings or talks to students or the larger community. However, they are primarily hired as instructors of creative writing.

In any of these four cases, residencies can be as short as a week or as long as a year or more.

Openings for writers in residence in the second and third categories listed above are usually advertised in the *AWP Job List* (see page 190 for details). Residencies in the first and fourth categories are *not* normally advertised.

With the exception of residencies at writers' colonies, writers in residence are paid a regular salary, usually $500 to $800 a week. Residencies at colleges—which are usually reserved for writers who have achieved at least a small national reputation—and residencies for very well-known writers can sometimes pay more, occasionally a good deal more.

Residencies in public schools are particularly accessible to newer writers. If you've published as few as half a dozen poems, stories, or articles in respectable magazines and/or newspapers, and are good at working with children and adolescents (or have had some successful teaching experience), your chances of landing a residency of this type are good. Most such residencies are offered through state arts councils, usually through programs called Artists in Education, Writers in the Schools, Writers in Education, Artists in the Schools, or Poets in the Schools. (Most programs with the word *Poet* in their names also hire writers of fiction and nonfiction.) School residencies are also offered through autonomous organizations that bear similar names. Occasionally local and regional arts organizations, such as COMPAS in Minneapolis–St. Paul, also sponsor such programs.

It is sometimes but not always necessary that you live in the same state or area in which a writer-in-residence program is based. For example, the Artists in Education program run by the Ohio Arts Council hires writers who live in other states; however, all the residencies are in Ohio schools.

A list of some residencies specifically for playwrights appears in *Dramatists Sourcebook;* see page 76 for details on this volume.

There's no reason why you have to stick to established programs, however. Many writers have arranged residencies at community centers, colleges, writers' centers, public and private schools, libraries, senior citizens' centers, and other organizations on their own. All you need is enthusiasm, the ability to sell yourself, a good written proposal, and a little chutzpah.

If you do approach an organization with a residency proposal, remember that you can offer a wide range of options. If a full-time three-week residency is too expensive, perhaps you can arrange a residency for only three days a week at $120 a day, or only four hours a day at $80 a day.

READINGS

If you are a writer of fiction, poetry, or creative nonfiction, you have the option of supplementing your writing income and building your literary reputation by giving public readings of your work. Being published helps, of course, since the more well known you are, the more attractive you are to reading sponsors. But being published is not always necessary.

There are two ways to arrange readings: through an established readings series, and on your own, on an entrepreneurial basis.

Here are some organizations that sponsor readings: state, local, and regional arts councils; writers' centers; writers' conferences and workshops; writers' clubs; colleges, community colleges, and universities; churches and synagogues; art centers; women's centers; community centers; bookstores, particularly literary bookstores (chain bookstores normally do not sponsor readings); museums and art galleries; libraries; YMCAs and YWCAs; senior citizens' centers; and coffee houses, restaurants, and bars.

It may also be possible to give readings at hospitals, prisons, high schools, and other organizations. In fact, there's no reason not to try any organization where you think you may find a receptive audience. If the organization hasn't offered readings in the past, you can make a pitch about why sponsoring a reading is a good idea (for example, it will bring in business or publicity). You might even suggest starting a reading series, with your own reading as the kickoff attraction—or the trial run.

Here are some things to keep in mind regarding readings:

• Expect to have to submit samples of your work to reading sponsors for evaluation. You may also be asked about your background, publications, and other credentials. Don't be too surprised if some organizations turn you down because you have few or no publications.

• No one gets rich off readings except the most famous of writers. Established reading series typically pay less-than-well-known writers $25 to $100 for a 30- to 60-minute reading. If you *do* become a reasonably well-known poet, fiction writer, or essayist, then you may be able to command $200 to $400 for a reading, plus travel expenses. Many reading series pay writers nothing at all, or pay them with something like a dinner and a $20 gift certificate to a bookstore.

• If you are trying to sell an organization on the idea of sponsoring a reading, don't insist that it come up with a fee for you. This is the surest way to be turned down, and it gives the organization the best reason in the world to say no: "We can't afford it." Instead, you might suggest that you be given a percentage—say, half—of the money taken in at the door. Or, in the case of a bookstore or café, suggest being paid with $25 to $50 in free books or food. Or, if the exposure is more important than the payment (and for many writers, especially poets, it may be), you can simply offer to give your reading at no charge.

• If your writing has a particular theme or focus, approach an organization that has the same (or a similar) focus. If your work has a feminist orientation, approach a women's center. If you've written a story about dogs, suggest to the organizers of a dog show that you read your story at the show.

• Colleges and universities each have several organizations through which readings can be arranged. Most readings are typically arranged through the English and/or creative writing departments, but if those departments turn you down, you have many other options. You can approach the Student Activities Board (sometimes called the Student Programming Board or the Events Committee). Or, depending on your religion, you can approach the campus Newman Center, Hillel House, and so on. Or perhaps you can get the Music Department to sponsor a reading of your short story about Gustav Mahler.

• You also have the option of sponsoring and arranging your reading yourself. You can rent or borrow a room in a church, school, or other building, put up flyers around town, and send out news releases to local media. You can then not only read your work but keep 100 percent of the admission fee. (Important: don't charge more than about $2 a head if you want people to show up.)

• If your book has just been published, giving a reading is an excellent idea. This helps promote the book, and your work in general. Be sure that the reading is scheduled for shortly *after* the book's publication so that copies are available. It is also a good idea to notify local bookstores a couple of months prior to the reading so that they will have copies of your book(s) ready to sell by the time the reading date arrives. Try to arrange a book signing (see pages 302–3 for details) for a day or two after your reading.

• Whenever you give a reading, bring copies of *all* your books to sell. Many people who like what they hear will plunk down hard cash on the spot for your work—though they might never take the trouble to go to a bookstore for it. Bring plenty of money to make change. Announce after you finish reading that the books are available, but wait until the other scheduled writers have finished reading to actually sell them. Obviously, you shouldn't sell your books at readings given in bookstores (unless the store sells out all its copies). You don't want to compete with your sponsor.

• Rehearse your reading thoroughly. Time it so you know exactly how long it will run.

• If you are giving a reading alone, it should run 40 to 60 minutes. If you are giving a reading with one or two other writers, 20 to 30 minutes a writer is standard.

• Your material should not only be worth listening to, it should lend itself well to being read aloud. Choose it carefully, and make sure it is appropriate for your audience.

• Make sure you read loudly and clearly, and that you can be easily heard by everyone in the room. It is not a bad idea to begin by asking, "Can you hear me okay in back?"

• Don't expect huge crowds at your reading. Twenty people is about average, and if you get thirty you're doing very nicely.

• Don't saturate the market with yourself and your work. You should give no more than two readings a year in any one city or area, and normally no more than one reading every year or two at the same organization or institution. Naturally, every time you read your work in the same city or locale, you should read different material.

• Once you've become fairly well known as a writer, you may be able to get on the reading circuit, where you can do anywhere from five to thirty readings a year, primarily at colleges. Many literary writers, particularly poets, make a good portion of their income through these reading tours.

• Poets & Writers, Inc., 201 W. 54th Street, New York, NY 10019, sells three publications that can help writers set up readings: (1) "The ABC's of Giving a Reading," a general overview of things to consider when doing readings; (2) *Author and Audience,* which lists several hundred organizations across the United States that sponsor readings; (3) *Literary Bookstores in the U.S.,* a list of the names and addresses of hundreds of these bookstores. It also includes a list of literary bars and coffee houses. All three are available from Poets & Writers by mail.

All of the information in this section also applies to storytellers who want to arrange storytelling gigs.

LECTURING AND SPEAKING

If you've published a reasonable body of work (at least one book or half a dozen short pieces) on a particular subject, you may wish simultaneously to promote your work, build your career, and earn some extra money by giving talks on that subject. This can be done locally (at libraries, colleges, high schools, YMCAs, and the other organizations listed on page 196) and in other cities. In fact, a good many writers make a major portion of their livings by going from city to city giving public talks, usually at colleges and universities, earning a sizeable fee (usually several hundred dollars, sometimes more) for each talk. You don't need to have been widely published to be a successful speaker (though it certainly helps). In fact, if you've published only one self-published book, that's often sufficient.

Arranging speaking engagements is much like arranging readings (see the previous section). However, lectures usually last longer (45 to 90 minutes), draw bigger audiences, and earn more money.

To sell yourself as a lecturer, it is best to assemble a press packet on yourself and your work. An excellent guide to putting together such a packet appears in Peggy Glenn's very helpful book, *Publicity for Books and Authors* (Aames-Allen Publishing Company).

If you attain some local recognition as a lecturer, and/or if your writing (in any genre) on a particular subject achieves some national notice, then you may wish to attempt a regional or even national speaking tour. You can set up such a tour yourself (perhaps combined with talk show appearances and/or newspaper and magazine interviews), though this takes an enormous amount of time and effort. Or you can hire a publicist (see page 301 for details), though this can be very expensive. Or you can approach a speaker's bureau or lecture agent with your press packet and a pleasant, professional-looking cover letter. Lecture agents arrange speaking gigs for writers and other people, and take a percentage of the speaker's earnings, just as literary agents earn commissions from books, plays, and so on. A good list of lecture agents that represent writers appears in *Literary Market Place*.

You may also wish to get yourself listed as a speaker in one or more of the following directories:

Speakers and Lecturers, edited by Paul Wasserman (Gale Research Co., Book Tower, Detroit, MI 48226).

Directory of Speakers, edited by Howard J. Langer (Oryx Press, 2214 N. Central Avenue, Phoenix, AZ 85004).

Directory of Experts, Authorities, and Spokespersons, edited by Mitchell P. Davis (Broadcast Interview Source, 2500 Wisconsin Avenue, Suite 930, Washington, DC 20007). Though primarily used as a listing of potential talk-show guests, this book is sometimes used for booking lecturers and speakers.

Write to the editors for information on being included in the next edition.

GHOSTWRITING

A ghostwriter is someone who writes—or collaborates on—a manuscript but receives no byline. Works that are supposedly the collaborative work of two writers but are actually written by only one of the two are also considered ghostwritten.

Most books supposedly written by politicians, TV or film personalities, or sports figures are ghostwritten. Sometimes the famous figure has done some of the actual writing; more often, he or she has provided notes, interviews, and/or diaries; occasionally the famous figure has done nothing more than lend his or her name to the project.

Financial arrangements for ghostwriters vary widely. Many writers receive a flat fee for their work; some receive a percentage of a book's royalties or total earnings; some receive both. Ghostwriters have received as little as a couple of thousand dollars for a book, or 10 percent of a book's earnings, and as much as half of a project's total revenues. Almost all terms are negotiable.

Whatever arrangements you make, you *absolutely must* draw up and sign a *written* agreement *in advance*, before any major portion of the writing begins. There must be no ambiguities in the terms. You must know exactly when and how much you will be paid, in percentages, dollars, or both. You must also agree, *in writing*, on what sort of byline, if any, you will be given. See pages 46–52 for more details on these agreements.

Ghostwriters are sometimes called in when an author is unable to complete a manuscript of satisfactory quality by the agreed-upon deadline, or complete it at all. Often a writer has produced a good outline of a project and has all the information readily available, but simply isn't a strong enough writer to produce a readable manuscript. In such cases the ghostwriter works from an outline and/or a first draft.

Sometimes an editor finds a ghostwriter to match with a particular writer or project, and the ghostwriter signs a contract directly with the publisher. Just as often the writer finds the ghostwriter, and the two make a private deal. In these cases, the publisher never knows that the book has been partly or entirely ghostwritten.

Ghostwriting pays very well if you can arrange to work with people who are already famous. Needless to say, this is very difficult for beginning writers. Much more common are projects by little-known people with good ideas but little writing ability. These pay decently but not spectacularly. Most common of all are projects by people with no writing ability and nothing worth saying who want to pay ghostwriters little or nothing for their services. When people learn that you're a writer, an amazing percentage of them will want you to write their life stories for them. Usually they "just know" such a story will be a best-seller; usually they are wrong.

Occasionally people will even put classified ads in newspapers or magazines with messages like, "Ghostwriter wanted for best-seller. Guaranteed earnings." Usually the "guarantee" refers to the fact that they "know" their book will be a best-seller; after all, won't everyone want to read about the trials and tribulations of a Milwaukee plumber? These people usually offer a percentage (often a tiny one) of the book's potential earnings—but rarely are they willing to pay writers cold cash up front for their efforts.

Here are some tips on negotiating a ghostwriting deal:

• Insist on being paid at least a flat fee for your efforts, regardless of whether or not the project sells. As a professional, you deserve to be paid for your time. Don't be swayed by assurances that the project is destined for great success, or that your coauthor has an "in" somewhere, even if they claim to be best buddies with the president of Doubleday. Never accept a project for which you'll be paid *if* it sells. Not only will you probably wind up with nothing, but your coauthor may even claim that the project didn't sell because you did a substandard job.

• Your flat fee may be based on the number of hours you actually work on the project; or, if you and your coauthor prefer, you may decide on a set fee to be paid regardless of how long the project takes. Two tips here: (1) if you charge on an hourly basis, $15 to $25 an hour is reasonable; (2) most projects take roughly twice as long as your best estimate; take this into account when quoting and negotiating an overall fee.

• You may want to ask for a percentage of the money the project earns in addition to your initial fee. There are many ways this can be arranged and negotiated. You might reduce the initial fee somewhat in exchange for a percentage (or a larger percentage) of the project's total earnings; or you might reduce the percentage in exchange for a higher initial fee. The up-front fee may be applied against the project's future earnings, or it may be in addition to a percentage of the total amount the project earns.

• Be careful about whom you work with. People who want to hire ghost-writers are often self-centered or egotistical; sometimes they're plain nuts.
• If you agree to a project and you later realize that either it or your relationship with your coauthor isn't going to work out, your best bet is to back out as quickly and gracefully as possible.

If you already have substantial writing credits, you may be able to work as a ghostwriter or collaborator through one or more editorial services or book packagers. These are listed under the headings Editorial Services and Book Producers in *Literary Market Place*.

For more information on ghostwriting, refer to these two interesting articles: "Giving Up the Ghost," *Publishers Weekly*, January 10, 1986, and "Underground Writing: Ghostwriting and Collaboration," *Coda* (now called *Poets & Writers Magazine*), May 1982. This article also appears in the book *The Writing Business* (Poets & Writers, Inc.).

STRANGE AND UNUSUAL ALTERNATIVES

You're not limited to the well-established ways of making money with your writing skills. Many writers make part or even all of their income in unique and innovative ways. For example:

• Detroit poet Raghudas writes original sonnets and, dressed in sixteenth-century garb, will recite one to anyone in Detroit for about $30.
• Todd Strasser wrote, manufactured, and sold Dr. Wing Tip Shoo's X-rated Fortune Cookies, which had risqué fortunes inside.
• One writer turns out clever messages for people's answering machines, usually in limerick or other poetic form.
• Poet Natalie Goldberg set up a booth at street fairs, art and craft festivals, and other community gatherings, where she wrote original short poems for $1 apiece. Another writer writes one-page "novels" that are actually brief plot synopses for $10 a crack.
• Writer Marcie Lee Musen writes custom-made greeting cards, inspirational letters, and other personal messages for a few dollars each.
• Writers with knowledge and interest in a particular area (cocker spaniels, investing in precious metals, HMOs, the Grateful Dead, etc.) have started their own newsletters for other people interested in the same topic.

Perhaps you can come up with an unusual product or service of your own to offer—something that people (or businesses) can use and appreciate but can't easily obtain elsewhere. This could be your route to writing success or at least some extra income.

SELLING YOURSELF

If you are serious about selling your ideas and services to others, then you will do well to prepare a short written proposal for each concept or service you want to sell. People in general, and executives in particular, respond far more favorably to written material than they do to ideas presented orally. Written proposals seem much more serious, thorough, and tangible, and provide documentation that can be shown to other people. Whether you want to teach a course in short story writing at the nearby YMCA, be hired by a large corporation to train executives to write more clearly, or write a new set of brochures for a hospital, a written proposal will be the most effective selling tool you can provide.

There is no standard format for such a proposal. I have found, however, that a three- to five-page, double-spaced proposal works well and is almost always well received. Longer proposals are difficult for some people to get through. If you are asked for more details, you can always provide them later.

If you can, make at least a portion of your proposal a list of information, rather than a continuous narrative. This makes the proposal easier to read and digest. This is particularly important if you are dealing with busy executives.

Be sure to stress in your proposal exactly what you propose to do or provide for the organization and how your services can benefit the organization and/or its constituency. Be very specific in each case.

The best way to present yourself and your ideas is to make an initial phone contact with the appropriate person, explaining your idea. If the person expresses some interest, send him or her your proposal and a resumé. Follow this up two to three weeks later with a phone call requesting an appointment. At the appointment, be prepared to answer questions and to give a more detailed oral pitch. Bring another copy of your resumé and proposal, just in case your interviewer can't find the material you sent earlier.

Selling yourself is of course an art. It's a combination of timing, tact, good manners, listening carefully, talking well, thinking fast, and even dressing appropriately. Keep in mind that how you present yourself and your ideas is at least as important as—if not more important than—the project you are offering.

If you can convince people and organizations that what you have to offer can be valuable to them, or to the people they serve, your chances of getting hired are excellent. Show them that they have a need that's gone unfilled (and possibly unnoticed), and that you're the person to fill it. Or offer them a service or skill that is entirely new, unique, or unavailable elsewhere.

Here are some things writers have done to sell their services, ideas, and talents to others:

• Approached corporate executives and offered to teach workshops for managers on writing clearer, more understandable memos, letters, and reports.

• Approached businesses and nonprofit organizations and offered to edit and publish newsletters and brochures for their employees, members, clients, or customers.

• Approached local businesses and offered to write and publish promotional flyers for them, and/or to write local radio or TV ads.

• Approached printers and offered to work as their associates when their clients need copy written or edited. The print shop could advertise writing and editing as two of its services, and it would take a percentage of the fee for each writing or editing job.

• Offered to serve busy executives as writer/secretaries by writing business (and sometimes personal) letters for them. An executive who would normally have to dictate a letter to a secretary could then simply say to a writer, "Write a letter to Helen Katzman telling her that everything she suggests is fine except for her proposal on freight charges. Tell her we've got a deal if we split the freight costs down the middle. At the end invite her for lunch next time she's in Chicago."

Don't be afraid to try something new, different, unusual, strange, or even wacky. It might be your key to success, or at least some earnings, as a writer.

HOW MUCH SHOULD I CHARGE?

If you are providing professional services (editing, copyediting, indexing, translating, or teaching, for example, as opposed to typing, proofreading, or answering the phone), under no normal circumstances should you get (or charge) less than $10 an hour, regardless of whether you are working on a salaried or freelance basis. In most areas of the United States, for most services, you should be getting a good deal more: $15 to $30 an hour is standard in most areas for freelance work, $10 to $20 for salaried jobs.

The general range of appropriate fees and wages for each of the writing and writing-related jobs listed at the beginning of this chapter appears in *Writer's Market* and in the booklet *Jobs and Opportunities for Writers*, available for $2.50 postpaid ($3.50 outside the United States) from *Writer's Digest*, 1507 Dana Avenue, Cincinnati, OH 45207.

Don't sell your services too cheaply. Some people and firms will plead poverty whenever they sense that you may be willing to lower your price; this plea of impoverishment may be an outright lie. Set a fair, reasonable fee as your bottom line, and stick to it. This may mean passing up some offers. Pass them up if you have to.

If you're asked to quote a fee for your services, don't quote a low one in the hope that you'll get the job because of your reasonable price. In practice, business people (especially executives in large corporations) are quite tolerant of moderate fees. In fact, they will be suspicious of quotes that seem too low.

WRITING YOUR RESUMÉ

Whether you are applying to fill an advertised vacancy or trying to hustle freelance jobs on your own, you need an effective, well-written resumé. A good resumé is especially important for a writer, because it serves not only as a summary of your experience but as a sample of your clearest, most concise writing.

Contrary to one common belief, a resumé should *not* be as detailed as possible. Rather, it should communicate your skills and experience quickly and succinctly, in one or (at the absolute most) two pages. Remember that your resumé will be read by a very busy executive, a bored personnel worker, or both. Neither will give your resumé more than a 30-second scan. Your resumé must communicate as much relevant information in that brief time as possible.

Another common but erroneous belief is that dolled-up resumés—those professionally typeset, offset-printed, duplicated on colored paper, or adorned with your smiling photograph—get the best results. In truth, none of this impresses anybody.

The resumés that consistently get the best responses are neatly typed on a standard typewriter or *letter-quality* printer, in a standard typeface, then photocopied on good paper.

Your resumé should be not only very easy to read but very easy to scan. Include nothing on your resumé unless it will have an immediate bearing on the job you are seeking. If you are only going to get a 30-second scan, you don't want any of those seconds spent on your social security number, hobbies, marital status, or date or place of birth. You *can* list any special interests or activities *if* they pertain to the job you're seeking.

Present all information in the simplest, most direct, and most readable way possible. Dot-points and lists work well; so do short sentences. If possible, avoid paragraphs of narration or description—these cannot be easily skimmed. Underlining key words and phrases adds contrast and makes resumés more skimmable; lots of white space and clearly defined borders, sections, and categories also help a good deal. A two- or three-column format usually works best.

Your resumé is itself an indication of your neatness, attention to detail, and ability to write clear, straightforward, concise English. So be sure to triple-check all your spelling, capitalization, and usage. Make sure, too, that the whole resumé is neat and looks good.

You will need an entirely different resumé for each different kind of job you are seeking. If, say, you are looking for freelance jobs as a writer, editor, and writing teacher, you will need a different resumé for each general area. But you may not need to rewrite anything; if you have designed your resumé carefully, you may be able to quickly create variations by cutting, rearranging, and pasting up a photocopy. However, you may need to type up a different list of professional references for each area of employment that interests you.

The resumé I use for teaching is reproduced on the next two pages. When I'm looking for a writing job, I use a resumé that places the Writing and Editing headings third and fourth, immediately below Books and Articles and Short Fiction. When I want an editing job, the Editing heading goes third and the Writing heading fourth.

The last item on your resumé should be References, under which you should type, "Available on request." Type up a separate list of business references for each area in which you are looking for work. Be sure to include complete addresses and phone numbers where people can be reached during business hours; if possible, list both work and home phones. Ideally, each list should have at least three and no more than five references. Enclose the appropriate reference list whenever you send out your resumé (even if it has not yet been requested).

If you are applying for a part- or full-time college teaching job, you

WRITER'S RESUMÉ

Scott Edelstein
179 Berkeley Street, #1
Rochester, NY   14607
(716) 244-0645

Books

Novel Approaches, Writer's Digest Books, 1989
Putting Your Kids Through College, Consumer Reports Books, 1989
The Indispensable Writer's Guide, Harper & Row, 1989
The No-Experience-Necessary Writer's Course, Stein and Day, 1988
Surviving Freshman Composition, Lyle Stuart, 1988
College: A User's Manual, Bantam Books, 1985
Future Pastimes (editor), Sherbourne Press, 1977

Articles and Short Fiction

Over 90 short pieces in a variety of literary and commercial magazines, news-papers, and book anthologies, including Glamour, Essence, Writer's Yearbook, Artlines, City Miner, Ellery Queen's Mystery Magazine, Science Fiction Monthly, and many others. Regular columns in Writer's Digest and The Artist's Magazine. Foreign appearances in England, Australia, Italy, Belgium, France, and elsewhere.

Teaching

State University of New York at Buffalo: Dept. of English, 1986-present
Ohio Arts Council: Writer-in-Residence, Artists in Education program, 1985-
   present
University of Akron: Lecturer, Dept. of English, 1985-6
University of Minnesota--Duluth: Adjunct Lecturer, 1982-4
Metropolitan State University: Adjunct Instructor, 1982-3
University of Minnesota--Minneapolis: Instructor, General College, 1979-80;
   Lecturer, Continuing Education for Women, 1979-83
The Loft: A Center for Literature and Writing: Instructor, 1981-3
University of Wisconsin--Milwaukee: Teaching Assistant, Dept. of English, 1980-1
Oberlin College: Teaching Intern, Dept. of English, 1978; Teaching Assistant,
   Creative Writing Program, 1974-5, 1977
Cuyahoga Community College: taught non-credit adult education class in writing,
   1978
Wilder Senior Citizens' Center, St. Paul: taught writing class, 1979

Education

Oberlin College: B.A. in Creative Writing, 1978
University of Wisconsin--Milwaukee: M.A. in English with writing emphasis, 1984

Awards

Bread Loaf Writers' Conference: Time Magazine Scholarship, 1978
Edward Albee Foundation: Fellow, 1978

Writing

The Taos News: Staff Writer, 1984
Artlines Magazine: Staff Writer, 1983-4
Writer's Digest: Columnist, 1985-present
The Artist's Magazine: Columnist, 1985-7
Freelance Writing: In addition to my own fiction and non-fiction, I have written
   and ghost-written material to order, including four ghosted books, many
   articles, brochures, and advertising copy.

Editing

The Taos News: Acting Arts Editor, 1984
Artlines Magazine: Managing Editor, 1983-4
Sherbourne Press/Aurora Publishers: Consulting Editor, 1974-6
Eternity Magazine: Assistant Editor, 1973-4
Witchcraft & Sorcery: Associate Editor of this horror magazine, 1973-4
The Dragonfly: Guest Editor for issue #15, 1976
Green Revolution: Guest Editor for special issue, 1977
Freelance Editing: Since 1978 have done freelance editing and rewriting on a
   wide variety of projects, both non-fiction and fiction.

Other   <u>Literary Agent</u>, 1982-4: Worked with clients to develop book projects, and
Relevant   represented those projects to publishers.
Experience   <u>The Loft</u>: A Center for Literature and Writing: Staff consultant and tutor,
                  1981-3; Chairman, Grants and Awards Committee, 1982-3
               <u>Minnesota Writers' Conference</u>: Lecturer and panelist, 1982
               <u>Public and Private Schools</u>: Have served as writer-in-residence in grades
                  K-12; have led in-services for teachers of all grade levels, 1986-present
               <u>Westwood Nursing Home</u>, Minneapolis: Tutor in creative writing, 1979

Readings   <u>SOMOS</u>, Taos, New Mexico, 1984
               <u>The Loft</u>, Minneapolis, 1982, 1984
               <u>University of Minnesota</u>, Minneapolis, 1983
               <u>St. Louis County Arts Center</u>, Duluth, 1982
               <u>Oberlin College</u>, 1978

Listings   Listed in the following reference books:
               <u>Contemporary Authors</u> (Gale Research)
               <u>Who's Who in U.S. Writers, Editors, and Poets</u> (December Press)
               <u>A Directory of Poets and Fiction Writers</u> (Poets & Writers, Inc.)
               <u>International Authors and Writers Who's Who</u> (Melrose Press/International
                  Biographical Centre)
               <u>Men of Achievement</u> (Melrose Press/Interntional Biographical Centre)

References   Available on request.

should refer to your resumé not as a resumé, but as a curriculum vitae or c.v.

LETTERHEAD STATIONERY, PART TWO

You'll recall from pages 143–45 how letterhead stationery, envelopes, and labels can help you succeed as a freelance writer. These items are far more helpful still when you are trying to sell yourself or your services to people other than editors.

To many white-collar folks, printed stationery and mailing labels signal that you're a competent, trustworthy professional. This one detail alone can be enormously helpful in getting freelance writing jobs from businesses and nonprofit organizations and for getting gigs as a lecturer, teacher, or writer-in-residence. If you will be marketing yourself outside of the publishing world, decent stationery is thus a virtual necessity. For similar reasons, business cards are also very important.

USEFUL AND USELESS APPROACHES

If you are trying to sell your services *as a freelancer* to an organization, it is essential that you avoid personnel offices and personnel workers. (The terms human services, human resources, and employee relations are synonymous with personnel office.) The primary tasks of these people are to screen out applicants and to keep their applications and resumés from bothering anyone higher up.

Furthermore, personnel workers have no authority over (or interest in) the creation of new jobs or in the hiring of professionals on a freelance basis. They are responsible *only* for dealing with applicants for jobs that already exist.

Therefore, if you approach a personnel office offering to sell your services as a freelancer, you will invariably be told that "no such position is available right now, but we'll be happy to keep your resumé on file." You will then be politely turned away.

If you want to sell your services and/or ideas to an organization, you must instead find out the name and position of someone who will have both an interest in what you have to offer *and the authority to hire you on a freelance basis.* This may take some calling around, but it is very important. Unless you can meet with someone who can genuinely use your services *and who is able to hire you,* you are going to be sent away—or worse, sent to the personnel office, which will in turn send you away.

Locating the right person isn't always easy. One good place to start is with an organization's switchboard operator. Suppose you decide you'd like to work as a writer or editor for Beatrice Foods. You might start by calling Beatrice's main number and asking, "What's the name of the office that publishes brochures and pamphlets for consumers?" Suppose the operator says, "The Consumer Education Division." You then ask, "Who's the head of that division?" Chances are very good that the operator will give you a name. Get that person's extension number, and you're on your way. You might also ask the operator, "Are there other divisions that are involved in writing and publishing?" This is very much worth asking, because the firm might publish a regular in-house newsletter, there might be a separate public relations office, and the Product Development Division might be putting together a series of cookbooks.

It is important to learn the name as well as the title of the proper person to speak with for the same reasons that it is important to write cover letters to editors by name. Knowing the right person's name will also help you get past secretaries and receptionists. If an operator won't give you the name you need, ask to be transferred to the proper office or division; then ask the secretary who answers for the name of the appropriate person.

If you are transferred to someone who in fact can't help you or isn't interested in what you have to offer, don't just say "thank you" and hang up. Instead, ask if the person knows anyone else, either at that organization or at another one, who might be interested in what you have to offer. Also ask if there is any other division or office within that organization that might need someone with your skills. Sometimes it will be necessary to follow a whole chain of inquiries before you reach someone who can help you or who is genuinely interested.

If a switchboard operator (or anyone else) asks why you want to know the names of certain people or offices, explain quite honestly that you're *a professional with consulting services to offer,* and that you're trying to locate the person or office that will be most interested in your services. Most operators will be understanding. Make sure that you call yourself a consultant, or otherwise make it clear that you are a professional interested in proposing a specific service to a particular person. If you sound as if you are merely looking for a job, you will immediately be referred to the personnel office.

All of the above also applies if you want to be hired on a salaried basis but are seeking to have a new job created for you. However, if you are applying to fill an opening that already exists, you needn't have any qualms about personnel offices.

STARTING OUT IN A SALARIED JOB

If you want a job in writing, editing, or some writing-related field, keep in mind that you will likely have to start out at or near the bottom. Typical entry-level positions include copy aide, proofreader, editorial assistant, and secretary.

Being a secretary or assistant is actually one of the fastest ways into many jobs. Let's say, for example, that you want to work in public relations, but you have no PR experience. When a public relations firm advertises for a secretary, apply for the job. If you get it, you will suddenly find yourself in the midst of lots of public relations activity. Within a few months you are going to know, through observation and osmosis, a great deal about the public relations business.

More important, if you do good work as a secretary, and can show that you are intelligent, capable, and interested in PR work, it is quite likely that you'll be given some PR duties and/or PR training. If you perform these duties well, you'll be given more and more PR responsibilities; eventually you'll know enough about public relations to apply for a full-fledged PR job yourself, either within your own firm or elsewhere. You may even get promoted automatically.

None of this is likely to happen unless you ask for it. So, either when you first apply for a secretarial job or soon after you've gotten it, let people (particularly your immediate superior) know that you'd like to learn the business and be given some responsibilities in that area. If you're not given such responsibilities and/or training at first, let the matter drop and do your secretarial job as well as you can. Then, after a few months, bring the subject up again. Once you've proven yourself to be bright and competent, you should have little trouble getting the increased responsibility—and you're on your way to the job you really want.

INTERNSHIPS AND VOLUNTEER WORK

If there is a particular salaried job you would like to land, or a particular field in which you want to work, there are two ways in through back doors: doing an internship and taking a volunteer position.

An internship will teach you a great deal about a field or job; give you contacts within an organization, some of whom may later be used as references; and earn you valuable experience, which can be put on your resumé and used to land a regular job in the field. Best of all, if you do good work as an intern, the organization may offer you a part- or full-time job when your internship runs out. The only negative aspect of being an intern is that most internships do not pay a salary.

If you call up someone at a corporation and say, "I'd like to get some experience in the ———— field. Can I work for you one day a week without pay?" the answer will almost always be no. But if you call up that same person and say, "I'm a student at ———— College and I'm interested in doing an internship with your organization," chances are fairly good that he or she will say, "Sounds interesting; come in and we'll talk about it."

To arrange an internship, locate the firm or firms you wish to work for; then determine the name and position of the person(s) you will want to work under. If you want to work as an editorial assistant, for example, contact an editor, explain that you're a student with an interest in editing and publishing, and that you're interested in doing an internship in the field.

To make such a statement true, go to your nearest state-supported college or university, or your nearest community college, and enroll as a nondegree undergraduate. This should be easy to do, as nondegree enrollment is usually open to everyone. (It makes no difference if you are 45 years old—or even 65. Colleges will let you enroll as a nondegree student regardless of your age, and employers know that college students nowadays can be any age.) Find the department that is most appropriate for the internship you have in mind. If you want to do an internship in public relations, the English and business departments would both be good possibilities. Fill out a registration form and register for a one-credit internship; this should cost you no more than $75, probably much less.

All you need now is a teacher to sponsor your internship. Speak to some faculty members in the appropriate department until you find one who will act as your sponsor. Be friendly and polite, and you should have little trouble.

There is another option for internships. A number of organizations (including publishers, public relations firms, advertising agencies, and many others) regularly offer internships of their own making to college students. Announcements for internships are normally posted on bulletin boards in or near the relevant college department. Writing, editing, and publishing internships are usually posted in or near the departments of English, creative writing, or journalism. Some colleges even have special internship offices, which keep on file lists of organizations that regularly take on interns.

It is also possible to earn valuable experience as an outright volunteer at some organizations. This is not an option at most profit-making firms, where people are very suspicious of (and even threatened by) anyone who offers them something for nothing. But nonprofit organizations and very small firms are often willing to take on part-time volunteers, who gain professional training and experience in exchange for their free labor. A nearby hospital's publications department, the local writers' center, a nearby university press, or an independent literary agent might be willing to have you work as a part-time volunteer if you can show that you're both intelligent and energetic.

In most respects, seeking an internship or volunteer position is very similar to job-hunting. For example, in each case it is important to approach the right person. Your initial contact by mail or phone should lead to a meeting or interview, at which the internship can be discussed. This interview should be treated like a job interview: dress appropriately, and bring a resumé with you.

The length and working hours of an internship or volunteer position are usually negotiable. Arrangements can be made to work as few as five hours a week, and as many as forty.

If you have worked as an intern or volunteer, you should of course include this experience on your resumé. However, don't call yourself an intern or volunteer; if your duties were those of, say, a copy editor, call yourself a copy editor. Nor do you need to mention that your position was part-time or unpaid. If you're asked about these things during a job interview, be honest; otherwise, remain silent about them.

USEFUL TIPS

Keep the following tips in mind while marketing your talents and services:

• When you meet with white-collar professionals, dress as you would for a job interview, and carry your papers and materials in an attache case or classy-looking leather folder.

• A telephone answering machine will enable potential clients to reach you at all times. This can make the difference between getting a freelance job and being passed over for it. A simple model costs less than $50, and it will pay for itself after recording one or two important calls.

• Whenever you complete and turn in a freelance job of any kind, give your client an invoice requesting payment within 14 or 30 days. Or you can simply type *Now due* on the invoice. Use your business stationery or plain paper for preparing invoices. If necessary, follow up with a "past due" invoice after thirty days. If your client is an organization rather than an individual, address your invoices to the accounts payable department. (See pages 140–42 for more details on invoices.)

• It is neither necessary nor cost-effective to get a separate business phone number for your freelance work. Nor is it worth being listed in the Yellow Pages.

• You do not need to be licensed or registered in any way to open up shop as a freelance editor, writer, researcher, teacher, translator, or other writing professional.

• You do not need to charge sales tax on any service you provide to anyone for a fee.

• Most salaried writing and writing-related jobs require a B.A. or B.S. in English, journalism, creative writing, or some writing-related field. In some cases, however, a bachelor's degree in any field will do; in some others, if you can demonstrate that you are energetic, intelligent, and a good writer, you may be able to get by without a college degree at all.

• If you wish to teach English or writing in a public school (grades K–12), you will normally need a teaching certificate acceptable in the relevant state. This certificate is *not* necessary for teaching in a private school.

• If you are looking for a *salaried* job, certain expenses (employment agency fees, transportation expenses, and the costs of preparing a resumé) are deductible on your federal income tax. However, these are deductible only on Schedule A, which is to be used only if you choose to itemize your deductions, and certain limitations apply. You must be looking for a new job in the same occupation as your previous job to qualify for this deduction. For details, contact the IRS or refer to its Publication 17.

• *All* your legitimate business expenses as a freelancer, including those incurred in drumming up freelance work, are 80 to 100 percent deductible on your federal income tax, Schedule C. See pages 426–33 for details.

USEFUL RESOURCES

Here are some resources that can be helpful in your search for writing and writing-related jobs.

• Two useful and thorough, if rather general, books on writing and writing-related careers are *Career Opportunities for Writers,* by Rosemary Guiley (Facts on File) and *Freelance Jobs for Writers,* edited by Kirk Polking and also published under the title *Jobs for Writers* (Writer's Digest Books). The latter volume is out of print but still available in libraries. Both offer overviews of dozens of traditional and nontraditional writing and writing-related occupations.

• Classified ads from firms and individuals that want to hire writers, editors, researchers, and other people with writing-related skills regularly appear in the back of *Publishers Weekly.*

• *Folio* magazine (6 Riverbend, Box 4949, Stamford, CT 06907), the professional journal for magazine publishing, also regularly runs ads for jobs in publishing, as well as for writing and writing-related jobs outside the industry.

• *Editor and Publisher* magazine (11 W. 19th Street, New York, NY 10011), the trade journal of newspaper publishing, publishes want ads for journalists in each weekly issue.

• *The Chronicle of Higher Education* (1255 23rd Street NW, Washington, DC 20037) regularly publishes ads for jobs in writing, editing, public relations, and other writing-related areas. Many, though not all, of these jobs are in academia. The *Chronicle* is published weekly.

• The New York local of the National Writers Union (see page 383 for details) offers a telephone job bank *for union members only.* This is a recorded announcement, updated regularly, of part- and full-time salaried and freelance jobs in writing, editing, researching, and other writing-related fields in or near New York. Some other local branches of the Writers Union also offer job banks for their areas.

• *The National Arts Job Bank* (207 Shelby Street, Suite 200, Santa Fe, NM 87501) publishes a wide range of job opportunities for writers and editors. Most of these are with the arts, public service organizations, or academia. This newsletter is published biweekly.

• *Writer's Digest,* the *Modern Language Association Job List* (see page 190), and the *Associated Writing Programs Job List* (see page 190) also run a few help-wanted ads fairly regularly, as do other writers' magazines and newsletters.

• People and organizations seeking to hire writers, editors, and other writing-related professionals often post notices at writers' centers and in or near college and university English, journalism, and creative writing department offices.

• Small lists of advertising agencies and public relations firms that do a fair amount of work for the publishing industry appear in *Literary Market Place* and *Magazine Industry Market Place.* These lists may be useful if you are interested in working in the publishing industry, advertising, or public relations.

• The National Education Service Center (Box 1279, Riverton, WY 82501) publishes a regular newsletter that lists openings for teaching jobs, including those in English and writing, on the elementary school through college level.

• Teachers & Writers Collaborative (5 Union Square West, New York, NY 10003) regularly hires writers to teach workshops and serve as writers-in-residence in and near New York City. Teachers & Writers publishes and distributes a wide variety of books on teaching creative writing and writing in general. It also publishes a regular magazine, *Teachers & Writers.*

• An excellent guide to job-hunting and careers in general is Richard Nelson Bolles's *What Color Is Your Parachute?* (Ten Speed Press).

7. ✎ ─────────────────────────────────

Building Your Reputation and Career

THE STEPPING-STONE PRINCIPLE

All of us have heard stories in which success seemingly fell into writers' laps. The first published books by Joseph Heller, Robert Pirsig, Judith Guest, and Mario Puzo, for example, all became best-sellers. What we *don't* hear about, though, are the years of effort that went into those books; or the many unpublished pieces those writers wrote before their blockbusters were published; or the number of major publishers that rejected some of these best-sellers before one finally agreed to take a gamble. Robert Pirsig's *Zen and the Art of Motorcycle Maintenance* was rejected over one hundred times. Viking Press held onto Judith Guest's *Ordinary People* for close to nine months before deciding to buy it. Joseph Heller's *Catch-22* did not sell especially well for the first couple of years after it was published.

While success has come quickly and magically for a few writers, for the vast majority of us success comes only as the result of hard work, persistence, chutzpah, and a little bit of luck.

Nothing can guarantee success for any writer. However, it *is* possible to carefully, deliberately, and systematically build your writing career. Your odds for success increase dramatically if you take such a step-by-step approach, starting small and slowly but steadily working your way upward, building on your previous accomplishments.

At any given time, your efforts should be focused primarily toward climbing *one step* higher, not jumping several steps at once or making a sudden leap to the top. If you have published articles in local publications, for example, most of your marketing energy should go toward submitting your work to special-interest national magazines, and/or to newspapers and magazines in other locales. There's no harm in shipping off an occasional piece to *Harper's* or *Ms.*, but you would be unrealistic to expect anything other than a rejection from either of these publications at this stage. However, if you have published several pieces in, say, *Working Woman* and *The Mother Earth News,* then magazines like *Ms.* might be within reach.

Keep in mind that even when you are firmly established at a given level, moving up to the next level is not often easy.

FINDING YOUR NICHE

What is it you know that nobody else knows?
What can you do that nobody else can?
What perspective do you have that is different or special?
What ideas do you have that are new or unique?

Make a list of possible answers to each of the questions above; then see if one or more of those answers provides some direction for your writing.

Have you developed a way to train cats to do tricks? Are you capable of writing African history in a manner that would appeal to a general readership? Can you put into words what it's like to grow up in the Alaskan wilderness? Can you see and express the humor in working in a morgue? If you have something unique to say, or some unique way of saying it, this could be your key to success. Writers as diverse as Erma Bombeck, William Faulkner, e.e. cummings, Philip Roth, Barbara Tuchman, Andy Rooney, Jorge Luis Borges, and Art Buchwald have built successful writing careers around their own special interests, approaches, viewpoints, or insights.

Don't put all your eggs in a single basket, though. Keep your options open. Feel free to pursue three or four different directions at once, so that you can choose whichever one(s) seem to be generating the most editorial enthusiasm—and so you've got a way to bail out if certain directions prove unproductive.

CREATING WRITING OPPORTUNITIES

One of the best and fastest ways to advance your writing career is to suggest to an editor or publisher that you write a column or regular feature for his or her publication. This enables you to achieve regular publication, build a readership, get your name known, and establish an ongoing relationship with an editor all at once.

Look back at the list you made of things that make you and/or your writing special. Is there a way to turn one or more of the items on that list into a column or regular feature?

The higher you aim, the more likely you are to be rejected, so your best bet is to start out small. Some excellent places are your neighborhood or suburban newspaper, your city's weekly entertainment newspaper or magazine, and other local publications.

It is perfectly acceptable to approach more than one publication at once with a column or feature idea; but it is *not* okay to write similar or identical columns for competing publications—that is, publications with the same or overlapping readerships—unless, of course, both publications agree to this.

One of my writing students approached several different local publications—all of them free, advertiser-supported weeklies—with about half a dozen different column ideas. Two of the magazines each liked a different idea, and for some time she wrote a weekly feature for each magazine, earning a total of $100 a week for a few hours of work—even though, until then, she wasn't widely published.

There's no standard way to go about suggesting a column or regular feature to an editor. If the publication is not based nearby, your best bet is usually to write up two or three sample columns and send them to the editor, along with a letter explaining their focus, intent, and likely audience. If the publication is a local one, you may prefer to give the editor or publisher a call to discuss your idea over the phone, or to set up an in-person meeting. (Make an appointment in advance; don't just drop in.) Again, present the editor with two or more sample columns or features.

There is nothing wrong with suggesting ideas for two or three different columns or features at once to the same editor or publisher.

It often works to suggest a new or additional direction for a publication. If your city has a weekly arts magazine, suggest to the editor that you write a cooking column for that magazine, since cooking is, after all, an art. If you write humor, suggest to the editor of your suburban newspaper that you write a regular humor feature for its lifestyle section.

THE FAST TRACK TO SUCCESS

Some aspiring writers have no burning desire to say something in particular—only the desire to earn their livings from putting words on paper, and/or to build their writing careers as quickly as possible. I advise most of these writers to find full- or part-time salaried writing (or writing-related) jobs.

For writers of this type who are keen on being freelancers, however, here is a step-by-step formula for freelance writing success:

First, most or all of your writing should be nonfiction. Nonfiction comprises the great majority of all published writing, and it is almost always the easiest material to sell.

Begin by approaching the editor of a small newspaper in your area. This should be your local paper if you live in a small town, a neighborhood paper or suburban weekly if you live in or near a large city. Offer to do some pieces for that paper on a freelance basis. You may need to write these on spec at first, and chances are good that payment will be small or nonexistent. Don't let that stop you. Continue writing for the paper until you can get published in it fairly regularly. You may also wish to offer your services as a part-time editor or layout and pasteup person. Usually this will be an unpaid, volunteer job.

Next, send some of your work to other local magazines, or suggest some assignments to the editors of those publications. Likely candidates here include weekly entertainment and arts publications, the Sunday supplement of your city newspaper, and, if your city has one, the slick monthly magazine that bears your city's name. When approaching the editors of these publications, be sure to mention your publications in the local paper. Include photocopies of some of your best published pieces. Here again, you may have to begin by writing on spec. Your goal is now to write regularly for one or more of these local magazines.

Once you've published several articles in local magazines, submit some pieces to national magazines oriented to specific subjects (coin collecting, cars, dogs, health, architecture, etc.). Always mention your previous publications in your cover letters. You might also try sending some pieces to feature editors at newspapers and Sunday magazines in other medium-size and large cities, particularly the ones near your home. You may suggest or request some assignments, although you should expect at least the first couple of sales to these publications to be freelance submissions or pieces written on spec.

Once you've sold a few pieces to national magazines, your next step is to write a book proposal using the guidelines in Chapter 9. *By far* the most salable book projects are how-to books, which show readers step-by-step how to complete a project, learn a skill, accomplish a task, or improve their lives. But for such a proposal to be salable, it must be unique in a way that is both significant and obvious. Books that take a material rather than a psychological approach are generally more salable. For example, *How to Survive Freshman Composition—and Earn a Higher Grade* is more salable than *How to Avoid College Burnout.* (I wrote and sold the former volume.) Other general nonfiction projects with new or unique themes or approaches are also often salable, though less so than how-to volumes.

Once you've completed the book proposal, contact some agents, following the guidelines in Chapter 8. Once an agent agrees to represent the proposal, move on to the next project—some more short pieces, and/or another book proposal. If you can't or choose not to get an agent for the project, market it yourself according to the guidelines in Chapter 2.

If you can write nonfiction reasonably well, and continue to have new and unique ideas for book projects, there is no reason why you cannot write and sell one nonfiction book proposal after another. A fair number of successful writers have done just this.

Keep these things in mind, however:

• No matter how good your ideas and proposals are, they are not all likely to sell. This is a basic fact of publishing life.

• Projects that do sell are likely to receive advances of $3000 to $10,000, with $7000 being about average. These sums aren't going to make you rich; but the royalties and money from the sales of subsidiary rights can mount up after the initial advance is earned back. Typically, however, you won't begin to see any of this money until fifteen to twenty-four months after delivery of a completed manuscript.

• Once you sell a book proposal, you still have to write the book, which means that much or most of your work is still ahead of you. Don't write and sell so many proposals that you've got more work than you can handle.

TO QUIT OR NOT TO QUIT YOUR JOB

A lot of aspiring writers are tempted to save some money, dump their jobs, and then work furiously to become full-time self-supporting freelancers. Some stout-hearted souls try to skip the step of saving money.

This approach has plenty of romantic appeal, but it is extremely unrealistic, and usually rather stupid. It takes most freelancers at least a few years, and frequently closer to a decade, to become fully self-supporting. Many writers who have quit their jobs too soon regret that decision when they find themselves looking for jobs again.

Your income from writing is likely to be zero, or close to zero, during your first year as a freelancer, and probably not a great deal more for one to three years thereafter. Don't gamble that you'll be that rarest of rarities—the writer who achieves immediate financial success. If you *do* somehow beat the odds and suddenly make a bundle of money, you can always give your employer two weeks' notice the next morning.

Quitting your job before you begin earning substantial sums from your freelancing *can* work if you have saved enough money to support yourself and your family for five years or more; if you have investments that will keep you and your family going; or if you can get a friend, relative, foundation, or other sympathetic person or organization to provide financial support until you can earn a living freelancing. If not, *keep your job*—or at least *some* job. Write in your free time and, if possible, let your hours as an employee decrease as your freelancing income grows. If your employer will not allow you to reduce your hours, ask about the possibility of job-sharing, where two (or more) people split the duties, hours, responsibilities, and pay of a single job.

Another option is working as a temporary. Temporary employment agencies match qualified workers with short-term assignments; as a temporary, you have the choice of working when you wish, and of turning down any temporary assignment. Jobs are available in many fields, including clerical and secretarial. Temporary agencies are usually listed under "Employment Contractors—Temporary Help" or "Employment Agencies—Temporary Help" in the Yellow Pages.

Substitute teaching is another viable option for writers. As a substitute, you can usually work as little or as much as you wish, and the pay is usually decent. In most cases, all you need are a bachelor's degree and a willingness to get up very early. Contact your local public school district(s) and/or private schools for details.

MAKING YOURSELF VISIBLE

Visibility is an important part of career-building. Here are some things you can do to become more visible to readers, editors and publishers, other writers in your field, and other people in publishing:

• Join the professional organizations for each writing field in which you are active (for example, Aviation/Space Writers Association, Associated Business Writers of America, or The Dramatists Guild).
• Volunteer to help with some of the routine tasks of these organiza-

tions—typing, answering the phone, responding to mail inquiries, orienting new members, helping organize events, and so on. Volunteer to work for, or be a member of, a committee. After you've been a member for a year or two, offer to chair a committee. After a couple of years, run for office in one of these organizations. But don't run for president, or for any other office normally reserved for senior members.

• Attend some of the regional or national meetings, banquets, conferences, or conventions that one of your writers' organizations holds.

• Join your local writers' club or center. Attend some of its meetings or events. Offer to help with some of its activities, or with some of its day-to-day tasks. Volunteer for one or more of its committees. Offer to give a lecture or reading, or to teach a class.

• Read the publications put out by the organizations discussed above. Offer to write one or more articles for these publications. After you've been a member for a year or so, offer to become an editorial assistant for one of them. This is one of the best ways to become visible quickly and make useful contacts within a particular field or locale.

• Get yourself listed in one or more of the directories mentioned below. Editors, publishers, producers, and other people often use these guides to locate writers and writing-related professionals. This will not only make you more visible, it will make your services as a writer widely available.

ASJA Directory   Published by the American Society of Journalists and Authors, 1501 Broadway, Suite 1907, New York, NY 10036. You must be a member of ASJA to be listed. To be a member you must have published a considerable amount of nonfiction. No charge for listings.

Directory of American Poets and Fiction Writers   Published by Poets & Writers, Inc., 201 W. 54th Street, New York, NY 10019. Open to poets and fiction writers. There is a minimum publication or production requirement. No charge for listings, but there is a one-time $5 fee to *apply* to be listed. A simultaneous listing in the Poets & Writers computer data bank is included.

Plays and Playwrights   Published by The International Society of Dramatists, Box 1310, Miami, FL 33153. Open to all playwrights, both produced and unproduced. No charge for listings.

Professional Freelance Writers Directory   Published by the National Writers Club, 1450 S. Havana, Suite 620, Aurora, CO 80012. Open only to Professional Members of the NWC. There is a minimum publication or production requirement. There is a $10 charge for listings.

The Working Press of the Nation   Published by the National Research Bureau, 310 S. Michigan Avenue, Chicago, IL 60604. There is a minimum publication requirement. No charge for listings.

To be listed in any of the resources above, write a brief letter expressing your desire to be included in the next edition. Enclose a resumé and/or list of your publications or productions. It is a good idea to mention in your letter your areas of writing interest and expertise (for example, fiction, travel articles, or health books).

If you can offer your services as a freelance editor, ghostwriter, book packager, public relations specialist, researcher, translator, or other writing-related professional, you may qualify for a separate listing in *Literary Market Place* and/or *Magazine Industry Market Place*. There is no charge for a listing. Write R. R. Bowker, 245 W. 17th Street, New York, NY 10011.

The following directories also publish information on writers. These books, however, are for writers who have already achieved some measure of success. Normally writers are listed only by invitation from the publisher, often through the recommendation of an editor, agent, or other third party. However, once you've built up sufficient credentials (for example, published a book, had a couple of off-Broadway plays produced, or published ten short pieces in magazines like *Harper's* and *Ms.*), it can't hurt to contact the publisher, explain what you've had published or produced, and ask to be included.

All of these directories publish both a brief biography and a bibliography for each author. There is no charge for listings.

Contemporary Authors (Gale Research)

Contemporary Poets (St. Martin's Press)

International Authors and Writers Who's Who (International Biographical Centre/Melrose Press)

Something About the Author (Gale Research). This work lists writers of material for children and young adults.

Who's Who in America (Marquis). There are also regional volumes, such as *Who's Who in the Midwest*, published by the same publisher.

Who's Who in U.S. Writers, Editors, and Poets (December Press)

The Writers Directory (St. James Press)

• Get your name known, and make your services available to editors, producers, and other people looking for writers, through a writers' referral service. The best-known of these is Writer Data Bank, Cassell Communications, Box 9844, Ft. Lauderdale, FL 33310, (800) 351-9278. Listings cost $25 a year, plus a 5 percent commission on any freelance jobs obtained directly from Data Bank referrals.

Be sure to update your listings in the above books and service whenever you change your address or phone number, or whenever you have additional major publications or productions.

OTHER TIPS FOR BUILDING A WRITING CAREER

The following tips will help you further your career as a writer:

• Be sure to let editors, publishers, and potential clients and employers know of your relevant writing success. If you are making an initial contact by phone or in person, include your most important credentials as you introduce yourself. For example: "Ms. Fleming? My name is Wanda Gold. I've published short pieces in several women's magazines, and I write a regular column for *American Artist.*" If you have to leave a message, leave your name, phone number, reason for calling, *and most important credentials.*

• One of the fastest and easiest ways to break into a publication (especially a small or local one) is to write reviews of books, movies, plays, records, visual art, fashion, restaurants, or whatever. While it certainly helps to have already been published, or to have some background or credentials in the field in which you are reviewing, with small publications often an interest and some basic writing ability are enough. Many writers do one or two reviews on spec; if these are intelligent and readable, they get published, and the writer continues reviewing for that publication. Local magazines and newspapers are usually open to reviews by new writers; the national magazines *The Bloomsbury Review* and *Library Journal* are always looking for book reviews by new writers.

• Don't be afraid to try unusual or out-of-the-way publications. Trade and professional journals, in-house newsletters, and even university publications may turn out to be viable markets. Public agencies such as the U.S.

Information Agency, the Department of Agriculture, or your local Chamber of Commerce may also be willing to buy (and even assign) freelance material.

• If you are just beginning your writing career, there is nothing wrong with publishing some pieces in publications that pay their writers nothing but free copies. However, if a publication does normally pay its writers, *never* offer your work or services to that publication for nothing. Whatever rate of payment a publication sets as its minimum, expect and insist on at least that minimum payment for your work.

• As much as possible, use the same name or pseudonym for all your published work, at least within any one field. The more work that appears under the same name, the more likely people are to recognize that name when they see it again. Similarly, avoid using different variations of your name, which could confuse readers, editors, and librarians.

• Remember that in many cases you can sell the same piece over and over. Newspapers are particularly open to publishing reprints; a piece that appeared in, say, the Minneapolis *Tribune* might well sell to ten or even twenty other newspapers, at $25 to $200 a crack.

• Write spinoffs. These are projects that are similar in content or concept to other projects you've written, but with a different slant, focus, or audience. Usually writing a spinoff requires little extra time and little or no additional research; it's simply a matter of presenting the same information or idea in a different way. For instance, if you've written a piece for a travel magazine called "Keeping Your Kids Happy on Trips," a minor rewrite might make it appropriate for a woman's magazine, under the title "Motherhood on Wheels." Another minor rewrite for an airline magazine might result in "Flying with Kids." Sometimes a spinoff can be more successful than the original project.

Spinoffs are considered new pieces, not reprints of earlier material, and they should receive the same rates of payment as other new pieces. Some writers, when approached by an editor to sell reprint rights to a piece, will suggest a spinoff piece with a new slant instead.

• Write sequels, follow-ups, and other such projects. If your book *Dogs of the Stars: Canine Companions of Hollywood's Biggest Celebrities* becomes a best-seller, you might want to write *Cats of the Stars*, and perhaps even *Farrah's Ferret and Seventeen Other Unusual Celebrity Pets*. The more successful a particular project is, the more likely a publisher or producer is to buy a sequel, and the more money and attention you are likely to earn from that sequel.

• Whenever a publication requests biographical information about you, send this information promptly. Make yourself sound as good as possible without lying, and be sure to mention all your appropriate publications and other credentials—and anything else that might interest readers. If you are sent a questionnaire, answer all its questions thoroughly. Add any additional information you think might be appropriate. *Anything* newsworthy about yourself is usually worth mentioning.

• If a publication requests a photograph of you, send one promptly. The photo should be taken by an experienced photographer with a 35mm camera. Unless you're informed otherwise, the photo should be black and white. It should make you look good, and, if possible, it should show you in an environment reminiscent of something in your piece. It's a good idea to send two or three different photos (at least one vertical and at least one horizontal), so that the publisher can pick the most appropriate shot.

• If you publish a book, send free copies to your contacts in the publishing world (particularly those who have been of help to you), to people in publishing you'd *like* to make contact with, to writers of your acquaintance, to writers you don't know but whose work you admire, and to anyone else you think can be helpful to your career. No accompanying note is necessary, though a short, simple one is permissible. You may invite comments, but don't outright ask for them. Staple your business card to the first page of each book, or at least write your name and phone number on each copy. If a play of yours is in production, send these people sets of tickets (always send tickets in sets of two)—again along with your business card.

• If your book, play, or movie will debut shortly, try to publish shorter material on the same or similar themes, or in the same genre, or for the same audience before your major work appears. These short pieces will help generate interest and attention in your longer work. Be sure to ask that some mention of your new book, movie, or play be made in the biographical note published with each piece.

• If time is a problem for you but money isn't, hire a publicist to publicize you and your work. Publicists can drum up attention for authors quite well, but they are usually expensive. A comprehensive list of publicists appears in *Literary Market Place.* (Details on publicists appear on page 301; the discussion relates to books but applies to other literary forms as well.)

If you want to do your own publicity, you should consult these excellent books on self-promotion and publicity:

Publicity for Books and Authors, by Peggy Glenn (Aames-Allen Publishing Company).

The Unabashed Self-Promoter's Guide, by Jeffrey Lant (JLA Publications, 50 Follen Street, Suite 507, Cambridge, MA 02138).

• Special tips on promoting your own book appear on pages 298–304.

THE LONG HAUL

When do you stop building your writing career? There are two answers: (1) never; and (2) when you have all the fame and fortune you can handle. For most writers, the two answers are synonymous.

Here are some additional things you can do to keep building your career once you have become reasonably well known in one or more fields of writing:

• Write cover quotes and endorsements for other writers' books.
• Review books in your field (and other fields) for magazines in and outside of your field, and for the nearest big-city newspaper.
• Write introductions for books by other writers whose work you enjoy or admire.
• Attend national and regional meetings and conferences of people in your field. Volunteer or apply to make presentations at these meetings or conferences.
• Go on a national reading or lecture tour every couple of years.
• Give a reading or lecture locally at least once a year.
• Do a benefit lecture, reading, or presentation for some charity, organization, or cause you believe in. Simply contact the organization and volunteer.
• Make local and national TV and radio appearances. Grant interviews to local and national media.
• Do book signings, both in your home town and elsewhere.

Although there is some tendency for a writing career to build momentum on its own, that momentum can get used up. It is often a big mistake to rest on your laurels, even if you have begun to make it big. When writers are on the way up, or at the top, they often think things will only keep getting better. But all too easily a writing career can peak, then fizzle out. A once-popular writer can become a has-been, even a poor has-been. You can avoid this by continuing to write, make and use contacts in publishing, and promote yourself to your readers.

8. ✎

Literary Agents:
The Complete Lowdown

THE AGENT'S ROLE

A literary agent (also called an author's representative) is a liaison between you and publishers and/or producers. Your agent will talk up you and your work, submit your projects to editors, negotiate details on your behalf, and in general serve as your advocate and representative in the publishing world.

Like publishers, agents are in business primarily or entirely to make money. While they may be interested in good literature and fine writing, their primary interest is in what sells—particularly what sells big and what sells fast. Like publishers and editors, they will be interested in you and your work precisely to the degree to which you can help them make money. The more money you can help them make (or they think you can help them make), the better they will generally treat you.

This may seem crass for people who represent writers, not publishers. But the fact is that, in a sense, agents represent publishers as well. Agents feel that their job is not to convince publishers to publish the best work possible, but to supply those publishers with exactly what they ask for, while at the same time securing for their writers the most money and best terms for that material. From a publisher's point of view, an agent procures talent and material and screens out writers who cannot turn out the kind of material the publisher seeks to publish.

Because good agents make their living solely from commissions, they will only represent work that is likely to sell to commercial publishers and producers. Some of the most prominent agents will represent only writers who earn more than $100,000 a year from their writing. And a few agents have enough profitable writers as clients that they don't take on new clients at all.

A good agent has these talents and resources: hundreds of contacts in publishing, television, film, and/or theater; the ability to deal effectively both with writers and with people in the publishing world; the ability to negotiate deals that are beneficial to (and acceptable by) all parties; plenty of know-how about the publishing and/or producing business; and a knack for knowing what material will appeal to which editors and publishers, and how much that material is worth to those publishers. As one high-level publishing executive once said, "What a good agent really knows how to do is find the right editor for the right book at the right house."

Any decent agent has far more contacts in publishing than most writers can hope to make in a lifetime. In fact, a great portion of an agent's time is spent making, reinforcing, and using those contacts. A good agent devotes regular time to lunching and dining with editors and publishers, attending publishing functions, giving and attending parties for publishing folk, and talking to editors on the phone. A great deal of business is conducted at these lunches, dinners, meetings, and parties.

Literary agents tend to reflect publishing trends almost as much as publishers and producers. If humor is big this season, and publishers are all scrambling to buy humor books, you can bet that's what agents will be scrambling to find, too. If humor is suddenly perceived by many publishers as a poor risk, few agents are going to represent humor books. They'll even tell hopeful humor writers, "Sorry, but humor is dead." (They'd be wrong, of course; a genre or topic rarely dies; usually it's just hibernating.) Agents rarely set (or even affect) publishing trends.

Many newer writers think that once they have agents, their troubles are over. This is not so. No agent is a miracle worker. A good agent can get your work to the most appropriate publishers and producers, get that work read in the most favorable light possible, and swing the best possible deal (almost always a better deal than you can arrange alone) *if* a publisher wants to buy the material. But no agent, not even the best one, can get editors to publish something they don't want to publish. In fact, much of the material an agent represents typically does *not* sell. Agents play the percentages, knowing that if they sell half the projects they represent, they're doing well. Most agents regularly take on new clients and new projects, and periodically get rid of those that aren't turning a decent profit.

Although you may wind up becoming friends with your agent, just as you may with an editor, your relationship will always be first and foremost a business one. Your agent will normally expect you to be concise and businesslike. Although no decent agent will neglect you, your agent's contact with you will be limited to the amount necessary to serve you properly. The less of your work your agent sells, the less contact with you will normally be necessary.

Your agent will expect you to sit tight while your work is being sent around. No agent likes to get eager phone calls that begin, "Have we had any luck yet?" When an offer has been made, your agent will get in touch promptly. Until then you're unlikely to hear much from him or her. It's fine to call or write three or four times a year to find out how things are going and what has been submitted (and/or rejected) where; but once a week, or even once a month, can be downright annoying. Trust your agent to do his or her job. If you don't have this trust in your agent, chances are you need a new one.

Although it is helpful to have previous publications or productions under your belt, it is quite possible to get an agent even if you've never published anything before. Since agents are interested in making money, they are willing to represent *any* projects they feel are salable. There has been a trend in favor of new writers in recent years. While some agents seek to represent only "career" writers, an increasing number are willing to take on a client on the basis of a single salable project, even if that writer has published nothing before and is unlikely to write another book or script.

WHO NEEDS AN AGENT?

In general, you need an agent if you wish to sell any of the following:

- A book or book proposal to be marketed to a major trade book publisher
- A full-length or one-act play intended for major production
- Anything to be marketed to major film producers
- Anything to be sold to major television producers and/or the networks

There are a few exceptions to this rule. Some major book publishers, and a few producers of plays, films, and TV shows, are willing to look at unagented material. Unagented books and proposals for children and young adults, and for adult readers of science fiction, mysteries, romances, male adventure, horror novels, and westerns, are normally given serious consideration by some (though by no means all) major presses that regularly publish books in these fields. And if you have an appropriate contact in any area of publishing, you may be able to have your work read without an agent's introduction.

However, major publishers and producers generally buy very little unagented material. If your work is agented, you are far more likely to receive serious consideration, your work is more likely to be accepted, and you are almost guaranteed better terms if a deal is made. Many of the larger trade book publishers, and most producers of TV, film, and major dramatic productions will return unagented material unread—possibly with a rejection slip that begins, "We have read the enclosed carefully."

If you have written a book or proposal that is appropriate for textbook, scholarly, professional, special-interest, literary, or smaller trade publishers, then an agent is not strictly necessary. One may be helpful, however. Some agents will represent a few books of these sorts; some will not. Often it depends on the book; if an agent believes it will sell a large number of copies over time, and/or earn a sizeable advance, then it is worth his or her while to represent it. If the project isn't much of a potential moneymaker, however, you will probably have to sell it yourself.

Some agents handle only TV and film scripts; some handle only books; some handle only plays; and some handle two or more of these types of literary properties. Some book agents specialize in certain areas or genres, such as science fiction or children's books. Some book agents also handle columns for syndication. Several agents in New York and Los Angeles specialize in computer software, and a few handle both software and literary properties.

Except under extraordinary circumstances, agents will *not* represent the following types of projects:

• Articles and essays
• Advertising copy
• Poetry, both individual poems and book-length collections
• Short stories or short-story collections, except by writers who are well known or who have strong publication records
• Greeting cards
• Cartoons, gags, ideas, or catch-phrases

In general, agents will not handle such material even if they represent you for books, plays, or TV or film scripts. The reason is simple: there's little or no money in it. *If,* for some reason, an agent feels he or she can make several hundred dollars or more selling your article or short story to *The New Yorker, Cosmopolitan,* or some other national magazine, then he or she *may* agree to take it on. In most cases, though, you will have to sell this material yourself.

There is one general exception to this: many agents will attempt to sell serial rights to excerpts from books that they have placed with book publishers.

WHAT MAKES SOMEONE A GOOD AGENT?

No two agents—not even two excellent agents—are alike in their personalities, contacts, or ways of doing business. The same agents who receive the highest praise from some of their clients (and who often manage to close astonishingly good deals for those clients) also receive the lowest ratings from other people they have worked with. The relationship between each author and each agent is unique, and the agent that may be perfect for Fred may be the worst possible one for Ethel.

However, there are some things all good agents have in common. All are reasonably prompt in reading and responding to material, and in getting that material out to editors and producers. All are reasonably available to both editors and authors by phone. All are responsive to questions, particularly, "What else have you sold, and to whom?" and "Where have you sent my manuscript, and who has rejected it so far?" All will work hard to make and keep useful contacts, to know the likes and dislikes of those contacts, to negotiate the best deals they can for their writers, and to look out for their writers' interests. All will vigorously push the works of *all* their authors, including the new and lesser-known ones. None will give up on a manuscript until they have given it a decent chance; normally this means until it has received at least fifteen rejections. All will pay their authors promptly and in full. None will insist on a kickback on earnings from sales you have made without their assistance. None will charge reading fees, submission fees, or other fees of any kind, and none will ask that you pay any of their normal business expenses.

There are some excellent agents out there. The majority are fair to middling. There are quite a few who are bloody awful. And there are several who are outright crooks.

An agent needs to make frequent contact with people in the industry. This is why most good book and play agents are in or near New York City and why most good film and TV agents are in Los Angeles. But it is possible to live elsewhere and still be a good agent. In fact, there are some highly effective agents in Chicago, Minneapolis, San Francisco, other large cities, and even a few small towns. However, a good agent must remain in close touch with the New York and/or Hollywood scene, and must make frequent business trips to either or both cities.

Most good book and play agents have Los Angeles affiliates who sell film and TV rights to their clients' work, and many film and TV agents have New York affiliates who sell book rights to scripts. Many of the better agents throughout North America have foreign affiliates (called sub-agents) who sell foreign rights to books and scripts. These affiliates can be of great help to writers in placing their works with foreign publications and earning them additional money.

GETTING AN AGENT

To get an agent, start by talking with other writers, editors, other publishing people, and any other useful contacts you have or can make, including bookstore owners, college creative writing instructors, and staff and members of writers' clubs and organizations. Magazine and newspaper editors with whom you have worked can be especially helpful.

For book authors, directors of writers' conferences can often be extremely helpful. Get a list of these conferences (see pages 389–90), call some of their directors, and say, "I've written a book on ———— and am looking for a good agent who represents work in that field." Much of the time you'll get a quick and useful recommendation.

Even better than having an agent recommended to you is having your work recommended to a good agent. If an editor, fellow writer, or anyone else who personally knows a good agent likes your work, ask him or her to write or call the agent with a recommendation. If an agent agrees to look at your manuscript as the result of someone's recommendation, send it along with a note saying something like. "This is the project Audrey Whitworth told you about, and which you asked to see."

Another useful place to begin looking for agents is the "Rights and Permissions" column that appears in most issues of *Publishers Weekly*. This column details some of the recent deals that have been made in book publishing, television, and film. Usually the names of the agents who made the deals, and the agencies they work for, are mentioned. An agent who made a deal on a book you admire, or a book in the same genre as yours, or a book on a similar subject, may be a good agent to contact.

Another approach to finding the name of the agent who sold a particular book is to call the editorial department of that book's publisher and ask, "Can you tell me what agent sold you ———?" (This approach will not work with TV or film producers.) Agents' names also sometimes appear on the acknowledgments page of books.

There are several good lists of agents:

• *Literary Agents of North America,* by far the best and the most comprehensive list, is published every other year by Author Aid Research Associates, 340 E. 52nd Street, New York, NY 10022.

• An excellent, though less comprehensive, list appears in the reference book *Literary Market Place.* Try to get the most recent edition, as changes occur in agents' offices as regularly as they do in the rest of publishing.

• Much less thorough, but still useful, is the list in *Writer's Market.* Again, try to get the current edition. If agents say in their *Writer's Market* listing that they are not taking on any new clients, don't take this too seriously; they're probably only trying to avoid a flood of manuscripts. It can't hurt to send a query about your project.

• *Literary Agents: A Writer's Guide* includes a small list of some agents. This book is published by Poets & Writers, Inc., 201 W. 54th Street, New York, NY 10019.

• Many, though by no means all, literary agents belong to one of two organizations: the Society of Author's Representatives (10 South Portland Avenue, Brooklyn, NY 11217) or the Independent Literary Agents Association (c/o Ellen Levine, 432 Park Avenue, Suite 1205, New York, NY 10016). No agent belongs to both; some very good agents belong to neither. Each of these organizations will send you a list of its members, including their addresses, on request, provided you enclose a stamped, self-addressed #10 envelope.

• The Dramatists Guild (234 W. 44th Street, New York, NY 10036) publishes a list of agents who handle plays. This list is available free to Guild members. A smaller list of members of the Society of Author's Representatives who handle plays is available to both members and nonmembers, at no charge, on request. A stamped, self-addressed #10 envelope should accompany the request.

• Lists of agents who handle plays also appear in *The Dramatist's Bible* and *Dramatists Sourcebook.* For details on these volumes, see pages 75–76.

• A list of about a hundred agents throughout the United States (but mostly in the Los Angeles area) who handle film and TV scripts is available for $1 postpaid from The Writers Guild, 8955 Beverly Boulevard, West Hollywood, CA 90048. This list is updated every few months.

Except as indicated, the resources listed above include agents throughout the United States and Canada. Most of these resources will indicate what kinds of material each agent handles or specializes in. (Some of these resources use the code letters *L* and *D*. *L* means the agent handles books; *D* means the agent handles scripts; *L-D* means the agent handles both.)

Lists of agents in countries other than the United States and Canada appear in these three reference books: *Directory of Publishing, International Literary Market Place,* and *International Writers' and Artists' Yearbook.* Information on these volumes appears on pages 75–78.

Many literary agencies have more than one agent, each with his or her own clients for whom he or she is solely responsible. As a writer, you may be represented officially by, say, Writers House, but in practice by a specific person at that agency. The same agency may therefore have several terrific agents and a couple of not-so-good ones. Bigger does not necessarily mean better. Although some of the best agents work for large firms, some of the best run their own one-person agencies. My own agent runs her own one-person agency out of a room in her home.

All of this means that you must not only pick a group of agencies to contact, but you must choose one particular agent to approach at each agency. If you have absolutely no way to know which agent to choose at any given agency, play a hunch.

If you must pick some or all of the agents you intend to approach at random or by intuition, only consider those in or near Manhattan (if you have a book, book proposal, or play) or Los Angeles (if you have material for film or television).

You should normally make your initial contact with agents by mail. A face-to-face meeting is fine *if* (and only if) it can be arranged through a contact you have. Keep such a meeting quite brief unless the agent wants it to go on longer; time is money, and your agent has other clients to serve. Making the initial contact by phone is warranted if your manuscript is extremely timely, if your project lends itself well to a brief verbal description, or if you are very good at using the telephone.

If the agent has been recommended to you by someone he or she knows, be sure to mention this at the beginning of your letter or call. If you just picked the agent out of a reference book or printed list, don't bring up the subject of how you got his or her name.

Your initial contact should be primarily devoted to outlining or synopsizing your project. If you are writing a query letter, it should be written in standard business form and style, and no longer than two pages. If your manuscript is fiction, journalism, or some other recounting of events, your letter should be largely composed of a synopsis of the plot or events. If your project is nonfiction, either an outline in narrative form or an annotated table of contents will serve well. For nonfiction projects, also *briefly* explain why your project is useful or important, who it will appeal to, and, most important, why it is special or unique. If you prefer, you may omit the synopsis or outline from the body of your letter and instead enclose it as an attachment. This should be no longer than a few pages. If it is written as narrative, it should be 1½- or double-spaced; if it's more of a list or table of contents, it should be single- or 1½-spaced.

If you have any previous publications, writing awards, or other writing credentials, mention these briefly. If you have any background, training, or expertise relevant to your project, mention this as well. And if you know anyone famous (in any field, for any reason) who will be willing to write an endorsement for the project, say so. Better yet, enclose such an endorsement.

Keep your tone businesslike and your writing concise. Your letter should *not* read like an advertisement or news release. Avoid mentioning who your influences are, what a great writer you are, and how your project is destined to be incredibly popular and a source of enormous income for both you and the agent. Just give the agent the necessary facts.

Wind up your letter by asking if the agent would like to look at the project. Enclose a stamped, self-addressed #10 envelope for a reply. If you like, and it seems appropriate, you may also enclose a resumé.

If you have more than one project, you may discuss two of them in your initial letter or conversation. If you have more than two, mention only the two best or most salable ones. If the agent takes you on as a client, you can then bring him or her additional projects; and if he or she turns down your first two, you can always write again about other manuscripts. In either case, though, don't overwhelm the agent with material.

Two sample letters to agents are reprinted here. Both letters were actually used by writers to approach agents at top agencies; in both cases, the agents expressed interest in the projects, and later represented them.

1220 Taransay Way
Henderson, KY 42420
502-827-3878

July 10, 1985

Mr. Sam Pulletter
The Word Merchants
9886 Lexington Ave.
New York, NY 10009

Dear Mr. Pulletter:

   One out of four families in the U.S. owns a VCR player
or recorder; according to reliable predictions, by 1987
one out of two homes will have a VCR. In 1984, there
were 304 million 24-hour video tape rentals in this
country--an increase of nearly 700% in four years. New
video tapes are coming onto the market at the rate of
100-200 each month. Industry estimates indicate that the
video boom is far from over, and that it will not peak
for several years, if then.

   As a result of all this, video tape rental stores have
become the entrepreneurial success story of the eighties.
One individual or couple, with only a small amount of
money, the willingness to work, and a little bit of common sense, can open and run a video rental store. Such
a store stands a very strong chance of growing quickly,
recouping the initial investment within months, and turning a steady profit thereafter.

   We've completed a proposal for a book called How to
Start and Run Your Own Video Rental Store, which explains
all the ins and outs of the video rental business, from
getting started to choosing and stocking the proper product to solving and avoiding possible problems. The book
will take readers step by step through such topics as
finding an appropriate store location, evaluating the
competition, preparing for the first day of business,
what a typical business day is like, dealing with customers, hiring and firing employees, and keeping income up
and costs down. It will be a complete do-it-yourself kit
for entrepreneurs who are considering opening up video
rental stores of their own. It will also provide useful
tips for readers who already operate video rental stores
and who wish to run their existing businesses more efficiently and profitably.

Ours is the first book on this topic; we have checked all of the appropriate sources carefully and have found no competitive titles.

Two of us, Frances and Rickie Gafford, have run our own video rental store, Preview Video, since the summer of 1984. Since we opened, Preview Video has become the fastest-growing and best-known video rental store in western Kentucky, tripling its business every month for the past eight months. The third member of our writing team, Louis Hatchett, is a writer whose work has appeared in several newspapers.

You were recommended to us as an agent who does a good and reliable job for your clients. If our project interests you, we'd be very happy to send the proposal your way.

Sincerely,

Louis Hatchett

Frances Gafford

Rickie Gafford

7307 W. Franklin Ave.
St. Louis Park, MN 55426
612-541-9827

August 19, 1984

Ms. Susan Example
Hy Pothetical Literary Agency
7244 Madison Ave.
New York, NY 10001

Dear Ms. Example:

I am a mystery writer who has sold five stories to
Hitchcock's Mystery Magazine in the past eighteen months.
The first of these stories appeared in the March 1983
issue; the last is not yet in print.

Two of the stories involve the hero of a murder mystery
I have written entitled MURDER AT THE WAR. The novel is
traditional in structure and set in an "exotic locale"--
a simulated medieval war. Every year 3000-plus members
of the Society for the Advancement of Medievalism gather
at a campground in western Pennsylvania to hold a mock
war. Everyone dresses in medieval garb (including steel
armor for the fighters), and the campground joyously
drops out of the twentieth century for a three-day weekend. During the course of a mock battle in the woods,
however, a man is found dead--really dead, not mock dead.
The woman who finds him becomes the chief suspect. She
also happens to be the wife of Peter Brichter, a police
detective from out of state.

The local law enforcement officers are startled at the
sight of all these oddly-dressed people, and half-con-
vinced they are some kind of cult. Brichter, trying to
clear his wife, begins his own unofficial investigation,
but the local police angrily call a halt to his activities and confine him to his encampment.

Meanwhile, the clues lead to a certain Lord Christopher,
who, dressed in armor, participated in a mock skirmish
beside the victim shortly before the murder. Lord Christopher's armor is found abandoned in the woods near the
body, and it seems that no one had seen or heard of him
before he appeared in the woods, dressed for battle.

All of this suggests that there is, in fact, no Lord
Christopher--that he was a SAM member who assumed that
persona (and armor) as a disguise only for a few minutes, for the specific purpose of killing his victim
and then escaping detection. There were two hundred
participants in the woods battle; any one of them might
have slipped away for a brief time.

While the local police struggle with the esoterica of
the Society, Brichter welcomes visitors in his tent,
fitting the pieces together in classic detective style.

There really is a medievalist society which holds an
annual mock war in Pennsylvania. I am a member, and
drew on my experiences at several of these wars in writing this book.

The novel is in finished form, about 90,000 words long.
Please let me know if you would be interested in reading
it with an eye toward representing it.

Sincerely,

Mary Kuhfeld

I have changed the agents' and agencies' names to hypothetical ones. *Murder at the War,* the novel introduced in the second letter, was sold by the agent to St. Martin's Press and published in 1987.

Write to agents by name in care of their agencies. Your letter should go to Edna McMurray, Sally Stephens Agency, not simply to either Edna McMurray or Sally Stephens Agency.

You may write letters to as many agents at a time as you wish. Ten is a good number. Each letter should be freshly typed, though attachments may be photocopied. Give agents five or six weeks to respond. A polite follow-up letter or phone call is appropriate if you've gotten no response by then.

If an agent writes or calls asking to see your work, send it off via first-class or priority mail, along with a short letter saying simply, "Thank you for your interest in my project, ————. I'm sending it on now, as you requested, and hope you find it both appealing and salable. Please feel free to write or call if you have any questions." Also enclose a return envelope and sufficient return postage.

If your project is a script, treatment, outline, or concept for film or TV, you will need to register it with the Writers Guild. See page 363 for details.

Although you may make an initial inquiry to as many agents at a time as you wish, you may send a particular *manuscript* to only one agent at a time. If several different agents express interest in seeing your manuscript, pick the one that sounds most promising to try first. If that one decides not to represent it, then try the next most promising agent, and so on. Don't tell the second agent that the first one turned it down, of course. Simply say, "Thank you for your interest in my project, ————. I'm sending it on now as you requested, and I'm sorry I wasn't able to get it to you sooner." It is permissible to send *different* projects to different agents simultaneously.

Occasionally, even though you have written a complete manuscript, an agent will ask to see only a portion of it—say, the first three chapters, or two chapters and an outline of the rest. Comply with this request if you can.

If the agent asks for something you don't have—if, for example, you've written a book proposal that has one or no sample chapters and the agent asks to see three chapters—use common sense. Either write some or all of the additional material, or send the agent what you've written so far, along with a note that says, "This is the material I've written to date. If you are interested in representing it but feel that you need to see more, I'd be happy to discuss the matter with you." If the agent asks for a synopsis but your finished project doesn't easily lend itself to one, it's fine to simply say so and send the full manuscript.

Once you have sent your manuscript to an agent, you should have a reply within five to eight weeks. After three months, remind the agent about your project through a polite note or phone call. If the agent has not responded after four months, write or call to say, "Please return the manuscript to me."

If an agent writes or calls you and says, "I like your project and wish to represent it," congratulations. But don't automatically say, "Great; we've got a deal." You need to make sure that the agent's terms are reasonable, and that he or she is both effective and trustworthy. So express your pleasure in the agent's interest; then ask the following questions, in a polite and friendly manner:

• What are some of the recent projects you have sold in the same medium as my project? What projects have you sold recently in the same genre as my project?
• Who are some of the publishers or producers you've sold work to *in the past year?*
• What is your commission on domestic sales? On foreign sales? On sales where subagents are involved?
• Do you sign a written contract with your clients, or do you simply make an oral agreement? What are the basic terms of this agreement?
• Do you have any affiliated agents who handle foreign rights for you? TV and film rights? Book rights?
• Do you charge any special fees of any kind?

If the agent's office is not in New York City and you have written a book, book proposal, or play, it is also a good idea to ask, "How often do you go to New York?" If the agent doesn't live in Los Angeles and your material is for film or television, ask, "How often do you visit LA?" The agent should make at least two to three such trips a year. If the agent has a good sales record over the past year, however, these questions may not be terribly important.

If the agent has had few or no sales within the past year or so, you've got good reason to be concerned. You want to be represented by someone who can *sell* your work.

It is a good idea to say to the agent after all your questions, "Is there anything you'd like to ask me?" This gives the agent a chance to get to know you a little more, and it makes the phone call more of a conversation and less of a one-way grilling session.

COMMISSIONS AND FEES

One of the best and quickest ways to tell whether an agent is legitimate and worth your while is to ask what commissions and fees he or she charges.

Any agent representing books, other print material, and/or computer software should charge absolutely no more than a 15 percent commission on most domestic sales, and no more than 25 percent on foreign sales and domestic sales in which an affiliated agent is involved. About 99 percent of subagent domestic sales will be to TV and film producers. Canadian sales are usually considered domestic sales; Canadian agents normally consider U.S. sales domestic sales.

Most agents representing plays charge 10 percent on most domestic sales; however, some good play agents charge as much as 15 percent, and commissions of up to 20 percent on sales to stock and amateur companies are acceptable, since there isn't much money in these sales. On foreign sales and sales in which a subagent is involved, the play agent's commission may go as high as 25 percent. No decent dramatic agent charges commissions higher than these.

Agents representing TV and film scripts, treatments, outlines, and concepts should charge no more than a flat 10 percent commission on any such project sold to any market. The 10 percent commission also applies to sales in which a subagent is involved.

There is one exception to the above. An agent who deals primarily with books, plays, and/or computer software but who agrees to represent a script, treatment, outline, or concept for film or TV will probably insist on his or her usual commission, whatever that might be. The reason: the agent will ship it off to Los Angeles to have his or her West Coast affiliate handle it. The affiliated agent will take 10 percent, and the rest of the commission will go to the first agent for making the connection. This is legitimate.

No decent agent should charge you a fee for reading or submitting your work, or for anything else. In fact, no legitimate agent takes *any* money from writers other than in duly earned commissions. Furthermore, no good agent collects a commission from any sale unless he or she was involved in that sale; you should not have to give your agent a kickback on anything you sell yourself.

When an agent agrees to represent a manuscript, he or she will normally wish to send anywhere from three to a dozen copies to publishers at once. You may, if you like, photocopy the manuscript yourself (and, in the case of material for TV, film, and stage, properly bind each copy) and send the copies to your agent for submission. However, the postage for this can be excessive, and many authors prefer to have their agents do the photocopying (and, for scripts, the binding). In such cases, the agent will ask and expect to be reimbursed for these costs. These are the *only* charges a decent agent will ask you for other than earned commissions.

Some agents charge a manuscript reading fee but offer to give a critique in exchange for that fee. This is fine if what you really want is a critique rather than representation. But if you are primarily interested in getting an agent rather than a critique, your response should be, "No, thank you. I'd simply like you to look the manuscript over and see if you'd wish to represent it. If you're willing to do this at no charge, I'd be happy to send you my manuscript." Other agents charge a reading fee but will refund it if they offer to represent the project and you agree to let them. This is *not* okay; do not pay a reading fee under any circumstances. Ask to have the fee waived; if the agent is intrigued enough by your query letter, he or she will say okay.

It is sad but true that one of the world's most famous and successful agents not only charges many potential clients reading fees, but regularly sends out brochures to thousands of writers, encouraging them to have him consider their work for representation—in exchange for a fee. This fee can run to several hundred dollars, and it entitles potential clients to a critique as well as consideration. (I have seen one of these critiques; I felt it was quite poor.) While this agent doubtless has a nice money-making sideline going, I *strongly* urge writers to respond to his offer by saying, "No critique is necessary. Would you care to consider the manuscript at no charge as a possible project to represent?" If the agent says yes, great; if he says no, try another agent.

An agent's commission is computed from the gross earnings of any project. That is, if your agent sells your novel for $8000, and you subsequently earn royalties and subsidiary rights income in three payments of $5000, $6000, and $11,000, your agent will receive commissions of $1200, $750, $900, and $1,650, respectively (based on a 15 percent commission rate). In each case, the publisher's check for the total amount is sent directly to the agent. The agent deposits the check, writes you a check for 85 percent of the amount from his or her own account, and sends that check to you.

If there are charges against your publishing earnings—for example, if your publisher charges you for the cost of indexing or for extra copies of your book—these won't affect your agent's total commission. Suppose your book earns $5000 in royalties, and you order 100 copies of the book at $6 each (60 percent of the full $10 retail price) and have the cost charged against your royalty account. Your agent will receive a check for $4400. But if the agent's commission is 15 percent, he or she is still entitled to $750, not $660.

AGENTS TO AVOID

Some folks who call themselves literary agents make their money primarily by charging writers fees for having their work considered, not by selling material to publishers. Some are outright crooks who charge their clients a fee for each submission; these "agents" will represent just about any author who can pay the submission fees. They rarely or never sell anything. And there are the "literary agencies" that are actually critiquing and/or rewriting services and that don't do any selling of manuscripts at all. These "agents" may offer to provide a critique that will supposedly help make your manuscript more salable—for a fee. Avoid all these folks. It is *not* true that any agent is better than no agent. A poor or crooked agent will be useless at best, and may even harm your career.

THE AUTHOR–AGENT AGREEMENT

Before an agent can officially represent you, you and the agent need to agree on the terms of that representation. Usually both parties sign a simple written agreement. A few agents prefer to make a simple oral agreement; this is fine, so long as the terms of the agreement are clearly understood by both parties. (To help ensure this, write down all the terms of this agreement, and keep this list on file.)

Every author-agent agreement will give the agent the sole right to represent a particular project, either on this continent or throughout the world. Every agreement will also specify the amount the agent is to receive as commission. The best author-agent agreements are open-ended on other matters. My own agent's standard agreement, which is reprinted on pages 248–49, is ideal in this respect.

Although an agent's primary responsibility is to look out for the interests of his or her clients, some author-agent agreements contain provisions that are clearly *not* in writers' best interests. Keep the following guidelines in mind:

• The specific terms of any author-agent agreement are usually negotiable.

• A good agent works on a project-by-project basis. Don't make an agreement that allows an agent to represent your entire literary output; this would give the agent the right to do anything he or she wished with each of your projects, including nothing at all. Many agents who make such "complete works" agreements with their clients do, in fact, often concentrate on selling only certain projects while letting others lie dormant. Such an agreement also obligates you to allow that agent to represent anything you write in the future.

There is nothing wrong with an agent wanting to represent more than one of your manuscripts, but you should make a separate agreement for each project. This allows the agent to turn down any project he or she doesn't want to mess with (rather than let it gather dust on a shelf) and frees up that project for you to market on your own, or through another agent.

• A good agent never wants money he or she did not earn. Beware of contract provisions that call for the agent to receive a percentage of your gross publishing receipts. This means that you owe the agent a commission on every dollar you make from writing, regardless of whether that agent (or one of his or her subagents) had anything to do with your earning that money. Insist on deleting this clause from any contract.

• Your agreement should specify that your share of any funds your agent receives on your behalf must be paid to you within one month of your agent's receipt of those funds. In the case of a check drawn on a foreign bank or paid in foreign funds, you should be paid within a month after the check clears.

• Many agents, including some good ones, have a "next work" provision in their contracts. This gives them the exclusive right to represent your next book or other writing project if they so desire. This can be harmful to you if your agent doesn't do a very good job with your first manuscript. Try to delete this provision. If the agent insists on keeping it, try to add

MRS. BOBBE SIEGEL
Rights Representative
41 West 83 Street
New York, NY 10024
(212) 877-4985

It is agreed that   (hereinafter referred
to as the Client) does grant Mrs. Bobbe Siegel (hereinafter referred to as the Agent) the exclusive right to represent the Client in any and all negotiations for the
sale of   (hereinafter referred to as
the Work) to a publisher and, thereafter, for the sale of
any and all rights related to the Work as well as all
other books and/or projects as shall be mutually agreed
upon.

The Client does hereby warrant that He/She is the author
and sole owner of the Work; that it is original and that
it contains no matter unlawful in the content nor does it
violate the rights of any third party; that the rights
granted hereunder are free and clear; and that the Client
has full power to grant such representation to the Agent.

The Client agrees that the Agent shall receive 15% (fifteen per cent) of the gross of all monies earned from the
sale of the Work. It is also agreed that the Agent will
receive from the sale, licensing option or other disposi-
tion of any foreign language rights (including British
rights) when negotiated without an overseas sub-agent a
commission of 15% (fifteen per cent) of the gross; when
foreign language volume rights (including British rights)
are negotiated with an overseas sub-agent the total commission will be 20% (twenty per cent) of the gross: 10%
(ten per cent) for the Agent and 10% (ten per cent) for
the sub-agent. Further, if the Agent should use the services of a sub-agent for the sale of movie and/or television rights the total commission shall be 20% (twenty per
cent): 10% (ten per cent) for the agent and 10% (ten per
cent) for the sub-agent...all from the gross.

.../see page 2

The Client does hereby empower the Agent to receive all monies due to him under any contractual arrangements related to the Work and the Agent warrants that her receipt shall be a good and valid discharge. The Client further empowers the Agent to deal with all parties on his behalf in all matters arising from the Work. The Client agrees that this agreement shall be binding on his/her estate.

The Agent agrees to remit all moneys due to the Client, less the Agent's stipulated commission, within thirty (30) days of the receipt of any moneys earned from the sale of any rights related to the Work if said monies are paid in U.S. currency. Otherwise, the Agent will remit all monies due to the Client, less the Agent's stipulated commission, within thirty (30) days of the conversion of said monies to U.S. currency.

If either Client or Agent should desire to terminate this agreement either party must inform the other, by certified mail, of such intent, and the agreement shall be considered terminated 60 (sixty) days after receipt of such letter. It is, however, understood that any monies due after termination whether derived from contractual agreements already negotiated or under negotiation by the Agent when the agreement is terminated shall be paid to the Agent who will then deduct her commission and remit to the Client as outlined above.

If the foregoing correctly sets forth your understanding please sign both copies of this letter, where indicated, retaining one copy for your files and returning the other copy to me for mine.

Yours sincerely,

Bobbe Siegel

AGREED

_____   Date:_____
   CLIENT

S.S. #_____

a phrase to it such as, "provided the agent sells the author's current project for terms acceptable to the author." Another option you have is to limit the type of project the agent has the unrestricted right to represent. For instance, you might give him or her the exclusive right to represent your next mystery novel or your next adult nonfiction book, rather than your next project of any kind. If you do sign a contract with a "next work" provision, you will need to make a new agreement covering representation for the subsequent work once it is ready for submission to editors. At that time you should insist that the "next work" provision be deleted from *that* agreement.

• The author-agent agreement should be subject to termination at any time by either party. This gives both you and your agent the right to back out if either of you doesn't trust or work well with the other. Beware of contracts that give the agent a specific amount of time to represent a particular work, or even everything you have written and will write in the future. Such a stipulation means that, for a certain period of time (usually one to three years), the agent can do whatever he or she pleases with your work, including nothing at all, and there's not a damn thing you can do about it until that time runs out. On the surface, this provision looks as if it compels the agent to continue submitting your work over a certain time period. But it doesn't; all it does is deprive you of all recourse in the event your agent does an unsatisfactory job. Get rid of this provision; if the agent insists on it, you should probably get rid of the agent. On the other hand, you *may* wish to go along with it *if* you set a term of representation of six months, or a year at the absolute most. If you do allow such a provision in your agreement, it should cover a particular project, not everything you have written or will write.

• If and when you and your agent decide to go your separate ways, your agent is still entitled to receive commissions on any money earned from deals that he or she made on your behalf. For example, suppose your agent sells North American and United Kingdom rights to your novel to Scribner's; shortly after you receive your advance, the two of you have a disagreement, and you get a new agent. The novel earns $5500 in royalties over and above the advance, and two years later Scribner's sells paperback rights and United Kingdom rights. Your original agent is entitled to a commission on all the royalties and both subsidiary rights sales, since all resulted from a deal that agent made. However, if you were to sell Japanese rights to the same book either on your own or through a new agent, your old agent would not be entitled to a commission since he or she was not involved in that sale directly or indirectly. Money earned from the original deal any time in the future would still be sent to your old agent, who would deduct his or her commission and promptly send you the remainder.

What is *not* fair or standard is a provision that entitles an agent to receive a commission on *all* money a project earns any time in the future, even money earned from sales you or another agent make after you and your first agent part ways. If such a provision appears in your contract, insist on its removal.

A reasonable provision in some contracts covers works submitted or under negotiation at the time the author-agent agreement is terminated. The agent may continue to represent you on these submissions *only* until a deal is closed or until all the submissions are rejected, whichever comes first. The agent would of course be entitled to a commission on all money earned from such a deal. An alternative provision, also reasonable, keeps the author-agent agreement in force for thirty or sixty days beyond one party's notice of intention to terminate that agreement.

If your agent works for a group agency rather than alone, your contract will be with the agency rather than your agent. If and when your agent leaves that agency, your agreement with the agency will remain in force. How this affects you is discussed in detail on pages 261–63.

Special Circumstances

• If your agent does not have affiliates in certain (or any) foreign countries, you may wish to arrange representation in those countries on your own through foreign agencies. However, you cannot give more than one agent the right to represent a project in a particular language, foreign country, or territory; and, if you have already given your U.S. agent the right to represent you in a country or language, you cannot arrange foreign representation in that country or language without your U.S. agent's approval.

You can approach foreign agents just as you would a U.S. agent, following these guidelines:

> • Foreign agents are perfectly happy to represent work that has been previously published, as long as it has not yet been published in the country or language in question, and as long as the appropri-

ate rights are available for sale. You may send either manuscripts or very clear photocopies of published materials.

• Work may be submitted either in English or in the appropriate foreign language. Most foreign agents, and many foreign editors, read English.

• Unlike U.S. agents, many foreign agents represent short stories, articles, and other short works as well as full-length projects.

• Enclose International Reply Coupons instead of return postage. Manuscripts are best sent airmail, as surface mail can sometimes take several weeks.

• Be sure to let foreign agents know who else represents you and what countries they represent you in.

The United Kingdom is by far the largest foreign market for material by U.S. writers. Other large markets include Australia, Japan, Israel, most European countries, and New Zealand.

• It is perfectly legitimate to have more than one agent representing you in the United States and Canada, each handling different properties. For example, you might have one agent in New York for books and another agent in Los Angeles, unaffiliated with your New York agent, for TV and film scripts. It is also okay to have two or more agents in this country, each representing different projects in the same medium. All of this is legitimate provided it doesn't violate any agreements you have made.

• Some agents—including a few otherwise decent ones—occasionally indulge in the very strange practice of submitting manuscripts to editors before arranging terms for representation with their writers. Here is a typical scenario: A writer sends in a manuscript for consideration. The agent reads it and likes it, makes photocopies, sends the manuscript to several different publishers, and only then writes or calls the writer and says, "I really liked your project, and I've sent it to these editors. . . ." In one case I know of, the agent (a well-known one) didn't get in touch with the writer at all. When the writer called after a couple of months to ask if the agent had read the book yet, the agent replied impatiently, "Of course I have. It's at Macmillan now."

If something like this happens to you, tell the agent, "Well, we need to agree on terms first, and I'd like to ask you a few questions." Spend a few minutes asking the questions on pages 243–44 and getting a feel for who the agent is and how he or she operates. If you do not want the agent to represent you or cannot work out acceptable terms, you have two choices: you can insist that the agent withdraw all the manuscripts sent out so far, or you can say, "You may represent me on the submissions you have sent out so far. However, please make no further submissions and return my manuscript to me." If none of those submissions leads to a sale, you can then (but not before) try another agent.

• Occasionally an agent will make no attempt to set forth any terms of agreement, either written or oral. In such a case, bring the matter up yourself. The agent may act surprised or even a little offended; don't let that stop you. Find out what his or her terms are so that there can be no misunderstandings. If the agent says, "My terms are standard for the industry," don't be satisfied with that. Find out exactly what he or she means by "standard."

• If any project your agent wishes to represent has been previously sold or published, in whole or part, in identical or substantially similar form, you must tell your agent where and when before you make an agreement on that project.

• If the project has previously been rejected, you must give your agent the names of both the publishers *and* the editors that have rejected it.

GETTING AN AGENT AT THE LAST MINUTE

If a book publisher, or a TV, film, or play producer, makes an offer on something you've written, and you don't have an agent, you can do one of two things: negotiate the deal yourself, or try to get an agent fast.

If the deal is a small one, you will probably have to work it out alone, because the potential commission won't be worth an agent's while. But if your project is likely to earn you at least $3000 over the first two years, there is enough potential commission in the deal that an agent should be willing to negotiate it for you.

If you're made an offer and feel you need an agent's help, do *not* agree to *any* of the terms of the deal, either on the phone or in a letter. In the case of a book, don't even agree to the amount of the advance. If you assent to anything, orally or in writing, your editor will consider that part of the deal closed and won't allow you or your agent to reopen discussion on it; so it is important to be noncommittal. Simply get the terms of the offer and write them down. Then say, "I'll need a bit of time to think these terms over. I'll get back in touch shortly."

Next, pick an agent using your contacts and/or the resources listed on pages 235–36. Use the phone—there's no time for writing letters and waiting for replies. Explain to whomever answers that you've got an offer and need someone to negotiate it for you. This will get you past the switchboard operator to the agent.

Explain to the agent the nature of the project on which the offer has been made, the terms of the offer, and the name, employer, phone number, and comments of the editor who made the offer. If the agent is interested in representing the project, you will need to ask the appropriate questions from pages 243–44, decide whether or not you want the agent to represent you, and make a verbal agreement regarding terms—all in a few minutes. Agreeing to terms over the phone can be a bit tricky, but you have no choice in these circumstances. You may need to make an oral agreement initially, to be followed by a written author-agent agreement later.

Once you've got an agent, he or she will handle the negotiations. You do not need to call your editor to explain that you've gotten an agent.

Strange as it sounds, one good way to find a respectable agent under these circumstances is to ask the editor who is making the offer to recommend one. Although you'd think this might represent a conflict of interest, in practice most editors (most book editors, at least) are quite happy to make recommendations, and usually their recommendations are decent ones.

Once the deal has been made, you have yourself an agent, the beginnings of an ongoing relationship, and the potential for other sales.

Never turn to an agent after trying to negotiate some or all of the terms yourself—or worse, after you have agreed to certain terms orally—or worst of all, after you have signed a contract. An agent can do little or nothing for you at these stages. Either get an agent before the negotiations begin, or handle the negotiations yourself.

You also have the option of hiring a literary lawyer to look your contract over and/or negotiate the deal for you. For details on this topic, see pages 372–74.

AGENTS AS CRITICS

Not every agent is willing or able to give helpful criticism, or even any criticism at all. Some agents view their role primarily or entirely as salespeople; these agents, like many editors, will simply turn down without comment any material that is not already in publishable or very close to publishable form.

Some agents, like some editors, will give suggestions for making your work more salable, though not necessarily better. Sometimes agents, like editors, will confuse quality with salability. They'll tell you that your manuscript needs certain changes to improve it, but what they mean is to make it sell more easily.

If an agent asks you for a rewrite, you have the right to say, "I consider the project finished, and must ask you to either represent it as is or pass it up." The agent, however, also has the right to say, "I insist on certain changes or I won't represent it."

Some agents may suggest future directions for your writing. This is fine, and can even be very helpful, but you are under no obligation to follow your agent's advice. Agents always have their eyes on the market, and it is not unusual for an agent to say something like, "Well, Anne, that biography you did on Mondrian was excellent, and I'm pleased we got a $7000 advance for it. How'd you like to write a family saga next, or maybe a mystery? They're really selling well these days." Take comments like these as suggestions, not as demands. If your own interests run in other directions, just tell your agent, "Thanks for the suggestions, but I'm working on something else."

STRIKING A DEAL

Once an agent has agreed to represent a literary project, he or she will usually tell editors about it, then photocopy several copies and send them out to the ones who express interest. For very big projects, those worth $50,000 or more, the agent may set up an auction, with a minimum bid (called a floor) and a set time period during which publishers can make their bids.

An editor who likes the project your agent submitted may call you to ask questions about it. If you get such a call, feel free to answer any questions the editor asks—except one: "How much money are you looking for?" If an editor asks you this, or tries to talk about *any* other contract terms, don't agree to *anything* and don't even discuss the matter. *Insist* (repeatedly, if necessary) that he or she bring all such matters to your agent. (*Don't* tell your agent to get lost and try to negotiate the deal yourself; if your agent made the initial submission, he or she is legally entitled to a percentage of the deal even if you part ways.)

If an editor is able to make an offer to buy your manuscript, he or she will bring it to your agent, who will then relate it to you—in some cases after an initial round of negotiation. Although an agent will negotiate on your behalf, *you* are the one who makes the final decisions. An agent may offer advice (usually "take it" or "hold out for more"), and you may take it or ignore it as you please. You should also feel free to ask the agent for advice, if you feel you need it, at any step in the negotiating process. But ultimately the agent is going to say, "All right. What do I tell the editor?"

Your options here go beyond "I'll take it" and "I won't." You can ask your agent to make a counter-offer or compromise, or you can say "I'll take the best deal you can make above $————," or you can simply say, "Just make the best deal you can, and I'll go along with it." Some writers tell their agents before the agents begin submitting a project, "Don't even bother to bring me any offers under $————."

If you turn down an editor's offer, the editor may make a better one, suggest a compromise, or say, "That's my best offer; take it or leave it." You also have the option of saying, "I don't really like the offer, but I'll take it if nothing better comes along. Can you leave it on the table for a while?" Most editors will let an offer stand under these circumstances.

If two or more editors are interested in the same project, your agent may set up an impromptu auction, with the project going to the editor who offers the best deal or the highest bid. You will be consulted at all times and given the chance to accept an offer at any point.

An editor's initial verbal offer will normally include only a few of the many terms of the written contract that will eventually be offered. In the case of a book or book proposal, the initial offer will normally specify only the amount of the advance, when that advance is to be paid, and perhaps some of the royalty rates. Although all other terms remain open to negotiation until a contract is signed by both parties, a verbal acceptance of a verbal offer indicates that both sides are committed in principle to working out a mutually acceptable deal. The terms that have been verbally agreed to normally cannot be altered in the final written agreement.

Once a verbal agreement has been reached, the publisher will draw up a contract and send it to your agent, who will then, if necessary, negotiate changes in that document. Once the contract satisfies your agent, he or she will send copies to you for your perusal and signature.

It is extremely important that you read all contracts carefully. If there is *anything* about a contract that you don't understand, that bothers you, or that you can't or won't agree to, call your agent promptly to discuss the matter. *Don't* sign any contract that you don't fully understand or that you are unwilling or unable to fulfill. You have the right to have your agent negotiate additional contract changes. It is your signature, not your agent's, that will appear on the contract and that will make the deal binding—and it is you who will be responsible for fulfilling the terms of that contract.

Before signing a contract negotiated by an agent, it is a good idea to discuss with your agent what kind of marketing job he or she can do for you overseas, either alone or through affiliates. You may then wish to grant your publisher publication rights in those countries in which your agent can't or won't try to sell your book. Or you might keep those rights and go hunting for one or more foreign agents.

Once a book deal is made (and in the case of book proposals, once the completed manuscript has been accepted by the publisher), a good agent will attempt to sell serial rights to magazines and newspapers. Once page proofs or prepublication copies of the book are available, a good agent will also get the project off to his or her foreign affiliates, who will market the project in their countries. If the project has other potential markets (such as film, TV, stage, or video) in this country, your agent will attempt to sell these rights as well. Any subsidiary rights sold to the initial publisher, however, will of course be marketed by that publisher rather than your agent.

WORKING WITH YOUR AGENT

Here are some tips that will help you and your agent keep up a strong and healthy working relationship:

• You are better off with an effective, honest, and obnoxious agent than you are with one who is warm, friendly, and poor at selling.
• Your agent should submit at least three copies of a completed book, or four to five copies of a book proposal, to editors at a time. If your agent doesn't, ask that it be done. Single submissions *are* common, and virtually the rule, in TV and film, however.
• Agents are perfectly willing to send you any rejection letters you may receive, or photocopies of them, and you are entitled as a client to receive them. However, agents do not send these letters automatically, as many writers prefer not to see them. You will need to ask, preferably when your agent first begins submitting the manuscript. Normally these letters will be sent in batches, three or four times a year.
• You have the right to know the names of any editors who have been sent your manuscripts, the publishers they work for, the dates the projects

were sent, and which editors rejected their submissions. Agents do not automatically give out this information to their clients, but it is always available on request. You may either request information after the fact or ask your agent to keep you informed of submissions and rejections on a regular basis.

• When your project is on submission, don't sit home nervously waiting for the phone to ring. And *don't* call any of the editors who have your manuscript to rush them or give them a sales pitch of your own. Trust your agent to do that job, and put your mind and energy elsewhere.

• Give your agent a decent chance to sell each of your projects. I wouldn't worry about a manuscript's salability or your agent's ability to sell it until it has received at least ten to fifteen rejections.

• Once you have an agent, it is not necessary to ask if he or she will look at other projects. You may simply send in other projects along with a short cover letter. However, don't inundate your agent with manuscripts. In general, agents don't want to send around more than two or three different projects by any one writer at a time.

• Your agent has the right to choose not to represent any project you may offer him or her. However, you also have the right to market it yourself or take it to another agent, unless you have specifically given up this right in a poor author-agent agreement. Even then any decent agent will bend the contract and allow you to take the project elsewhere, since he or she obviously isn't going to market it for you.

• Don't send your agent a project in the first place unless you think it has a decent chance of selling. Don't submit your fourth-grade diary in the hope that just maybe your agent can sell it to Knopf.

• If an agent (either one you are initially approaching or one who already represents you) turns down a project, don't expect or ask for any reason or explanation.

• Your agent should read and respond to any new project you send him or her within two to three months at the latest. After three months, a polite reminder by telephone or mail is appropriate. If your agent has not read your new project within four months, it's time to call and say, "Is there some problem?" After five months, you should take the project back. You may wish to take back your other projects as well.

• No decent agent (or publisher or editor, for that matter) will ever call you collect. You should not call your agent collect either.

• If you have an idea for a project and want to discuss it with your agent to see if it sounds salable, or to get his or her advice, feel free to do so.

However, such discussions should normally be brief—no more than ten to fifteen minutes. You should also feel free to discuss future projects (at more length, if need be) by correspondence.

• Even though you have an agent, it is still a good idea to continue to make, and make use of, other contacts in the publishing world. If you send your agent a new book manuscript, for example, it can be helpful to call up the book editors you are friendly with, tell them about your new project, and ask them if they'd care to see it. Then give your agent the names of those editors who have asked for a look.

• If your agent gets excited about something you've written, great. But don't get too excited about it yourself until it actually sells. And don't be surprised if, after that project has been rejected a few times, your agent's excitement starts to wane. After a few more rejections, the agent's contacts with you, and even the agent's number of submissions, may also wane.

• There is nothing wrong with agents keeping a low profile, provided they keep your manuscript in circulation and answer all your legitimate inquiries. But if they don't answer your letters, take or return your phone calls, or keep your work going out to editors, you've got a problem.

• If a genuine problem does arise between you and your agent, or you feel you're not getting proper service, write or call to discuss it. Calling is usually best, as it gives you the chance to resolve the matter on the spot. Explain calmly what the problem is, and suggest possible ways of resolving it if you can. Don't get angry or accusatory or fail to be polite.

• If you have a project that's not selling and your agent starts talking about "looking ahead to your next project," chances are your agent has given up, or is almost ready to give up, on the earlier project. Find out if it's still in circulation and which editors have it at the moment, and encourage your agent to keep it in circulation a little longer.

• An agent who doesn't sell a project within a year, or after fifteen to twenty rejections—whichever comes first—as likely as not will give up on it and return it to you. This doesn't mean *you* should give up on it, though. Have your agent return it to you immediately, so that you can market it yourself if you wish.

• An agent who gives up on a project before it has received, at the very least, ten to fifteen rejections, is not being persistent enough. Say so, or think about getting a new agent.

• It is quite possible that you'll be able to sell a project on your own that your agent couldn't sell for you. If your agent does return an unsold project to you and you succeed in getting an offer for it from an editor, feel free to call your agent and say, "I've got a bite on my project. Interested in negotiating the deal for me?"

• If your project will require any special terms or assistance from a publisher or producer—for example, if you must have your travel or research expenses paid for, or if you insist on retaining British Commonwealth rights—let your agent know before he or she sends the project out.

• If your agent bills you for photocopying and/or binding charges, pay these charges within ten days—twenty at the latest.

• Some agents will rarely or never get excited about a project, no matter how salable or potentially lucrative it may be. Some won't give you the slightest word of praise, but will simply agree to represent it. This is nothing to be concerned about; it's just certain agents' way.

• Agents tend to deal only with those editors they know personally (though any good one knows at least several dozen and is always working to know more). Book agents tend to stick to the hundred biggest houses and avoid the smaller and more specialized ones. If you know any editors you think might be interested in your project, or if you know of any small or specialized houses that might be especially appropriate for your project, tell your agent about them.

• If your agent is unable to sell any of your projects over the course of a year or so, don't be surprised if he or she chooses to drop you as a client. Don't be insulted or take it personally. Agents are in business to make money, and if your work isn't making any, the smart thing for them to do from a business standpoint is cut their losses. It may well be the smart thing for you, too, since the agent hasn't sold any of your work. You may continue to offer that agent future projects, of course.

• Your agent is your official representative in the publishing world. If you are having trouble with a publisher or editor and are not able to resolve the problem on your own, your agent may be able to resolve it for you.

• Feel free to ask your agent for advice on business matters and for information on publishing practices and terminology. You may even ask for advice on magazine and newspaper deals that you have made (or are in the process of making) on your own. Agents will normally offer such advice as a courtesy, at no charge.

• If you will be out of town or otherwise unavailable for more than a few days, let your agent know in advance. If possible, leave phone numbers of where you can be reached.

BREAKING UP

If your agent decides to drop you, or you realize you must drop your agent, it is by no means the end of the world. In fact, if things aren't going so well with your agent, getting free and moving on could be the best thing for your career. A great many writers change agents, and some have gone through several before they found one they liked.

If you want to end the relationship, a polite letter to your agent expressing this desire is all you need. You don't have to supply a reason for wanting to go separate ways, and you don't have to feel guilty about it.

If your original agreement specifies terms for termination, these terms must of course be adhered to. If no terms have been agreed on, then technically the author-agent relationship ends the moment either party says, "Let's forget it." In practice, however, it is fair and reasonable to give your agent sixty days' notice, or to allow him or her to continue to represent you on any submissions that are still "live" as of the date of termination.

Terminating the author-agent relationship usually isn't difficult or sticky. However, there *is* one circumstance that is both sticky and absurd: when an agent moves from one group agency to another. If your agent works for a group agency and later leaves that agency, his or her clients must stay with the agency. In fact, agents are legally forbidden to ask, or even suggest, that any of their clients remain with them when they leave a group agency. They can tell their clients that they are leaving and where their new offices will be, but they must also inform their clients that they now "belong" to someone else at the agency. The departing agent is not allowed to even hint that he or she would like to continue representing any of his or her clients.

What can you do under these circumstances? If you have signed an author-agent agreement that gives the agency the right to represent certain works, or even all of your writing, for a set period of time, then you must stick with that agency until that time runs out. If your contract gives the agency the right to represent your next project, then you must give your new agent that chance. However, if neither provision is part of your agreement, you may simply "jump ship" at any time and follow your old agent elsewhere, provided you give proper notice as stipulated in your agreement.

The moment you are free of the agency—but not a moment before—

you have every legal and ethical right to sign up with your old agent once again—though if your agent is with a new group agency, you must again sign up with that agency rather than with your agent. And if your agent leaves *that* agency, you will have to go through this whole process again.

If you do wish to follow your old agent to a new agency, it is important to discuss the terms of representation again, since these terms have been set by the new agency, and they may not be the same as your previous terms.

Your other option is to build a good relationship with your new agent. This may be to your benefit if you weren't very happy with your old agent. In this case, follow up as you would with a new editor. Call a few days after the new agent takes over. Be businesslike but friendly. Give the agent a list of all your projects that he or she has inherited, and, in a sentence or two, describe each project and explain what makes it unusual or special. Explain the marketing handle of each nonfiction project. Ask the new agent a few questions about their own background and interests: what kind of projects they most like to represent, what projects they have sold in the past year or so, what editors and publishers they have sold work to, and so on. Give them your address and home and work phone numbers, and tell them you're available to answer any questions they might have.

Follow up this phone call with a brief letter that lists by title all the projects of yours that they're now representing. If you like, in this letter you may ask them to inform you of any submissions they make, to send you copies of rejection letters, and/or to return to you any manuscripts they don't intend to try to sell. (They are not obliged to continue marketing any projects they do not feel are salable.) If you have any other reasonable requests (such as "Don't even bring me any offers under $5000"), make them here. Enclose your business card if you wish.

When an *independent* agent goes to work for a group agency, none of the strange protocol above applies; these agents can take any clients along that they like, provided the clients want to go. However, the clients have to sign a new agreement with the agency—and if the agent later leaves that agency, the clients are still attached to the agency.

When you terminate your relationship with an agent, no matter what the arrangement or reason, you are entitled to receive, on request, a complete listing of all the publishers that considered each of your projects, and the names of the editors at those firms who saw your work. Getting a list of both publishers *and* editors is very important in the event that you or a new agent wish to submit the project elsewhere. The names of the particular editors are necessary because editors move from one house to another with great frequency. You are also entitled to ask for and receive any of your manuscripts, including photocopies, in the agent's possession.

What do you do if you dump an agent who has done a lousy job and get another one, and your new agent turns out to be no better than the first? You have two choices: market your work yourself; or grit your teeth, start looking for agent number three, and hope that you get lucky. I know one writer whose first two books went unsold despite the efforts of no less than three agents; her fourth agent sold those same books very quickly to a major publisher.

9. ✎

Selling and Publishing Your Book

THE WORLD OF BOOK PUBLISHING

Most book publishers, like most other publishers, go for the money. The big publishing houses are more interested in outbidding each other for Jackie Collins's new novel or the ghostwritten autobiography of a television star than they are in publishing a literary novel or a history of American vice presidents. Although most of the bigger houses are also interested in that novel or history book and willing to pay a reasonable advance—$5000 to $10,000—for either one, they will focus most of their energy, attention, promotion, and spending on the books that appeal to the largest and widest readerships. It's simple economics. Whether you and I like it or not, there's a lot more money in trashy books than in serious ones.

Most books, however, don't earn their authors a great deal of money; the average advance is about $7500 for a trade book, even less for a nontrade volume. But if your book does catch on, you can make a good deal of money, get your name known, and build a solid writing career.

There are three kinds of trade books: hardcover, trade paper, and mass-market. Mass-market books are the inexpensive pocket-size paperbacks sold at newsstands, airports, drugstores, and supermarkets. They are sometimes called *rack size* books. Trade paperbacks (also called *quality* or *large-format* paperbacks) are larger paperbound volumes, usually printed on better paper, with a stronger binding, and carrying a higher cover price.

Individuals aren't the only book buyers. Libraries, schools, service groups, and other organizations buy them, too, often by the thousand. It's possible to earn $50,000 or more in royalties just from the sale of a widely used reference book to libraries.

There are many other outlets for books. Gift shops, card shops, and office supply stores often sell books. Books on special themes can be marketed through retail stores selling related products. For instance, a book on kids' fashion might be sold in children's clothing stores, and a guide to word processing might be sold through retail computer dealers. Sales to these markets are called *special sales*. Books are also sold to employers, professional societies, clubs, and other organizations, which then sell or give them away to employees, members, or clients. These are called *premium sales*.

Direct mail also accounts for a large percentage of the books sold in this country. This is when flyers, brochures, or catalogs are sent directly to a targeted group of people, and interested buyers order directly from the publisher.

The amount of money a book earns its author is the result of three factors: the advance, the royalties, and the sale of subsidiary rights. An *advance* is a lump sum paid to an author by a publisher, normally prior to publication. Advances are applied against a book's future earnings. The size of a book's advance is based almost entirely on its projected sales. *Royalties* are moneys the publisher pays an author based on the sale of copies of his or her book and calculated as a percentage of the book's wholesale or retail price. *Subsidiary rights* are rights of publication and/or production that have not yet been exercised; for example, book club sales and excerpts sold to magazines are subsidiary rights.

Let's say you've written a book called *Getting the Most from Your Job*. You're given a $10,000 advance for the book, which is published in hardcover at a price of $14.95. Your contract calls for a royalty of 10 percent of the cover price on the first five thousand copies sold through U.S. retailers, 12½ percent on the next five thousand, and 15 percent thereafter. The day you sign a contract for the book, an account is set up for that book at your publisher. When the advance is paid, the amount in your account goes from zero to minus $10,000. Let's suppose that in the first six months your book sells exactly five thousand copies, all through U.S. book retailers. You would earn $7475 during that period. This would not be paid directly to you, but credited to your account. Your balance would now be minus $2525.

Suppose that in the next six-month period your book sells exactly five thousand more copies. You would earn an additional $9344, based on a 12½ percent royalty. This sum would be credited to your account, leaving you with a positive balance of $6819. This is the amount your publisher would be required to pay you or your agent.

In practice, computing royalties gets a great deal more complicated than this. Books sold through direct mail, special sales, and nontraditional outlets typically receive reduced royalty rates, as do books sold in certain foreign countries and those sold in the United States at discounts of 50 percent or more. Furthermore, if an unsold copy of your book is returned to your publisher, the royalty for that book that was credited to your account when the copy was originally sold gets deducted from your account. To protect themselves against the possibility of future deductions, publishers withhold a *reserve* from most royalty payments. This ranges from 15 to 35 percent of the total royalties (but not subsidiary rights money) earned during that period (35 to 55 percent for mass-market paperbacks). The typical rate of actual returns for hardcover and trade paperbacks is about 20 to 25 percent; the rate for mass-market paperbacks is usually 35 to 50 percent. The amount withheld is credited to the author on the following royalty statement.

Two or three times a year, publishers issue new catalogs, which go out to bookstores, other retail outlets, libraries, and agents across the country. These introduce the books to be published during the four to six months to come, called the publisher's *frontlist*. Catalogs sometimes also include a list of previously published titles still in print (that is, still available), called the *backlist*. All these books together form the publisher's complete *list*.

Each season a small group of books—and sometimes one book in particular—is chosen to be a publisher's *lead title(s)*. These receive the most advertising and publicity, get pushed the hardest by book sales reps, and usually have the largest print runs. Books other than lead titles are called *midlist books*.

When a book stops selling adequately, or when stock in it runs low or out and the publisher deems it financially unfeasible to reprint it, the publisher will declare the book *out of print* (or *OP*). This means that the book will no longer be available for sale through that publisher, that returned copies from booksellers and wholesalers will only be accepted for a few more months, and that any remaining copies will be destroyed or sold off at a large discount as *remainders.* The publisher will print an out-of-print notice in *Publishers Weekly* and inform the author.

BOOK PROPOSALS

There are two ways to sell a book: with a complete manuscript or with a *book proposal.* A proposal consists of an outline of the project and several items of supporting material. These may include any or all of the following: one or more sample chapters; an introduction; a rationale for (or overview of) the project; a table of contents; a short biography of the author; samples of the writer's previously published (or accepted) work; a resumé; endorsements and/or a preface from one or more authorities, celebrities, or other writers; a list of competing books and an explanation of why the proposed book is different or superior; a discussion of likely readers or markets; and drawings, charts, graphs, and/or photographs.

A good proposal should, first and foremost, give the reader a clear, unambiguous sense of the book's focus, approach, contents, and tone or style—in short, the "feel" of the project. It should also clearly demonstrate to editors that you're a capable writer, and that you can finish the book successfully.

Proposals can be any length, provided they fulfill the criteria listed above. I've written and sold proposals that ranged from less than ten pages to nearly a hundred. Most proposals run from twenty-five to seventy-five pages.

In general, the fewer credentials and previous sales and publications you have, the longer your proposal will need to be to win editors over. If you're a veterinarian with a previously published book or a dozen published articles in major magazines, your proposal for *Home Health Care for Dogs and Cats* need not be lengthy, and it need not include a sample chapter, so long as it *does* contain a comprehensive outline. If you haven't published or sold anything before, editors will almost certainly insist on seeing at least one sample chapter, and possibly several. And if you haven't published anything and you're not even a vet, just a vet's assistant, your proposal will have to be still more thorough, because you've got to convince editors that you have not only a viable idea and sufficient writing talent but the specific knowledge to write the book.

Most books can be sold through proposals, but there are a few general exceptions. Editors are often reluctant to buy first novels based on proposals, since they have no real way to know whether you can do a good job with your book. Even if an editor does want to publish your first novel, his or her colleagues are more likely to veto it if all they've seen is a proposal. Some houses even have a policy against buying first novels based on proposals.

However, it is quite possible to sell a genre novel (science fiction, romance, etc.) through a proposal even if it is your first book, especially if you have already published short fiction in that genre. General-interest novels can also be sold through proposals if you have previously published a nonfiction book or book of short stories, and/or if you can get some major endorsements for your novel (see pages 287–91 for details).

By their very nature, collections of short stories or poems normally cannot be sold through proposals. Essay collections are also difficult to sell through proposals. (Exceptions are sometimes possible, however, if your book has a single central theme, location, or character.)

Anthologies can sometimes be sold via proposals (see pages 286–87 for details).

Certain books (including some novels) simply don't lend themselves well to proposal form. If this is true of your own project, don't try to force it to fit. Finish it first and then get it out to publishers.

Most writers prefer selling their books on the basis of proposals for five reasons: it means doing far less work before striking a deal; if a book sells, it earns its author a portion (usually half) of the advance up front, before the bulk of the writing has begun; it virtually guarantees receipt of the second half of the advance if the project turns out acceptably; it means less time and effort go down the tube if the proposal doesn't sell in the first place; and it means that they can claim the book sale on resumés and in letters to editors and prospective employers, even though the book hasn't been completed yet.

Selling a book by proposal is also very helpful if putting your book together is going to require the cooperation of other people—interviewees, public officials, contributors of original material, and so on. You are going to get a good deal more cooperation from these people if you can tell them that your book is under contract, not some pie-in-the-sky project.

The drawback of selling a book through a proposal is that you have committed yourself. You must write your book for that particular publisher, and you must meet a deadline.

Keep in mind that you are not usually required to follow your own proposal outline to the letter. Editors understand that a book may naturally undergo some change as it gets written. This doesn't mean you have the right to change the central focus of your project, however. If you feel a significant change is necessary, contact your editor promptly.

There are many different ways to write a good book proposal. The overall quality and persuasiveness of a proposal are far more important than adherence to specific rules. However, the following guidelines should be helpful:

• The first item in your proposal should be your cover page; prepare this according to the directions on pages 33–35. Next should come your "about the author" page, as described on page 285. If you feel a special need to establish yourself as an authority in a field, you may next include a resumé.

• If you have a statement of rationale for the book, a general overview of the project, and/or a discussion of likely markets or readers, these should come next.

• Next comes your table of contents, then your introduction (if any). The next two items should be your sample chapter(s) (if any) and a chapter-by-chapter outline. These two can go in either order; put first the one that yields the most logical, attractive, or convincing result.

• To prepare each copy of your proposal for submission to an editor or agent, purchase a paper two-pocket 9-by-12-inch folder, the kind without a gusset (a strip used for binding in three-hole notebook paper). Remove the price tag (carefully!). Neatly type the title of the proposal and your byline on a blank stick-on label; stick this to the front of the folder. If you like, you may also attach a label with your name, address, and phone number(s) on the front. Place your proposal inside the folder, in the right-hand pocket. In the left-hand pocket, place endorsements or prefaces from other people and/or samples of your previously published or accepted work. If you're including both these items, put the endorsements first. If you're enclosing slides, these (and lists of captions and photo credits) also go in the left-hand pocket, behind this material. Clip return postage to the outside of either pocket.

• Your cover letter may be placed in front of your cover page (as if it were page zero) so that it is instantly visible when an editor opens the folder; or it may be placed in a business envelope on which you have typed the editor's name, and placed in either pocket, sticking halfway out. Some writers like to clip their cover letters to the front of the folder, either flat and face up or in a business envelope with the editor's name typed on it. This is fine.

• If you are enclosing no endorsements, preface, or writing samples, you may, if you wish, place your author's biography, resumé, and/or cover letter in the left-hand pocket. If you choose to put your cover letter here, it should go on top; otherwise these items can go in any order.

SPECIAL GUIDELINES FOR NOVEL PROPOSALS

Your sample chapter(s) should give the reader a strong sense of your style, a close look at one or more major characters, and a reasonable piece of the plot. Although most novel proposals include the first one, two, or three chapters, it is perfectly acceptable to include one or more later chapters instead of or in addition to earlier ones. Sample chapters need not be consecutive or clearly related; they can even introduce two different characters and two different subplots. I have seen novel proposals with as few as thirty pages of sample chapters (this should be considered a minimum), and others with as many as one hundred twenty. Forty to seventy pages is about average.

In addition to your sample chapters you should include an "outline," which is actually a narrative synopsis of the plot. Normally this should cover the entire plot from beginning to end. However, if you have included the first chapter(s) in the proposal, you may, if you like, begin your synopsis where these leave off. If you choose to do this, the sample chapters should physically precede your outline in the proposal.

Stick firmly, even religiously, to the plot—to what happens. Don't include explanatory asides like, "Here there will be a long, moving scene in which Denise confronts her own fears of intimacy and finally comes to realize that she fears Tom more than she loves him." This doesn't show the reader anything of the scene itself. Instead, give the reader in synopsis form the specific external events that occur. (For example, "Denise runs outside, crying, and disappears into the forest.") Don't tell the reader what your character feels; describe the events as they are played out, moment by moment—though in synopsized form. Similarly, avoid long narrative descriptions of people and places. Physical descriptions of characters should be kept to an absolute minimum.

The great majority of novel outlines are written in the third person *present*—for example, "Denise leaves work early and visits Tom in his office." Third person past ("Denise left work early") is also acceptable, though it is usually best avoided because it can sound flat, singsong, and dull. Synopses written in the first person ("I left work early"), either in the past or present tense, are unusual but acceptable, provided they're appropriate for your book. Use whatever best represents the strengths and special qualities of your novel.

Pay special attention to the beginning and ending of your outline. They should *read* like a beginning and ending, even in synopsis form.

In essence, your outline should be a heavily condensed version of your entire novel. Outlines for novels can run anywhere from six to fifty double-spaced pages; fifteen to twenty-five pages seems about average. Outlines may be broken down by chapter, or they may be single extended narratives.

If you like, you may begin your outline with a cast-of-characters page, which provides a list of the major and supporting characters and a one- or two-sentence description of each person's situation, dilemma, or relationship with other characters. This item is optional.

SPECIAL GUIDELINES FOR NONFICTION BOOKS AND PROPOSALS

When it comes to nonfiction projects, book publishers are most concerned with these three questions: Who is the book for? (What is its intended readership?) What books already in print, or scheduled for publication, might compete with it? What makes the book different, unique, special, or better than any of its competitors? You should know the answers to these questions when you (or your agent) submits your project to editors. The answer to the third question is especially important.

Here are some ways to make your nonfiction book special, unique, or clearly superior to other, similar titles:

• Take a different tack, approach, or slant. Instead of writing yet another general health book, write *How to Get the Most from Your Doctor*.

• Narrow your focus. Your recipe book, *World's Favorite Cookies*, isn't going to sell because there are already a dozen books just like it. But a publisher might go for *One-Hour Christmas Cookies*.

• Combine ideas, fields, approaches, or focuses into a synthesis or an interdisciplinary approach. The world doesn't need yet another exposé of the politics and economics of the movie industry. But it might go for *A*

Day in Studio C, a close look at everything that goes on over a twenty-four-hour period on one Hollywood sound stage.

• Appeal to a different or more specific audience. When Lynne Burmyn wanted to write a book on astrology, she knew that general astrology guides were a dime a dozen. So she wrote *Sun Signs for Kids,* which she sold to St. Martin's.

• Present new ideas or information.

• Make your project more thorough, more detailed, more careful, or more complete than anything else available. That's what I did to sell the book you're reading now.

To make your book different from its competitors, or to find out if the project you've already begun is unique, you are going to have to identify your competition. It's important to be very thorough about this. Check bookstores, libraries, publishers' catalogs, *Subject Guide to Books in Print* (and any appropriate specialized *Books in Print* volumes listed on page 80), *Publishers Weekly, Library Journal, Forthcoming Books, Publishers' Trade List Annual,* and/or *Publishers' Catalogs Annual.*

To let editors know how and why your book is special, your book or proposal must convey an easily identifiable and immediately recognizable focus. Book publishers consider such a focus absolutely central to a book's salability. In fact, publishers insist that each book have its own *marketing handle*—a one-sentence (or shorter) description that sales representatives can use to sell the book to bookstores, and that advertisements can use to arouse reader interest. Your book's title and/or subtitle should express your book's handle quickly and clearly. (If you don't need a subtitle, don't use one.) Chapter titles should also be clear, concise, and immediately meaningful.

Next to your title and subtitle, the part of a nonfiction book that should most clearly telegraph your marketing handle—and the part that editors will pay the most attention to—is your introduction. Your book will need an introduction unless your title and subtitle say absolutely everything about your handle that needs to be said.

Your introduction should be written to attract and hold your potential reader. It should explain to the reader, in somewhat more detail than your title and subtitle, exactly what your book is about; who it is for; why it's worth reading; why you're qualified to write it; and what makes it unique, special, different, or better than anything else available in book form. If there *is* nothing else available, your introduction should say so. However, it should not stoop to an overt hard sell or advertising gimmickry, and it should be clear, concise, readable, and to the point.

In a proposal for a nonfiction book, the outline may take any form that is logical and clearly readable. An annotated table of contents often works well. Some writers prefer to write chapter-by-chapter outlines listing topics and subtopics, as I did in the proposal for this book. Others write narrative descriptions of each chapter; these may be in either the third person ("This chapter looks at . . .") or the first ("In this chapter I intend to . . ."). It is a good idea to outline every chapter, including those already written and included in the proposal.

If you have written a nonfiction book that details a more or less chronological sequence of events, such as a novel does, then your outline may (and probably should) be written as a plot synopsis, just like a novel outline. If you've written the story of your years growing up in a Moscow orphanage, you'll probably move readers (and editors) more with a novelistic outline than with a mere listing of facts and details.

A sample chapter is not always necessary, although usually one will help. The more extensive your outline is, the less important a sample chapter becomes. If you do include sample chapters, they need not be sequential or the first ones in the book.

Portions of two book proposals follow. Pages 274–78 contain portions of my original proposal for the book you are now reading. (Note some of the changes the book has undergone since then.) The full proposal contained an author biography, an introduction, one sample chapter of thirty-five pages, and an outline of each chapter (including the sample chapter). The complete proposal ran to eighty pages.

Pages 279–84 contain portions of my proposal for a humor book, *How to Have More Sex Than You Can Stand or Imagine.* Note that my author biography is very different here, because a different tone and emphasis are necessary. Here the contents and outline have been merged into one. The complete proposal runs thirty-five pages, and also includes two sample chapters and an introduction by Blanche Knott.

Before submitting your proposal to agents or editors, carefully consider exactly how long it will take you to complete the project. Add a couple of months to give yourself some leeway. Also, estimate carefully what your expenses, if any, will be. These might include costs of travel, hotels, office supplies, secretarial services, photocopying, illustrations, graphs and charts, photos, preparation of an index, writings by other people, and so on. If you don't know the cost of an item, get an estimate. It's important

Scott Edelstein
c/o Bobbe Siegel
41 W. 83 Street
New York, NY   10024
212-877-4985

BEHIND THE LINES

All the Important Things No One Else Will Tell
You About Freelance and Professional Writing

by Scott Edelstein

Projected length: 60,000 words

SCOTT EDELSTEIN has published over seventy short pieces (half fiction, half non-fiction) in magazines ranging from <u>Writers' Yearbook</u> to <u>Swank</u> to <u>Ellery Queen's Mystery Magazine</u> to <u>Artlines</u>. His previous books include THE STUDENTS' BOOK OF SECRETS (Bantam, 1985), a street-wise guide for college students, and FUTURE PASTIMES (Sherbourne Press, 1977), a science fiction anthology.

Since 1972 Mr. Edelstein has worked as an editor for several magazines, two book imprints, and two newspapers. He has also been a writing consultant, a literary agent, an arts administrator, a ghost writer, a freelance editor, a writing tutor, and an instructor at several universities. He lives in Kent, Ohio, where he continues to do freelance writing and editing.

BEHIND THE LINES

All the Important Things No One Else Will Tell You
About Freelance and Professional Writing

by Scott Edelstein

Contents

(Chapter 11, Taxes for Writers, appeared in slightly different form in the
1985 Writer's Yearbook, under the title "Income Taxes for the Successful
and the Unsuccessful Writer.")

Chapter 2

Researching the Markets

Contents:

--Why personally researching your potential markets is crucial to your success as a writer, and why it can make the difference between acceptance and rejection.

--Why reference books and writer's magazines alone will not tell you enough about any market.

--Where to do your market research.

--How to do your market research more effectively and efficiently.

--Getting started.

--The importance of looking through current issues of magazines and newspapers that may be potential markets.

Being sure that the publications are still alive and well.

Learning the publications' slants, approaches, preferred lengths, and audiences.

Noting any policy changes.

Being aware of changes in staffs or addresses.

Deciding whether a publication is one you genuinely want your work to appear in.

--Why any publication unavailable in a major library or a major newsstand is probably not worth submitting your work to.

--Locating the proper editor to send your work to.

Why this is crucially important.

How to do it.

--Deliberate misinformation fed to prospective writers by editors.

How to spot it.

Where it appears.

What forms it takes.

What to do about it.

--The importance of continuing to look at current issues of magazines and newspapers.

Keeping abreast of new departments or areas of interest.

Staying aware of policy changes.

Keeping up with changes in staffs or addresses.

Being sure that a publication is still alive and well.

--The book market: the importance of reading Publishers Weekly.

--Little-known but useful resources, and where to find them.

SCOTT EDELSTEIN
Literary Services
179 Berkeley St., Suite 1
Rochester, NY 14607
Telephone: 716-244-0645

HOW TO HAVE MORE SEX THAN YOU CAN STAND OR IMAGINE

by Jerry Fiocca

Introduction by Blanche Knott

Author of TRULY TASTELESS JOKES I, II, III, IV, V, VI, and VII

Projected length: 40,000 words

About the Author

JERRY FIOCCA is the leading authority on sex in Ohio. He was appointed to this position by the Governor of that state shortly after the publication of his study, "The Function of the Orgasm in Residents of Cleveland." Mr. Fiocca hopes someday to shake the Governor's hand, provided it has first been washed in soap and water.

Under his real name, Scott Edelstein, he has written regular humor columns for two national magazines. "Question Mark" has been appearing monthly in Writer's Digest since its October 1985 issue. "Ask Arty" has appeared regularly in The Artist's Magazine.

Over eighty of Scott's short stories and articles--many of them humorous-- have appeared in dozens of other publications, including Glamour, Essence, Writer's Yearbook, Ellery Queen's Mystery Magazine, Swank, Artlines, Science Fiction Monthly, and many others.

When he wants to, Scott can write serious non-fiction. He has six such volumes out or forthcoming: COLLEGE: A USER'S MANUAL (Bantam, Fall 1985); SURVIVING FRESHMAN COMPOSITION (Lyle Stuart, Spring 1987); PUTTING YOUR KIDS THROUGH COLLEGE (Consumer Reports Books, Fall 1988); THE NO-EXPERIENCE-NECESSARY WRITER'S COURSE (Stein and Day, Fall 1988); THE INDISPENSABLE WRITER'S GUIDE (Harper & Row, Spring 1989); and NOVEL APPROACHES (Writer's Digest Books, Spring 1989). He is also the editor of an anthology about the future of entertainment, FUTURE PASTIMES (Sherbourne Press, 1977).

Scott has worked as a book, magazine, and newspaper editor; an art and theater critic; a ghost writer; and a college writing teacher. He is not kidding about any of the information in these last four paragraphs.

BLANCHE KNOTT is the pseudonym of a husband-and-wife team living in New York City. Ms. Knott is the author of seven bestselling humor collections, TRULY TASTELESS JOKES I, II, III, IV, V, VI, and VII, which have sold well over four million copies. She is also the author of a volume of TRULY TASTELESS ETIQUETTE (St. Martin's Press).

<u>Targeted markets for HOW TO HAVE MORE SEX THAN YOU CAN STAND OR IMAGINE</u>:

<u>SPECIFIC TARGETS</u>:

    --Readers of Blanche Knott's bestselling books (her seven collections of TRULY TASTELESS JOKES plus TRULY TASTELESS ETIQUETTE).

    --Readers of Richard Smith's bestselling books (THE DIETER'S GUIDE TO WEIGHT LOSS DURING SEX, etc.).

    --People who would enjoy seeing sex experts, from Dr. Ruth to Alexandra Penney, lampooned.

<u>GENERAL TARGET</u>:

    --Anyone interested in sex who also likes to laugh.

HOW TO HAVE MORE SEX THAN YOU CAN STAND OR IMAGINE

by Jerry Fiocca
Introduction by Blanche Knott

Contents

that you know more or less what your costs will be so that you can negotiate an appropriate advance.

BIOGRAPHICAL AND SUPPORTING MATERIAL

When you submit your book or proposal, include a short "about the author" statement which substantiates your claim to expertise on your subject and/or your ability and status as a professional writer. It should be concise, straightforward, to the point, and no longer than four hundred words. Half this length is ideal. The tone should suit your book or proposal. See pages 275 and 280–81 for examples.

Do whatever you need to do to make yourself look as good as possible—without lying. If all you've sold so far are three very brief articles to neighborhood newspapers, and your only formal training has been an associate's degree in English from the University of Akron, your biography might read:

> HORACE QUINN is a writer whose work has appeared in several newspapers. He has a degree in literature from the University of Akron. He currently lives in Rochester, New York, where he continues his activities as a freelance writer.

If you have very few (fewer than Horace Quinn) or even no appropriate credentials at all, you should omit an "about the author" statement altogether.

If your book or proposal includes a preface or introduction written by someone else, include a short biography of that writer on a separate page. This should go immediately after your own biography. Stress that person's expertise and/or writing credentials.

When submitting a book or proposal, it is often a good idea to include samples of earlier work you've sold or published. These show editors you're a professional. Both completed short pieces and excerpts from previous books are fine. Indicate on the first page of each piece where and when it appeared (or will appear). Your samples should be as closely related to your book as possible. Don't include samples unless they'll make you look good; don't include pieces published in your church newsletter, neighborhood newspaper, or other very small publications.

If you're submitting a finished book, biographies and writing samples should appear immediately after your cover letter. Be sure to state in that letter what supporting materials you're enclosing.

PREVIOUSLY PUBLISHED MATERIAL

It is perfectly acceptable to submit to editors or agents a book that has previously been published, in whole or part, in magazines, anthologies, and/or newspapers. It is just as permissible to submit works that have been self-published or that have been previously published in book form by other houses and are now out of print. You may submit work in manuscript, and/or photocopies of published pieces. If the material has been previously published as a book, you may send either a manuscript or a copy of the printed book. However, when you send the book to publishers or agents, you must let them know what rights you have already sold to what portions of the manuscript. Those rights must of course be specifically excluded from any contract you sign.

ANTHOLOGIES

An *anthology* is a group of pieces by three or more different authors, usually on a particular topic or theme, assembled into book form by one or more editors. This is different from a *collection,* which is a book of short pieces by a single author (or a single set of collaborators). A *treasury* is another name for an anthology.

Anthologies may be sold via either completed manuscripts or proposals; they may contain new or reprinted material, or both.

Rights to works by other authors must be purchased for use in an anthology, and there are three ways in which these rights may be acquired:

1. You handle all the details yourself. You assume the legal responsibility for securing the necessary items and the financial responsibility for paying for them. You make these payments out of the money you receive from your publisher, which is enough to cover the payments and still leave a reasonable sum for you.

2. You and your publisher agree in your written contract that the publisher will set up a separate budget (called a permissions budget) to pay contributors. You are responsible for making the contractual arrangements for each item to be used. The cost of these items is paid by your publisher, up to the limit of the budget.

3. The publisher agrees to arrange and pay for all the necessary items. No effort or expense is required from you. This situation is ideal, and not terribly likely.

Unless your publisher is taking care of all the permissions for you, you'll need to draw up a permission form (or standard permission letter) to send to your contributors. Before you actually send out these forms, however, it is a good idea to submit a copy to your publisher's contracts department for approval and a critique. The contracts people will be able to catch any possible problems that could arise, and will make good suggestions for revising your form, if necessary.

Big names cost big money. On the other hand, big names are a big help in selling books and proposals to editors. If you are editing an anthology, it is often a good idea to include the work of one to three famous people if you can, or at least one to three people who are prominent in your book's subject area. However, it is generally prudent to avoid getting *lots* of big names, because the permissions costs can become exorbitant. (You never know for sure, though: I once got permission to reprint a piece by one of today's best-known and best-selling writers for $50. It doesn't hurt or cost anything to find out an asking price, or to make a fairly low offer and hope.)

You do not need to obtain permission from authors to submit their previously published pieces to editors as part of an anthology or anthology proposal. Simply photocopy the published pieces and include them in your manuscript. However, once you sell the anthology to a publisher, you must of course negotiate and obtain written permission from the author to publish each piece (or get your publisher to agree to do this).

What do you do if a piece you planned to use turns out to be unavailable, or if its selling price turns out to be much higher than you expected? You should of course first try to negotiate with the seller; but if that brings no results, contact your editor and explain the situation. Unless the piece is by some prominent or famous person, there should usually be no problem in substituting a piece by a different author. It may also be possible to locate a different piece by the same author that is cheaper.

ENDORSEMENTS, INTRODUCTIONS, AND COLLABORATIONS

Although any book must ultimately stand on its own merits, the fact is that agents, editors, and readers will look at your project more favorably if the name of someone they respect or admire (or someone who is already well-known) is associated with it. Such association can take one of three forms: endorsement; the writing of an introduction, foreword, or preface;

or collaboration or pseudocollaboration. Although such an association is neither expected nor required by editors, the less of a reputation (or the fewer publications) you have, the more helpful someone else's name can be in getting your book sold.

Endorsements

Endorsements are quotes from recognized authorities or other prominent people that praise your book or your writing in general. Used on book jackets and covers, and in press releases, advertisements, and catalogs, they can do wonders to help sell books. They are even more useful in arousing interest from editors and agents. If you can get Roger Tory Peterson to endorse your book on birds, or Grace Paley to endorse your novel, your book becomes much more attractive in editors' eyes.

An endorsement must be from someone of recognized authority or national prominence, at least in the appropriate field. If you've written a book about recent breakthroughs in medicine, the endorsement of your family doctor will be worthless. But words of praise from the president of the American Medical Association, or from any one of its ex-presidents, will be worth a great deal. An endorsement from art dealer Leo Castelli will help sell your art book, but it will do nothing to help sell your history of Uruguay.

If someone is famous enough, however, his or her endorsement will help sell a trade book of *any* sort. Praise from Bryant Gumbel, Carl Sagan, Erma Bombeck, Nancy Reagan, Ella Fitzgerald, Howard Baker, Steven Spielberg, or Connie Chung will catch editors' (and readers') eyes regardless of the kind of book the praise is for.

Here are a few items of protocol regarding asking people for endorsements:

• Never ask anyone to lie. Ask people to give their honest reactions, even if they're negative. Naturally, don't use their comments unless they're positive. It is okay to use only the most positive excerpts from someone's comments.

• Explain why you're asking for the endorsement. Make sure people understand how important their few words can be in selling your book; most people don't realize just how difficult it is for a little-known writer to get published.

• Be polite. *Never* be obnoxious, demanding, or pushy.

The best endorsement is a concise, eloquent letter of praise signed by the endorser. But if what you get is an oral endorsement, or a written statement that needs editing or excerpting, feel free to type the appropriate portions of the quote, double-spaced, on a separate sheet of paper. You will need the endorser's oral permission (written permission is even better) to use the endorsement as a selling tool. A simple endorsement page appears on page 290.

If endorsers are not likely to be known to editors by name, be sure that the letters or endorsement pages include their titles or primary credentials—for example, "President of the American Association of University Professors" or "Author of the novels *Cat's Paw, Holy Night,* and *Mainline,* all published by McGraw-Hill."

Occasionally, busy but prominent people may ask you to write their endorsements for them. This goes on all the time, and there's nothing wrong with it. Be sure that they see and approve any endorsement before you use it.

When enclosing endorsements with a proposal or book, put them in a prominent place—either just under your cover letter or cover page, or in the left-hand pocket of your proposal folder. Each endorsement should be on a separate page. One strong endorsement from a well-respected endorser is often sufficient for a proposal, but if you can get three or four, that's even better.

To give you an idea how important endorsements can be, when I was an agent I got a call from an editor at a major publishing house who said, "I like this proposal you sent me, but I don't think I can get it through unless you can get me some endorsements from famous people. Can you?" I did, and the book sold. The editor told me later that it was the endorsements that did it.

Publishers routinely send out dozens of prepublication copies of books to prominent people who might respond with usable quotes. Once you've sold your book to a publisher, you can help secure further endorsements by giving your editor a list of well-known people in your field, everyone prominent or famous whom you know personally, and anyone else you think might provide a useful endorsement. Always include people's titles or positions, addresses, and, if possible, phone numbers (both work and home).

You can also, if you like, send copies of your published book to people and ask for their reactions. Any favorable comments on this book (or on your writing in general) can be used as endorsements to help sell your next

Jerry Fiocca's HOW TO HAVE MORE SEX THAN YOU CAN STAND OR IMAGINE is crazy, uproarious, and as surprising as it is funny. I recommend it heartily to anyone who has sex, used to have sex, or is thinking about having sex.

W. Shakespeare

one. Published comments from reviewers can also be used as endorsements for future projects. You may either type up endorsement pages using pertinent excerpts from reviews or photocopy the reviews in their entirety. You do *not* need reviewers' permission to do this.

Introductions, Prefaces, and Forewords

Even more valuable than endorsements are introductions from experts, recognized authorities, and famous people. The guidelines for getting someone to write an introduction are more or less identical to those for getting people to write endorsements, with one exception: some people will expect you to pay them for their introductions. You needn't offer money when you first bring up the idea; but don't be surprised if your potential introducer asks for some. The size of the fee, and the terms, are usually negotiable.

Sometimes a complete unknown with a useful title can provide an introduction that will make all the difference to editors. For instance, if you've written a diet book and don't have a background in the health sciences, an introduction from *any* M.D. will lend credence to your book. If you've written a scholarly study of Emily Dickinson but are not a college graduate, an introduction from a professor of literature at a well-known college or university will make a big difference.

If you do have someone else write an introduction, preface, or foreword for your book, be sure that both of you sign a written agreement setting forth the terms of its use. Get permission to use the introduction in *all* editions of your book. A simple agreement of one or two sentences is fine; for example: "In exchange for the right to publish your introduction to my book *Silent Thunder* in all editions of that work throughout the world, I agree to pay you $200 on execution of this agreement, and 5 percent of all the monies I receive from that book in the future, after agent's commissions, within thirty days of my receipt of said monies."

As with endorsements, you may be able to work out an arrangement whereby you write the introduction yourself and simply have someone else sign it.

Collaborations

The best way of all to make use of someone else's name and status is to collaborate on a project with him or her. The second best way is to pretend to.

Collaboration can mean actually working on the project together. It can mean asking your collaborator to put in a token effort, such as writing one chapter, or critiquing the project, or editing it, or helping you with some difficult spots. It can also mean getting your collaborator to do nothing more than lend his or her name to the project, simply to make it more salable.

Here are some sample situations:

• You've written your first novel (or a proposal for it) but have published nothing previously. You have a friend who has already published three novels with major houses. You add his name to the byline (with his permission, of course) to make the book more attractive to editors.

• You've written a proposal for a fitness guide but do not have a background in medicine or health. You get your physician to add her byline to yours, suddenly giving your book credence.

• You've written *anything at all* and have a friend who is a famous actor or politician. His name added to yours makes your book instantly attractive to trade book editors.

In such cases, nothing about the book need have changed except the byline.

Naturally you shouldn't expect anyone to sign on as your collaborator, or even your pseudocollaborator, unless you can offer payment in return. It is crucial that whatever terms you and your coauthor agree upon be put explicitly in writing and signed by both parties. Exactly how much to pay your coauthor or pseudocoauthor will depend on the size of their contribution and the degree of their prominence or fame. However, most of the money from the project should go into your pocket unless your collaborator genuinely puts in a major share of the work.

No one is going to agree to become your coauthor or pseudocoauthor who doesn't like and approve of your book or proposal. So don't be secretive with it. Let potential collaborators look it over carefully, at their leisure.

Be sure to get from your collaborator a resumé and/or a list of all his or her relevant credentials and publications. Type up an "about the authors" page that includes two short biographies, one for each of you. Be sure to emphasize in your collaborator's biography all those credentials you don't have yourself, so that, together, you appear to be an ideal team to write the book.

Whose name goes first in the byline? Generally, I'd suggest putting the name of the better-known or better-credentialed person first, both on the title page and on the "about the authors" page.

More details on collaborations appear on pages 46–52.

ROYALTY STATEMENTS

Once your book has been published, you should normally receive royalty statements twice a year, even if you are not owed any money, until the book is declared out of print. (A few scholarly and smaller presses issue statements only once a year.) If your book was sold through an agent, each royalty statement will be sent to your agent, who should promptly send you a copy. If you (or your agent) are due any money, a check for the amount due should accompany the statement. (Actually, the term *royalty statement* is inaccurate, since a statement should include information on the sale of subsidiary rights as well as royalties.)

All of the following information should appear in a royalty statement:

• The number of copies sold through regular retail outlets in the United States, its possessions, and in some cases the Philippines; in Canada; in other foreign countries; through mail order, as premiums, and through other unusual means; and at an unusually high discount (usually 50 percent or more)

• The applicable royalty rate in each of the above cases, and the total royalties earned in each case

• The number of copies returned to the publisher unsold; debits against your account for those returns; and the total of those debits

• The amount withheld, if any, as a reserve against future returns

• A credit for the amount of the previous period's withheld reserve

• A list of all income (if any) received by the publisher from the sales of subsidiary rights; your percentage of that income; and the total such income due you

• The total amount due you, after any advances have been subtracted— or the amount of any advance remaining unearned

Figures should apply to the most recent royalty period. Cumulative totals covering all royalty periods since the book's publication should also appear.

If a license has been granted to another firm to publish your book or a portion of it, either a copy of this license or a description of its terms should be sent to you by your initial publisher. It is your right to receive one of these, so if you don't receive one automatically, call the subsidiary rights department (also known as the rights and permissions department) of your publisher and request it. If you have to, insist on it, or have your agent insist on it.

Whenever you receive a royalty statement from any publisher, look it over *very* carefully, item by item. Check all math. If the statement lacks any information, if any information on it seems questionable or incorrect, or if you have any other question about the statement, contact the royalty department of your publisher immediately for clarification or explanation. You have a right to this information. If you are not given the information you want promptly, continue to press for it—politely at first, less politely thereafter if necessary. If you have to, insist on speaking to someone's superior, and if necessary the superior's superior. Have your agent do this for you, if you have one. This is part of an agent's job, and he or she can often get better results.

Be especially careful in noting the amount withheld as a reserve against returns. Many publishing contracts allow publishers to withhold a "reasonable" but otherwise undefined sum of royalty money against returns; but the amount actually withheld on a royalty statement may be much more than is reasonable. A genuinely reasonable reserve is 35 percent or less of the royalty (but not subsidiary rights) earnings for that period, 45 percent for mass-market paperbacks—but I have seen publishers try to withhold much more.

If, even after your (and your agent's) best efforts, you are still not satisfied that your royalty statement is accurate, you have the right to hire an accountant to audit your publisher's records. This can be expensive, so I wouldn't recommend it unless you believe your publisher has made a large error in its favor, or unless you think your statement has been deliberately falsified. Most book contracts require publishers to pay for this audit if their accounts are found to be in error by more than 5 percent in their favor; they must also, of course, promptly pay you the amount in error. A clause stipulating this should appear in your contract (see page 349 for details).

Royalty statements and checks will usually be mailed out on the last possible contractual day. If your contract calls for your statement and check to be mailed "sometime during March," expect it to be mailed on March 31, possibly in the late evening. If your royalty statement is more than a week late, call (or have your agent call) the royalty department of

ROYALTY STATEMENT FORM

F&W Publications, Inc.
1507 Dana Avenue
Cincinnati, Ohio 45207
513-531-2222

WRITER'S DIGEST/NORTH LIGHT BOOKS

Agent/Author: Title:

Royalty Statement for period ended _____ , 19_____

	U N I T S			NET RECEIPTS	ROYALTY EARNINGS		TOTAL COPIES SOLD
	Sales	Returns	Net		%	$	
Trade							
Cloth							
Paper							
Direct to Consumer							
Cloth							
Paper							
Canadian Sales							
Book Club Sales							
Cloth							
Paper							
Book Club Premiums/ Bonuses							
Special Sales:							
Subsidiary Rights:							
Total Earnings:							

Adjustments

Net—negative balance—
  Carry forward to
  next period   _____

Net earnings;
  Check enclosed   _____

ROYALTY STATEMENT

DOUBLEDAY & COMPANY, INC.

7371/1/N/0000/07134   ROYALTY STATEMENT

PAGE 1

FOR THE 6 MONTHS ENDING   10/31/86   TITLE YOUR DOWN SYNDROME CHILD

SOC/SEC OR TAX I.D.   00000000   ISBN   23023 0

PUBLISHED DATE   08/15/85   AUTHOR MCCLURG EUNICE

TO   SCOTT EDELSTEIN LIT
      219 SOUTH PEARL SUITE 1
      KENT, OH 44240

BOOK SLS SOURCE	RETAIL PRICE	ROYALTY PERCENT	RATES	COPIES SOLD	COPIES RETURNED	NET COPIES	ROYALTY EARNED
DOM.	15.95	10.00	1.5950	4,070	29	4,041	6,445.40
CAN.	15.95	5.00	.7975	369	18	351	279.92
EXP.	15.95	8.00	1.2760	1		1	1.28
SPEC.	.00	5.00	.0000	101		101	80.55

NET EARNINGS DOUBLEDAY BOOK SALES   6,807.15

NET TOTAL OF ALL EARNINGS   6,807.15

ADJUSTMENTS TO CURRENT EARNINGS

TRANSACTION	DATE	ADDITIONS	SUBTRACTIONS
ADVANCE	11/84	.00	3,750.00
ADVANCE	09/85	.00	3,750.00
CHARGE FOR INDEXING	08/86	.00	207.37

NET UNEARNED   900.22

ROYALTY STATEMENT

DOUBLEDAY & COMPANY, INC.
6868/17N/0000/07134   ROYALTY STATEMENT

PAGE 1

FOR THE 6 MONTHS ENDING   04/30/87   TITLE YOUR DOWN SYNDROME CHILD

SOC/SEC OR TAX I.D.   000000000   ISBN   23023 0

PUBLISHED DATE   08/15/86   AUTHOR MCCLURG EUNICE

TO   SCOTT EDELSTEIN LIT
179 BERKELEY ST SUITE 1
ROCHESTER NY 14607

BOOK SLS SOURCE	RETAIL PRICE	ROYALTY PERCENT	RATES	COPIES SOLD	COPIES RETURNED	NET COPIES	ROYALTY EARNED
DOM.	15.95	10.00	1.5950	960	492	468	746.46
CAN.	15.95	5.00	.7975	32	96	64—	51.04—
M/O.	15.95	5.00	.7975	5		5	3.99
SPEC.	.00	5.00	.0000	15		15	11.96

NET EARNINGS DOUBLEDAY BOOK SALES   711.37

NET TOTAL OF ALL EARNINGS   711.37

ADJUSTMENTS TO CURRENT EARNINGS

TRANSACTION	DATE	ADDITIONS	SUBTRACTIONS
UNEARNED BALANCE FORWARD	01/87	.00	900.22

NET UNEARNED   188.85

your publisher and politely but firmly insist that it be sent immediately. Keep careful track of the dates when statements are due.

Normally a publisher will supply royalty information *only* in official statements. You can try calling the royalty department for information, but don't be surprised if you can't get anything over the phone and are simply told to wait for your statement. It *is* both reasonable and wise, however, to ask your editor to let you know whenever a subsidiary rights sale is made (and the details of that sale), and whenever your book goes into a new printing (and the size of that printing). Most editors will be willing to give this information to you. But don't ask them for a lot of detailed information, and don't badger them with monthly calls asking, "How's the book doing now?"

On page 295 is a blank royalty statement from F&W Publications. This is an unusually easy royalty statement to read. Note, however, that it computes royalties on net receipts rather than on retail or invoice price, which is somewhat unusual. (The *Net Receipts* column would simply be changed by hand to *Retail Price* for any author who was entitled to receive a royalty based on the retail price.)

On page 296 is the first royalty statement Eunice McClurg received for her Doubleday book, *Your Down Syndrome Child.* On page 297 is the royalty statement she received six months later. Note that you need the first statement to be able to understand and check the accuracy of the second.

When a new edition of a book is issued—even a slightly updated edition published in the same format—sales of that new edition are computed separately, not cumulatively. For example, suppose your contract entitles you to a hardcover royalty of 10 percent on the first five thousand copies, 12½ percent on the next five thousand, and 15 percent thereafter. The initial edition of your book sells twelve thousand copies in the first two years. Your publisher then asks you to do a slightly revised, updated edition. You do, and the publisher issues it in an identical-looking hardcover format. The first five thousand copies of this new edition will *not* receive a 15 percent royalty, but only 10 percent; the next five thousand will receive 12½ percent; and only thereafter will you receive 15 percent once again.

PROMOTING YOUR OWN BOOK

Promotion is another word for *advertising and selling.* In general, the more your publisher promotes your book, the more copies it will sell. Each publishing season, a few books are promoted very heavily; but the vast majority receive only minor promotion—perhaps a press release and a few small ads.

Every publisher sets an initial promotion budget for each of its books. When that has been spent, promotion usually ends, unless the book meets or exceeds sales projections, in which case additional promotion *may* be ordered. Indeed, books that receive little initial promotion but that sell like crazy anyway sometimes receive major promotion only *after* they have sold well for some time.

Most writers tend to sit at home and let the publishers handle all the details of promoting their books. If you are serious about your book doing well, you must take a more active approach. First, work with your publisher to encourage promotion on your book. Second, promote your book on your own.

About five months before your book is to be published, get in touch with your editor to say that you will be happy to do whatever is required to help promote your book. Spend some time thinking about ways of promoting it, places where it can be promoted, and audiences it can be promoted to. Perhaps you know of a group of potential sales outlets or readers your publisher doesn't even know exists. If you come up with any bright ideas (and you should), send them in a letter to your editor for forwarding to the firm's promotion people. Or if you prefer, find out the name of the people in charge of promotion and publicity and write to them directly.

If your publisher sends you an author's questionnaire to complete (and most will), fill it out very thoroughly and carefully. Take time to think about each question, and provide as much information and detail as you possibly can.

You can also help your publisher promote your book by supplying the following lists:

• All the specialized publications in your field that might be good places to advertise your book. Include addresses.

• Groups, businesses, and organizations that might be interested in selling or giving away copies of your book to their members, employees, or clients. Again provide addresses.

• All the places you've lived since you were born. The media in each of these towns can tout you as a local author. If you've lived in small towns, also indicate the nearest big cities.

• Book clubs that you believe might be interested in your book.

• Periodicals (especially little-known or specialized ones) that might be interested in publishing excerpts from your book.

• Names and addresses of publications in your field that might review your book.

• Names, addresses, and phone numbers of *people* you know who might review your book. You can list many of your writer friends and acquaintances here.

• Names, addresses, and (if available) phone numbers of people who might provide endorsements for your book.

• Names and addresses of any bookstores where you are known (as either author or customer), with which you have some connection, or where you know one of the owners or managers. Where possible, provide owners' or managers' names.

• Any previous experience you have had being interviewed for radio, TV, magazines, and/or newspapers. If possible, enclose photocopies of print interviews or articles.

• All your significant publications.

It's also helpful to send a couple of photos of yourself (see page 227 for details).

If your publisher is a very small one, you might also volunteer to write cover copy, a press release, and/or ads for your book.

I make a point of visiting a publisher four to six months before it will publish my book. I call my editor a few weeks in advance and ask him or her to set up a meeting with people from publicity, promotion, and sales. This enables me to meet them face to face; and it gives them the chance to ask me questions about myself and my book, to get a feel for how "promotable" I am, and to think of me as not just another author but a living, breathing person. It gives me the chance to explain my book's strong points, potential audience, and special features. It enables the promotion people to tell me exactly what is being planned to help sell my book. And it enables all of us to brainstorm, exchange ideas, make suggestions, get to know one another, and, if we're lucky, get to like each other. On top of all this, I usually get taken out to lunch at a good restaurant. I recommend such a trip each time one of your books is forthcoming, even if you keep the same publisher for book after book. All these trips are 80 to 100 percent tax deductible.

It is also an excellent idea to promote your book on your own, at your own (tax-deductible) expense. Chapters 5, 6, and 7 provide many excellent tips for promoting yourself and your work. Here are some additional tips concerning books:

• There now exists an independent book promotion firm called Sensible Solutions (6 E. 39th Street, Suite 1201, New York, NY 10016, 212-532-5280), which is run by Judith Appelbaum (author of *How to Get Happily Published*) and Florence Janovic. Sensible Solutions provides promotion for books of all sorts. Its services are cheaper and much more tuned into the book industry than those of advertising agencies—but they are not inexpensive. For each book project, Sensible Solutions can design an entire promotion scheme, which may include direct mail flyers, ads in periodicals, and/or special promotions. It is also possible to purchase its services on a more limited basis for an hourly fee.

• *Promotion* is the art of advertising and selling a product. *Publicity* is the art of getting authors and their works into the public eye via the media. One good way to help you and your book get noticed is to hire a publicist. This person sends out news releases; arranges interviews with newspapers, magazines, TV, and/or radio; arranges appearances such as book signings; and generally touts you and your work. A publicist's job is to generate attention and interest—and thereby generate sales and still more attention.

Publicists, unfortunately, are very expensive. Don't expect to spend less than about $1500 for publicity for one book, and don't be surprised if the costs run a lot higher. It's a good idea to shop around and get quoted some hourly rates or rates for specific services. Ask each publicist for samples of previous work, such as news releases, and for the names of some of his or her other clients. *Literary Market Place* contains a list of publicists who work largely or primarily for writers under the heading "Public Relations Services." Local publicists are listed in the Yellow Pages under "Public Relations."

If you are thinking of hiring a publicist, keep in mind that not every book needs or deserves publicity. Most trade books can benefit from publicity, since they are written for a general audience. But textbooks, scholarly books, and other projects with a limited or specialized readership really don't need to be publicized. The average reader simply isn't going to be interested in things like *An Introduction to Fluid Mechanics* or *Sculpture in the Middle Ages.*

• Don't arrange any publicity or promotion on your own until you know exactly what efforts your publisher will be putting forth in these areas. It's wasteful to duplicate anything your publisher is already doing; more importantly, if your publisher knows you're willing to pay for publicity and promotion on your own, it may well choose to scrap or reduce its own plans for pushing your book. So, shortly before publication of your book, find out *exactly* what is being done by way of promotion and publicity. Ask to be sent copies of all ads and news releases for your book, and find out where those ads and news releases are going. Then, *after* the publisher's own promotion and publicity efforts have run their course, usually a few months after publication, and *if* you feel more needs to be done, hire someone on your own.

• Publishers tend to put most or all their publicity and promotion efforts into a book shortly before and after its initial publication; but you can keep a book selling, and perhaps selling well, by continuing to promote it on your own.

• Interviews and appearances on radio and TV can often be quite helpful in spreading the word about your book. If your publisher doesn't arrange any of these for you, you can arrange them yourself by following the steps in *Publicity for Books and Authors,* by Peggy Glenn (Aames-Allen Publishing Company). Being listed in the talk-show directory *Directory of Experts, Authorities, and Spokespersons,* edited by Mitchell P. Davis (Broadcast Interview Source, 2500 Wisconsin Avenue, Suite 930, Washington, DC 20007) can also help.

• Do book signings. Simply call up the managers of bookstores, explain who you are, what you've published, and who published it, and ask to do a signing. Many bookstore managers will be happy to oblige, and normally they'll publicize the event for you. Be sure to set up signings three to four months in advance, so that bookstores have enough time to order and receive copies of your book(s). Let the bookstore know of (and encourage it to order) *all* your published books, including any self-published ones— not just the newest one. Book signings typically run two to four hours; the author receives no pay. Keep some extra copies of your book(s) in your car in case the bookstore runs out or, God forbid, the books it ordered don't arrive in time.

It is normally proper to do no more than one book signing per town or metropolitan area, though in very large metro areas it is okay to do more, provided they are far apart. For example, it's all right to do signings in Manhattan, Stamford, Newark, and Wantagh.

• With a little money (about $250–$300) from you or your publisher, you can make a book signing into a publication party. You'll still sign copies of your new book, and the bookstore will still set up a promotional display; but the event will be much more of a celebration. Invitations will go out in advance to your friends, colleagues, people you want to get to know, likely buyers, and anyone else who might be interested or who you'd like to have come. Good food and drink—wine, champagne, good cheese and bread, etc.—are served, and the whole event is rather festive. Ask your publisher whether it will spring for a publication party at a local bookstore or at least split the cost with you. If it won't, you can of course arrange a publication party with the bookstore yourself.

• If your book is fiction or poetry, arrange a reading in or near your hometown. Better yet, arrange a series of readings in many different cities. See pages 195–98 for details.

• A few months before your book is to be published, ask your publisher to make up a simple flyer advertising it. This should include a mail-order form. Ask for a few hundred of these to be sent to you. You can then distribute them whenever you give a reading or lecture or whenever you run into someone who might be interested in your book. You can also easily include a flyer with any letter you write to anyone. This is a very inexpensive way to generate awareness of your book and of course an easy way to generate orders. Many publishers will be happy to do up such a flyer for you—*if* you ask them to. (Harper & Row produced a flyer for this book—but only after I asked for one.) When your supply of flyers runs low, simply photocopy more.

• Some writers who have written books that they feel have major sales potential have gone so far as to become partners with their publishers in promoting and publicizing their projects. One novelist I know, after learning what the promotion budget would be for his book, called up his publisher and said, "I'll contribute an equal amount to promotion, and we'll work on an ad campaign together." The publisher agreed, and the author even wrote some of the ads himself. This same writer also spent the money to have his manuscript set in type as soon as it was completed; he then sent these "pregalley" galleys to dozens of famous writers, asking for endorsements to be used in ads and on the book's cover. Another writer spent $6000 to test-market several potential titles for his book; the title people responded to most positively was the one he ultimately used.

• Publisher's Services (Box 51103, Seattle, WA 98115, 206-527-2693) offers several promotional and publicity services: *Spotlight,* a nationwide publicity newsletter targeted at radio stations that interview writers; *Spotlight Northwest,* a publicity newsletter targeted at all media, serving the northwestern United States; *Focus on Books,* a newsletter for reviewers and librarians that announces and describes small-press books for children and books on women's and family issues; mailing lists of reviewers, librarians, and other groups; and direct mailing of flyers and other ads for children's books and books on raising and caring for children.

• Some good books on self-promotion and publicity:

101 Ways to Market Your Books, by John Kremer (Ad-Lib Publications, 51 N. 5th Street, Fairfield, IA 52556)

Publishing, Promoting, and Selling Your Book for Self-Publishers and Impatient Writers, by John C. Bartone (ABBE Publishers' Association, 4111 Gallows Road, Annandale, VA 22003)

BOOK PACKAGERS

Book packagers, also called book producers, provide writing, rewriting, collaboration, ghostwriting, and editorial services to publishers. They also typically provide the basic concepts for many books and, in some cases, layout, illustrations, covers, and book design as well. Some even supply printing and binding.

Book packagers work in two ways. They may approach publishers with a finished manuscript (with or without artwork), or with a proposal or idea for a book or series. This may have been staff-written, it may be the work of an affiliated freelancer based on an idea of the packager's, or it may be the work of a writer the packager is representing, just as an agent would. The publisher then works out a deal and signs a contract with the packager, much as it would with an individual author. However, book design and artwork, and often typesetting, are often included in the package.

Alternatively, a publisher may approach a packager with an idea, a proposal, or part or all of a manuscript and say, "Make this into a finished book (or a book ready to go to the printer) for us."

It is possible to approach a book packager with a book or proposal just as you would an agent or editor. However, keep the following points in mind:

• A packager typically takes a much higher percentage of a project's earnings than an agent. A 25 to 50 percent share is standard, but 50 percent should be considered the absolute maximum.

• In general, packagers are interested only in the following kinds of books: potential best-sellers (either fiction or nonfiction); series (or books that might spawn a series); books that are highly unusual in form, content, and/or design; books that are (or will be) heavily visual or that rely heavily on design; and humor books, especially unusual ones. Book packagers handle only trade books and trade book proposals.

• If a book packager agrees to represent your project and offers you a contract, look this contract over *very* carefully. Make sure you are not paid only a flat fee for your work, that you do not do the project "for hire" (see pages 364–66), and that you do not have to supply anything other than a typewritten manuscript (and perhaps illustrations, if appropriate). Review "The Author-Agent Agreement" on pages 246–53. If necessary, have a literary attorney look over the agreement the packager offers you.

If you have appropriate publishing credits, you can also contact packagers to try to be hired as a staff writer or to write freelance projects based on the packager's ideas.

Book packagers are listed in *Literary Market Place* under the heading "Book Producers." For an excellent history and overview of book packagers, see the article "Book Packaging and the Big Time" by Charles Salzberg in the August 9, 1985, issue of *Publishers Weekly*.

MISCELLANEOUS TIPS FOR BOOK AUTHORS

Here are some further helpful tips:

• The average length of time between acceptance of a finished manuscript and publication is eleven months. Eighteen months is not uncommon. Six to seven months is generally the minimum.

• Most book contracts will allow you to buy copies of your own book at a 40 percent discount, provided you do not sell them. In practice, however, publishers don't mind if you sell these copies, so long as you sell them to individuals (people attending your readings, members of your writers' group, etc.) and not to stores or distributors.

• Picture books for children and other illustrated books (and proposals for them) may be submitted with or without illustrations. If illustrations are enclosed, editors have the right to offer to publish only the text and to commission illustrations from another artist. This is fairly common in children's publishing, where publishers like to hire well-known artists to illustrate books by little-known writers, so that parents and librarians will recognize at least one name on the cover. (If the illustrator chosen by the publisher is well known, he or she can command as much as 50 percent of a book's earnings, occasionally even more.) It is also possible that an agent may offer to represent only the text of a book for which you have also submitted illustrations or photographs. Book packagers may do the same, and/or insist on providing visual material by one of their own artists.

• Most book publishers issue new catalogs two to three times a year; catalogs of mass-market paperbacks are issued four to twelve times annually. Your editor should automatically send you at no charge at least two copies of the catalog that announces the publication of your book. If you haven't received these by three months before publication, ask your editor to send you copies. Most editors will also be happy to send you additional copies on request, at no charge.

• If you will be out of town or otherwise unavailable anytime during the six months before your book is published or the three months afterward, let your editor know in advance. If possible, provide phone numbers of where you can be reached.

• Some miscellaneous terms:

El-hi books: textbooks for children in kindergarten through twelfth grade.

Juveniles: books for children under age 12.

Young adult books: books for children ages 12–17.

RECOMMENDED BOOKS

For readers desiring more detailed information on the book publishing industry, the following books are recommended:

How to Get Your Book Published, by Herbert W. Bell (Writer's Digest Books). Especially useful for the authors of texts, professional books, and scholarly volumes.

In Cold Type, by Leonard Shatzkin (Houghton Mifflin). An overview and critique of the book publishing industry.

A Writer's Guide to Book Publishing, by Richard Balkin (Dutton/ Hawthorn). A thorough and very readable guide.

Book Publishing: What It Is, What It Does, by John P. Dessauer (Bowker). Perhaps the most comprehensive look at book publishing available, by one of the field's leading experts.

The Blockbuster Complex, by Thomas Whiteside (Wesleyan University Press). A close look at commercial book publishing and distribution.

10. ✎

Publishing Contracts and How to Negotiate Them

CONTRACT BASICS

A contract between a writer and a publishing firm can take any of the following five forms:

- A written contract signed by both parties. Each party keeps a copy. In some cases (most often, book contracts) a witness to each party's signature is required; the witnesses must also sign the agreement. A publisher's standard, unamended printed contract is called its *boilerplate*.
- A formal letter of agreement written by the editor or publisher to the author setting forth the terms of publication—in essence, a formal contract in letter form. It is offered in duplicate; the author signs the letter, returns one copy to the publisher or editor, and keeps one copy.
- An informal letter of agreement. This is identical to a formal agreement letter except that the author need not sign or return a copy.
- An agreement printed on the back of a publisher's check. Endorsing the check constitutes acceptance of the agreement.
- An oral agreement between the writer and the editor or publisher.

All of these forms of agreements, including oral agreements, are legally binding, provided the terms have been clearly and unambiguously agreed to by both sides. The seal and signature of a notary are neither useful nor required.

Any publishing agreement, whether written or oral, should specify, at minimum, what rights are being purchased, who is purchasing them from whom, how much money will be paid in exchange for these rights, when this money will be paid, and where and when the piece will be published.

If a written or oral agreement does *not* specify what rights are being sold, or if no specific agreement is made at all concerning the publication of a piece, then under U.S. copyright law, the seller automatically conveys to the publisher *only* the nonexclusive right to publish that piece in that particular publication in whatever territory it is normally distributed. The publisher *can,* however, publish that piece as many times as it wishes in that particular publication without getting the author's permission and without paying the author any more money.

When you make a deal with a publisher or editor, normally you should insist on some form of written agreement setting forth the terms of publication, even if it is only a handwritten note on company stationery from the editor to you. If your publisher doesn't give you a written contract and you feel one is necessary, feel free to write one yourself, make and sign two copies, and send them to your editor for signing.

In some cases, however, an oral agreement is sufficient. These general principles apply:

• The smaller a publication and/or its audience, the more reasonable and acceptable an oral agreement is. If you write some articles for a neighborhood or small-town newspaper, or have your play produced by a college or community theater, or give a reading of your work at a writers' center or on a local cable TV channel, you should neither expect nor insist upon a written agreement. You should always, however, sign a written agreement for the publication of a book, no matter how small the publishing house may be.

• Some large newspapers and magazines make only oral agreements with writers. This is normally fine.

• Literary magazines and scholarly journals, especially some of the smaller ones, often make only oral agreements with writers. This is legitimate. However, if a literary or scholarly press wants to publish your book or chapbook (a small book of fifteen to eighty pages), you should execute a signed formal agreement.

If you do make only an oral agreement with an editor, it's important to do three things. First, jot down all the terms you've agreed to so that you have a written record of them. Second, once the deal has been closed, orally review the terms with the editor to make sure both of you understand them clearly. Third, *save* your list of terms, just in case there is a disagreement later. It is also often an excellent idea, once the deal has been made, to type up that list of terms in a letter and send it to your editor (keeping a copy for yourself), so that both of you have a written record of your agreement.

From the moment you create a piece of writing, you own and control all rights to that piece. A publication contract involves the transfer of some or all of those rights from the author to a publisher, usually in exchange for a specified amount of money.

Rights are commonly sold or transferred according to five sets of conditions: geographical area, form of publication, language, time, and exclusivity. If you sell first North American serial rights to a piece, you're selling the exclusive right to publish that piece for the first time in a periodical distributed throughout North America. (*Serial* is another word for *periodical; exclusive* means that no one else in that territory may exercise this right.) If you sell worldwide German language rights to your book, you are selling the right to publish and sell a German language translation of that book throughout the world. If you sell one-time nonexclusive British Commonwealth serial rights to that same book, you are selling the right to publish part or all of that book anywhere in the British Commonwealth countries once in any single periodical. Because you have sold these rights on a nonexclusive basis, you can sell the same rights over and over again, in or outside of the British Commonwealth. If you sell all rights, you are selling all present and future rights to publish, perform, or otherwise use the piece throughout the universe.

Rights that a publisher purchases but does not itself exercise are called *subsidiary rights.* If you sell an article's first North American and British Commonwealth serial rights to a magazine distributed only in the United States and Canada, that magazine has the right to sell your piece to British Commonwealth magazines and pocket all the money from such sales. If you sell a book's North American publication rights to Random House, it will most likely publish your book in hardcover and attempt to sell the paperback rights to another firm. It will split the proceeds with you if a paperback sale is made.

U.S. and Canadian rights are almost always sold together, as a package. Mexico and the Philippines are sometimes thrown in, too. The Virgin Islands, Puerto Rico, and other U.S. possessions are normally considered part of the United States in publishing contracts.

The sale of rights to a manuscript in any foreign country or language will typically earn 10 to 50 percent of the amount they would bring from a U.S. publisher. This can vary greatly depending on the piece, the publication, and the territory or language in question. The more people who live in that territory or speak that language, the more money you're likely to receive. The British Commonwealth is by far the largest foreign market. Money from such sales can range from 25 to 50 percent of U.S. earnings.

General tips on contracts:

• Any rights not specifically transferred in a written or oral agreement remain yours.

• If you make an oral agreement or receive an informal letter of agreement, then later sign a formal contract or formal agreement letter with the same publisher for that piece, the formal document supersedes the earlier agreement. Read this formal document carefully. If it doesn't reflect the terms you and your editor agreed on earlier, or if it has additional provisions that you object to, don't sign it. Instead, promptly call your editor and negotiate any appropriate changes. The same goes for an informal letter of agreement that follows an oral agreement.

• Always keep a copy of every publication agreement you sign, including informal agreement letters.

• If an agreement does not specify whether a group of rights has been granted on an exclusive or nonexclusive basis, exclusivity is implied.

• The terms *first serial* and *second serial* each have two different meanings. In book publishing, *first serial* means *in print in any periodical(s) prior to initial book publication in that territory; second serial* means *in print in any periodical(s) following first book publication in that territory.* In all other fields of publishing, however, *first serial* means *in print in a periodical for the first time in that territory; second serial* means *one-time use in a periodical following the piece's first periodical publication in that territory.* Note that in either case, there is no such thing as third serial rights; if you sell nonexclusive second serial rights to a periodical and then sell six more one-time reprint uses to six more magazines in that same territory, each of those six times you are still selling nonexclusive second rights.

• If someone approaches you with a request to publish something you have written, and the rights you are asked to sell no longer belong to you,

you must refer that person or firm to whoever *does* control those rights. If someone approaches your publisher to reprint a piece of yours and the publisher doesn't control the rights the buyer wants, it will refer the buyer to whoever owns those rights.

• In general, avoid selling all rights to something you've written. When you sell all rights to a piece, you no longer have the right to do *anything* with that piece. If you want to reprint your own piece in a collection of your own work, you'll have to ask (and perhaps *purchase*) permission to do so from whoever bought the rights from you.

• Several organizations, such as The Authors Guild and the Writer's Union, have published model contracts for book and magazine publication, and sets of guidelines for contract negotiation. In the great majority of cases, these reflect a highly idealistic and unrealistic view of the publishing world. Although these models and guidelines are far from useless, they imply that publishers are much more generous and flexible than they actually are. This also applies to some of the other books that deal with publishing contracts and contract negotiation.

• It takes most publishers four to eight weeks from the time a final agreement is reached to mail a check. If you are turning in a piece written on assignment, the check may take a few weeks longer, as some time may pass before your editor reads it. If you are turning in a book manuscript contracted for on the basis of a proposal, or rewritten to editorial order, give your editor four to eight weeks to read it; upon deeming the book acceptable, he or she will order a check, which will usually take four to eight weeks *more* to be sent. If the check is being sent to your agent, add two to four more weeks for the money to make its way to you.

SAMPLES OF PUBLISHING AGREEMENTS

Samples of publishing contracts appear in this book as noted below:

F&W Publications, Inc.
1507 Dana Avenue
Cincinnati, Ohio 45207

Writer's Digest Books / North Light Books

AGREEMENT

THIS AGREEMENT dated the   , between
F&W Publications, Inc., dba Writer's Digest Books/North Light Books, 1507 Dana Avenue,
Cincinnati, Ohio 45207 (hereinafter referred to as "Publisher") and

(hereinafter referred to as "Author"), whose address is:

1. EXCLUSIVE PUBLISHING RIGHT

The Author hereby grants and assigns to the Publisher the exclusive right to produce and publish
in book form, and sell directly or through others, a work to be prepared by the Author now tentatively titled

(hereinafter referred to as "the Work"). The Author also hereby grants to the Publisher the right
to produce and sell, and to permit others to produce and sell, reprint and book club editions, adap-

tations, abridgments, condensations, and selections from the Work, motion pictures, radio and television broadcasts, or recordings based on the Work, novelty or commercial use of the Work, and use of the Work in any means of storage, retrieval, dissemination, and reproduction of information (the "subsidiary rights"). Publisher's right to publish, and the subsidiary rights herein granted, shall be exclusive worldwide in all languages.

2. COMPETING WORKS

While this Agreement is in effect, the Author shall not, without the prior written consent of the Publisher, write, edit, or publish, or cause to be written, edited, or published, any other work or any other edition of the Work, whether revised, enlarged, abridged, or otherwise, nor shall the Author permit the use of his name or likeness in connection with any such work.

3. AUTHOR'S WARRANTIES

The Author warrants and represents to the Publisher that:

(a) the Author is the sole and exclusive owner of the rights herein granted to the Publisher;

(b) the Work has not heretofore been published, except as follows:

(c) the Author has not heretofore assigned, pledged, or otherwise encumbered the rights herein granted to the Publisher;

(d) the Work violates no copyright, either in whole or in part, and the Author will obtain and forward to the Publisher all necessary permissions and licenses for the use of copyrighted text or illustrations contained in the Work, for all editions and uses of the Work throughout the world;

(e) the Work is not in the public domain;

(f) the Work contains no matter which would be libelous or defamatory, or infringe any trade name or trademark, or invade any right of privacy or proprietary right, and it contains no injurious formulas or instructions;

(g) all statements of fact contained in the Work are true or based upon reasonable research;

The foregoing warranties and representations shall survive any termination of this Agreement, and at all times the Author shall, at his expense, indemnify and defend the Publisher, and hold the Publisher and its licensees harmless against any claim, loss, or liability sustained by reason of a breach of any of the foregoing warranties and representations. The Publisher shall promptly notify the Author of any claim or suit which may involve any of the foregoing warranties and representations, and the Author will cooperate fully in the defense thereof; provided, however, the Publisher and its attorney shall have the right to control the defense, or with the Author's consent, the settlement thereof. The Author shall, in all events, be entitled to employ his own attorney, who shall cooperate with the Publisher's attorney in all proceedings hereunder.

If such claim or suit is not finally sustained, the Publisher shall bear one-half of the counsel fees and other costs incurred, except where the Author, prior to publication, had refused to revise the manuscript in connection with such matter at the Publisher's request.

Without limiting any other remedies which the Publisher may have, any payments that would otherwise be due the Author under Paragraph 11 may be offset by any liability or expense the Publisher may incur as a result of a breach of the foregoing warranties and representations.

These warranties do not apply to any material inserted in the Work by the Publisher.

4. PERMISSIONS

The Author shall obtain permission for use of copyrighted text and/or illustrations contained in the work and such permission shall be in the form of world rights in all languages for all editions of the Work, and all such permissions shall be submitted with the manuscript.

If the Author fails to deliver all the completed permissions with the manuscript on the delivery date specified under Paragraph 5, the Publisher will assist in the process of obtaining permissions and all costs shall be charged against payments otherwise due Author under Paragraph 12.

5. MANUSCRIPT

(a) The Author shall deliver to the Publisher not later than two complete copies (the original and a duplicate) of the typewritten, printed out, or disks of the manuscript of the Work, which shall contain approximately words and be acceptable in form, style, and content to the Publisher, and the Author shall retain a third copy of the manuscript. Whether the manuscript is typewritten or printed out, it shall be double-spaced, clean, and readily legible, and if printed out, it shall be provided in separate pages, not a single continuous printout sheet.

The Author will supply with the manuscript and permissions: table of contents, preface, foreword, if any; bibliography or glossary, if any; and the following illustrations, acceptable in form, style, content and of good reproduction quality together with all captions they require:

If the Author shall fail to do so, the Publisher shall have the right to supply said illustrations and charge the cost thereof against any sums that may accrue to the Author under the terms of this Agreement.

Time is of the essence in the Author's obligation to deliver an acceptable manuscript, and if delivery is not made on or before the stipulated date, the Publisher may, at its option at any time after sixty (60) days following such date, terminate this Agreement by notice to the Author.

The Publisher shall, within ninety (90) days from the date of its receipt thereof, accept the manuscript, or reject it, or return it for correction or revision. In the event the Publisher returns the manuscript to the Author for correction or revision, the Author shall make such corrections or revisions within the time and in the substantive form and editorial style required by the Publisher, and the Publisher shall have the right, upon the Author's failure or refusal to do so, to terminate this Agreement by notice to the Author.

(b) Upon such termination, the Author shall return to the Publisher all amounts theretofore advanced by the Publisher to the Author on account of the Work, and upon such repayment, the Publisher shall reassign to the Author all rights granted to the Publisher under this Agreement.

(c) In the event that the Author shall become unable to carry out his responsibilities under this Agreement or shall die at any time before completion of the Work or of all revisions deemed necessary and desirable by the Publisher, the Author or the Author's representative shall appoint an appropriate person, acceptable to the Publisher, to complete the Work and/or all necessary revisions. In the event that the Author or the Author's representative declines to designate someone to perform these functions, the Publisher shall have the right to do so, and all fees or costs incurred in the completion and/or revision of the Work by the designated person shall be charged against the amounts otherwise accruing to the Author under this Agreement.

6. AUTHOR CORRECTIONS

The Author shall have the right to review the copyedited manuscript and shall return it to the Publisher with corrections noted within fourteen days after receipt thereof by the Author. If the Author fails to return the copyedited manuscript within such period, the Publisher may publish the Work without the Author's corrections.

7. INDEXING

The Publisher will engage the services of others to do an index for the Work, and the cost of this service shall be charged against payments otherwise due Author under Paragraph 12.

8. PUBLICATION

The Publisher will publish the Work at its expense, except as otherwise provided herein, within eighteen (18) months after acceptance by Publisher of the completed, acceptable manuscript as required under Paragraph 5. In the event Publisher is prevented from publishing the Work within such time for extraordinary causes beyond its control, the publication date shall be extended for the amount of time during which Publisher was so prevented from publishing.

The Publisher shall have the right to publish the Work in such form as it deems best suited to the sale of the Work; to fix or alter the prices at which the Work shall be sold; and to determine the methods and means of advertising, publicizing, and selling the Work, the number and destination of free copies, and all other publishing details. All of the Publisher's decisions about format, design, editorial style, and production specifications shall be final.

The Publisher may use the Author's name and likeness or photograph in connection with the advertising and promotion of the Work, and the Author will make himself available, upon the Publisher's request, to publicize and promote the Work.

9. COPYRIGHT

The Author owns the copyright in the Work. The Publisher will print the Author's name as the copyright owner on the copyright page of every copy of the Work, in the correct form to comply with the U.S. Copyright Act and the Universal Copyright Convention. Within three (3) months of first publication, the Publisher will register the Author's name as "claimant" with the United States Copyright Office. Any license granted by the Publisher to a third party to reproduce and distribute copies of the Work will require the licensee to print the appropriate copyright notice in the Author's name in all copies, and the Publisher shall make any additional registrations or applications necessary to protect the Author's copyright in any subsidiary uses of the Work.

If any registered copyright therein shall be in the name of any person or party other than the Author, the Author shall deliver to the Publisher legally recordable assignment or assignments of such copyright or copyrights before the book goes to press.

If this Agreement has not by then been terminated, the Publisher shall apply for any necessary renewal or extension of the copyright in the Author's name.

10. INFRINGEMENT

If either party desires to make a claim for infringement of the copyright in the Work or other unauthorized use of the Work by another, such party shall notify the other party of such claim prior to or as promptly after asserting such claims as is reasonably possible. Publisher and Author shall have the right to prosecute jointly any claim for infringement or unauthorized use, provided that the party notified of such claim shall within ten (10) days of such notification notify the other party of its intention to proceed jointly. If the parties proceed jointly, the expenses and recovery, if any, shall be shared equally. If either party refuses to proceed jointly, the other party shall have the right to proceed alone and shall bear all expenses thereof and shall be exclusively entitled to any recovery. and if the Author refuses to so proceed, the Publisher may assert such claim or file suit in the Author's name.

11. REVISION AND UPDATING

The Author shall, upon the Publisher's request, revise or update the Work from time to time after publication to keep the material current. Should the Author be unable or unwilling to perform such revision, or should the Author be deceased, the revision shall be performed by the revisor designated by the Author. If the revisor or revisors designated by the Author are unable to perform such revision, or if the Author has not designated a revisor, it shall be performed by a revisor chosen by the Publisher in consultation with the Author's personal representative. Any compensation paid by the Publisher or expenses incurred in connection therewith shall be charged against payments otherwise due the Author under Paragraph 12, and the Publisher may display in the revised Work, and in advertising, the name of the person or persons who revised the Work.

If the revision is of a nature and scale as to require extensive rewriting and retypesetting, and the Publisher plans to republish and promote the Work as a revised edition, an advance proportionate to the extent of the necessary revision will be negotiated, and the provisions of this Agreement shall otherwise apply to such revision as though that revision were the Work being published for the first time.

12. ROYALTIES AND OTHER PAYMENTS TO AUTHOR

The Publisher shall pay to the Author the following advances, royalties, and payments:

ADVANCE

(a) An advance against all monies first accruing to the Author under this Agreement, of payable as follows:

one-third upon receipt by the Publisher of a copy of this Agreement signed by the Author;

one-third upon receipt of the complete and final manuscript and art acceptable to the Publisher, together with all necessary permissions, illustrations, and captions; and

one-third upon the Publisher's receipt of the reviewed copyedited ms.

ROYALTIES ON THE SALE OF COPIES

(b) On sales of any hardcover edition of the Work published by the Publisher and sold in the United States through normal book trade retail and wholesale channels, a royalty of:

ten percent (10%) on copies 1–10,000

twelve and one-half percent (12½%) on copies 10,001–20,000

fifteen percent (15%) on copies 20,001–30,000, and

twenty percent (20%) on all copies sold thereafter

based on Publisher's net receipts. As used in Paragraph 11(b) of this Agreement, net receipts means Publisher's list price less distributor's or bookseller's discount, returns, and credits.

(c) On sales of any paperback edition of the Work published by the Publisher and sold in the United States through normal book trade retail and wholesale channels, a royalty of:

ten percent (10%) on copies 1–20,000

twelve and one-half percent (12½%) on copies 20,001–40,000, and

fifteen percent (15%) on all copies sold thereafter

based on Publisher's net receipts. As used in Paragraph 11(c) of this Agreement, net receipts means Publisher's list price less distributor's or bookseller's discount, returns, and credits.

(d) On copies of the work sold at 60% or more discount, one-half the royalties specified in 12(b) and (c) above.

(e) On copies of the Work sold by the Publisher direct to consumers, a royalty of ten percent (10%) of Publisher's net receipts.

(f) On copies of the Work used as textbooks or premiums in the Publisher's own correspondence courses, a royalty of three percent (3%) of Publisher's list price.

(g) Should the Publisher find itself with an overstock of the Work on hand when, in its sole judgment, the demand for the Work would not use up the stock within two (2) years, it shall have the right to sell such copies at the best price it can secure. The Author shall have first option to buy any such overstock, in minimum quantities of 25 copies, at the best price obtainable from any third party. If such overstock is sold at a price below manufacturing cost, no royalty shall be paid on copies thus sold. If sold at a price above the manufacturing cost, but at a discount of seventy percent (70%) or more, the Author shall receive a royalty of ten percent (10%) of net receipts, except that the Author's royalty shall not reduce the Publisher's net receipts below the manufacturing cost. No overstock sale of copies of the Work shall occur prior to one (1) year from the date of first publication hereunder, nor shall any such sale be construed as declaring the Work either "out of print" or "off sale" in regular distribution.

(h) If the Publisher finds it necessary to remainder its entire stock or the remaining copies of an edition which has become obsolete and is being replaced by a revised edition: If the remainder selling price is less than the manufacturing expense, no royalty will be paid the Author. However, if the remainder selling price exceeds manufacturing expense, the Publisher will pay the Author ten percent (10%) of the actual cash received over manufacturing expense, for such a sale. No remainder sale may take place before one (1) year from the date of first publication of the Work in book form, and Author shall have first option to purchase "remainder copies" of the Work at the best price obtainable from any third party, or the cost of manufacture, if there is no such offer.

ROYALTIES ON THE SUBSIDIARY RIGHTS

(i) On a license of the right to another to publish a paperback or hardcover edition of the Work, fifty percent (50%) of Publisher's receipts.

(j) On a license to book clubs to produce the Work, either in whole or in condensation, and distribute it to their members: fifty percent (50%) of Publisher's receipts.

(k) On copies of the Work sold to the Publisher's own book clubs as main or alternate selections, a royalty of five percent (5%) of Member's Price. On books used as new-member inducements or bonus books in any of the Publisher's own book clubs, a royalty of two and one-half percent (2½%) of Member's Price will be paid.

(l) On copies of the work sold to other book clubs, 50% of the royalty received by the Publisher.

(m) On a sale of the right to publish the Work in English outside of the United States, or the right to translate the Work and publish it in other languages, fifty percent (50%) of the Publisher's receipts.

(n) On a sale of First Serial rights to the Work, the Author shall receive fifty percent (50%) of Publisher's receipts, except that on a sale of any serialization or excerpt from the Work to one of the Publisher's own periodicals, the Author shall receive one hundred percent (100%) of the fee paid for such a use.

(o) On a sale of the right of Second Serialization, the Author shall receive fifty percent (50%) of Publisher's receipts, except that in the case of a sale of Second Serial rights to one of the Publisher's own periodicals, the Author shall receive one hundred percent (100%) of the fee paid for such a use.

(p) The Publisher may permit others to reprint selections from the Work and the Author shall receive fifty percent (50%) of the Publisher's receipts.

(q) If any part of the Work is included in an anthology, compilation or digest published by the Publisher, the Author shall receive a fee based upon the percentage the Work's material bears to the contents of the said volume.

(r) On bulk sales of the Work or any part of the Work for use as premiums or promotions, a royalty of ten percent (10%) of net receipts.

(s) On a license, with the Author's approval, for products or novelties based on the Work, or taking their name from the Work, the monies received shall be divided as follows: ninety percent (90%) to Author and ten percent (10%) to Publisher

(t) Audiovisual or audio recording rights to the Work: If such rights are exercised by the Publisher, the Author shall receive ten percent (10%) of the Publisher's net receipts; if such rights are licensed, fifty percent (50%) of the Publisher's receipts.

(u) A royalty of fifty percent (50%) of Publisher's net receipts for granting to others any of Publisher's rights with respect to the Work hereunder not specified in Sub-paragraphs (a) through (t) above.

13. ROYALTY-FREE PROVISIONS

(a) No royalty shall be paid on free copies of the Work furnished to the Author or to others for purposes of review, sample, or similar purposes, or on damaged copies sold at or below manufacturing cost, or on copies which are destroyed by the Publisher.

(b) The Publisher shall have the right to permit others to publish or broadcast over radio or television selections from the Work without royalty, if the Publisher determines that such publication or broadcast will benefit sales of the Work. And the Publisher may use photographs or illustrations from the Work to promote or advertise the Work without making any payment to the Author.

(c) The Publisher is authorized to permit publication of the Work in Braille, or other reproduction of the Work for the physically handicapped without payment of fees and without compensation to the Author, providing no compensation is received by the Publisher.

(d) The Publisher may grant permission to publish extracts of the Work containing not more than five hundred (500) words, without compensation to Author or Publisher.

14. NOTICE OF LICENSE AGREEMENTS

The Publisher shall promptly furnish to the Author copies of any agreements in which the Publisher grants a license or other rights in the Work to others.

15. FREE COPIES

Upon publication, the Publisher shall deliver to the Author twelve (12) free copies of the hardcover edition of the Work, twelve (12) free copies of any paperback edition of the Work published by the Publisher, and six (6) free copies of each substantially revised edition.

16. COPIES PURCHASED BY AUTHOR

The Publisher shall sell to the Author copies of any edition of the Work for resale or other purposes in quantities of less than 200 copies, at a discount of forty percent (40%) from the Publisher's list price; in single-order nonreturnable quantities of 200 or more copies, at a discount of forty-six percent (46%) from the Publisher's list price; and in single-order nonreturnable quantities of 1,000 or more copies, at a discount of fifty percent (50%) from the Publisher's list price, FOB the Publisher's warehouse or bindery.

The Author's purchases of any edition of the Work, up to a total of one thousand dollars ($1,000.00), may be charged to the Author's royalty account upon request, as long as the advance has been earned back and the account is not in a negative balance.

17. STATEMENTS AND PAYMENTS TO AUTHOR

(a) After publication, the Publisher will render to the Author semiannual statements, on February 28 and August 31 of each year following the first publication of the Work, which shall show all payments due Author hereunder for the six-month period ending on the preceding December 31 and June 30, respectively, and the basis for the determination thereof. Payments due the Author as shown thereon shall accompany such statement.

(b) If in the opinion of the Publisher, it is likely that credits for returns in a following royalty period will exceed income from sales and subsidiary rights income in that royalty period, then the Publisher may withhold from payment a reserve not to exceed fifteen percent (15%).

(c) If the Author's royalty account is in a negative balance for three or more six month periods, the Publisher may apply any other monies due Author against the negative balance until it has been earned back.

(d) The Author or the Author's designated representative shall have the right, upon thirty (30) days notice to the Publisher, to examine the Publisher's books of account relating to the Work. Such examination shall be at the Author's cost unless any additional amount found to be due Author upon such audit shall exceed five percent (5%) of the amount due Author as originally determined by the Publisher, in which case such audit shall be at the Publisher's expense.

18. RIGHT OF TERMINATION BY AUTHOR

The Author, at his election, may terminate this Agreement in the event of any of the following, in the following manner:

(a) if the Work is not published within the time specified in Paragraph 7, by notice to the Publisher, effective six (6) months after receipt thereof by the Publisher, unless the Work is published prior to the expiration of such six-month period;

(b) if the Work is not for sale in at least one edition (including any revised edition or reprint edition) published by the Publisher or under license from the Publisher and, within six months after written demand by the Author, the Publisher or its licensee fails to offer it again for sale, then this Agreement shall terminate and all rights granted to the Publisher in it shall revert to the Author;

(c) if the Publisher fails to deliver the semiannual statements or make any of the payments provided for herein, by notice to the Publisher effective thirty (30) days after receipt thereof by the Publisher, unless the Publisher delivers such statements or makes such payments within thirty (30) days after receipt of such notice;

(d) if the Publisher shall become bankrupt or file a petition for an arrangement under the Federal Bankruptcy Acts, or if it shall make a general assignment for the benefit of creditors, or if a trustee or a receiver shall be appointed of all or substantially all of the Publisher's assets, or if the Publisher shall take advantage of any insolvency law of any state of the United States, or shall commence the liquidation of its business, then immediately upon the happening of any of the said events, upon written notice by the Author to the Publisher, the Publisher's rights under this Agreement shall terminate.

19. EFFECT OF TERMINATION

Upon the effective date of the termination of this Agreement by the Author, or as soon thereafter as possible:

(a) The Publisher shall reassign to the Author all rights granted to the Publisher hereunder, with the exception of licenses theretofore granted. After such reversion, the Publisher shall continue to participate to the extent set forth in this Agreement in any license previously granted by it.

(b) The Author shall have the option to purchase the printing materials from the Publisher, if available from the printer, at the cost of retrieval and shipping, and any or all of the remaining sheets or copies of the Work at a price not to exceed the manufacturing cost. If the Author shall not have exercised his option to acquire such printing materials, sheets, or copies within sixty (60) days of the effective date of such termination, the Publisher shall have the right to destroy or to sell such remaining materials at cost or less, without payment to the Author on such sales, except as provided in Paragraph 11(u) of this Agreement.

(c) All accounts between the Author and the Publisher shall be adjusted and paid, except for any unearned advances.

20. INTERPRETATION

This Agreement shall be interpreted under the laws of the State of Ohio and of the United States of America.

21. ASSIGNMENT

Except as provided below, neither party may assign his or its rights or obligations in this Agreement or any portion thereof without the consent of the other:

(a) The Author may assign and transfer any monies due or to become due under this Agreement.

(b) The Publisher shall have the right to assign the Work to its own subsidiary or affiliated companies, and to authorize and sublicense publication or use of the Work throughout the world as set forth in Paragraphs 1 and 11 of this Agreement.

22. WAIVER

Failure by either party to promptly enforce any of his or its rights hereunder shall not constitute a waiver of those or any other rights or of strict compliance by the other party of its obligations hereunder, or in any way affect any other terms or conditions hereof.

23. MODIFICATION

No waiver, modification, or amendment to this Agreement shall be valid or enforceable unless it is in writing, signed by the parties.

24. ARBITRATION

Any controversy or claim arising out of this Agreement or the breach thereof shall be settled by arbitration in Cincinnati, Ohio, in accordance with the then-effective rules of the American Arbitration Association. The decision of the arbitrator(s) shall be binding upon the parties, and judgment thereon may be entered in any court of competent jurisdiction.

The Author has the right to refuse arbitration in case of the Publisher's failure to pay royalties, and to pursue other legal remedies in such a case.

25. NOTICES

Any notice required or permitted under this Agreement shall be in writing and delivered in person or by ordinary mail to the parties at their respective addresses set forth above, or to any other address as changed by notice in writing; provided, however, that notices of termination shall be delivered in person or by certified mail, return receipt requested.

26. FIRST REFUSAL

The Author hereby grants to the Publisher the right of first refusal to publish his next

on terms not less favorable than those contained in a bona fide offer to publish tendered to the Author by any third party. The Publisher shall exercise such right by notifying the Author of whether or not it wishes to publish said Work not later than thirty (30) days after receipt by Publisher of the manuscript or proposal/outline and complete sample chapters and art, if appropriate.

27. AGENT

All sums due the Author under this Agreement shall be payable to the Author's agent, and shall be sent to such agent at the address indicated on Page One of this Agreement. The delivery of such sums to such agent shall be a full and valid discharge of the Publisher's obligations herein.

28. BINDING EFFECT

This Agreement shall be binding upon and inure to the benefit of the respective heirs, personal representatives, successors, and assigns of the parties.

IN WITNESS whereof, the parties hereto have executed this Agreement in duplicate on the date and year first above written.

WRITER'S DIGEST BOOKS/NORTH LIGHT BOOKS

AUTHOR: (A Division of F&W Publications, Inc.)

_____   By _____

_____

Social Security or Federal ID Number

CONTRACT FOR FIRST PUBLICATION IN AN ANTHOLOGY

(0)   MEMORANDUM OF AGREEMENT

RE: "A STORY" by Walter W. Writer

Between Jack Dann and Jeanne Van Buren Dann of _____, _____
New York 13903, Editors of an Anthology tentatively entitled IN THE FIELDS
OF FIRE, hereinafter referred to as the ANTHOLOGISTS, and _____
_____, whose address is_____
_____
_____

hereinafter referred to as the AUTHOR.

1.   The Author grants permission to include the story in the above
mentioned volume to be published in the United States by TOR Books and in
other editions throughout the world.

2.   The Anthologists offer an advance of _____
and a   pro rata share of the anthology's earnings, if any, beyond the
initial advance, earnings to include income from trade, book club, reprint,
translations and foreign sales or any other subsidiary earnings received
by the Anthologists from sales of the Anthology. Fifty percent of the
earnings actually received by the Editors will be distributed to the Authors
of the stories in the volume at least once each calendar year, as soon as
such earnings exceed $5.00 per story.

3.   The Author agrees not to publish or permit others to publish his/her
story in any form prior to its publication and appearance in the Editors'
anthology for a period of one year after the appearance of the paperback
edition without the prior written permission of the Anthologists/and or
publisher.

4.   The Author represents and warrants that he/she is the sole author(s)
of the story, and that no one has received the rights granted in this
agreement; also that the story does not contain any libelous material and
is not in violation of any rights of privacy or any other rights of third
persons, and does not violate any existing common law or statutory copyrights, and has not been published before in any form.

5.   All rights not specifically granted in this agreement are reserved
by the Author.

6.   It is understood that permission is granted for transcription of
the story into Braille, tape, talking, or oversized book in case that book
or your story is selected for such transcription by a non-profit organization
for the disabled.

7.   The Author shall receive one free copy of the edition; and, wherever
possible, one free copy of all other editions.

8.   The Author's literary agent, to whom all earnings under this Agreement
should be paid is_____
_____

AGREED: (Please indicate your acceptance by
                                 signing and returning two (2) copies
                                 of this agreement)

_____   Date:_____
Author/Literary Agent

                                         _____
                                         Author's Social Security Number

_____   _____
JEANNE VAN BUREN DANN   JACK DANN

FORMAL AGREEMENT FOR FIRST MAGAZINE PUBLICATION

DAVIS
PUBLICATIONS, INC.

380 LEXINGTON AVENUE · NEW YORK, N.Y. 10017 · 212-557-9100

Dear

We are pleased that you have submitted your work to

_____

(the "Magazine") and we acknowledge receipt of your manuscript entitled

"_____ " (the "Work").

We agree to pay you (or your duly designated agent if one is listed below) the sum of

_____ ($ _____)

Dollars in consideration for your work and the rights and agreements enumerated below. We ask you to confirm by your signature the following:

A. You warrant that the Work (i) was created solely by you, (ii) is entirely original, (iii) was not copied from any other source, (iv) has not been previously published in any form in any medium, (v) does not defame or violate the rights of privacy or publicity or any other rights of any person or institution, (vi) is not libelous, and (vii) does not infringe upon any copyright. You further warrant that neither the Work nor any rights in it has been sold previously, and no one but you possesses any rights in or to it

(except _____).

B. In consideration of our payment to you of the sum set forth above, you grant us, our successors and assigns, the following world-wide publishing, distribution and other rights in the Work:

1. First English language publication rights and translation rights for use in various editions of the magazine.

2. First anthology rights, whether with respect to hardcover or paperback anthologies containing the Work which are sold to consumers by any means, including, but not limited to, mail order, coupon, or radio or television advertising, for which, when exercised, you will be compensated as follows: $50 for first North American anthology rights; $40 for subsequent anthology use; $25 for foreign anthology rights; and a pro rata share of 50% of the royalties received by Davis Publications, Inc. ("DPI") if the anthology is chosen by a United States book club, payable upon receipt of such royalties by DPI. You agree to ensure that following publication of the Work in the Magazine, DPI will receive suitable credit as publisher of the Work if the Work is subsequently published in an anthology other than one published by DPI.

3. The right to license others to reprint the Work in any language in magazines and newspapers other than those published by DPI, for which we will pay you 25% of the amount set forth in the initial paragraph hereof.

4. The right to illustrate the Work, change its title, and to condense and edit the Work in a manner consistent with the editorial standards of the Magazine and the right to copyright the Work in our name as part of the Magazine. Copyright in the Work shall be transferred to you upon request on or after one year from the initial date of publication of the Work by DPI, subject to reservation and retention of all rights granted us in this Agreement.

5. (a) The first right to adapt, produce, distribute and exhibit the Work and to exploit any of the dramatic, musical or other allied rights in the Work (i) via radio, motion picture, television or other audio-visual mechanical reproduction media, now or hereafter known (all such rights being hereinafter referred to as the "Subsidiary Rights"), or (ii) in cartoon or filmstrip versions, for which you shall receive a sum to be negotiated and agreed upon by you and us prior to any such adaption, production, distribution or exhibition.

(b) The right to license third parties to exercise or exploit the Subsidiary Rights, for which you shall receive payment of a sum equal to 80% of the amounts received by DPI pursuant to such license.

(c) If prior to our exercise of the rights specified in Section B.5(a) or B.5(b) hereof you receive a bona fide, written offer for the acquisition of any of the Subsidiary Rights from a party with whom DPI or its agents has not initiated negotiations or from whom DPI or its agents has not solicited offers to purchase any Subsidiary Right, DPI shall have the right to pay to you the dollar amount and meet the other financial terms of such offer and thereby acquire the Subsidiary Rights for our exclusive benefit and the benefit of our licensees, with no further payment to you pursuant to Sections B.5(a) or B.5(b) hereof. You shall not initiate negotiations with or solicit offers from any person with whom DPI or its agents has had such contact with respect to the license of the Subsidiary Rights.

6. The right to develop or license the development of special projects, including, but not limited to, games, toys and t-shirts, based upon characters from the Work, for which we shall pay you a sum equal to (i) 50% of the revenues received by DPI from such projects, net of any production, development or distribution costs incurred by DPI with respect thereto.

7. The right to use the Work, your name, your biography and your likeness in connection with the Work, and in our advertising and promotion, or to license such use in connection with the rights granted pursuant to Section B.5 and Section B.6 hereof.

C. If you incorporate any copyrighted material in the Work, you shall procure and deliver to us simultaneously with delivery of the manuscript, at your expense, signed written permission to reprint such material from the copyright proprietor.

D. You shall hold us, our licensees and assigns harmless against any claims or suits (including costs, expenses and reasonable attorney's fees) arising out of a breach of your warranties or agreements hereunder. This Agreement shall be binding upon and inure to the benefit of the parties hereto and each of their respective heirs, executors, administrators, successors and assigns.

E. This Agreement is governed solely by New York law and can only be changed by an agreement in writing, signed by each of us.

Very truly yours,
DAVIS PUBLICATIONS, INC.

By_____

AGREED:

_____
AUTHOR

_____
SOCIAL SECURITY NO.

_____
AGENT

4-82

TERRY CARR

Your permission is hereby requested to publish

_____

in _Universe 16_, to be published by Doubleday & Co., Inc. It is understood and
agreed that Doubleday & Co., Inc., shall have the right to distribute copies of its
edition, and those of its licensees, throughout the world.

I offer payment of _____ for such use, as an advance against a pro-rata share
of 50% of all payments I receive from any and all editions of the book.

You warrant that your material, as heretofore named, is an original work that has
never been published previously, and that it is in no way in violation of any
existing copyright, is not libelous or otherwise has caused or will cause injury
to anyone or is in violation of any law, and you agree to indemnify me and Doubleday
& Co., Inc., its licensees and any seller of the work against damages and expense
arising by reason of any breach of these warranties.

You agree that until six months after the appearance of a paperback reprint edition
of said anthology, or two years after original hardbound publication by Doubleday
& Co., Inc., whichever is first, you will not publish without written permission
from me any material in book, newspaper, magazine, or pamphlet form based upon the
work. Anthologies of the year's best science fiction or fantasy shall be exempt
from this agreement.

Please enter your Social Security Number or Tax Identification Number in the space
provided, as required by Federal law, and return two countersigned copies of this
memorandum of agreement to me. Thank you.

Sincerely,

Terry Carr
Terry Carr

AGREED:

Ronald Anthony Cross

_____

Social Security Number or Tax Identification
Number

ROSE ADKINS, ASSOCIATE EDITOR

9933 ALLIANCE ROAD
CINCINNATI, OHIO 45242
TEL. 513-984-0717

April 11, 1984

Scott Edelstein
Box 6138
Taos, New Mexico 87571

Dear Scott:

Sorry to have taken so long with the INCOME TAXES article
you submitted.

We'd like to buy the manuscript for $600, first North
American serial rights, one-time use only. We plan to
use it in Writer's Yearbook '85. You'll see Author Galleys
for final OK. If you'll fill out the enclosed Author
Information Form, return it to us, we'll get a check out
to you right away for the article.

We'll have a few questions when we edit the manuscript,
and we'll be doing some rearranging. Primarily, we may
pull about three sections out of the main text and convert
them to sidebars. But Author Galleys will be mailed to
you for your final verification.

Thanks for the good work on this feature, Scott.

Cordially,

Rose

CONTRACT NEGOTIATION

Whenever you negotiate a publishing agreement, you are making a business deal—even if the person you are negotiating with is your best friend. Your editor or publisher is, at base, the opposition—sometimes the friendly opposition, but the opposition nevertheless. Even if you trust your editor or publisher completely—and he or she trusts you just as much—that is no reason to be less than careful and clear. After all, your editor might quit, get fired, or die. Or the publication he or she works for might be sold to a less than reputable person or firm (publications, and whole publishing firms, get bought and sold all the time).

Negotiation is an art, and some people are better at it than others. If you are not by nature a wheeler-dealer, or if you've had little or no negotiating experience, you will find contract negotiation complicated, slippery, and ambiguous at first, and you may find yourself getting outwitted, outmaneuvered, or talked into corners. Don't despair over these initial failures. As you acquire negotiating experience, and as you sell more of your work, you'll find yourself getting more of the terms you want.

Your manner is an important part of negotiating an agreement. As in all business dealings, remain calm, polite, and businesslike at all times, no matter how the person you are negotiating with may act, and no matter how you may feel inside. Stick to the issues, and don't get sidetracked onto topics such as how poverty stricken the publication is. Don't wander from the specific terms of your agreement.

It is essential that you enter into negotiations with these two attitudes: (1) it is in the best interest of both parties to come to agreement, and you will work in good faith to make such an agreement; *but* (2) if a decent agreement cannot be reached, you will be willing and able to forget the whole thing. Without the first attitude, reaching any agreement at all will be difficult. Without the second, you've got no bargaining position. If at heart you want to be published so badly that you'll make an agreement that is unfair to you, your editor may sense it and not give an inch (or more than a few inches) in negotiations. I deal with this by deciding in advance what I can live with and what I cannot; I go into negotiations knowing what will cause me to say, in all sincerity, "I think we'd better just forget this. I don't think we can reach an equitable agreement."

Here are some other useful tips on contract negotiation:

• An offer to publish your piece may be initially made by either mail or phone. Negotiations may then be conducted in either manner, or both.

• You *don't* usually have to accept terms exactly as they are offered, even (perhaps *especially*) if editors tell you they are offering their publication's "standard contract." It never hurts to ask for better terms and/or more money; the worst you'll be told is, "No. Either take the terms as offered or leave them." Usually, however, at least some terms are negotiable.

• No decent editor will ever attempt to punish you for asking for more money or better terms. I have *never* heard of an editor who withdrew or reduced an offer because a writer tried to get it improved.

• *Don't* sign a contract unless you can live with its terms—because once you've agreed to them, you *will* have to live with them.

• Don't expect to get everything you ask for in a contract. Compromise is often necessary; in fact, properly used, it's a virtue in contract negotiation. If you can get one-third of the extra money and better terms you ask for, you are doing nicely.

• If a contract you are offered fails to cover a particular circumstance, by all means ask your editor to include a provision covering it. If you like, suggest the specific wording for that provision yourself.

• *Never* agree to anything you don't fully understand. If you have a question about anything in the contract (no matter how "trivial"), by all means ask your editor about it. Also feel free to ask your agent and/or a literary attorney. If anything in a contract, even a punctuation mark, is unclear or ambiguous, don't sign the contract until it has been changed so that the sentence or paragraph is no longer unclear or ambiguous. It is *not* enough for your editor to explain to you what it means.

• If something in an agreement is unacceptable as written, tell your editor exactly why. Suggest alternative language of your own.

• From the time your editor says, "I'd like to use your piece" until both parties have signed an agreement (or made a final oral one), be restrained, even bland. Don't express any excitement or enthusiasm, *even if your editor does.* At most, calmly say that you're pleased. The more excited you act, the weaker your bargaining position will become. Acting a little bored conveys this message: "I'm a professional, and this is just another dull business deal. I've done it all before and I'm used to it." Believe it or not, editors will respect you for adopting this attitude.

• A similar negotiating technique is to act a little unsatisfied with a deal, even if it suits you perfectly. For instance, if a book editor offers a $10,000 advance, you might respond, "Ten thousand is less than I'd like, but I can live with it." This puts you in a better bargaining position over matters like subsidiary rights and royalties; since you don't seem too pleased with the advance, the editor may want to be more flexible in negotiating other parts of the contract.

• If you have *any* doubts about a deal at all, take at least a day or two to think it over before telling the editor your decision. This won't endanger the deal in any way.

• What one editor may readily agree to another may unconditionally refuse, and vice versa.

• Negotiations often go quickly, but they can sometimes take time, especially for book contracts. The editor may have to check with the contracts department and/or the publisher or editor-in-chief, perhaps several times. If one or more of these people are out ill or on vacation, the whole process can grind to a temporary halt. Be patient. Don't try to rush negotiations; and most certainly don't give in on any key points just to get the business over and done with.

• Although in many cases some or all of your negotiation will precede the drawing up of a document, sometimes you will simply receive a written agreement without any prior negotiation. If this document is unacceptable as written, it is your job to contact the editor and say, "I'm sorry, but I can't accept the agreement as it's currently written. Here are the changes I'd like to see made."

• A piece of writing doesn't have a fixed value. What you should negotiate for (and expect to get) depends on what the publication can afford and is willing to pay. If I write a three-thousand-word mystery story and send it to *Playboy,* and *Playboy* responds with a contract offering me $600, I'll turn it down and ask for $1500, because I know *Playboy* pays a great deal more than 20¢ a word. But if *Playboy* bounces the piece, I send it to *Hitchcock's Mystery Magazine,* and *Hitchcock's* offers me $400 for it, I'll take the deal, because I'll be getting close to *Hitchcock's* top rate. (Of course, *Playboy* wouldn't actually offer a mere $600 for the story; they'd offer a reasonable fee from the start.)

• If the amount of money you have been offered is too small, it is acceptable to either make a counter-offer or simply say, "It's not enough."

• One good negotiating technique is to ask an editor flat out, "What's the absolute highest you can go?" After he or she responds, say, "So if I don't agree to that amount, we can't make a deal at all?" If the answer is yes, the editor probably means it. But if the editor beats around the bush, then he or she can probably go at least a little higher.

• If a small publication doesn't offer you any money for your piece, or a small book publisher doesn't offer you an advance, that doesn't mean you can't ask for some money up front. In fact, some of these publishers are perfectly able to pay writers something in advance. So ask.

• If a set of terms is not acceptable to you as offered, or if an editor asks you, "How much do you need?", *don't* begin negotiations by stating your minimum acceptable terms or price. If you do, chances are you won't get them. Instead, ask for 25 to 75 percent more than you need or expect to get. This allows your editor to talk you down, and the two of you to work out a compromise that both of you can live with. If you are offered $500 for a piece and you feel you need at least $700, ask for $900 or $1000, and chances are pretty good that you'll get your $700. But if you only *ask* for $700, the editor may assume that you're actually looking for $600, and that will probably be his or her final offer.

• If you're asked, "What's the least you'll take?" *don't* answer honestly, because whatever amount you say is probably exactly what you'll end up with. There are three standard responses to this question: (1) the counter-question: "What's the most you can offer?" (2) the nonanswer: "It all depends on the other terms we work out," and (3) the outright lie.

• If an editor won't go along with a large change, suggest a smaller one. If he or she says no to a $100 increase in a fee or a 1 percent hike in a royalty rate, suggest a fee of $50 (or even $25) more, or an extra ½ percent royalty. (Dealing with quarter-percentage points and amounts of $5 or $10 is *too* picky, however.)

• Remember the value of trade-offs. Occasionally you may get something for nothing in a contract negotiation, but sometimes you'll have to give a little in one area to get something in another. Proposing trade-offs yourself can be helpful; for example: "I need a 7½ percent royalty on the trade paperback. Give me that and I'll let you have 50 percent on British Commonwealth rights instead of 25 percent."

• Don't be afraid to ask for what you genuinely feel is reasonable. This doesn't always mean you'll get it, of course.

• If an editor says, "We've never done anything like that before," or "We don't work that way," or "My boss will never go for that," or even "Our policy forbids that," don't assume the policy is genuinely inviolable. Say to your editor, "Well, would you please ask about it?" (If it seems appropriate, you may want to add, "I think an exception is warranted in this one particular case.") Sometimes, to your editor's surprise, his or her superior will say okay.

• If you and your editor come to an impasse on a certain point, the wisest thing to do is say, "Let's come back to that later." Finish negotiating your other points, and then return to the item or items that proved stickiest. With the negotiations nearly completed, both of you will be inclined to be a bit more flexible.

• Everything above notwithstanding, know when it's time to give up on a certain point. An editor's no in the early stages of negotiation may mean maybe, but when you've returned to an item for the third time and the editor still says no, he or she probably means it.

• Be reasonable. Don't ask for a great many changes unless the contract is truly abominable; don't ask for changes that are of little or no importance; and don't drag the negotiations on longer than you have to.

• Sometimes the addition or deletion of one word, or even one comma, can make a big difference. Feel free to negotiate such small changes if you have to.

• If an editor makes a variable offer, such as an advance of "four to six thousand dollars," ignore everything but the highest figure. Assume that this is the amount offered, and take your negotiations from there.

• If you have to tell an editor, "Sorry, we're too far apart; no deal," and you later decide that you should have taken the terms that were offered, there's no reason why you can't write or call the editor and say, "I changed my mind. Can we strike a deal now?" Naturally, the editor has the right to say, "Sorry, it's too late," but some editors will say, "Sure."

• Once a deal has been made, don't try to remake it by bringing up other items or by trying to reopen negotiations on things you've already agreed to. Once it's done, it's done.

• Some editors and publishers will be friendly and cooperative about everything except contract negotiations, during which they will be aggressive, gruff, defensive, impatient, and even nasty. Some editors are cooperative throughout contract negotiations except when it comes to the matter of payment, at which point they turn ugly and/or plead horrendous corporate poverty. These are usually just negotiation techniques, and nothing personal is intended, even if it seems to be. Remain polite, assertive, and businesslike, and stick to the real issues at hand.

• A few editors, purely as a negotiating tactic, will try to intimidate writers by accusing them of being unprofessional. If this happens to you, look carefully at what you're asking for. Would a little more flexibility on your part be genuinely more reasonable? If so, show that flexibility. But if, after careful consideration, you believe you should stick to your guns, tell the editor, "I'm sorry if you feel that what I'm doing is unprofessional, but I stand by my position."

- Be sure your agreement includes a deadline for publication. Otherwise, the publisher can withhold publication indefinitely—for decades, if it so chooses. If you've sold first rights to that publisher, this delay also forces you to withhold the sale of reprint rights for as long as the publisher delays publication of your piece. Generally, newspapers should be given six to nine months after acceptance of a manuscript to publish it; magazines and newsletters should be given one year; book publishers, eighteen months. If the publisher fails to publish your piece by the specified deadline, then the agreement is voided and all rights to your piece return to you; you keep the money you've been paid so far, and the publisher must once again obtain your permission (presumably in exchange for another fee) before publishing the piece.

If a publisher in fact does not publish your piece within the time specified in your agreement, write your editor a letter explaining that time has run out and that a new agreement will need to be made. Be polite and friendly, and suggest a reasonable fee for extending the agreement— perhaps half the original one. (If the publisher doesn't overshoot the deadline by much, though—say, by a few weeks—you might want to simply let the matter go.) It is also a good idea to let your editor know when the deadline for publishing your piece is only two months or so away.

- Avoid signing contracts that call for payment partly or entirely on publication. Always try to be paid in full on acceptance for all completed works and all magazine, newspaper, and newsletter assignments, and half on signing and half on acceptance for books sold through proposals. If a publisher agrees to pay you on publication, it may not only withhold payment for as long as it delays publication; it may *also* choose not to publish the piece at all and return it to you without paying you a penny! This is why publishers are so keen on paying writers on publication, and why you should be even keener on being paid no later than on acceptance.

- If a publisher absolutely refuses to pay you on acceptance, suggest that a specific date for payment be set; for example, July 17, 1989, or "within three months after acceptance." This way the publisher must pay you by a certain date whether or not it publishes your piece by that time (or at all). One strategy you might try is to ask, "When do you expect to publish my piece?" Suppose the answer is "By late May." You can then say, "All right. Let's add a clause to the contract that stipulates that I be paid on publication or by June 1, 1989, whichever comes first." Another option is to ask for half the money on acceptance (or shortly thereafter), half at a later specified date.

• If you sell any subsidiary rights to a piece along with first publication rights, try to retain at least a 50 percent interest in the earnings from the sale of those subsidiary rights. For example, if you sell first and second serial rights to a short story, try to add a clause that says, "In the event that second serial rights shall be sold to another firm, the author shall receive 50 percent of the money thus realized within thirty days of receipt of said money by the Publisher."

• Remember that publishers want to protect their interests as much as you want to protect yours. If something in a contract is unacceptable to you, try to determine why the publisher put it there in the first place—you can even ask your editor why. Then see if you can come up with language that protects the publisher just as well but that is acceptable to you. For example, suppose in a book contract there is a clause that says, "The author may not publish any other work on this subject before or while the Work is in print." The publisher is probably only worried about competitive *books,* but the contract says "any other work" just to be safe. If you want to publish an article on the subject in a professional journal, ask that the words *in book form* be inserted after the word *subject.* Naturally, this request should be made *during* contract negotiations, not after the contract has been signed.

• Religious, scholarly, and textbook publishers use the same negotiating techniques as commercial publishers. Don't treat them any differently.

• If an editor or publisher offers to publish your piece but wants you to "contribute" to the cost of publication, or even foot the entire publishing bill, your response should be, "No. If you'd like to publish my work at no charge to me, fine; let's work out an agreement. Otherwise, please return my work to me immediately." Don't let yourself get sucked into a subsidy or vanity publishing deal. (See pages 93–95 for details on this subject.)

• Sometimes you just can't get what you want; occasionally, you can't even come close. When my agent sent my creative writing book, *The No-Experience-Necessary Writer's Course,* to publishers, I told her I hoped for a $15,000 advance but would consider offers of $10,000 or more. The first offer, from a very large publisher, was for $6000. I turned it down, and she tried a new group of editors. This time we got an offer of $7500. I made a counter-offer of $9000, which was turned down. I was told, "Seventy-five hundred—take it or leave it." The question finally became: "Would you rather take a $7500 advance for this book or have it go unsold?" I took the $7500.

• If you are offered a contract from a TV or film producer, a major book publisher, or a major play producer, I strongly urge you to get an agent or literary attorney to negotiate the contract for you (see pages 253–54, "Getting an Agent at the Last Minute," and pages 372–74, "Literary Attorneys," for details).

• You don't *have* to ask for more money or better terms. If the agreement you are offered seems fair, by all means sign it without discussion or negotiation.

• For more details and tips on contract negotiations, I highly recommend reading Richard Balkin's *How to Understand and Negotiate a Book Contract or Magazine Agreement* (Writer's Digest Books) and *Negotiating a Book Contract,* by Mark L. Levine (Moyer Bell).

ALTERING A WRITTEN CONTRACT

Suppose you receive a written contract or letter of agreement, but find some of its terms unacceptable. Here's what to do: first, reread the document carefully and make a list of the specific items that need changing. If an item needs rewriting to make its terms fairer, think up a suggested revision. Write this down on a separate page. Don't make any changes on the document itself.

Then do one of three things: call the editor and discuss all these items one by one over the phone; type up a list of all your suggested changes and mail them to the editor along with a polite letter; or make a photocopy of the document, amend the *photocopy* in the ways that you would like the original amended, and send the editor the photocopy. Also enclose a letter explaining that you have the original, unaltered document in your files and that the photocopy contains the changes you would like to see made.

If the editor doesn't agree to all your suggestions, some further negotiation may then take place. Eventually, though, you'll reach a final set of terms. The letter or contract must then be altered to reflect these terms.

If you were initially sent an *informal* letter of agreement, you should ask your editor to send you a fresh agreement letter reflecting these new terms. This letter must be dated later than the earlier letter so that it legally supersedes the earlier one. If you like, you may ask the editor to include a sentence in this new letter such as "This agreement letter supersedes the letter dated ———."

If you were initially sent a formal contract or formal agreement letter, then you and your editor have three options: the editor can draw up a new contract or letter and send it to you for your signature; the editor can amend the existing document (or have it amended by the contracts department) and send it to you for your signature; or you can amend the document yourself so that it reflects the terms agreed upon, sign it, and return both copies to the editor. The editor will then initial the appropriate changes and send you a copy.

If you are permitted to make changes in a document, follow these guidelines:

• Before you make any correction, make a photocopy of the unaltered document. If you make an uncorrectable error on the original, you can then remove that page and use a photocopy of it in its place.

• Use a black pen with waterproof ink or a clear, dark black typewriter ribbon. These make the cleanest, highest-contrast, most permanent corrections, and they photocopy best.

• It is fine to make corrections in the margins, between lines, and even between words.

• Make all changes neatly, clearly, and readably.

• If the document requires both your signature and that of someone from your publisher, *each* change in that document must be initialed in the margin by both parties to become valid.

• If you wish to add provisions to a contract, you may add them as *riders* at the end. Simply type in the language you wish on the last page of the contract, or add one or more pages. If the sections or paragraphs of your agreement are numbered, number your riders appropriately. For example, if the last paragraph in the printed contract was 28, and you have two riders, they would become paragraphs 29 and 30. All riders must be initialed by both parties.

• If there isn't room in the margin for a particular change or addition, you may place a symbol (such as %, #, *) at the spot where the change belongs. It's fine to do this in midsentence, if necessary. Elsewhere on the page you should type the symbol again and follow it with the words you wish to add. If there's not even room for this, follow the symbol with the words "See rider on page ———." Then add a rider at the end of the contract. Identify this rider with the appropriate symbol and reference;

for example, " # Rider to subsidiary rights paragraph, page 2" or "%
Rider to paragraph 9." Be sure both parties initial the change.

• Triple-check each copy of the document before sending it back to your
editor. Go through it word by word, and punctuation point by punctuation point, to catch errors and omissions. Compare all copies against each
other.

• When you finally have in your hand a copy of the agreement that has
been signed and initialed by both parties, check everything again. Take
special care to see that the other party initialed the agreement in every
necessary spot.

Look back at the sample publishing agreements on pages 323–27. Most
of these agreements require no changes, except perhaps the addition of
a sentence guaranteeing the author some (or more) free copies. In my
opinion, however, the Davis Publications letter of agreement would be
unacceptable in its standard form. Here are some of the changes I'd ask
for:

B.2.: Change *First anthology rights* to *Anthology rights to anthologies
published by Davis Publications, Inc.; $40* to *$40 for each; for foreign
anthology rights* to *for each foreign anthology use; royalties* to *royalties and
advances* (in two spots).

B.3.: Change *The right* to *The nonexclusive right.*

B.4.: Add *You shall have the right to examine and approve all editing,
such approval not to be unreasonably withheld.*

B.5.: Change *The first right* to *The nonexclusive right* in (a); change
(b) to read *The nonexclusive right to license third parties or exploit the
Subsidiary Rights, under the same terms as in 5(a) above;* omit (c) entirely.

Are these unreasonable requests? Absolutely not. Mystery writer Mary
Pulver Kuhfeld asked for all of these changes, except the one noted in
B.4., when making a deal for one of her stories—and Davis agreed to all
of them.

Next take a look at the book contract from F&W Publications on pages
312–22. This is F&W's "boilerplate," its standard unamended printed
contract. Although in many respects it is a fair contract, there are a few
major items that beg for negotiation and alteration. For example, the
boilerplate gives F&W all rights to the author's book; unless you've
written a highly specialized title and/or are not being represented by an
agent, you probably won't want to give up all rights. I would also make
several important changes in Paragraph 12.

MAGAZINE, NEWSPAPER, AND NEWSLETTER AGREEMENTS

Listed below are points specific to magazine, newspaper, and newsletter agreements:

• The terms *serial rights* and *periodical rights* are identical. Both refer to publication in magazines, newsletters, and newspapers.

• If the piece you are selling has not previously been published, you should normally sell nothing more than first North American serial rights. If the publication to which you are selling your piece is normally sold both within and outside of North America, however, you should sell either first world serial rights or first North American and first British Commonwealth serial rights.

• Vigorously oppose attempts by publications to purchase first serial rights in any language or territory in which that publication is not published or distributed. Otherwise you are giving the publisher the right to sell foreign first rights to your piece without paying you a penny.

• Some publications buy all rights but return all but first serial rights to the author, either automatically or on written request, on or shortly after publication. The purpose of this is to guarantee that you won't sell any reprint rights to the piece until after its initial publication. There is nothing wrong with this, provided the rights are returnable no later than three months following publication, and provided the agreement sets a specific and reasonable deadline for the piece's initial publication. If a written request is required on or after publication for the remaining rights to be returned to you, be sure to make such a request promptly; the publication will formally return the rights to you in a letter. If you don't get such a letter promptly, press for one. Save this letter for your own legal protection.

• If a publication tries to buy all rights, and no return-of-rights provision is included in your agreement, *don't* go along with the terms unless the payment is truly enormous, and perhaps not even then. Instead, call or write your editor and suggest that *all rights* be changed to *first serial rights*—or better still, *first North American serial rights.* If this is refused, suggest a return-of-rights provision as described above. Many publications that initially try to buy all rights will go along with one of these options—provided you ask for it.

• Some contracts may include a stipulation preventing you from selling or publishing your piece elsewhere until that publisher has published it, or until a short time after such publication. Here again the publisher is simply trying to guarantee itself exclusivity. If the time limits are reasonable, this is fine. If the restriction is on *selling* the piece, I normally wouldn't let this limitation extend beyond the date of publication, and certainly no more than three months thereafter. If the restriction is on *publishing* the piece elsewhere, however, this means you are free to sell reprint rights to that piece at any time, provided that you can get other editors to agree to abstain from reprinting it until a certain date. This should ideally be six months after initial publication, and definitely no later than one year.

• Some publications do not send authors letters of agreement or contracts, but stamp or print the terms of agreement on the backs of authors' payment checks. Endorsing the check constitutes endorsement of the terms on that check. If you get such a check and the stamped or printed terms are acceptable, then you have no problem: simply sign the check, and cash or deposit it. This constitutes a legal agreement binding on both parties. However, if the terms are *not* acceptable, or if they do not cover everything you feel they should (for example, if they don't specify a deadline for publication), do *not* sign, cash, or deposit the check. Instead, call your editor, explain that you cannot cash the check or accept the terms being offered, and do your best to negotiate terms that are acceptable.

Once you have come to an agreement on terms, you *still* should not cash the check. Ask that you be sent a letter (or offer to draw one up yourself) specifically setting forth all the terms you've agreed to on the phone. Insist that this letter contain a sentence that says, "This letter supersedes the terms printed on the back of our check #————." This is very important. *After* you have received such a letter, you may cash or deposit your check.

Alternatively, you may take a pen and amend the agreement on the back of the check to reflect the new terms you have negotiated *if* your editor (or someone in the contracts department) gives you permission to do so. You can then simply sign and cash the check; no letter from the publisher is necessary. Some authors have dealt with contracts printed on the backs of checks by depositing the checks without signing them, or by altering the terms in pen without first consulting with editors or contracts people. But it is better to avoid ambiguity and potential conflict by calling your editor and working out terms that are mutually acceptable.

Some firms have a contract or formal letter of agreement that they offer to writers who are smart enough to refuse the terms printed on their checks. If a publisher wants to send you such an agreement, fine. However, look that agreement over carefully, too, and be willing to negotiate changes in it if necessary.

• Many agreements contain "right to edit" clauses. These can specify any of the following terms: (1) the publication may edit your piece as it sees fit; (2) the publication may edit your piece as it sees fit, but shall do so with great care; (3) the publication may edit your piece as it sees fit, provided such editing is reasonable and appropriate; or (4) all editing on your piece shall be subject to your approval, such approval not to be unreasonably withheld. The fourth set of terms is ideal. The third is most common, and it's a pretty good compromise between the needs of publishers and the rights of authors. If your editor won't let you approve the editing of your piece, these are the terms you should propose. The first and second sets of terms both give editors *carte blanche;* the phrase "but shall do so with great care" means nothing at all. If your agreement contains one of these two provisions, ask that it be changed to the third or fourth provision listed above. If your agreement doesn't say anything about editing at all, then the third set of terms is implied. However, if you want to play it safe, you may want to ask for the third or fourth provision to be added.

• If your piece is accompanied by drawings, maps, and/or photographs, you should receive an additional fee. Be sure your agreement specifies the terms of the use of both written *and* visual material. The terms should be similar or identical for both.

• When you sell reprint rights to a piece that has previously appeared in that same territory (for example, North America or the British Commonwealth), you should try to give up only one-time nonexclusive rights within that territory. However, if a publication wants one-time exclusive rights within a certain field (for example, art and architecture, sports, or pets), I see no reason not to agree. This is reasonable, because a publication geared to a specific audience doesn't want you selling the same piece to one of its competitors.

• Some publications may want to buy some reprint rights at the same time they purchase first serial rights. There is nothing wrong with this so long as you are reasonably paid for those rights. Insist that all reprint rights be sold on a nonexclusive basis *only.* Your agreement should specify this clearly and unambiguously. You want to be able to sell reprint rights to other publishers on your own.

ANTHOLOGY CONTRACTS

If someone wishes to use something you've written.in a book anthology, the guidelines above concerning use in a periodical generally apply. Here are some exceptions and additions:

• You will be selling not serial or periodical rights but anthology rights. If your contract simply specifies first publication or reprint rights rather than anthology rights, this is fine.

• The fee for anthology use should reflect the territories in which the book will be published. If the editor wants to buy the right to publish your piece in all editions of the anthology worldwide, you should expect to receive (and should ask for) a heftier fee than if you are just selling one-time North American anthology rights. Alternatively, you can sell only the right to publish your piece in all North American editions of the book; use in other editions must then be negotiated separately. Or your contract might cover both North American and foreign rights, but call for an additional fee to be paid if and when a foreign edition is published by that publisher or foreign rights are sold to another publisher.

• You have two additional items to use as leverage in negotiations: royalties and subsidiary rights income. If the fee you are offered seems too small, you might suggest that you receive a prorated percentage of the anthology's royalties and/or subsidiary rights earnings. (This should *never* be less than 50 percent.) You can, of course, ask for a share of these earnings even if the fee you are offered seems just fine. For details on prorating, and on royalty and subsidiary rights income from anthology use, see page 375.

• If your piece has not previously appeared in print, you should normally expect a much larger fee—at least twice as much as for a similar reprint use.

• The lead time (the amount of time between the purchase of rights and publication) is generally longer with books than with periodicals. The deadline for publication should reflect this reality. Let your editor have two years from the signing of your contract, or eighteen months from the time the final manuscript of the book is accepted by the publisher, to publish the anthology.

• Because books are more expensive than magazines, it's appropriate to have a clause in your contract covering author's copies. Try to get three copies of the first edition on publication; settle for two copies if the anthology will first be published in paperback, one copy if it will first be published in hardcover. It is also worth asking for one copy of each subsequent edition of the book; but don't be surprised if this request is refused. You may, if you like, also try to write in a provision that allows you to purchase additional copies of the first edition from the editor at 40 percent off the retail price.

BOOK CONTRACTS

Book contracts can be as brief as one or two pages or as long as fifteen; five to eight legal pages is about average. Because each book contract is so detailed and complicated, and because each firm offers its own version, there is always a good deal of room for negotiation. You should expect to negotiate quite a few points—at least five or six, perhaps as many as twenty—in any book contract. These negotiations are not only permitted but expected; I've never known a book publisher to offer a contract on a "take it or leave it" basis.

Negotiating a Book Contract

When an editor at a trade publisher gets the go-ahead to make a deal on your book, he or she will call you or your agent to ask, "How much of an advance do you need?" and to offer some basic terms—usually the advance and U.S. royalty rates. The territory in which the editor wants to acquire rights (North America, North America and the British Commonwealth, the world, etc.) may also be a matter of discussion at this stage. The first round of negotiation will involve coming to some agreement on these basic terms. If no agreement can be reached at this stage, the deal will be scuttled without further ado.

Once the basic terms have been orally agreed to, the publisher will draw up a formal contract, which will then be sent to you or your agent. At this stage, the size of the advance, the basic royalty rate, and anything else agreed to orally are no longer negotiable. However, everything else is open to discussion. The main negotiations take place after you or your agent have received and looked over the written contract, which usually takes two to six weeks to arrive.

Some text, professional, scholarly, and reference book publishers follow the procedures discussed above. Most of these publishers, however, as well as some literary presses and some tiny trade publishers, may skip the phone call and simply send a contract and a letter of acceptance.

Here are some tips which, along with the general tips beginning on page 328, will help you negotiate a book contract:

• Although your editor probably will not specify this, any royalties initially offered, and any final oral agreement on basic royalty rates, refer to *royalties paid on copies of the book published by that publisher and sold in the United States at discounts of less than 50 percent to regular retail outlets (such as bookstores, department stores, newsstands, and drugstores).* Royalties paid on sales of books published by other publishers, on books sold outside the United States, on books sold at a 50 percent or higher discount, and on books sold by direct mail, as premiums, or through special outlets, are usually lower. No royalty is usually paid on copies given away or on copies you purchase yourself.

• Before your negotiations on a book begin—but after the offer of an advance and royalty rates is made—ask your editor these four questions: (1) In what format or formats do you plan to publish the book initially? (2) What will be the cover price of the book? (3) How large do you estimate your first printing will be? (4) What do you project for first-year sales? It's very helpful to get answers to these questions before beginning negotiations, because they will give you some idea of what the book is worth to the publisher.

• If an editor asks you, "How much of an advance are you looking for?" ask for about 150 percent of the advance you think you are likely to get.

• Remember that the initial advance offered for a trade or professional book will usually equal 50 to 80 percent of the book's anticipated royalty earnings in its first year of publication, or from its first printing. Scholarly books, and trade books published by literary houses and very small presses, tend to receive smaller advances, or no advances at all. It may, of course, be possible to negotiate a higher advance, or a small advance if one is not offered at all.

• The advance, royalties, and other terms you negotiate should be based on the *kind* of book you're selling, not the kind of publisher that will be publishing it. If Oxford University Press wants to publish your trade book, you should expect at least a small advance and standard trade royalties. But if Oxford wants to publish your book called *Prose Styles of Nineteenth*

Century Jewish Writers, expect royalties for a scholarly volume and no more than a tiny advance, perhaps $1000—if that much.

• If an editor's best offer on a book is too low, or if you have trouble agreeing on other terms, you have the right to say, "I don't like the deal you're offering, but I'll take it if nothing better comes along. Can you leave your offer on the table for a while?" Some editors will say yes. Ninety days is a reasonable period to ask for.

• When negotiating an advance, you may use increments of $1000, $500, $250, or even $100. Dealing with smaller increments is too picky. When negotiating royalties, you can deal in increments of 2½ percent, 2 percent, 1 percent, or even ½ percent. In fact, making compromises based on half a percentage point is quite common. Indeed, half a percentage point can make a big difference if a book does well.

• It is possible to negotiate a contract to death. Although most book contracts can be improved in fifty different ways, your best bet is to pick the five to ten most important items and work at negotiating those.

• Once you and your editor have agreed to an advance and basic royalty rates, you have made an agreement to negotiate in good faith on a final written contract. However, if you cannot negotiate a written contract acceptable to both sides, you have a right to say, "Sorry, but we don't have a deal" and end the matter.

Provisions of a Book Contract

Advance   If you are selling a finished manuscript, you should expect payment of the full advance on signing. If you are selling a book proposal, you should normally expect (and, if necessary, push for) half the advance on signing and half on acceptance of the completed work.

If your publisher absolutely insists on paying a portion of the advance on publication, push hard to get the bulk of it no later than acceptance. If you are selling a proposal, suggest 40 percent on signing, 40 percent on acceptance, and 20 percent thereafter. Push hard to change payment on publication to payment on publication or one year from acceptance, whichever comes first.

Make very sure that once you have received the full amount of the advance your publisher cannot reclaim any part of that advance if it cancels its plans to publish your book. Also make very sure that if your book fails to earn out its advance, you are not required to pay back the unearned portion and that any unearned portion may not be deducted from earnings from any other book that you may sell (or have sold) to that publisher.

Royalties   Some basic terms bear discussion here: the *cover price* (called the *catalog price* in some book contracts) of a book is the price usually printed on the cover. The *invoice price* is the cover price less a freight allowance (usually 50¢), which the bookseller keeps as reimbursement for the cost of shipping books to the bookstore. Some publishers pay the cost of shipping themselves; when this is the case, the invoice price is no different from the cover price. *Net receipts* and *wholesale price* refer to the amount received by the publisher from the book dealer, distributor, or wholesaler. This can range from 40 to 80 percent of the cover price. Trade book royalties are usually based on the cover or invoice price; royalties on other types of books are most often based on net receipts.

Here is a general outline of the basic royalty rates you should expect, ask for, and, at times, insist on:

• *Hardcover trade books for adults*   The standard royalties are 10 percent of the cover or invoice price for the first five thousand copies sold; 12½ percent for the next five thousand; and 15 percent thereafter. A few major publishers set their breakpoints at seventy-five hundred and fifteen thousand copies.

• *Hardcover trade books for children and young adults*   Royalties can range from a flat 10 percent of the cover or invoice price to the same terms as for hardcover trade books for adults. Ask for 12½ percent after ten thousand copies and 15 percent after twenty thousand copies; avoid taking less than a flat 10 percent.

• *Trade paperbacks for adults*   Royalties range from 6 to 8 percent of the cover or invoice price. The beginning rate can be anywhere from 6 to 7½ percent. Ask for a rate of 7½ percent to start and 8 percent after fifty thousand copies. Under no circumstances take less than a flat 6 percent.

• *Trade paperbacks for children and young adults*   Royalties are equal to or slightly lower than those for adult trade paperbacks. Ask for a flat 7 or 7½ percent of the cover or invoice price. Some publishers offer starting rates as low as 5 percent, but you shouldn't have to take less than 6 percent.

• *Mass-market paperbacks for adults*   A flat 8 percent of the cover price is standard, though some publishers will try to start you out at 6 percent. Try for 8 percent; if you absolutely have to, take 6 percent, with an escalation to 8 percent as soon as possible—say, at twenty thousand copies. A flat 6 percent is the minimum.

• *Mass-market books for children and young adults*   Ask for 8 percent of the cover price, though you may have to settle for a beginning rate of 6 percent with an escalation to 8 percent at one hundred to two hundred thousand copies.

• *Exceptions and qualifications regarding trade books*   Royalty rates may be lower on art books, children's picture books, and other books that are very expensive to produce. Royalties for books published by very small presses, particularly some literary presses, may also be lower.

There's nothing wrong with a contract that bases trade royalties on net receipts, provided the amounts you'll earn are reasonable. For example, a hardcover royalty based on net receipts of 15 percent for the first five thousand copies, 20 percent for the next five thousand, and 25 percent thereafter is fine, because it's roughly equivalent to the standard 10 to 12½ to 15 percent royalties based on cover price.

• *Textbooks*   Royalties are normally computed on net receipts. Royalties for college texts can range from 8 to 20 percent, but 10 to 15 percent is the normal range for both hardcovers and paperbacks. Ask for a flat 15 percent of net receipts and see how close to that figure the publisher will go. Try not to settle for a flat 10 percent; try to at least get an escalation to 12 percent or 12½ percent, either at ten thousand copies or on the second printing. Royalties on elementary, junior high, and high school texts may be lower, perhaps considerably so.

• *Professional, technical, and medical books*   Royalties are usually computed on net receipts, and range from 10 to 15 percent for both hardcovers and paperbacks. Ask for a flat 15 percent of net receipts and settle for as close to that figure as you can get, but certainly no less than a flat 10 percent.

Some publishers base royalties for these books on the cover or invoice price. When dealing with such a publisher, suggest the following royalties: paperbacks, a flat 10 percent; hardcovers, 10 percent to five thousand copies, 12½ percent for the next five thousand copies, and 15 percent thereafter. You may wind up having to take a flat 10 percent on all copies sold.

• *Scholarly books*   Royalties are usually based on net receipts, though some publishers will pay royalties based on the cover or invoice price.

Either way, your royalty should be in the 10 to 15 percent range for hardcovers. You'll probably have to start at 10 percent, but shoot for 12½ percent at twenty-five hundred copies and 15 percent at five thousand. You should be able to get at least one escalation. Paperback royalties range from 5 to 10 percent; you should be able to start at no less than 6 percent. On certain scholarly works that are almost guaranteed to lose money for the publisher, or at best break even, you may be asked to forego royalties altogether on the first printing, or on the first thousand to twenty-five hundred copies. If your book or monograph is very specialized or obscure, I'd say go along with such a request. However, if your project has more than a very narrow, specialized readership, push hard to be paid royalties from the beginning.

Reduced Royalties   On books of *all* types, royalties are typically lower for all of the following sales:

• Books sold outside the United States
• Books sold at a discount of 50 percent or more, including books sold to wholesalers, distributors, and book clubs
• Books sold by the publisher via mail order
• Books sold as premiums—that is, to businesses and other organizations for distribution to their members, clients, employees, or customers
• Books sold through other unusual means (for example, sold by the publisher through the National Park Service)
• Books sold as remainders (copies of a book remaining in the publisher's warehouse when it is declared out of print)
• Books sold as overstock (large numbers of unsold copies that are taking up space in the publisher's warehouse)
• Unbound books or "printed sheets" (that is, the complete contents of a book sold unbound to another publisher, which in turn binds those pages into books on its own)

In each of the above cases, royalties tend to range from 50 to 70 percent of the otherwise appropriate rates specified in your contract. For example, your contract may call for a royalty rate of 7½ percent of the cover price on the trade paperback edition of your book, but only 7½ percent of the net receipts for premium sales.

No royalty is normally paid on books sold at or below cost, or on books given away for any reason.

Some book contracts reduce the author's royalty by 25 to 50 percent for books published in *reprintings* of twenty-five hundred copies or less. The purpose of this reduced royalty is to allow the publisher to make a reasonable profit on small reprintings, and thus keep books that are in fairly low demand in print. This is okay, with one exception: if such a reduced royalty clause appears in a contract for a scholarly book or from a small literary press, insist that it be omitted. These presses routinely have very small print runs (often under twenty-five hundred copies), and they are perfectly willing and able to keep slow-selling books in print without having to reduce your royalty.

Rights Purchased/Subsidiary Rights   You should try to hang onto any rights that you think you have a good chance of selling elsewhere—either on your own, through your domestic agent, or through one or more foreign agents. But if you doubt you can sell a certain group of rights, it *may* be better to grant those rights to your publisher, *provided your contract entitles you to at least 50 percent of the money from your publisher's sale of those rights.* For example, if you don't have an agent, there's not much point in trying to hang onto film and TV rights to your novel, since you have no way to market them.

Rights that you can't do much with yourself can be used as excellent bargaining chips in contract negotiations. For example, if you don't have a British agent, you can initially try to keep British Commonwealth rights—then offer to give them up in exchange for, say, higher royalties.

Although your contract should entitle you, at minimum, to 50 percent of all money from the sale of most subsidiary rights, you should usually be able to keep 90 percent of the money from the sale of TV, movie, stage, and radio rights, and 85 percent of first serial money. It is also usually possible to retain 75 percent of all money from foreign rights sales. You may, of course, not have to give up any of these rights at all.

Do keep in mind that your share of money from your publisher's sale of subsidiary rights is *not* paid directly to you; instead, it is credited to your publishing account (see pages 293–94 for details).

It is worth trying to insert a provision that requires the publisher to notify you of any subsidiary rights sale within thirty (or at most sixty) days of that sale. The publisher should be required to tell you what was bought (for example, an excerpt, or the whole book), what rights were bought, how much money changed hands, and when it changed (or will change) hands.

Royalty Statements Also called statements of account, these statements cover *all* a book's earnings, including both royalties *and* income from subsidiary rights sales. A complete discussion of royalty statements appears on pages 293–98. Here are some things to keep in mind when negotiating a book contract:

• Each statement and royalty check should be sent no later than four months after the close of the royalty period. This is the *absolute maximum* delay you should permit. A three-month delay is better.

• Your contract will allow your publisher to withhold a reserve against returns of each edition. This reserve must be held *only* against royalty income, *not* against subsidiary rights money. Most contracts simply state that a "reasonable" reserve may be withheld; try to change this phrase to a specific percentage. Suggest 15 percent (25 percent for mass-market paperbacks). If a percentage *is* specified, it should be no more than 25 to 35 percent of royalty income for the royalty period—for mass-market paperbacks *only,* 40–45 percent. It is also acceptable if your contract calls for reserves to be based on actual returns for the current or previous royalty period.

• *Don't* agree to any clause that puts limits on the amount of money you can be paid in any six-month or one-year period. This is nothing more than a way for your publisher to hang onto money that is rightfully yours. If you really want to reduce your income during any royalty period, your publisher will be *delighted* to withhold some or all of your money on request. But don't get stuck with a clause that *forces* a payment ceiling on you.

• Your contract should give you the right to have an accountant examine your publisher's accounts at your expense, *and* the right to be fully and promptly reimbursed for the accountant's expenses by the publisher if there are errors in your account to the publisher's advantage by more than 5 percent. The contract should also call for you to be promptly paid the amount in error. Insist on adding these provisions if necessary; they're very important, as they keep your publisher honest.

• Because many publishers' royalty statements are confusing or incomplete, it is an excellent idea to get the following sentence added to your contract: "At the Author's written request following receipt of any statement of account for the Work, the Publisher shall supply complete information as to the number of copies of the Work printed, sold, and returned in all editions at all prices, as well as the current reserve for returns for all editions at all prices."

• You should be entitled to receive royalty reports (and, if appropriate, payments) for *every* royalty period in which copies are sold. Your contract should state this specifically; it should *not* say, "Royalty reports shall be rendered until the book goes out of print." This second stipulation allows your publisher to declare your book out of print on the last day of a royalty period, to not issue a royalty statement for that period, *and* to keep for itself all of your earnings for that period *plus* any previously held reserve against your returns.

Delivery Date   If you are selling your book on the basis of a proposal, make sure your deadline for submitting the finished book gives you plenty of time. Add a couple of extra months just to be sure. Nine to twelve months is standard for most trade books; however, publishers are aware that certain projects can take longer. Keep in mind that if you miss your deadline, your publisher has the right to cancel the contract and be repaid any advance and expense money you've received for the project. Make sure that your contract does not attach any penalty (other than potential cancellation of the agreement) to late delivery of a manuscript. Late delivery should not entitle the publisher to reduce the amount of your advance.

Simultaneous Projects   Get rid of clauses that say things like "The Author warrants that the Work shall be his or her next project, and that he or she shall not work on or agree to write for any other publisher any other project until the final manuscript of the Work is accepted." If you're selling a book on a proposal basis, such a clause limits your other writing activities unfairly and unnecessarily; if you're selling a completed manuscript, the provision is meaningless. Tell your editor to dump this; few will object.

Competitive Works   Your contract may require that you not publish any book that will complete or conflict with the project you are selling. This is reasonable, but it is a good idea to try to change "conflict with" to "directly conflict with," just to be safe. (Incidentally, if you're selling a western novel, selling another western to another publisher does *not* constitute a conflict with the first book. But if you sell *The Homeowner's*

Guide to Lawn Care to one house and *How to Have a Beautiful Lawn* to another, those two works would probably be considered competitive.)

Manuscript Form   Your contract should *not* require you to submit your text in copyedited, typeset, or camera-ready form. Even if your project is an art or illustrated book, your publisher should bear the cost of copyediting, typesetting, and formatting.

Length   If your contract specifies a length for your project, make sure that it is reasonable and appropriate.

Publication Deadline   Your publisher should have no more than eighteen months from the acceptance of the completed manuscript or the signing of the contract, whichever comes second, to publish your book or license another publisher to do so. If your publisher absolutely insists on more time, *very grudgingly* allow two years, but try to get something else you want in exchange for it. Make sure that *some* time limit is specified; one major house tries to get away with setting no publication deadline at all. Most contracts extend the deadline for publication in the event of flood, fire, water, acts of God, and other disasters. This is reasonable so long as such an extension is limited to the length of the actual delay caused by the disaster.

Previous Publication   If all or part of your book has been previously published or any rights to all or part of the book have previously been sold, any such sales, publications, and copyrights should be clearly indicated.

Indexing   If your book is nonfiction, it may need indexing. Your contract will have a clause covering this. Here are the possible terms, from best to worst:

• The publisher will provide an index at its own expense. You can ask for this, but you probably won't get it. You might be able to trade something else for it, though. Your chances of getting this are *better* if you aren't being paid in advance.
• You have the option of either preparing the index yourself or having the publisher prepare it for you, with the cost of such preparation to be charged against your publishing account.

• You have the option of either preparing the index yourself or having the publisher prepare it for you, with the cost of preparation to be billed to you and payable immediately.

Option two is a good compromise, and most publishers will go along with it.

It is *sometimes* possible to split the cost of preparing an index with the publisher. Again, try to have your share of the cost charged to your account rather than billed directly to you.

Some indexing clauses will give the publisher the choice between billing you for the indexing costs *or* charging them to your royalty account. Try to change this to option two above; most publishers, given the chance to be paid in cash for indexing, will ask you for the money.

Right of Refusal   If you're selling your book on the basis of a proposal, your publisher will want the right to cancel the contract if your finished manuscript is "unacceptable in form or content." Here are the various commonly offered options for such a provision, listed from best to worst:

• The publisher may cancel the contract; the author keeps all moneys received so far but is entitled to no more.

• The publisher may cancel the contract; the author must repay the publisher some or all of the money received for the project *only if and when* he or she receives such amounts from one or more other publishers in exchange for the right to publish the project. This is quite common, and worth pushing for. It provides you with at least partial protection against capricious rejection, and most publishers can live with it.

• The publisher may cancel the contract; the author must repay all moneys received for the project on the publisher's demand. Avoid this if at all possible.

Everything else aside, your contract should give you the right to be told why a manuscript is unacceptable, and the right to revise it to the publisher's specifications. The publisher still has the right to reject the revision, but you at least have a chance to salvage the deal.

Right and Responsibility to Edit   Your contract should guarantee that no editing shall be done without your approval. Don't permit any clause that allows an editor to overrule your own editorial judgment.

Libel   Every book contract will have a libel clause, invariably weighted heavily in the publisher's favor. Usually the publisher has the right to require that libelous material be deleted and/or to cancel the contract if the book contains anything libelous. While publishers can usually be flexible about things like rights and royalties, they usually stand firm (on the advice of their attorneys) when it comes to protection from lawsuits. If your book is not potentially libelous, let the libel clause stand as is unless it is truly outrageous. If your book *is* potentially libelous, I urge you strongly to either eliminate or modify the libelous parts, or take both your book and the contract to a literary lawyer for advice before you close the book deal.

Cover Design and Cover Copy   In most cases you will have no control over what your book cover or dust jacket will look like or say. But if you feel strongly about the issue, ask that your book's cover design and/or cover copy be subject to your approval. Your chance of getting this is slim. More likely you'll be given the right to be consulted on the cover, but not the right of approval.

Author's Alterations   Most contracts require authors to pay any costs of making changes in a manuscript once it has been typeset, *if* those costs exceed 10 percent of the original cost of typesetting. This provision is fair, as it prevents you from making enormous changes at the last minute. Try to have any such costs charged to your publishing account.

Copyright   Insist that your contract specify that the publisher will copyright the book in your name (or if you prefer, in your pseudonym). With the exception of a few textbook publishers, you should have no trouble getting this.

Author's Copies   Your contract should give you *at least* ten free copies of *each* edition of your book on publication. Ask for twenty-five; you'll usually get them. Make sure your contract also has a provision allowing you to purchase additional copies at the wholesale price or less (at least 40 percent off for trade books). Ideally, your contract should allow you to charge the cost of these copies to your publishing account.

Editions for the Handicapped   Some contracts call for the author to forsake royalties on special editions or reproductions of the book for the physically handicapped. This is fine *provided that the publisher makes no profit on these editions and reproductions and is merely reimbursed for its actual expenses.*

Bankruptcy   Your contract should contain a provision such as this one: "In the event of the bankruptcy or liquidation of the Publisher, this agreement shall terminate and all rights granted to the Publisher not heretofore exercised shall automatically revert to the Author." If no bankruptcy clause appears in your contract, try to insert the clause above as a rider. If your publisher wants different wording, work out a reasonable compromise, but *some* sort of bankruptcy clause *must* be a part of your agreement. It is very important that in the event your publisher files for bankruptcy, all unexercised rights revert to you *automatically,* without any notice required. Otherwise, you can lose both your rights to your book *and* all future income from it.

Option   Your publisher may want the right of first refusal on your next manuscript—that is, the right to see and make an offer on your next book before any other publisher does. Some publishers are willing to dump this provision when asked; most are willing to negotiate it. If your editor insists on keeping an option on your next book, keep these tips in mind:

• The contract should *not* give the publisher the right to buy your next book on the same terms as the current volume. In fact, it should give you the right to turn down an unacceptable offer. The clause should say something like this: "The Publisher shall have first option to publish the Author's next book, provided that the Publisher's terms for that book are acceptable to the Author." Or, "The Publisher shall have the first option to publish the Author's next book, provided its terms for that book are fair and reasonable."

• You should have the option of submitting either a completed manuscript "or a comprehensive outline of the project" (that is, a proposal) for your next book. Don't let your contract require you to submit a finished manuscript.

• The publisher should have no more than sixty days (ninety at the absolute most) from receipt of your next manuscript or proposal to make an offer on it.

• Get rid of any stipulation that ties the publisher's deadline for making an offer on your next work to acceptance or publication of your *current* book. This could allow the publisher months or even years to hang onto your next project without making a decision, while preventing you from taking it elsewhere.

• One excellent way of limiting the effect of an option clause is to limit the kind of works it refers to. For instance, if your contract is for a romance novel and your publisher insists on an option for your next book, try to change "the Author's next book" to "the Author's next romance novel." Alternatively you can suggest "the Author's next fiction book," "the Author's next adult fiction book," "the Author's next adult trade book," and so on.

Revision   Book contracts typically have two revision provisions. The first concerns revision of a manuscript prior to publication; the second deals with revision of a published book for a new edition. Neither provision should *ever* give the publisher the right to revise the work without your permission.

The publisher may *request* certain revisions prior to the book's publication; but if you are unwilling or unable to make these revisions yourself, the publisher should not have the right to make them without your consent.

Don't allow a provision in your contract that permits the publisher to publish a revised or updated version of your book without your consent. Any revision or updating should be by mutual agreement. If your publisher does wish to publish a revised or updated edition, you should ask—and expect—to be paid a new (though smaller) advance for putting together the revision.

Out of Print   Your contract *must* have a clause that requires your publisher to return any unexercised rights to you if and when your book goes out of print. Although this is a standard provision in most contracts, at least one of the very biggest houses doesn't offer such a clause unless authors ask for it. Under most out-of-print clauses, the author can write to the publisher when a book is out of print and ask for the book to be put back into print. The publisher then has six to twelve months to republish it or license another publisher to do so. If no such publication or licensing takes place by that time, then any unexercised rights revert to the author. A good out-of-print clause allows you to reclaim U.S. publication rights if your book is out of print in this country, even if it is still in print elsewhere. This is worth asking for, though you won't always get it.

Author's Right to Purchase Remainders   If your book is declared out of print, your publisher will try to sell off the remaining copies (at 5 to 50 percent of the book's wholesale price) to discount booksellers, mail-order dealers, discount department stores, and other cut-rate outlets. Some authors would rather purchase these copies and try to sell them themselves. If you feel this way, try to add a provision to your contract that says, "The Author shall have the first option to purchase any or all remainders at the remainder price." If you like, you might also try to add, "The Author may also purchase any remaining unbound sheets and/or the plates used for printing the Work, if he or she so chooses." Once your book has been declared out of print, you may sell copies of the book to anyone you want, including bookstores, organizations, or even other publishers.

Your contract should also give you the first option to purchase overstock—copies gathering dust in the publisher's warehouse that it decides to sell at a reduced price. (Overstocked titles remain in print, however.)

Arbitration   Because going to court can be so time-consuming and expensive, some writers and publishers like to include an arbitration provision in each book contract. This is a good idea for everyone. Here is some suggested language: "Should an unresolvable difference arise between the Publisher and the Author, the matter may be referred to a mutually acceptable mediator. Should the mediator fail to solve the problem, a panel shall be formed of one representative of the Author, one representative of the Publisher, and a third party agreeable to both sides. The panel's decision on the issue shall be binding on both the Author and the Publisher."

Agency Clause   Your agent, if you have one, will insist on adding a provision requiring that all payments be made to him or her. This is reasonable.

TV AND FILM OPTIONS

TV and film rights to books (and to plays, short stories, and other literary forms) can be sold in two ways: directly, and through *options*.

A direct sale is much like the sale of any other form of rights: the TV or film producer negotiates a contract with a writer or (in the great majority of cases) the writer's agent; the producer and writer sign the contract; and the writer gets paid a fee. Sometimes additional fees and bonuses may be written into the contract.

An *option* is not the sale of TV or film rights, but the exclusive right to purchase those rights. An option gives a producer a specific amount of time (usually a year) to purchase movie or TV rights (or both). During this time, the writer may not accept an offer for those rights from anyone else, nor may the writer accept an option from anyone else.

Options typically sell for $2000 to $5000 a year, though they can go as high as $50,000 for successful books. If a producer actually purchases film or TV production rights, the price can range from $25,000 to $200,000, occasionally higher.

11. ✎

Legal Matters

COPYRIGHT

Copyright is a complex issue. However, for most writers a working knowledge of the key points of United States copyright law is sufficient. These key points are discussed below.

Copyright law differs from country to country. When a work is published or performed in a country outside the United States and its possessions, in some cases a separate copyright must be obtained in that country. This is normally done by the foreign publisher of the work. Some international copyright protection does exist under a copyright agreement signed by the United States and a number of foreign countries; when you, your agent, or one of your publishers sells foreign rights to a piece, you can assume that proper copyright protection in that country or countries either already exists under the international copyright agreement or will be obtained by the foreign publisher or producer.

The remainder of this section refers to U.S. copyright law only.

Copyright law covers publication and certain other forms of public distribution or display. It protects *all* forms of creative work including books, articles, plays, poems, songs, scripts, tapes, records, videotapes, photographs, illustrations, computer software, paintings, sculpture, and so on. It covers both unpublished or published manuscripts and unperformed or performed works.

Once you have created a work (for example, written a short story), that work and all rights to it immediately become your property, and immediately become protected by U.S. copyright law. (For a list of the very few exceptions, see below and on page 360.) *You do not need to register something you have created with the Copyright Office prior to its publication.* You do not need to mail a copy to yourself or put a copy in a sealed envelope in a safe deposit box. You own that work completely until and unless you decide to sell off one or more of the rights to it.

Although unnecessary, copyright registration *is* available for pieces that have not yet been published. You may, if you wish, assemble a collection of your own manuscripts (published, unpublished, or both) and register the entire work with the Copyright Office. This work can be any size, and can be composed of work in any genre or combination of genres. It can include written material, visual material, or both. The single copyright that you obtain for this collection (for a fee of $10) will cover every unpublished selection in that collection as well as the collection as a whole.

If you do choose to register your own unpublished writings, you need not place a copyright notice on your unpublished manuscripts. In fact, I advise against this, as it looks amateurish to some editors. (Previously published material, however, whether submitted in manuscript or clipping form, *should* contain a proper notice of copyright.)

Once something you have written has been *published* in the United States, it *must* be officially registered with the U.S. Copyright Office to continue to receive copyright protection. Registration involves filing a form, paying a small fee, sending two copies of the work to the Copyright Office, and publishing a proper copyright notice on or in the published work. With *very* few exceptions, you can expect your publisher to handle these details for you automatically.

If you have self-published (or plan to self-publish) one or more of your works, you will need to register it with the U.S. Copyright Office yourself. To learn which of the several different registration forms you will need, call (202) 479-0700, or write to the Copyright Office, Library of Congress, Washington, DC 20559. To request specific forms, write to the same address or call (202) 287-9100. Forms are free; instructions accompany each form. Works may be registered any time following publication; however, the sooner after publication the better. However, if you register an unpublished work, then later self-publish all or part of that work, you must reregister it as a published work on or after its publication.

Nothing intangible can be copyrighted. Thus, manuscripts, published books and magazines, tapes, films, records, paintings, and photographs receive copyright protection; but ideas, discoveries, melodies in your head, conversations, improvised speeches, and so on cannot receive copyright protection until and unless they are written down, filmed, taped, or otherwise recorded.

Names cannot be copyrighted. This includes the names of people, pseudonyms, titles of creative works (yes, that's right—the title of your book *cannot* be copyrighted; anyone else can use that same title on another work at any time), names of organizations or groups, names of businesses, and names of products or services. Catchwords, catchphrases, slogans, and short advertising phrases cannot be copyrighted; nor can recipes, formulas, or lists of ingredients. However, the items listed above *are* in certain cases eligible for patents and/or trademarks through the Office of Patents and Trademarks. In certain other cases, they are protected under U.S. trade law whether or not patents or trademarks have been obtained. In other words, you can't market your own brand of typewriter and call it Smith-Corona, even though the name isn't copyrighted. You can, however, name a character in your short story Marilyn Smith-Corona, or mention Smith-Corona typewriters in a piece you're writing, without first having to get permission from the Smith-Corona Corporation.

Rights are different from *copyright.* The holder of a work's copyright may or may not actually control a particular right or group of rights to that work. For example, I own the copyright to this book, but Harper & Row owns second serial rights to it. This means that if someone asked to buy second serial rights from me, I'd have to refer him or her to Harper's subsidiary rights department. (However, although Harper & Row controls the rights, it must pay me half the money earned from the sale of those rights.)

The author of any piece owns all rights to that piece not specifically conveyed to another party from the moment of its creation until the moment copyright protection expires. Revisions and new editions do not alter this. The only exception is a work made for hire; see pages 364–66 for details.

If you have written a piece that appears in a magazine, newspaper, or newsletter, normally the entire contents of that periodical will be copyrighted in the name of the publisher. There is nothing wrong with this, and it affords you full protection under U.S. copyright law. It does *not* grant to the publisher any right that you have not expressly granted to it already. If your piece is published in an anthology, the anthology may be copyrighted in the editor's *or* publisher's name. However, the same stipulations apply.

If one of your pieces is published separately (for example, as a book, chapbook, record, or map), the copyright may legally be registered in your name, the pseudonym of your choice, or the publisher's name. This is a matter for negotiation between you and your publisher. It is best to have the work copyrighted in your name or pseudonym. If your piece is *published* pseudonymously, you may *copyright* it in either your own name or your pseudonym. This name will appear on the copyright page. If you copyright it in your own name, you may use any variation you like; for example, S. Edelstein, Scott Samuel Edelstein, or S. S. Edelstein.

If you have collaborated on a work with someone, all the collaborators are coowners of the copyright unless they make an agreement to the contrary.

Copyright protection for both published and unpublished works begins at the moment of the work's creation and ends fifty years after the death of the author, regardless of whether the work is published, when it is published, who owns the rights, and the name in which the work is copyrighted. The only requirement for this protection is that *if and when* the work is published or otherwise publicly distributed, it must be properly registered with the Copyright Office.

If a work is a collaboration, the copyright runs out fifty years after the death of the last surviving collaborator.

In all of the above cases, copyright protection extends until the end of the calendar year in which the copyright would otherwise expire. In other words, if I die on February 2, 2050, the copyright to this book will expire at midnight on December 31, 2100.

If a work is anonymous, a work for hire, or *copyrighted* under a pseudonym, copyright protection lasts for seventy-five years beyond publication or one hundred years beyond the work's initial creation, whichever comes first. Again, copyright protection extends until the end of the calendar year in which the copyright would otherwise expire. However, if a work is published pseudonymously but copyrighted in the author's real name, or if it is published and copyrighted pseudonymously, but the author's true identity is revealed to the Copyright Office on the copyright registration form, the copyright expires at the end of the fiftieth calendar year following the author's death.

Copyright of each separate contribution to a periodical or anthology is distinct from copyright of the entire work. If I reprint an essay by Norman Mailer in a book I've edited, I can (and should) legally copyright the entire book in my name. This does not in any way affect Mailer's separate copyright for that essay, or the copyright of the magazine that first published that essay.

U.S. copyright laws were changed in the late seventies. Works published before January 1, 1978, fall under a different set of regulations. In general, copyrights on these pieces endure for exactly twenty-eight years. These copyrights may be renewed for an additional forty-seven years by filing a renewal form with the Office of Copyright; indeed, they *must* be formally renewed to prevent expiration. For complete information, contact the Copyright Office.

Physical possession of a creative work in no way effects ownership of rights or copyright. For example, if I buy the original manuscript of *Ragtime* from either a manuscript collector or E. L. Doctorow himself, I have not purchased the right to publish it in any way, shape, or form. Publishers normally do the opposite: they buy only the right to publish the piece, not the physical manuscript itself, which they sometimes return to the author.

What constitutes a proper copyright notice depends on the kind of work being copyrighted. In general, copyright notices for written and visual material follow the same form as the copyright notice for this book (which appears on the back of the title page).

Once a copyright has expired, that piece goes into the *public domain*— that is, anyone can use it at any time, in whole or part, without securing permission from anyone.

One of the best sources of information on copyright law is the Office of Copyright itself, which operates a telephone information service. You can have any question about copyright law answered at no charge (except the cost of the phone call) by calling (202) 479-0700.

The Copyright Office publishes dozens of documents on copyright and copyright law; most of these are free. For a complete list of government publications on copyright, order Circular 2; other general documents available at no charge include Circular 99, "Highlights of the Current Copyright Law," and Circular 1, "Copyright Basics." Request them by writing the Information and Publications Section, LM-455, Copyright Office, Library of Congress, Washington, DC 20559 or calling (202) 287-9100. Other forms and circulars are available from the same address and phone number.

Unusual or complex copyright questions are often best dealt with by a copyright or literary attorney.

Several excellent books cover copyright and other legal issues of interest to writers:

Every Writer's Practical Guide to Copyright Law: 50 Questions and Answers, by Ellen M. Kozak (Inkling Publications, Box 65798, St. Paul, MN 55165)

How to Protect Your Creative Work, by David A. Weinstein (Wiley)

Law and the Writer, edited by Kirk Polking (Writer's Digest Books)

A Writer's Guide to Copyright, by Caroline R. Herron (Poets & Writers, Inc., 201 W. 54th Street, New York, NY 10019)

A SPECIAL NOTE FOR WRITERS OF MATERIAL FOR FILM AND/OR TELEVISION

For all that I have said above about the protection that U.S. copyright law provides, the nature of the television and film industries makes additional protection necessary for TV and film material.

If you have written a television or film script, treatment, or concept, you normally should (and normally will be expected to) register the work with the Writers Guild, the professional organization for TV and film writers, before it gets submitted to producers. You don't have be a member of the Writers Guild to use the registration service. You need not register your work before it goes to an agent; however, the Guild recommends that you do so. Once an agent agrees to represent the work, you *must* register it before it is sent to producers.

Material for radio may also be registered with the Guild; however, in my opinion, registration is not necessary for this material. Registration is not available, or useful, for commercials, news reports, public service announcements, and so on.

For complete information on registration, contact the Writers Guild West, 8955 Beverly Boulevard, West Hollywood, CA 90048, (213) 550-1000, or the Writers Guild East, 555 W. 57th Street, New York, NY 10019, (212) 245-6180.

More information on the Writers Guild appears on page 385.

FAIR USE

U.S. copyright law permits anyone to publish brief quotes or excerpts from other people's writing without acquiring permission to do so. This is known as *fair use.*

Copyright law sets no specific length limit on fair use. The Copyright Office insists that each set of circumstances is unique, and that what would be considered fair use in one case might not be in another. In fact, the definition of fair use is circular: anyone can print a brief quote or excerpt without permission so long as doing so doesn't violate anyone's rights. How do you know when someone's rights have been violated? When a judge decides in that person's favor in a rights violation lawsuit.

In practice, brevity is almost always an important consideration, and so are good judgment and common sense. Two to three hundred words of prose is often the upper limit for fair use (except in cases where the piece being quoted or excerpted from is itself very brief).

Poems and songs can be trickier; while many writers have no problem with others quoting entire verses or stanzas from their work, some writers have objected to others quoting as little as a line or two without permission. Again, the length of the quote and the length of the piece it is taken from are both important.

Fair use boils down to this: if someone uses an excerpt from something you've written without permission and you feel your rights have been violated, you can ask or insist on some financial compensation and/or take that person to court. And if *you* wish to use a quote or excerpt by someone else and are unsure whether the passage is brief enough to use without obtaining permission, your best bet is to play it safe. Get in touch with the rights holder and request permission. Don't offer any money, though; chances are you'll be allowed to use it without charge.

When a fair use quote or excerpt is published, no copyright information or acknowledgment of previous publication need accompany it. However, the author and title of the piece from which it is taken should be indicated.

WORK FOR HIRE

Earlier in this chapter I explained that once a work is created, all rights to it belong to its creator until and unless he or she sells or gives them away. There is one exception to this: when the writing of a piece is a part of your regular duties as a part-time or full-time *employee* (not a free-lancer), all rights to that piece belong to your *employer,* not to you. This is known as *work for hire.* When you create a work for hire, your employer is legally empowered to copyright the work in its (or his or her) name, and under copyright law your employer, not you, is legally considered the author of the work.

Generally, any work you do for your employer during your regular work hours, or during extended hours for which you are paid your standard overtime rate, qualifies as "regular duties," even if the specific task you are carrying out is a one-time, unusual assignment. However, the rights to any writing job you do on the side—that is, as a freelancer hired to do a specific project—remain yours until you sell them.

When you sell or give up *all* rights to something you've written *in exchange for a flat fee,* this is *also* known as work for hire. "All rights" means just that: the exclusive right to publish, license, or otherwise use the piece in any way, shape, or form, at any time, anywhere in the universe, for the duration of the copyright. A flat fee means a single, one-time payment. This is distinct from, say, a book contract where you receive an initial payment *and* a royalty on copies sold and a share of money earned from the sale of certain rights to other parties. If you give up all rights to a piece but are entitled to royalty or subsidiary rights money, or if you give up less than all rights for a flat fee, the work you have done *cannot* be considered work for hire—unless it was done as part of your regular salaried job.

If there is any doubt about whether you are being asked to do a project for hire or on a freelance basis—or if there is any doubt about which rights to a freelance project someone wishes to purchase from you—bring up the subject. Make sure everyone understands the terms under which the project will be completed. Unless you are doing the project as part of your regular employment, you should sign a written agreement that sets forth specifically what rights you are selling, how much and when you will be paid, and so on.

There is nothing wrong with doing work for hire provided you are genuinely doing it as part of your job. Nor is there anything wrong with doing *certain* freelance projects for hire. For example, if the U.S. Department of Agriculture wants you to write a pamphlet called "Tips for Mustard Growers" for free distribution to farmers, it is appropriate that the Department should control all rights to that pamphlet, and equally appropriate that it should pay you nothing beyond your initial fee for writing it. The same would be true if the Chrysler Corporation commissioned you to write a brochure called "Getting the Most from Your Dodge Colt." It is legitimate to have freelancers do work for hire on projects that will be used in-house, given away free, or sold at low cost as a public service.

However, if you are offered a work-for-hire contract and you think that subsidiary rights to the project can be sold, and/or that royalties on it can be earned, *don't* sign that contract. Instead, suggest that you be allowed to hang onto some or all of the most valuable rights. Or ask to be cut in for a share of the profits—through royalties, a percentage of subsidiary rights earnings, or both. You'd be surprised at how many firms will first offer work-for-hire contracts, knowing very well how unfair they are, in the hope that you'll be naive or desperate enough to sign them. Some of these firms will offer you reasonable terms, but only if you ask for them.

There is one other circumstance when doing work for hire is acceptable, and that is when the flat fee you are offered is positively enormous. Even if the fee offered is enormous, however, it is always worth trying to get at least a small share of a project's earnings. The worst a publisher can do is say no.

PROBLEMS

Most writers' legal problems fall into one of three categories: contract violation, libel, and theft.

Contract Violation

If you feel a publisher has violated its contract with you, your first and best course is to call your editor. Politely but assertively explain what the problem is, and ask that the situation be corrected promptly. If this does not yield satisfactory results within two to four weeks, or if your editor won't speak to you (this occasionally happens), write your editor a civil but no-nonsense letter outlining the problems and urging their resolution. Send the letter by certified mail with a return receipt requested, and keep a copy of the letter for your files. Make sure that your return receipt requires the date of delivery, the address to which your letter is to be delivered, and the signature of the person accepting the letter. You may want to require that the letter be delivered *only* to your editor. Also explain the situation to your agent, if you have one, and have him or her get on the editor's back as well. Send your agent a copy of the letter you sent your editor.

Alternatively—or simultaneously—you can ask one or more of the writers' organizations to which you belong (such as the National Writers Union or the Society of Children's Book Writers) to put pressure on the errant publisher. Most of these organizations have a grievance or advocacy committee or officer that handles such problems.

More often than not, one of these steps will put an end to the problem without your having to go to a lawyer.

Suppose, however, that these efforts prove ineffectual. One month after sending your letter, give your editor one last call. If you get through, politely explain that if things can't be resolved shortly, you may be forced to file suit. Whether you get through or not, shortly after making the call send your editor a certified letter containing the message in the previous sentence. Again get a return receipt, and again ask your agent and/or one or more organizations to do everything they can. Send your agent and/or the organizations each a copy of the second letter.

Wait another month to six weeks. If things haven't improved, contact an attorney. See pages 372–74 for details on locating and using a literary lawyer.

This doesn't mean you'll have to go to court. Sometimes just a curt phone call or letter from an attorney can nudge a publisher into compliance. In fact, even if you have no intention of actually filing suit, it may be worth the $20 to $50 investment to have an attorney write a letter or make a call.

If this doesn't work, you may be stuck with filing suit and perhaps going to court. Arbitration is also a possibility in some cases, especially those where the publisher is at least responsive, though not agreeable. Certainly it's considerably less expensive, time-consuming, and difficult than suing. Discuss this option with your attorney and/or with your publisher.

One qualification to all this: if your publisher is cooperative, and the dispute is basically a matter of interpreting some contractual point, you may not want to take a hard line. Perhaps you can suggest a compromise, and invite your publisher to do the same.

If you do get involved in a disagreement with a publisher—and especially if you sue—try not to let the matter get in the way of your other writing projects, or your nonwriting interests and activities. Before you sue, or get all wrapped up in a fight with your publisher, think carefully about what you have to gain and what you have to lose. Money is not your only consideration. Time, happiness, emotional stability, and freedom from aggravation also have value. Sometimes the smart thing to do is let the matter drop, even if you've been deliberately and shamelessly cheated. Look at the matter from a business point of view. If going through with a lawsuit will take up so much time, or cause so much heartache, that you'll lose more money from missed work than you'll make by winning, maybe you're better off forgetting about the whole issue.

You are almost always better off treating small problems lightly. If a check from your publisher arrives a month late, your publisher may have technically breached the contract; but generally I'd say cash the check, write your editor a polite note explaining that the check was late and that you expect to be paid on time in the future, and forget about the matter.

In disputes over small sums of money—for example, if a magazine fails to pay you the $300 it owes you—you can take your publisher to small-claims court. This costs little or nothing, and you won't need an attorney. However, you'll need to file suit in the county or city of the publisher's official place of business. Unless you live nearby, this often isn't worth the trouble.

Important: also see "Some General Words of Wisdom on Lawsuits" on page 372 before you sue a publisher.

Libel

To libel a person is to write and publish something that maliciously exposes or brings contempt upon him or her. Satire and parody are thus usually not libelous, but they can be if they attempt to cause someone genuine harm. Truth is rarely libelous, but it can sometimes be libelous if presented in a misleading or malicious way.

When a libel suit is filed, it is usually filed against both the author and the publisher of the allegedly libelous piece.

Libel is a very sticky legal issue in publishing. Generally, common sense prevails: if you see nothing libelous in something you've written, there probably isn't anything libelous in it. But if you feel that something in your piece *could* be libelous, or could be taken as libelous, then you're probably better off changing it, omitting it, or speaking to a literary attorney about it before sending it out.

None of these precautions can actually *prevent* you or your publisher from being sued for libel; indeed, each year a number of meritless nuisance suits are brought against writers and publishers.

Some book publishers have responded by providing their books and authors with free libel insurance. You can also, of course, purchase libel insurance on your own if your publisher refuses to provide it for you and if you think your piece might draw a libel suit. Ask your editor or agent to provide you with the names of the companies that offer such insurance coverage. Rates and deductibles vary widely from policy to policy and from company to company, so be sure to comparison shop.

Theft

Most new writers are very concerned about having their work or ideas stolen. Some take elaborate precautions against this, and some are downright paranoid.

The fact is that plagiarism is pretty rare in publishing, somewhat less rare in film and television. I have *never* heard of a case (outside of *The Phantom of the Opera*) in which someone actually stole another writer's work and published it under his or her own name. But if the near-impossible does happen to you and somebody swipes your work, you can sue the thief; your work is fully protected by U.S. copyright law.

More common are cases where publishers print authors' works without bylines, or with the proper bylines but without their permission. Usually this involves a small publisher reprinting a piece without first securing reprint rights. *Much* less frequent are the cases where publishers receive submissions and publish them without first making arrangements to do so with the authors.

The best way to respond in any of these situations is to send a certified letter to the publisher or president of the publication by name. (Find out his or her name by consulting the publication itself, checking the appropriate reference source from the list on pages 88–91, or simply calling up the publication and asking.) Be sure to purchase a return receipt for your letter that includes the date and address of delivery and the signature of the person accepting the letter. It is also a good idea to require that the letter be delivered *only* to the publisher or president. A sample letter appears on page 370.

Such a letter often will generate an apologetic response and a check: some less than honest publishers make an informal policy of publishing work without permission, then making amends with the few writers who catch them red-handed.

Because you've caught the publisher with both hands in the cookie jar,

SCOTT EDELSTEIN
Literary Services
179 Berkeley St., Suite 1
Rochester, NY 14607
Telephone: 716-244-0645

February 7, 1989

Mr. Edmund Newkirk
Publisher, <u>Newkirk's Newsletter</u>
80 Gable Drive
Crookston, MN 55676

Dear Mr. Newkirk:

I was pleased to discover, quite by accident, that you felt my article, "Tips for Spouses of Diabetics," was worthy of reprinting in your February issue.

I was <u>not</u> pleased, however, that you chose to reprint the piece without first purchasing the appropriate rights from me, as is both standard in the publishing industry and required by law.

However, I see no reason not to grant you this one-time non-exclusive use retroactively in exchange for a permissions fee of $600.

Upon my receipt of this sum <u>within thirty days</u> of the date of this letter, I grant you the one-time non-exclusive right to publish (in this case, to have previously published) "Tips for Spouses of Diabetics" in <u>Newkirk's Newsletter</u>.

I hope and expect that you will reply promptly, thereby settling this matter.

Sincerely,

Scott Edelstein

you should deliberately ask for a lot of money (from 150 to 200 percent of what would normally be appropriate for the right to print or reprint the piece) in exchange for your retroactive permission.

Once the check has cleared—not a moment before—it may be possible to begin a normal, honest working relationship with that publisher. Suggest that the two of you work together more legitimately in the future, and if you like, mention a few ideas for pieces that you'd like to do for him or her.

If the publisher is a hard-core crook, he or she won't respond to your letter at all—or will agree to pay and won't, or will send you a check that bounces or is stopped. If you haven't been paid a month after you send your letter, it's time to either take the scoundrel to court or get an attorney to make a threatening call or send a threatening letter.

In general, the larger, better-known, or more prestigious a publication is, the less likely it is to cause you any of the troubles discussed above.

As for ideas, they are stolen all the time. Sometimes they are stolen deliberately—most often in TV and film, much less often in other genres. More frequently, they are stolen accidentally or unconsciously. After all, who can keep track of all the ideas he or she encounters each day? Quite often writers and editors come up with "original" ideas that they ran across months or years ago, then forgot about.

For better or worse, there is nothing you can do—legally or otherwise—to prevent your literary ideas from being stolen, or to obtain restitution from someone who does swipe them. If you have an idea for an invention or process, you can protect it with a patent. But you can't patent a literary idea.

Most editors and publishers try hard to avoid swiping ideas. But if you send an editor a badly written article on the history of the Staten Island ferry which the the editor rejects, and a well-written piece on the same subject turns up two months later, he or she is going to buy it without any qualms.

Or suppose you ask an editor if you can do an interview with Barbara Bush. The editor's been thinking about commissioning an interview with Mrs. Bush for some time but wants George Will to do it. Will says he'd be happy to do it a few months from now. The editor rejects your interview idea, and six months later publishes Will's Bush interview. Did the editor steal your idea and give it to Will? No. Is what the editor did fair and legitimate? Yes.

Some General Words of Wisdom on Lawsuits

If you do decide to file a lawsuit against a publisher for any reason, don't expect the matter to be resolved quickly, easily, or cheaply. If the amount of the suit is large enough, *and* you have a good enough case, you *may* be able to get an attorney to represent you on a contingency basis. This means the attorney gets nothing if you lose, and a hefty share (usually around 30 percent) of the money you receive if you win. However, in most cases, you will have to pay your attorney by the hour. You can sue for attorney's fees in addition to damages, but you still have to pay your attorney yourself; you'll get reimbursed *if* you're awarded those fees at the trial and *if* you collect the money you're awarded. And there are other costs beyond your attorney's time. There may be interrogatories, depositions, and other documents that must be prepared, for example.

In short, lawsuits can take a long time and cost a lot of money. The one time I had to sue a publisher (over a sum of about $15,000, of which my attorney took almost $4000), it took almost two years from the time I hired an attorney until the case actually went to trial.

Furthermore, don't think that if you win, the matter is over when the trial is. The publisher may appeal. Even if it doesn't, that doesn't mean you'll get a certified check for the amount awarded a week later. I won the case mentioned above in November of 1978; I actually got my money from the publisher, after much hassling and pressure from my attorney, in the summer of 1980.

LITERARY ATTORNEYS

Several hundred lawyers in the United States and Canada specialize in literary law (also called publication law). Some of them specialize in a particular area of publication law—for instance, libel law or copyright law—but most are qualified to handle a wide range of literary legal matters.

Here are some of the things a literary attorney can do:

• Look over and/or negotiate a publishing contract on your behalf
• Look over, negotiate, and/or write other publishing-related agreements (such as agreements between collaborators, contracts between writers and ghostwriters, and TV and film options)
• Provide advice on libel, particularly in regard to projects that may be of a legally sensitive nature

• Provide legal advice and representation in the event of a lawsuit, contract violation, or other legal problem
• Serve as an arbitrator in a legal dispute
• Pressure publishers into paying past due money or otherwise complying with the terms of an agreement
• Provide legal advice on a variety of other publishing matters

Some literary attorneys are also agents, and thus offer their clients both literary and legal representation. Most of these agent-attorneys handle only writers who are already making $50,000 or more a year from their writing, though some have been known to take on new writers occasionally. Usually these attorney-agents charge the standard commission for agenting, plus an hourly rate for legal services, though often they'll offer advice or write occasional nasty letters to publishers at no charge.

Most literary attorneys are not agents, however, and thus will not submit your work for you. But many *will* negotiate a contract for you if you've already gotten an editor or publisher to say, "We want to use your work; let's strike a deal." You do not need to have already established a relationship with an attorney for him or her negotiate on your behalf; most are happy to work for strangers. You should, however, only hire an attorney whom you trust and who you feel will do a good job. A good literary lawyer can negotiate a contract as competently as a good agent.

Attorneys normally charge by the hour for their services. Charges range from $25 to over $150 an hour; you should be able to get a good literary attorney for $50 to $75 an hour.

Important: it is generally not a good idea to bring publishing contracts or legal matters of a literary nature to a general-practice attorney, even one who has done an excellent job representing you in other matters. In part this is because publication law has its own distinct terminology (for example, galley proofs, second serial, or statements of account), which general-practice lawyers may be unfamiliar with; in part it's because general-practice lawyers aren't often aware of the standards and practices of the publishing industry. For example, a generalist isn't going to know that a 5 percent royalty on a trade paperback is too low, or that the great majority of libel clauses in book contracts are heavily weighted in favor of publishers.

Most literary attorneys have their offices in the New York City and Los Angeles metropolitan areas. However, most major cities have at least a few such attorneys. There's no reason why your literary attorney has to be in your home town. In fact, if you are contemplating filing suit against a publisher, you will want to find an attorney who practices in the same city as the one in which that publisher has its editorial (or main) office, as you will most likely have to file suit in that city.

To locate literary attorneys in a specific area, call the Bar Association in that area, or ask your regular attorney, who should be happy to provide the referral at no charge.

Volunteer Lawyers for the Arts (1285 Avenue of the Americas, Third Floor, New York, NY 10019, 212-977-9270) is a nationwide network of lawyers who provide legal advice, information, representation, and referrals to writers and artists. Information and answers to arts- or writing-related legal questions are available to all writers at no charge through VLA's ARTLAW line, (212) 977-9270. Services of a VLA attorney are available free or at a reduced rate to writers who meet certain income guidelines. Volunteer Lawyers for the Arts also offers useful workshops and publications on arts-related legal issues.

Many legal questions require nothing more than a brief consultation with an attorney, either in person or on the phone. Many attorneys charge very little for such consultations—usually $15 to $35.

PERMISSIONS

If you wish to use all or part of a piece someone else has written in a work of your own, you must secure permission to do so from whomever controls the rights you wish to purchase. This might be the writer, the writer's agent, his or her estate, or one of his or her publishers.

Normally you'll have to pay a fee for permission to print or reprint the piece. You'll also have to draw up and sign a written agreement that sets forth the terms of its use; the rights holder must also sign this agreement. This written contract should specify the agreed-upon payment, when such payment is to be made, and the rights you are purchasing. It is *always* best to try to purchase the right to publish the piece in *all* editions of your work anywhere in the world. This saves you the time and expense of later negotiating additional agreements and paying additional fees. Some agents, writers, and publishers will go along with this. They may, however, ask for, or even insist on, a higher fee (or a share of royalties and/or subsidiary rights money in addition to a fee) than if they were selling only English language or North American rights. If you cannot buy nonexclusive world rights, try to buy at least nonexclusive British Commonwealth rights as well as North American rights, since these are the most common foreign rights purchased.

Sometimes a writer, agent, or publisher will refuse to grant more than world English language rights, or North American rights, or even one-time North American rights to a piece. In such a case, I suggest accepting the limited territory but insisting that the following paragraph be part of your agreement:

> In exchange for the rights specified above, the Editor shall pay to the Author/Publisher a fee of $————. Should the Editor wish to use the Author's Work in other editions, the Editor may do so upon payment to the Author/Publisher of an additional fee for each such use; the size of this fee shall be mutually determined, but in no case shall it be more than $———— for each such use.

Fill in the second blank with a figure you can both agree on. Suggest 50 percent of the initial fee; 75 percent is a fair compromise; under no circumstances should it be more than 100 percent.

If you are reprinting a piece, you will probably only want to use it on a nonexclusive basis; that is, a basis that also allows other people to reprint it at any time in any country or language. Your permissions agreement should specify this. If you are using a previously unpublished piece, and the fact that it is being published for the first time is important, your agreement should specify that the piece may not be published elsewhere until a certain amount of time (usually six months) has passed beyond its initial North American publication. This constitutes temporary exclusive use, and nonexclusive use thereafter.

Sample permissions letters appear on pages 326, 327, and 376.

If you are publishing a book, one bargaining chip you can use in negotiating permissions is future income. While traditionally the rights holder receives only a flat fee for granting permission, you may wish to offer a percentage of future royalties and/or subsidiary rights income from your project in addition to an initial fee. For example, instead of paying the requested $500 for permission to use a piece, you might offer $400 as an advance against a prorated share of 50 percent of all the money you receive from your book (after your agent's commissions), beyond your own initial advance. Prorated means that the 50 percent share will be divided among all contributors, based on either the number or length of each person's contributions. This arrangement is especially common with pre-viously unpublished material. If you do use or suggest such an arrange-

SCOTT EDELSTEIN
Literary Services
179 Berkeley St., Suite 1
Rochester, NY 14607
Telephone: 716-244-0645

January 22, 1989

Mr. James Retton
105 Morningside Blvd.
Milwaukee, WI   53212

Dear Jim:

I'd like to reprint your short story, "Grandma
Goes to Neptune," in my science fiction anthology,
Octogenarians in Space.

In exchange for the right to reprint this piece
on a non-exclusive basis in all domestic and foreign
editions of the aforementioned volume, I agree to
pay you, on execution of this agreement, $150. This
shall be an advance against a pro-rated share of 50%
of all the monies I receive, after agent's commissions, over and above my own initial advance for the
book. Such additional monies shall be paid to you
within thirty days after my receipt.

I shall provide you with one copy of the initial
edition of my book, to be published by Pluto Press.

If these terms are acceptable, please sign both
copies of this letter and return one to me.

Sincerely,

Scott Edelstein

I agree to the above:

                                    Date:_____

_____
James Retton

                                    SS #:_____

Copyright data: the above piece was originally published in the _____ issue of _____ and is
copyright _____ (year) by _____.

ment, the standard split is 40 to 50 percent for you, 50 to 60 percent prorated among the contributors. Fifty percent is considered the minimum fair share for contributors.

To obtain permission to reprint a piece, you first need to find out who owns the rights you want to buy. Start with the person in charge of permissions at the magazine, newsletter, newspaper, or book publisher that previously published the piece. This person is known as the permissions or subsidiary rights director. If the publisher does not control the rights, the permissions person will tell you who does and how to contact him or her.

Alternatively, you can contact the author or his or her agent directly. To obtain addresses or phone numbers, use one or more of the reference books listed on pages 223–25, or contact one or more of the referral services listed on pages 387–89. The organizations listed on pages 384–85 can also supply addresses and phone numbers of members or their agents. The writer or agent will either negotiate with you directly or refer you to whoever does control the rights.

All of the above advice also applies if you wish to use drawings, photographs, or other visual material by (or owned or controlled by) someone else in a project of your own.

Other tips regarding permissions:

• If material is in the public domain—that is, if it was published in the United States more than seventy-five years ago—it is no longer protected by copyright. You can reprint it anywhere, in whole or part, any time, at no charge, without first obtaining anyone's permission. Material published more recently but never copyrighted (rare except for certain government publications) is also in the public domain.

• If you wish to reprint a piece or excerpt from an advertisement, government report, or other publication normally distributed free, the right to do this can *usually* be secured from the publisher at no charge. Correspondence also can usually be published at no charge. In all these cases, however, you must nevertheless obtain written permission; a simple letter from the holder of rights to you will do. You may draw up such a letter and enclose it with your request if you like; the rights holder simply signs it and returns it to you. Your best bet in such cases is to request permission without even bringing up the matter of money; the rights holder who wants money will ask for it.

• You are expected to publish a proper copyright notice for each item you choose to print or reprint in whole or part, except for pieces in the public domain and excerpts and quotes considered fair use. It is also a standard courtesy to acknowledge by name (and, if appropriate, by issue date and/or number) the publication in which each piece originally appeared. Be sure to obtain copyright information and other necessary details at the time you secure permission to print or reprint a piece.

• It is a good idea to get the social security number of any person whose work you use. This is important because you will be required to report to the IRS the name and social security number of any person whose work you use and to whom you pay $600 or more during any calendar year. See pages 439–40 for details.

WILLS FOR WRITERS

Every adult needs a will. A writer needs a will even more than other people, because each piece of writing (whether finished or unfinished) is a literary property that can be edited, completed, sold, and published—or not, depending on what the author's will specifies.

A standard will gives each piece of your personal and real property (your home, car, furniture, clothing, etc.) to one or more heirs. Each literary project you have written or begun, and each project you will write or begin, is also a piece of property, and the rights to it can be given to whomever you choose. (The physical manuscript itself—as opposed to the rights to publish or perform it—can also be given to whomever you please. It is possible to will the physical manuscript to one heir and the publication rights to another.) Even an unfinished piece may have value if your work becomes popular enough.

Your will, therefore, should specify who shall inherit the rights to each of your literary creations and who shall inherit the physical manuscripts themselves. Remember that on your death you will still control some rights to pieces that have already been published.

Here are some other considerations for your will:

• Copyrights in your name registered before 1978 will need to be renewed at the appropriate times; who will you appoint to handle this?
• Rights to unpublished and published pieces can be sold to publishers throughout the world through appropriate channels; someone will need to arrange these sales. This person will need to know the value of each group of rights for each piece, what rights remain available, the means

of selling these rights, the appropriate markets, and some general information about how the publishing world works.

• Which pieces—both published and unpublished—do you want marketed? Are there any markets or editors that must be approached first, or avoided entirely? Which pieces should not be permitted to see print at all?

• May pieces in progress be published in unfinished form? May they be finished by anyone else and then published? Who may and who may not finish these works?

• Who, if anyone, may edit your unpublished pieces prior to submitting them?

• May any or all of your letters be published?

• What may be thrown away? What must not be?

• May physical manuscripts, letters, other papers, and/or your personal library be sold and/or given away to individuals or institutions (for example, universities)?

• What rights and responsibilities exist regarding collaborations, pieces you've ghostwritten or had ghostwritten, and/or anthologies you edited?

• What projects, previously published or produced, continue to earn royalties? When and from whom are those royalties due?

• Who will receive future earnings from your work? How will these earnings be divided? Who will inherit which rights to which pieces?

To have your wishes carried out after your death you will need to keep clear, careful, thorough, and accessible records while you are still alive. It does your daughter no good to learn that she has inherited all the remaining rights to your novel *Daddy Goes to Heaven* if she has no idea what rights remain.

The best and easiest way to keep such records is to start a file for each piece you complete (or better yet, for each piece you begin). In each file you can keep notes, drafts, copies of correspondence (both sent and received), contracts and letters of agreement, a written list of terms agreed to orally, royalty statements, and all other matters concerning the piece. The first item in each file should be a list of all the editors, publishers, and publications that have rejected the piece, and the approximate dates these rejections occurred. The second item should be a list of all the editors, publishers, and publications worldwide that have published the piece in whole or part, and the approximate dates on which publication occurred. (If only a portion of the piece was published, this sheet should indicate which portion.) This sheet should also indicate what rights were purchased in each case—or it should refer to the appropriate written agreement (or the list of terms of an oral agreement) kept in that same file. Ideally, all these files should be kept together, along with a master list (kept at the front of all the files), which lists all of the literary properties in the file. All the files in this collection should be kept current.

If you can't bring yourself to go to such trouble and detail (and many of us can't), *at least* keep all your literary records and manuscripts in easily accessed files, and if possible make a master list of all your literary works.

You will need the help of an attorney to draw up a good, clear will that will "stick." Don't try to do it on your own unless you're a lawyer yourself. However, any good general-practice attorney can handle this for you. It is not necessary to hire a literary lawyer.

You will need to name an executor in your will. This is the person who will take charge of—and arrange distribution of—your assets after your death. If your executor is not well versed in the business of writing and publishing, it is an excellent idea to name two executors—one to handle your literary assets, and one to handle everything else. You don't want your son selling off all rights to everything you've written for $5000—not when North American book rights to a single novel might alone be worth $15,000. Find a literary executor who knows the publishing field, knows your work, and knows what it is worth. It's also a good idea to list in your will the names of people who will serve as executors in the event that one or more of your original executors are no longer alive at the time of your death.

You should name someone as an executor only if you have received that person's permission to be so named. The responsibilities of an executor are large and serious ones. Also be sure to let each of your executors know where they will find your manuscripts, files, and other important papers upon your death.

12. ✎

Programs, People, and Institutions That Help Writers

WRITERS' ORGANIZATIONS AND CLUBS

There are five kinds of writers' organizations:

• *Professional organizations*—national societies of professional writers, usually in particular genres or fields, which provide information and advocacy to their members. The best-known of these are the Writers Guild (for TV, film, and radio writers), The Authors Guild (for writers of prose and poetry), The Dramatists Guild (for playwrights), the American Society of Journalists and Authors (for writers of nonfiction), PEN (for authors of books of literary merit), the Society of Children's Book Writers, and the Associated Writing Programs (for writers affiliated with academia). More specialized organizations include the Baseball Writers Association of America, Western Writers of America, the Society of American Travel Writers, et al. Most (though not all) of these organizations admit as members only those writers who have achieved some success—that is, had work published or produced—in the appropriate fields. Many of these societies give out annual awards for the best works in their fields.

• *General organizations*—national organizations providing information and advocacy to writers in many different fields and at all stages of their careers, from beginners to seasoned professionals. The two best-known of these organizations, and the two with the most members, are the National Writers Union and the National Writers Club. Both are open to unpublished writers.

• *Special-interest groups*—organizations providing information, services, and/or advocacy for a particular group of writers or for writers sharing a particular interest. Examples here include the International Women's Writing Guild, the Black Writers United Club, and Poets for Peace. These are usually open to anyone with the appropriate background or interest.

• *Regional organizations*—literary groups that focus their efforts on a particular geographic area. This can be as large as a country—for example, Playwrights Canada—or as small as one city—for example, the Santa Barbara Writers Consortium. Regional organizations are usually open to all interested writers. Occasionally national writers' organizations will have regional or local branches in various cities; PEN, Writers Club, and the National Writers Union all have such branches.

• *Writers' clubs*—typically, these do not provide advocacy or professional services for writers. They are, instead, usually places for writers to meet and talk, to hear speakers, and/or to read and critique one another's work. They are usually informal and almost always local in membership and orientation. Writers' clubs are normally open to just about anyone.

Some organizations provide information and services to all writers on request, often at no charge. Most, however, offer services and benefits only (or primarily) to their members.

The cost of joining writers' organizations varies greatly. Those in the first two categories, since they have a strong professional orientation and typically offer a wide range of services, charge dues of $40 to $150 a year. An initiation fee may also be charged. Organizations in the next two categories usually charge much less, from $10 to $50 annually. Writers' clubs usually charge minimal dues or nothing at all.

Professional and general organizations typically offer these items:

• A regular newsletter
• Up-to-date market news (If the organization covers a particular field, usually the market information will be limited to that field.)
• Advocacy/grievance procedures (to put pressure on editors and publishers who aren't treating members properly)
• Professional advice on marketing, ethics, contract negotiation, copyright, and other helpful topics, in the form of publications, responses to telephone inquiries, or both
• A directory of members

Some of the other benefits often available through these organizations include:

- Legal services
- Banquets, lunches, and parties
- Meetings, conclaves, and/or conferences
- Lectures and panels
- Classes and seminars
- Annual awards
- Grants and/or fellowships
- Press cards and membership cards
- Author referral services (provided to editors and others seeking to hire writers or solicit manuscripts)
- Discounts on books, computers, magazine subscriptions, furniture, typewriters, car rentals, air fares, and innumerable other items
- Health insurance plans
- Other insurance plans, such as dental, life, or disability
- Funds providing money for writers in emergency situations, who are disabled, or both (see pages 414–15 for details)
- Model contracts for books, magazine pieces, ghostwriting, etc. (Note: all of these contracts that I have seen are almost laughably unrealistic.)
- Referrals to literary agents, attorneys, accountants, and other professionals

One organization, the National Writers Club, also offers manuscript criticism, correspondence courses, a savings plan, and complete publishing services, including design, illustration, typesetting, printing, and binding. Both the eastern and western branches of the Writers Guild offer members all the advantages of a union, including collective bargaining, a pension plan, and two insurance plans. Some local branches of the National Writers Union run job banks, listing freelance and salaried jobs available in the region in writing, editing, researching, and other writing-related fields. These services are for union members only.

One good-sized, if less tangible, benefit of membership in a professional writers' organization is that you can list your membership on your manuscripts (see page 32 for details). This establishes you as a professional at first glance.

Organizations in the third, fourth, and fifth categories usually offer a considerably narrower range of services and benefits.

Membership in any of these organizations is of course both voluntary and optional—with one exception: TV and film writers *must* normally belong to the Writers Guild if they are to sell their work to producers.

It isn't necessary to belong to a writers' organization. I now belong to only one organization—Associated Writing Programs, the professional organization of college creative writing teachers. I do, however, recommend that writers in a particular genre join the professional association for that genre. For example, if you're a mystery writer, it will probably be very helpful to be a member of Mystery Writers of America.

The most complete list of writers' organizations available is John Hall's *International Directory of Writers' Groups and Associations,* which lists organizations in the United States, Canada, and dozens of foreign countries. This book is available in many libraries, or from Inkling Publications, Box 65798, St. Paul, MN 55165. A considerably less complete, but still useful, list of writers' organizations appears in the reference book *Literary Market Place,* under the heading "Literary and Writers' Associations." A good listing of organizations that serve playwrights, composers, lyricists, and librettists appears in *The Dramatist's Bible.* See pages 75–76 for details on this volume. Poets & Writers, Inc., 201 W. 54th Street, New York, NY 10019, publishes a partial list of organizations that offer information and services to writers. This list, entitled "Helping Writers Help Themselves," is available for $1 plus a #10 self-addressed stamped envelope. (For more information on Poets & Writers see page 387, under the heading "Writers' Centers.")

Here are the names, addresses, and phone numbers of some of the largest and most useful organizations for writers. Organizations with special requirements for membership are so noted.

American Society of Journalists and Authors, 1501 Broadway, Suite 1907, New York, NY 10036, (212) 997-0947. For writers of nonfiction. There is a publication requirement for membership.

Associated Writing Programs, Old Dominion University, Norfolk, VA 23508, (804) 440-3839. For college writing teachers, students in college writing programs, and anyone else interested in writing and academia.

The Authors Guild, 234 W. 44th Street, New York, NY 10036, (212) 391-9198. For writers of fiction, nonfiction, and poetry. There is a publication requirement for membership.

The Dramatists Guild, 234 W. 44th Street, New York, NY 10036, (212) 398-9366. For playwrights, composers, and lyricists.

National Writers Club, 1450 S. Havana, Suite 620, Aurora, CO 80012, (303) 751-7844. For all writers.

National Writers Union, 13 Astor Place, New York, NY 10003, (212) 254-0279. For all writers.

New Dramatists, 424 W. 44th Street, New York, NY 10036, (212) 757-6960. For playwrights. Requires evidence of ability as a playwright, based on the submission of a full-length script, for membership.

PEN American Center, 568 Broadway, New York, NY 10012, (212) 334-1660. For writers and translators of "books of literary merit." There is a publication requirement for membership.

Poetry Society of America, 15 Gramercy Park South, New York, NY 10003, (212) 254-9628. For all poets.

Society of Children's Book Writers, Box 296, Mar Vista Station, Los Angeles, CA 90066, (818) 347-2849. For writers and illustrators of material for children in all lengths, formats, and genres, and for anyone interested in children's literature.

The Writers Guild. For television, film, and radio writers. Members must normally have sold at least one TV, film, or radio script. Writers east of the Mississippi should join the Writers Guild East, 555 W. 57th Street, New York, NY 10019, (212) 245-6180. Writers west of the Mississippi should join the Writers Guild West, 8955 Beverly Boulevard, West Hollywood, CA 90048, (213) 550-1000.

OTHER HELPFUL ORGANIZATIONS

A few organizations also exist that serve not only writers but the entire community of freelancers, artists, and/or self-employed people. One such organization is the Foundation for the Community of Artists (FCA), 280 Broadway, Suite 412, New York, NY 10007, (212) 227-3770. The FCA is open to all writers and artists, and provides these services: information, referrals, income tax filing and consultation at reduced rates, seminars and workshops, and group medical insurance. The FCA also publishes two magazines, *Art and Artists* and *Artist Update* (see page 75), and several books.

Another organization is Support Services Alliance (SSA), Box 130, Schoharie, NY 12157, (800) 892-8925; (800) 322-3920 within New York State. Although anyone may join SSA, it is intended primarily for people who are largely or entirely self-employed or working in small organizations. SSA provides group health, disability, and life insurance; a legal referral service; a credit union; loan guarantees on college loans for members and their children; travel services; computerized record-keeping services; and a variety of publications, including a regular newsletter. Membership is currently $20 a year.

Still another helpful organization is the Small Business Service Bureau (SBSB), Inc., 554 Main Street, Box 1441, Worcester, MA 01601, (800) 222-5678; (800) 262-2981 within Massachusetts. This organization provides information and services to small businesses and self-employed individuals; membership is $75 a year, and all writers who are partly or entirely self-employed may join. The SBSB offers the following group insurance plans to its members: medical, life, disability, and accidental death and dismemberment. The SBSB also offers HMO coverage. It publishes two regular newsletters and a variety of pamphlets, books, and cassettes on small business topics. The SBSB also has a telephone information line, which members with business-related questions may call.

WRITERS' CENTERS

A writers' center is an organization that provides information and advocacy to writers; that offers conferences, workshops, seminars, and/or readings; that publishes its own newsletter, magazine, books, pamphlets, and/or regular announcements; that has its own office, telephone, and staff; and that offers its services and programs to everyone. A writers' center, then, serves both writers and the general public.

It is normally possible to become a member of any writers' center for a small annual fee; in return, members typically receive a regular newsletter, discounts on center-sponsored events, and so on. However, it is not necessary to be a member, or even a writer, to make use of a writers' center's services, or to attend its programs and functions. The one national writers' center, Poets & Writers, Inc., does not accept members at all; its services are available to anyone and everyone.

Each writers' center offers its own array of services and programs. These can include any or all of the following:

• A regular newsletter listing news of literary events
• Readings by local and/or nationally known writers
• Open readings
• Lectures, panels, and talks

• Workshops, seminars, conferences, and/or classes
• Support groups
• Referrals to editors, publishers, resource materials, other organizations, and other writers
• Discounts on books, magazines, computers, typewriters, etc.
• A literary magazine and/or book press. (These usually publish work by both members and nonmembers.)
• Manuscript criticism
• Grants and/or fellowships
• Contests and/or awards
• Books and magazines (usually of a literary nature) for sale
• A library or reading room
• Information. Most writers' centers can provide answers to a wide variety of questions about writing and publishing. Simply call and ask.
• Publishing services, such as typesetting, word processing, design assistance, and printing. (At present only the Writer's Center in suburban Washington, D.C., offers these services.)

The largest and best-known writers' center in the country is Poets & Writers, Inc., 201 W. 54th Street, New York, NY 10019, (212) 757-1766. (This address and phone number will change in early 1989.) It is also the only nationally oriented center; all the others are primarily regional. Poets & Writers focuses its efforts on the dissemination of information. It has a telephone Information Center, which is open from 11 AM to 3 PM on weekdays; P&W staff will answer any questions during these hours at no charge. Poets & Writers also publishes a regular newsletter, *Poets & Writers* (see pages 78–79 for details); an excellent directory of poets and fiction writers; books and article reprints for writers; and much more. You may get on Poets & Writers' mailing list at no charge, on request.

The two largest regional writers' centers, and the ones that offer the widest array of services and programs to writers and readers, are The Loft, 2301 East Franklin Avenue, Minneapolis, MN 55406, (612) 341-0431, and the Writer's Center, 7815 Old Georgetown Road, Bethesda, MD 20814, (301) 654-8664. Each of these centers offers the great majority of items in the list above.

Other regional writers' centers that offer a wide range of services and programs include:

Beyond Baroque Literary/Arts Center, 681 Venice Boulevard, Box 806, Venice, CA 90291, (213) 822-3006

Greenfield Review Literary Center, 2 Middle Grove Road, Greenfield Center, NY 12833, (518) 584-1728. This center also has its own publishing house, Ithaca House.

Just Buffalo, 111 Elmwood Avenue, Buffalo, NY 14201, (716) 885-6400

Konglomerati Foundation, Box 5001, Gulfport, FL 33737, (813) 323-0386

Niagara-Erie Writers/Western New York Literary Center, 7 West Northrup Place, Buffalo, NY 14214, (716) 836-5287

North Carolina Writers' Network, Box 954, Carrboro, NC 27510, (919) 967-9540

The Poetry Center, 92nd Street YM-YWHA, 1395 Lexington Avenue, New York, NY 10128, (212) 427-6000, ext. 176 or 208

The Poetry Project at St. Mark's Church, 10th Street and Second Avenue, New York, NY 10003, (212) 674-0910

Poets House, 351 West 18th Street, New York, NY 10011, (212) 627-4035

The Thurber House, 77 Jefferson Avenue, Columbus, OH 43215, (614) 464-1082

Woodland Pattern, 720 E. Locust Street, Milwaukee, WI 53212, (414) 263-5001

Writers & Books, 740 University Avenue, Rochester, NY 14607, (716) 473-2590

There are also quite a few smaller organizations throughout the United States which provide a much smaller selection of the services listed above; typically, these include readings, workshops, and perhaps an irregular newsletter.

All the above writers' centers are oriented primarily toward prose and poetry, and toward the people who write in those genres. There also exists one large national center for playwrights, composers, lyricists, librettists, and others connected with drama and music: the Theatre Communications Group (TCG), 355 Lexington Avenue, New York, NY 10017, (212) 697-5230. TCG provides information and referrals to writers and holds regular conferences and seminars. It also sponsors a number of special projects, including the Hispanic Translation Project and the annual Playwrights USA Awards. TCG publishes several books on an annual or biannual basis. These include the *Dramatists Sourcebook* (see page 76 for details); *New Plays USA,* an anthology; and two theater directories. TCG is also an important resource center for directors, play producers, actors, and other nonwriters connected with theater.

A few regional playwrights' centers also exist. The biggest and best known of these is probably the Playwrights' Center, 2301 East Franklin Avenue, Minneapolis, MN 55406, (612) 332-7481.

Regional centers providing information and services to both artists and writers can be found throughout the country. Two of the largest are the Artists Foundation, 8 Park Plaza, Boston, MA 02116, (617) 227–2787, which offers free information, referrals, workshops, and fellowships to writers and artists living in Massachusetts, and United Arts, 411 Landmark Center, 75 West Fifth Street, St. Paul, MN 55102, (612) 292–3222, which offers workshops, information, referrals, and consulting services to writers and artists in Minnesota and nearby states.

CONFERENCES

First some definitions: a writers' conference is any organized meeting of writers lasting one month or less. Conferences are sometimes called seminars, workshops, conclaves, colonies *(sic)*, retreats, festivals, and institutes. They are places to meet—and in some cases work with—well-known writers, editors, agents, other publishing professionals, and writing teachers. Most conferences run two to seven days, though some are as brief as a single day and others as long as four consecutive weeks. The great majority of conferences are held annually between the months of May and August.

The cost of attending a writers' conference can vary tremendously, from $30 for a one-day conference to $1500 (including room and board) for a month-long program. The quality can range just as widely.

The following resources will help you learn of writers' conferences in your area and throughout North America:

The May issue of *The Writer* publishes a good list of upcoming conferences; advertisements for some of these conferences appear in this magazine throughout the year.

The May issue of *Writer's Digest* publishes an equally good list of conferences; conference ads appear throughout the year in this magazine, too.

The May issue of *AWP Newsletter* (see page 75 for address and details) also publishes a list of conferences; conference ads appear here, too.

Poets & Writers, Inc. (see page 387 for address and details) publishes a good list of upcoming writers' conferences each March. This list is available for $5.00 postpaid.

Somewhat less useful and less comprehensive lists are available in two reference books: *Literary Market Place* and *International Directory of Writers' Groups and Associations.*

You can get details on any writers' conference—including lists of faculty, costs, and a conference schedule—at no charge, simply by requesting this information from the sponsoring organization.

The most famous and prestigious writers' conference in North America is the Bread Loaf Writers Conference, held in Vermont for twelve days each August. It is expensive, though some scholarships and fellowships are available. For information, contact Bread Loaf Writers Conference, Middlebury College, Middlebury, VT 05753, (802) 388-3711, ext. 5286.

CREDIT AND NONCREDIT WRITING COURSES

Colleges, universities, and community colleges now offer a vast array of courses in writing, editing, and publishing. Almost every conceivable topic and subtopic is available. Courses are available for graduate credit, for undergraduate credit, and on a noncredit basis. (Courses normally offered for credit can always be taken on a noncredit basis by enrolling as an auditor. The cost can range from 20 to 100 percent of the cost of regular credit registration; contact the school's registration office for details.) Noncredit courses are typically cheaper, shorter, easier, and more informal than credit classes.

In addition to their regular daytime courses, colleges and universities offer a plethora of credit and noncredit courses through special programs. These programs are typically titled Continuing Education, Adult Education, Summer Program, Community Education, Evening College, Lifelong Learning, Weekend College, New College, and so on. Sometimes special programs will be offered for senior citizens, women, or other targeted groups. Some universities and colleges may have more than one such program, each with its own separate course listing.

At most schools, you may enroll in any class, including those for academic credit, simply by registering. You do not need to apply for admission to the college, nor do you need a high school diploma. You will, however, be a nondegree student, ineligible for a degree unless you apply for admission to a degree program and are accepted.

Writing courses are most likely to be found in the departments of English, composition, creative writing, journalism, and/or rhetoric, but they may also be found in other departments and colleges. There may be a course in medical writing in the College of Health, a course in technical writing in the School of Engineering, or a course in television scriptwriting in the School of Communications. Sometimes journalism is not a department but an entire separate college.

Noncredit (and sometimes credit) courses in writing, editing, and publishing are also regularly offered by high schools, writers' centers, art centers, community centers, YMCAs and YWCAs, corporate learning centers, senior citizens' centers, and dozens of other public-service organizations. See page 191 for a complete list.

COLLEGE PROGRAMS IN WRITING, EDITING, AND PUBLISHING

In the past fifteen years there has been enormous growth in the number of programs in writing and publishing offered by colleges and universities. Years ago there were only programs in literature, plus a few programs in creative writing. Today programs leading to certificates, undergraduate degrees, and graduate degrees are available in the following areas:

• Creative Writing (poetry, short stories, novels, plays, essays, and scripts for TV and film). Degrees available: B.A., B.F.A., M.A., M.F.A., D.A., Ph.D.

• Nonfiction Writing (sometimes called Expository Writing or Rhetoric—includes essays, criticism, technical writing, magazine features, reviews, etc.). Degrees available: B.A., B.J., M.A., F.M.A., D.A., Ph.D.

• Journalism (print, television, and radio). Degrees available: B.A., B.J., B.S., M.A., M.S., Ph.D.

• Professional Writing (fiction, nonfiction, and scripts for stage, film and TV). Degrees available: B.A., B.J., M.A., M.P.W.

• Editing (for books, magazines, and newspapers). Degrees available: B.A., M.A., M.S.

• Publishing Studies (all areas of book, magazine, and newspaper publish-

ing, including editing, marketing, design, publicity, and distribution).
Degrees available: B.A., M.A., M.S.

• Literature (approaches include the traditional survey of English and
American literature, comparative literature, contemporary/modern literature, foreign literature, American studies, women's studies, and ethnic
studies—Chicano literature, Jewish literature, Native American literature, and so on). Degrees available: B.A., M.A., D.A., Ph.D.

• Linguistics. Degrees available: B.A., M.A., M.S., D.A., Ph.D.

• Public Relations (with copy writing emphasis). Degrees available: B.A.,
B.S., M.A., M.S.

• Advertising (with copy writing emphasis). Degrees available: B.A., B.S.,
M.A., M.S.

• English Education (for prospective teachers of literature and/or writing on the elementary, secondary, and/or college level). Degrees available:
B.A., M.A., M.S., M.A.T., D.A., Ed.D., Ph.D.

A GUIDE TO THE
ABBREVIATIONS
OF DEGREES

B.A.—Bachelor of Arts. The standard undergraduate degree.
Sometimes abbreviated A.B.

B.J.—Bachelor of Journalism. Equivalent to a B.A.

B.S.—Bachelor of Science. Equivalent to a B.A.

B.F.A.—Bachelor of Fine Arts. Awarded by a few schools to
creative writing majors, usually playwriting majors. Equivalent to
a B.A.

M.A.—Master of Arts. Sometimes abbreviated A.M. Although
the M.A. is an advanced degree (that is, higher than a
bachelor's), it is not usually considered a "terminal"
degree—that is, the highest and final degree in a particular field.

M.S.—Master of Science. Equivalent to an M.A.

M.F.A.—Master of Fine Arts. Awarded to writers in some
graduate creative writing programs. A few programs award the
M.F.A. for work in nonfiction as well as for work in the
traditional creative genres. There is a heated debate in progress

as to whether the M.F.A. is or is not a terminal degree. Some schools consider it such; some do not. It is a more advanced degree than an M.A., M.S., or M.A.T., but less advanced than any doctorate.

M.P.W.—Master of Professional Writing. Most often awarded to nonfiction writers, it can also be given to writers of fiction, poetry, drama, TV, and film. Some people regard the M.P.W. as equivalent to an M.A.; others see it as equivalent to an M.F.A.

M.A.T.—Master of Arts in Teaching. Someone holding this degree has completed the equivalent of an M.A. plus sufficient work in the Education field to be certified as a public school teacher.

D.A.—Doctor of Arts. D.A. programs are designed to train people to teach college; in practice, though, most four-year colleges refuse to hire people with D.A.s and insist on hiring only holders of M.F.A.s and Ph.D.s. The D.A. is a higher degree than the M.A., but—depending on who is making the judgment—it can be considered less than an M.F.A. or equivalent to a Ph.D.

Ed.D.—Doctor of Education. For specialists in English Education. One step below a Ph.D.

Ph.D.—Doctor of Philosophy. The highest and most prestigious academic degree in the liberal arts.

Associate of Arts (A.A.) degrees—two-year undergraduate degrees—are also available in some of the above fields.

Programs differ widely—sometimes very widely—from one college to the next. One school might require a strict regimen of ten specific courses, from studies in Chaucer and Shakespeare to a survey course in twentieth century British literature, of all students wishing to earn the B.A. in English; another might allow students to design their own programs, or might simply require eight English courses of the student's choice. One school's M.F.A. might require less work than another's M.A. College A might award an M.A. in English but allow students to do most or all of their graduate work in creative writing; College B might award the M.A.

in Creative Writing but require that half or more of the work be in literature. Some schools require M.A. students to write a thesis; others make the thesis optional. The variations are endless.

Master's degrees can require as little as a single academic year of full-time study beyond the bachelor's degree, though one-and-a-half to two years is more common. Doctoral degrees require two to five years of full-time study beyond the bachelor's, and one to four beyond the master's. Most schools and programs permit both part- and full-time study. Part-time students and students holding teaching assistantships usually take longer to complete degrees.

Some doctoral programs require a master's degree for admission; others accept students with bachelor's degrees. In exceptional circumstances, it is sometimes possible to be admitted to a graduate program in writing without a bachelor's degree.

Financial aid is almost always available. It can take a wide variety of forms, including federal grants, state grants, grants directly from the college, work-study grants, loans, scholarships, assistantships, and fellowships.

A few schools offer fellowships for undergraduate students with special abilities or potential in writing; these usually pay all expenses and a stipend of several thousand dollars a year. Most schools also have merit scholarships and fellowships available for undergraduate students of high all-around academic promise. However, the great bulk of financial aid awarded to undergraduates is based on need, not merit.

In graduate programs, the opposite is true. Low-interest loans are available to most graduate students, and grants and work-study arrangements are sometimes available on the basis of need; however, most of the financial support goes to the most talented graduate students, regardless of financial need. In graduate writing programs, money is usually awarded to the best writers, regardless of their financial status or undergraduate academic records; in other English programs the determining factors are usually undergraduate grades and recommendations. Some schools give preference to students who have already been enrolled in the graduate program for one or more academic years.

Although some graduate assistantships and fellowships do not require recipients to render any services to the college, the great majority do. About 10 percent of the assistantships involve working in the English Department office, doing research for a professor, or editing a literary magazine; 90 percent involve teaching one or two undergraduate classes a term, usually freshman composition. The option of teaching upper-level composition courses, technical writing, literature, or creative writing is sometimes available. The average assistantship covers all tuition and pays about $6000 for nine months, but the range is from $1500 to $14,000 a year.

Because programs can differ so greatly in both approach and quality, it is essential that you research a program carefully before applying to it, or at least before enrolling. Write to the schools and departments for information.

One excellent place to start researching college programs is with the *AWP Catalog of Writing Programs,* published by Associated Writing Programs, Old Dominion University, Norfolk, VA 23508. This guide lists over three hundred graduate and undergraduate writing programs at colleges and universities throughout the United States and Canada.

Writers interested in academic programs in playwriting should also consult *The Dramatist's Bible* (see pages 75–76 for more details on this volume).

The following schools offer degrees or certificates in *professional* writing—that is, writing for publication or production:

The Professional Writing Program, WPH 404, University of Southern California, Los Angeles, CA 90089, (213) 743-8255. Offers the M.P.W. in fiction, nonfiction, drama, TV writing, poetry, and film.

Graduate Office, English Department, Carnegie-Mellon University, Pittsburgh, PA 15213, (412) 268-2850. Offers the B.A. and M.A. in Professional Writing. Also offers work in creative writing.

English Department, Hofstra University, 1000 Fulton Avenue, Hempstead, NY 11550, (516) 560-5454. Offers the B.A. in all areas of writing and publishing, including professional writing.

Department of Writing, Literature and Publishing, Emerson College, 148 Beacon Street, Boston, MA 02116, (617) 578-8750. Offers the B.F.A. and the M.A. in Professional Writing. Also offers graduate and undergraduate programs in creative writing.

The following schools offer programs in editing and publishing:

Master of Science in Publishing, Pace University, 1 Pace Plaza, New York, NY 10038, (212) 488-1416 or (212) 488-1417. Offers the M.S. in Publishing.

Department of Writing and Publishing, Emerson College, 148 Beacon Street, Boston, MA 02116, (617) 578-8750. Offers the B.A. and M.A. in Publishing and Professional Writing.

English Department, Hofstra University, 1000 Fulton Avenue, Hempstead, NY 11550, (516) 560-5454. Offers the B.A. in Publishing Studies.

Publication Specialist Program, Center for Continuing Education, George Washington University, 801 W. 22nd Street NW, Room T-409, Washington, DC 20052, (202) 994-7036. Offers a one-year nondegree program leading to a certificate in Publishing Studies. These courses do not carry academic credit.

Programs in Publishing, School of Continuing Education, New York University, 48 Cooper Square, Room 108, New York, NY 10003, (212) 998-7219. Offers a five-course noncredit certificate program in book publishing and a 16-credit diploma program in magazine publishing. Both programs are nondegree; the magazine publishing courses carry academic credit.

Certificate Program in Publishing, University of California Extension, 2223 Fulton Street, Berkeley, CA 94720, (415) 642-4231. Offers a nondegree, 210-classroom-hour certificate program in publishing. Courses carry academic credit.

Stanford Communications Workshop Series, Stanford Alumni Association, Bowman House, Stanford, CA 94305, (415) 725-1083 or (415) 723-0544. Offers a continuing series of noncredit workshops (and a noncredit certificate program) in many different areas of publishing and communication.

Education in Publishing Program, City University of New York Graduate Center, 33 W. 42nd Street, New York, NY 10036, (212) 575-1493. Offers a continuing series of noncredit evening seminars on a wide variety of publishing topics.

Publishing Program, Office of Continuing Education, The University of Chicago, 5835 S. Kimbark Avenue, Chicago, IL 60637, (312) 702-1727. Offers a continuing series of noncredit seminars and one-day workshops on a wide range of publishing topics.

Chicago Book Clinic/Professional Publishing Education, 100 E. Ohio Street, Suite 630, Chicago, IL 60611, (312) 951-8254. Offers an ongoing series of noncredit seminars through Northwestern University.

These cover a huge range of publishing topics not limited to book publishing.

Although the great majority of writing, literature, and publishing programs require students to be in residence for at least one academic year, there are a few exceptions. The following three schools offer M.F.A. degrees in creative writing that require only two weeks in residence on campus every six months; students spend the rest of their time writing and working with instructors by mail and phone. All three colleges are accredited.

M.F.A. Writing Program, Box 510, Vermont College of Norwich University, Montpelier, VT 05602, (802) 223-8750

M.F.A. Writing Program, Warren Wilson College, 701 Warren Wilson Road, Box 300, Swannanoa, NC 28778, (704) 298-3325

M.F.A. Writing Program, Goddard College, Plainfield, VT 05667, (802) 454-8311

These programs are virtually identical in structure. Each takes about two years to complete.

Nonresident B.A., M.A., and Ph.D. degrees are also available in various fields—including literature, nonfiction writing, creative writing, and many others—through several dozen different institutions. The majority of these, however, are "degree mills," which are not accredited and whose degrees are worthless. A few (such as Columbia Pacific University in California) are legitimate but nevertheless unaccredited. Below is a list of accredited, legitimate institutions that offer degrees in writing and English for study that is done primarily or entirely on a nonresidential basis:

Antioch University, Box 500, Yellow Springs, OH 45387, (513) 767-2661. Offers self-designed M.A. programs.

Antioch University/Los Angeles, 4800 Lincoln Boulevard, Marina del Rey, CA 90292, (213) 578-1090. Offers self-designed B.A. programs.

Antioch University/Seattle, 2607 Second Avenue, Seattle, WA 98121, (206) 441-5352. Offers self-designed B.A. programs.

Goddard College, Plainfield, VT 05667, (802) 454-8311. Offers self-designed B.A. and M.A. programs.

Union for Experimenting Colleges and Universities (UECU), 632 Vine Street, Suite 1010, Cincinnati, OH 45202, (513) 621-6444. Offers self-designed B.A. and Ph.D. programs.

Vermont College of Norwich University, Montpelier, VT 05602, (802) 223-8701. Offers self-designed B.A. and M.A. programs.

Self-designed *residential* programs are available from other accredited colleges and universities, such as Empire State College in New York and Metropolitan State University in Minneapolis/St. Paul. Some traditional colleges and universities offer a self-designed program option, often through offices called University Without Walls. For a complete listing of nontraditional, nonresidence, and low-residence college degree programs, see John Bear's *Bear's Guide to Earning Non-Traditional Degrees* (Ten Speed Press).

There are also a few schools that offer graduate degree programs in English which can be completed primarily or entirely through summer study. These include Colgate University, Indiana University of Pennsylvania (not to be confused with Indiana University of Indiana), and Middlebury College.

CORRESPONDENCE COURSES

You've no doubt seen the ads in writers' magazines—and elsewhere—that begin "We're Looking for People to Write Children's Books" or "Do You Have the Desire to Write?" These ads are usually touting correspondence courses for writers. There are about ten well-known organizations that teach writing through the mail. Some of these courses teach general creative writing skills; others focus on particular areas or genres, such as children's literature, nonfiction, romance, and so on. These schools are usually profit-making institutions that award diplomas but not academic credits or degrees.

Almost invariably, these schools are legitimate, and they supply helpful instruction from qualified teachers. Almost invariably, they rely on high-pressure and persistent sales techniques to get people to enroll. And almost invariably, they are expensive.

You are probably not going to be cheated if you enroll in one of these courses. However, you may not be getting the most for your money. Often your dollars will be better spent on a writers' conference or class. Compare prices; typically the cost of a six-week noncredit class will be only 15 to 25 percent of the cost of a correspondence course.

Some colleges and universities (the Universities of Tennessee and Minnesota, for example) offer correspondence courses in writing. Topics range from composition to creative writing to technical writing to journalism. These courses normally carry academic credit, and they are usually a good deal less expensive than those offered by profit-making schools.

PUBLISHING WORKSHOPS

About a dozen colleges offer professional and preprofessional workshops in the occupations of publishing. Most of these focus on book publishing, but some deal with magazine and newspaper publishing as well. While many workshops are devoted largely to editing, some are also devoted to design, marketing, rights and permissions, distribution, and other less literary aspects of publishing.

These workshops are excellent places to learn about careers available in the publishing field, to meet publishing professionals, and to learn how the publishing world works. Attending a publishing workshop is an excellent first step for anyone contemplating a career in any area of publishing.

Seven major publishing workshops are held each year. They run from ten days to seven weeks. All except the University of Pennsylvania's are held during the summer, on the campuses of major universities. College credit, if desired, is available in most cases, as are housing and board. These workshops are:

University of Denver Publishing Institute, 2075 S. University Boulevard, #D-114, Denver, CO 80210, (303) 871-2570

Howard University Press Book Publishing Institute, 2900 Van Ness Street NW, Washington, DC 20008, (202) 686-6498

New York University Publishing Institute, School of Continuing Education, 48 Cooper Square, Room 108, New York, NY 10003, (212) 998-7219

Radcliffe Publishing Procedures Course, 6 Ash Street, Cambridge, MA 02138, (617) 495-8678

Rice University Publishing Program, Office of Continuing Studies and Special Programs, Rice University, Box 1892, Houston, TX 77251, (713) 520-6022

Stanford Publishing Course, Alumni Association, Stanford University, Stanford, CA 94305, (415) 725-1083

University of Pennsylvania Publishing Institute, 3803 Walnut Street, Philadelphia, PA 19104, (215) 898-6479 or 6493 (held September through November)

In addition to the major workshops, Vassar College offers a week-long Publishing Institute during the summer that focuses on children's books. For information, contact Publishing Institute, Box 300, Vassar College, Poughkeepsie, NY 12601, (914) 437-5900.

The reference book *Literary Market Place* publishes a larger list of programs and courses in editing and publishing, under the heading "Courses for the Book Trade."

GRANTS AND FELLOWSHIPS

Here is a list of most of the *major* grants and fellowships available to writers:

• George Bennett Fellowship, English Department, Phillips Exeter Academy, Exeter, NH 03833, (603) 772-4311. One fellowship of $5000 plus food and housing is awarded annually. Winners must live at Exeter for the entire fellowship period, which consists of one nine-month academic year. No teaching is required; fellows work on their own writing projects. Previous publication is not necessary.

• The Thurber House, 77 Jefferson Avenue, Columbus, OH 43215, (614) 464-1032. Awards three fellowships of $5000 annually, one to a fiction writer or poet, one to a playwright, and one to a writer of journalism or other nonfiction. Fellowships run approximately eleven weeks; fellows must live at the James Thurber House (a two-bedroom apartment with a writing studio is provided at no charge) and teach one writing course at Ohio State University. Nonfiction writers must also serve as part-time writing coaches at the newspaper *The Columbus Dispatch*. Fellowships for nonfiction writers may sometimes run an additional eleven weeks, for which writers are paid an additional $5000. Poets and fiction writers must have published a book; playwrights must have had a play produced or published by a major organization; nonfiction writers must have significant publications.

• Wisconsin Institute Fellowships, Ronald Wallace, Institute for Creative Writing, Department of English, 7161 Helen C. White Hall, University of Wisconsin-Madison, Madison, WI 53706, (608) 263-3705. Two fellowships of $15,000 to $17,000 are awarded annually to poets and fiction writers who have received a master's or doctoral degree in creative writing and who have not yet published a trade or university press book. Fellows must live in Madison (or nearby) for one academic year (August 15 to May 15), must teach one creative writing course a semester, and must give a reading; the remainder of their time may be used as they please.

• Wallace Stegner Fellowships, Creative Writing Office, Department of English, Stanford University, Stanford, CA 94305, (415) 723-2637. Twelve fellowships (six in fiction, six in poetry) of $8000 are awarded each year. Fellows must be in residence near Stanford for one academic year and must take one advanced writing course a term (for which there is no charge). Previous publication is helpful but not necessary.

• D.H. Lawrence Summer Fellowship, D.H. Lawrence Fellowship Committee, English Department, Humanities Building, University of New Mexico, Albuquerque, NM 87131, (505) 277-6347. One three-month (June through August) fellowship is awarded annually to a creative writer in any genre. Fellows must live at the D.H. Lawrence Ranch in the Sangre de Cristo Mountains fifteen miles north of Taos for at least four weeks of the fellowship period. Free housing and a $2100 stipend are supplied. Writers may bring their families. There is no publication or production requirement.

• Fellowships for Creative Writers, National Endowment for the Arts, Literature Program, 1100 Pennsylvania Avenue NW, Washington, DC 20506, (202) 682-5451. About a hundred fellowships are awarded annually to writers of fiction, other creative prose, and poetry. Fellows receive $20,000 and have no obligations other than to pursue their own writing projects. Applicants must have some previous publications. The NEA also awards Translation Fellowships of $10,000 to $20,000 to translators through the Literature Program.

• Fellowships for Playwrights, National Endowment for the Arts, Theater Program, 1100 Pennsylvania Avenue NW, Washington, DC 20506, (202) 682-5425. About twenty one-year fellowships for playwrights are awarded annually; these range from $12,500 to $20,000. Some two-year fellowships of $37,500 are also available. Applicants must have work previously produced or in production.

• Guggenheim Fellowships, John Simon Guggenheim Memorial Foundation, 90 Park Avenue, New York, NY 10016, (212) 687-4470. A few dozen large (usually around $25,000) fellowships are awarded annually to writers of fiction, poetry, creative prose, criticism, and drama. Fellowships

402 The Indispensable Writer's Guide

are also awarded to researchers, scholars, and artists in many other fields. Over two hundred fifty fellowships in all are awarded. Fellowships are given to persons of exceptional ability; Guggenheim fellows have usually achieved some recognition through significant publication or production.

• Rockefeller Fellowships, Rockefeller Foundation, 1133 Avenue of the Americas, New York, NY 10036, (212) 869-8500. For playwrights. Contact the Foundation for details.

• PEN/Nelson Algren Fiction Award, PEN American Center, 568 Broadway, New York, NY 10012, (212) 334-1660. One fellowship of $1000 is given annually to a writer who needs financial assistance to complete an unfinished novel or short-story collection. Writers must spend a month at the writers' colony run by the Edward Albee Foundation (see page 408 for details).

• Fine Arts Work Center, 24 Pearl Street, Box 565, Provincetown, MA 02657, (617) 487-9960. Several fellowships are awarded annually to creative writers. Fellows must live at the center from October 1 to May 1. Previous publications are helpful but not required. Because of its requirement that fellows be in residence, I have also listed this center and its fellowships in the following section, "Writers' Colonies."

• Arts Awards Service, Canada Council, Box 1047, Ottawa, Ontario K1P 5V8, Canada, (613) 598-4365. Sponsors several grant programs for creative writers and writers of criticism who are Canadian citizens or permanent residents. Contact the council for details.

Certain other fellowships cannot be applied for by individual writers; you must instead be nominated by an editor, publisher, or other writer. Examples include MacArthur Fellowships, the Rome Fellowship, and the National Endowment for the Arts' Senior Fellowships.

In addition, many public and private organizations offer grants and fellowships in very specific areas such as the translation of Scandinavian literature into English, film criticism, and publication design.

All of the above programs, except as noted otherwise, are open to writers across the United States (and in some cases from other countries as well), regardless of sex, age, religion, academic background (or lack thereof), race, organizational affiliation, state of residence, and so on. There are, however, well over a hundred other grant and fellowship programs available to creative writers that carry some restrictions. Here are some examples:

• Most states (and Canadian provinces) offer fellowships for writers who are legal residents of those states and provinces. These are usually administered through state and provincial arts councils. Awards specifically for criticism, scholarship, and/or translation may be available from state and provincial humanities councils as well. There are also a few fellowships administered by local and regional public arts organizations.

• Several private foundations sponsor grants or fellowship programs for writers living in particular states or regions. Examples here include the Bush Fellowships and the Loft/McKnight Fellowships, both available only to residents of Minnesota, and the Artists Foundation Fellowships, available only to residents of Massachusetts.

• Some writers' organizations give grants, fellowships, and/or awards to writers chosen from their own membership. For example, the Society of Children's Book Writers sponsors several grant programs solely for its members.

• Some grants and fellowships are specifically earmarked for particular groups of people, such as women, blacks, Chicanos, and so on.

• A good many fellowships and scholarships are available to student writers. The great majority of these are given out by colleges to their students (see pages 394–95 for details), though a few are privately administered and nationally competitive, and a few others are sponsored by the federal or state government.

To research the grants and fellowships that are available and appropriate to you, check the following books:

Grants and Awards Available to American Writers (PEN American Center, 568 Broadway, New York, NY 10012).

National Directory of Grants and Aid to Individuals in the Arts International, by Nancy A. Fandel (Washington International Arts Letter, Box 12010, Des Moines, IA 50312). The strange, contradictory title of this book is nevertheless accurate: it lists grants and fellowships available to writers and artists through both national and international programs.

The Dramatist's Bible (International Society of Dramatists, Box 1310, Miami, FL 33153). This volume provides an excellent and comprehensive list of grants and fellowships available to dramatists, lyricists, librettists, and composers.

Dramatists Sourcebook (Theatre Communications Group, 355 Lexington Avenue, New York, NY 10017). This also contains a list of grants and fellowships available to dramatists, librettists, lyricists, and composers.

Another excellent resource is The Foundation Center, an organization that provides extensive information on fellowships and grants to individuals and organizations throughout the world. The Foundation Center maintains libraries in New York City, Washington, D.C., Cleveland, and San Francisco. These are open to the public and may be used at no charge. The Foundation Center also maintains a collection of seven basic volumes on grants and foundations at over 150 locations (mostly libraries) in virtually every state, as well as in Toronto, London, Mexico City, and several other locations. For a complete list of locations, or to learn of the one nearest you, call (800) 424-9836.

The following reference books (which are described on pages 75–82) contain very limited lists of grants and fellowships: *Literary Market Place, Poet's Market, The Poet's Marketplace,* and *The Writer's Handbook. Literary and Library Prizes,* edited by Olga S. Weber (R. R. Bowker) also includes a list of some writers' grants. *Artist Update,* the *AWP Newsletter* (see page 75 for both), and many writers' magazines also publish a limited amount of information on grants and fellowships. The bimonthly *Washington International Arts Letter* (Box 12010, Des Moines, IA 50312) regularly publishes information on grants and fellowships for writers.

Here are some things to keep in mind regarding fellowships and grants:

• Some programs will require you to live in a particular city, town, or facility during all or part of the fellowship period. Some programs will permit you to bring your family with you, but most will not. You may, of course, always have visitors.

• Taxes on grants and fellowships can be confusing. See pages 437–38 for details.

• It may or may not be possible to hold more than one grant or fellowship simultaneously. However, it is always perfectly Kosher to apply for several at once. The chances of receiving two or more at once is very slight, but if this does occur, discuss it frankly with the program administrators. You may be able to arrange to have one grant begin immediately after the other ends. The worst that can happen is that you will have to decline one of the grants. You will *never* be penalized for having applied to two or more grant or fellowship programs simultaneously.

• If you are turned down for a grant or fellowship, you can always apply for it again the following year. The fact that you made previous application will not hurt your chances of getting the grant later.

• Many grants can be received more than once. Some writers have won as many as three or four NEA fellowships over a period of years. If you do receive a grant or fellowship and wish to apply for it again, check with the sponsoring organization to see if repeats are permitted. Even if they are, many organizations have an official or unofficial requirement that two or more years must pass before a second grant or fellowship can be awarded to the same person. Ask about the length of this waiting period.

• It is perfectly fine to apply for a grant from one organization while you are receiving one from another. Many writers have received back-to-back grants. In fact, getting one grant or fellowship tends to increase your chances of getting another.

• Some grants are paid monthly; others are paid semiannually; others are paid in a lump sum.

• The great majority of grants and fellowships for writers are available only to writers who work in the English language.

• While there may be some bias or favoritism here and there, the great majority of grants and fellowships are awarded fairly and honestly, and on a genuinely competitive basis. In many cases, writing submitted is judged anonymously—that is, the judges don't know who wrote each manuscript.

• Decisions on who gets (and who doesn't get) a grant or fellowship are usually made by a committee, not a single individual. This means that an application that four out of four judges find pretty good may well win a grant, while one that three judges love but one despises might get passed over.

• Be as careful in writing, editing, and proofreading a grant or fellowship application as you would be with a manuscript. The better an application looks and the easier it is to read, the more favorable an impression you may make.

• Statistically, your chances of getting a grant or fellowship are fairly slim: usually one in eight to one in fifty applications receives funding. (The exceptions here are academic scholarships and fellowships. The odds of getting one of these are far better.) National Endowment for the Arts Literature Fellowships typically go to one out of fifteen applicants.

• Grants and fellowships are intended to provide writers with needed financial support to work on literary projects that they would otherwise be unable to write (or write as quickly or as well) because of the pressures of earning a living. If you've already got plenty of money, or if you don't intend to use a grant or fellowship to further your writing, you shouldn't apply for one.

One final item bears discussion here: literary fellowships given out by book publishers. Each publisher that sponsors such a fellowship normally gives out only one a year; the best known of these is the Houghton Mifflin Literary Fellowship. In most cases, these fellowships are awarded to new writers who are publishing their first books. Writers can apply for one of these by submitting a completed book manuscript. Fellowships normally consist of a standard publishing contract and a medium-sized advance for the book, plus (in some cases) a cash award.

These fellowships are quite legitimate, but I advise against applying for one, for the same reason that I recommend against entering more than a few contests. Most publishers receive hundreds of entries annually for each fellowship. Your book will be judged against all of these other entries, and only the best of the whole group can win. But if your manuscript is submitted to an editor at that same publishing house by a legitimate agent, it will be judged entirely on its own merits, not in comparison to other writers' works. Your chances of getting published by that publisher are best, therefore, if you make a standard submission rather than apply for a fellowship. Furthermore, the advance you will earn for your book, if it is sold through a standard submission, is likely to be as large or larger than the advance you would receive if you won the fellowship.

WRITERS' COLONIES

Writers' colonies offer writers places to write, uninterrupted and free from distraction and obligation, for a short period of time. The average residency runs one to three months, though one colony allows writers to stay only one to three weeks, and another requires writers to stay for seven months. Some are open only part of the year; others operate year-round.

Typically, writers are given comfortable (though not luxurious) living quarters in pleasant physical surroundings. Sometimes a separate writing studio is provided. Meals are usually provided, and people on special diets can normally be accommodated. Some colonies permit writers to bring their spouses or families, but most insist that writers come alone. Brief visits from family and friends are of course permitted.

Financial arrangements vary from one colony to another. Most offer free housing and meals; a few pay a monthly stipend. Several charge residents a weekly or monthly fee; however, some of these will waive part or all of this charge for writers in financial need. Travel expenses to and from the colony are almost never paid by the colony.

You must formally apply well in advance—anywhere from two to twelve months ahead—for a residency at a writers' colony. Six months ahead is average. Call or write the colonies that interest you and ask to be sent an application and a description of the facilities. (If you make your request by mail, include a #10 self-addressed, stamped envelope.) Admission is granted to those writers who demonstrate strong talent. Most colonies do not require applicants to have had their work published or produced, though this usually helps. Those that do have a publication or production requirement will say so.

If you are turned down by a writer's colony, you may reapply the following year without prejudice.

It is possible and permissible to attend more than one writers' colony, and it is permissible to apply for and be given a second or third residency at the same colony. However, some colonies require that two or more years pass before a writer may return.

Writers' colonies are not for everyone. Here are some things you should consider:

• Solitude makes some people productive, but it makes others' creativity dry up. You'll need to consider how well you are likely to work in an unfamiliar environment, away from your family, friends, and things you find familiar. Some writers grow lonely, unhappy, and unable to produce at colonies.

• A residence in a writers' colony isn't your only option, and it isn't necessarily your best one. I've known writers who have achieved the same solitude by renting separate office or studio space (without a phone); by checking into a hotel, motel, or cabin for a week or month at a time; by declaring a certain room of their house off limits to other family members; or by renting a carrel (see "Writer's Studios" below). In all of these cases, the writers didn't have to leave their home towns.

• Consider the costs (in money, time, energy, and anxiety) of traveling from your home to the colony and back again. Even if your room and board are being provided free, the costs of transportation and incidentals may make the residency a decent-sized (though tax-deductible) expense. If you live in Denver, and what you want is a month of isolation, you may be smarter to rent a cabin in the Rockies for a month than to travel to upstate New York for a month-long residency at a colony. (*Writer's Digest* magazine even publishes an occasional feature called "Writer's Hideaway," which carries classified ads for lodges, cabins, farms, desert islands, and resorts that offer seclusion and relaxing surroundings for writers.)

• Even though you may be charged nothing for your stay at a colony, you may thereafter be asked (perhaps repeatedly) to make charitable contributions to the colony to keep it operating for other writers.

• A few colonies have long waiting periods for residencies. At least one is so backed up that writers have to wait two years after being accepted before their residencies may begin.

• A few organizations that call themselves writers' colonies aren't. One in Ontario, for example, is actually a writers' conference. You'll be able to tell quickly from an organization's own information whether it is genuinely a colony or something else.

• Most colonies are open to writers of fiction, poetry, plays, and other forms of creative writing. A few admit journalists, essayists, scholars, and other writers of nonfiction—but most do not. (Many colonies admit visual artists and/or composers as well as writers.)

A list of writers' colonies in North America follows. All residencies run three months or less unless otherwise noted.

ACT I Creativity Center, Artist and Writers Colony, 4550 Warwick Boulevard, #1201, Box 10153, Kansas City, MO 64111, (816) 753-0208. Housing and meals provided; a weekly fee is charged. Financial aid is available. Residencies are in rural Missouri, on Lake of the Ozarks.

Edward Albee Foundation, 14 Harrison Street, New York, NY 10013, (212) 226-2020. Housing provided; no charge. The colony is in Montauk, Long Island.

Blue Mountain Center, Blue Mountain Lake, NY 12812, (518) 352-7391. Housing and meals provided; no charge.

Centrum, Box 1158, Port Townsend, WA 98368, (206) 385-3102. Housing and a $75 per week stipend are provided.

Cummington Community of the Arts, Cummington, MA 01026, (413) 634-2172. Housing and food provided; a monthly fee is charged. Financial aid is available. Residencies run up to six months.

Djerassi Foundation, 2325 Bear Gulch Road, Woodside, CA 94062, (415) 851-8395. Housing and meals provided; no charge.

Dorland Mountain Arts Colony, Box 6, Temecula, CA 92390, (714) 676-5039. Housing provided. There is a small charge. Financial aid is available.

Dorset Colony House for Writers, Box 519, Dorset, VT 05251, (802) 867-2223. Housing provided; a weekly contribution is requested.

Fine Arts Work Center, 24 Pearl Street, Box 565, Provincetown, MA 02657, (617) 487-9960. Housing provided; no charge. Pays a monthly stipend. Residencies run for seven months: October 1 through May 1.

Hambidge Center, Box 339, Rabun Gap, GA 30568, (404) 746-5718. Housing and meals provided; a weekly fee is charged. Financial aid is available.

Leighton Artist Colony, Banff Center, Box 1020, Banff, Alberta T0L 0C0, Canada, (403) 762-6370. Housing and meals provided; a fee is charged. Financial aid is available.

MacDowell Colony, 100 High Street, Peterborough, NH 03458, (603) 924-3886 or (212) 535-9690. Housing and meals provided; a weekly fee is requested, but not required.

Mantalvo Center for the Arts, Box 158, Saratoga, CA 95071, (408) 741-3421. Housing provided; a monthly fee is charged. Some financial aid is available.

Millay Colony for the Arts, Steepletop, Austerlitz, NY 12017, (518) 392-3103. Housing and meals provided; no charge.

Niangua Colony, Route 1, Stoutland, MO 65567. Housing and food provided; a monthly fee is charged. Most residencies run two to eight weeks, but long-term residencies are sometimes possible.

Northwood Institute Creativity Center, Midland, MI 48640, (517) 832-4479. Housing and meals provided; no charge. Pays a small weekly stipend.

Oregon Writers Colony House, Box 15200, Portland, OR 97215, (503) 771-0428. Housing provided; a weekly fee is charged. Financial aid is available. Residencies are in a small lodge on the rural Oregon coast.

Palenville Interarts Colony, c/o Bond Street Theatre Coalition, 2 Bond Street, New York, NY 10012, (212) 254-4614. Housing and meals provided. A weekly fee is charged; some financial aid is available. The colony is in upstate New York.

Ragdale Foundation, 1260 North Green Bay Road, Lake Forest, IL 60045, (312) 234-1063. Housing and meals provided; a weekly fee is charged. Financial aid is available.

Rockefeller Foundation, 1133 Avenue of the Americas, New York, NY 10036, (212) 869-8500. Housing and meals provided; no charge. Residencies are at the Bellagio Center in the Italian Alps, on Lake Como.

Ucross Foundation, 2836 U.S. Highway 14-16 East, Clearmont, WY 82835, (307) 737-2291. Housing and meals provided; no charge.

Virginia Center for the Creative Arts, Sweet Briar, VA 24595, (804) 946-7236. Housing and meals provided; a daily fee is charged. Financial aid is available.

Helene Wurlitzer Foundation, Box 545, Taos, NM 87571, (505) 758-2413. Housing is provided; no charge. Residencies may extend to six months.

Yaddo, Box 395, Saratoga Springs, NY 12866, (518) 584-0746. Housing and meals provided; no charge.

Several colonies for writers have closed their doors in the past few years. These include Creekwood in Alabama, the Ossabaw Island Project in Georgia, and the Rhode Island Creative Arts Center.

Although writers' colonies provide a degree of solitude, they do not provide complete privacy: you're there with at least a couple of other writers. However, Writers & Books, the Rochester, New York, writers' center, has recently established The Gell House, which it calls a writers' retreat. The Gell House is a comfortably furnished three-bedroom home in rural New York about forty miles south of Rochester that is rented to writers who desire complete isolation to work on their writing. Writers may stay from one night to several weeks; a very reasonable fee is charged. Writers must do their own cooking, and may either come alone or bring their families. It is also permissible for two or three writers to rent The Gell House together, and split the cost. Applicants must submit a writing sample. Contact The Gell House, Writers & Books, 740 University Avenue, Rochester, NY 14607, (716) 473-2590.

WRITERS' STUDIOS

Some writers have trouble finding an adequate spot in which to do their writing. Those who cannot make such a spot in their own homes sometimes rent offices, studios, lofts, or other spaces; rooms in boarding houses and industrial space are both popular, because they are inexpensive. Other writers have rented attics, basements, and storefronts.

Some art and cultural centers offer studio space to writers and visual artists, either at no charge or for a small fee. Libraries (especially those at colleges and universities) can also supply writers with cubicles or carrels, again for little or no money. New York City has two well-known organizations that provide small workspaces especially for writers: The Writers Room, 153 Waverly Place, Fifth Floor, New York, NY 10014, (212) 807-9519; and The Writers' Studio, Mercantile Library Association, 17 E. 47th Street, New York, New York, NY 10017, (212) 755-6710. Space at either organization must be applied for in advance.

Many small businesses and nonprofit organizations (local colleges and community centers, for example) have vacant offices or storerooms, and some will be pleased to rent out an empty space to a writer for a small (and perhaps even token) fee.

EDITORIAL SERVICES AND FREELANCE EDITORS

These people and agencies do writing, rewriting, and editing to order. Some will also provide one or more of these services: collaboration, research, ghostwriting, and manuscript evaluation and critiquing.

Typically, these firms make their services available to both authors and publishers, though some work only with one or the other. For authors, they help get manuscripts in the best possible shape for submission; for publishers, they help improve projects already completed, or complete stalled ones. Often editorial services are hired by publishers to handle some of the tasks of an in-house editor.

Some services charge by the hour, some by the page, and some by the project. Rates vary widely, so shop around and get several quotes. Larger firms tend to charge more than individuals, since they must split the fee between the editor/writer and the management; such a firm might charge $20 to $50 an hour. An editor or writer working alone might charge only $12 to $30 an hour; $15 to $25 is average. If a project requires collaboration or ghostwriting, some people and firms may charge a percentage of the project's total earnings in addition to or instead of a flat fee. This can go as high as 50 percent; the percentage is often negotiable, however.

A good listing of these services appears in *Literary Market Place* under the heading "Editorial Services." Some services are listed under the heading "Consultants." Some of these firms and people work only with books and proposals, but they should be able to refer writers of other material to professionals who can be of help.

Before hiring a writer, editor, or editorial service, ask for some credentials. Normally the person should be (or have been) an editor or staff writer for a reputable magazine, newspaper, or book publisher. Or, he or she should be widely published by reputable publishers. If a firm has several writer/editors on its staff, feel free to specifically request someone with the appropriate credentials.

Before hiring a writer, editor, or editorial service, you should also know exactly how much you will be paying, either for the whole project, or by the hour or page. If you are being charged by the hour or finished page, you may want to get an estimate of the cost of the project. Or you might want to tell the writer or service that you're setting a ceiling on the total bill. For example, "I'll pay at most 10 percent over your estimate for the finished project" or "I'll pay up to $800 for the project—no more." In some cases, it may be possible to negotiate a lower fee or rate than what is quoted—but usually it is not.

Some editors and editorial services will turn down projects that they feel have slim chances of getting published, even with editing, revision, or collaboration.

If you've got a fair amount of experience as an editor, or are a fairly widely published writer, you can of course hire yourself out as a freelance editor, and/or set up your own one-person editorial service. All you need are business cards (see pages 182–84) and a little advertising. Printed stationery is also recommended.

If you have strong editing and/or publishing credentials already, you also have the option of approaching one of the established editorial services with a resumé and a letter. Some of these services are interested in adding new writers and editors to their salaried and freelance staffs. In some cases, you need not live near the firms' offices, but can work via mail and/or modem.

CRITIQUING SERVICES

A number of firms and individuals (including some agents, ghostwriters, and editorial services) offer manuscript critiques to writers for a fee. Some of these critiques are concerned primarily with the literary quality of manuscripts. Others are concerned primarily or entirely with their salability; some may even include a list of suggested markets. Some critiques are concerned with both. Before engaging the services of a paid critic, be very clear about whether you want a literary or commercial evaluation—or both. Also make sure that the critic is able to provide what you want.

Manuscript critics may charge by the hour (the range is $10 to $30 an hour, with $10 to $20 being fairly standard), by the page (50¢ to $4 a page), by the project, by the one hundred or one thousand words, or by the line. Before you purchase a critique, find out exactly what the critic's rates are. If possible, get a firm quote before you agree to a critique; if you will be charged by the hour, get an estimate of how long the project will take. It is also a good idea to say something like "I'll pay you for your time up to the amount of your estimate" or "I'm not willing to spend more than 10 percent over your estimate." Feel free to shop around and get quotes from several different critics or services.

It's impossible to know in advance what kind of a job a critic can do for you, but you *can* ask some probing questions. Find out what experience the critic has in the way of writing, editing, and/or teaching writing. Someone who is (or used to be) a professional editor or a college writing teacher, or someone who has published widely, is probably worth taking a chance on. If the service has several people on its staff, you may wish to specifically request someone with a particular background.

Some critiquing services advertise in writers' magazines. If you are seeking a paid critic, consult the back pages of these magazines and/or the agencies listed in *Literary Market Place* under the heading "Editorial Services."

You should of course send any critic a photocopy of your manuscript, keeping the original for yourself. This allows the critic to write comments and make changes directly on the manuscript.

If you'd like to *become* a paid critic—and are both competent and qualified—all you need are business cards (see pages 182–84), notices on bulletin boards, and/or ads of your own.

RESEARCHERS

Writing often requires research—sometimes a great deal of research. If you don't have the time or the inclination to do the research yourself, you can hire a professional researcher to do some or all of it for you. These researchers usually do a thorough job, but they can be expensive. Rates range from $15 to $50 an hour, with $15 to $25 being fairly standard.

To locate researchers, look under the heading "Editorial Services" in *Literary Market Place,* or ask your editor or agent. It is also a good idea to call the reference librarian at a large public or university library; often he or she can recommend one or more researchers in your area. The library may even have a staff of researchers who work for an hourly fee.

EMERGENCY MONEY

Below are some organizations that can offer help in the event of financial and/or medical emergencies. Write or call for more details and application materials.

• The Actors Fund, 1501 Broadway, 24th Floor, New York, NY 10036, (212) 221-7300. Provides grants to people in the entertainment industry (including writers) in emergency situations.

• American Academy and Institute of Arts and Letters, Artists' and Writers' Fund, 633 W. 115th Street, New York, NY 10032, (212) 368-5900. Provides grants of up to $3500 to writers in the event of illness, disability, or emergency. Writers *must* be recommended for the grant by a member of the Academy or Institute, though grant recipients need not be members themselves.

• Authors League Fund and Dramatists Guild Fund, 234 W. 44th Street, New York, NY 10036, (212) 391-3966. Provides interest-free loans to professional writers in emergency situations. Open to both members and nonmembers.

• Carnegie Fund for Authors, 330 Sunrise Highway, Rockville Centre, NY 11570. Provides grants for writers in verifiable emergency situations. Writers must have published at least one book with a commercial publisher. Telephone inquiries are discouraged.

• Change, Box 705, Cooper Station, New York, NY 10276, (212) 473-3742. Provides grants of up to $500 to writers in emergency situations. Also sponsors a program to cover medical expenses.

• The Llewellyn Miller Fund, c/o American Society of Journalists and Authors, 1501 Broadway, Suite 1907, New York, NY 10036, (212) 997-0947. Provides grants of up to $2500 for writers who are unable to produce because of age or disability, or who are experiencing an extraordinary professional crisis that a grant can help alleviate. Open to both members and nonmembers of ASJA.

• PEN Fund for Writers, 568 Broadway, New York, NY 10012, (212)

334-1660. Provides grants and loans of up to $1000 to writers in emergency situations. Open to both members and nonmembers of PEN.

You must make formal application to the above programs. Grants and loans are given on the basis of need, and not all applications are approved. Applications may take several days to several weeks to be processed. In most cases, you must have achieved some success as a writer (for example, published at least one book or had at least one full-length play produced) to be eligible; in some cases, you must have been a full-time professional writer for at least a short period of time.

Grants do not need to be repaid; loans do. If you are awarded a grant, however, you are encouraged to make a donation of equal or larger size to the fund that gave you the grant as soon as you are financially able to do so. This enables the fund to help other writers in need in the future.

Never apply for money from any of these funds unless you are suffering a genuine disability or emergency, unless you genuinely *need* the money, and unless other options are unavailable.

Certain other state, federal, and private programs provide general and emergency assistance to low-income individuals. See below for details.

INSURANCE, SOCIAL SECURITY, AND OTHER ASSISTANCE FOR WRITERS

Salaried employees normally receive a variety of perks, which include comprehensive medical, disability, and unemployment insurance. Freelancers, unfortunately, receive none of these perks automatically, but a wide variety of options are available.

Insurance Basics

Insurance costs and coverage differ greatly from plan to plan and from company to company. It pays to shop around, look at several different plans, and get several different price quotes. Be sure you understand clearly exactly what coverage is provided by each plan. It is generally a good idea to consult at least one independent insurance agent—that is, one who sells policies from a variety of insurance companies. This agent can help you select the plan that best suits you, regardless of which company offers it. An agent working for a single company, on the other hand, can only sell that one company's offerings.

Group plans may or may not be more expensive than equivalent *individual* plans, so it pays to compare these two options as well. However, if your health history shows repeated illness or one or more chronic problems, you may not be able to get complete (or even any) medical coverage through an individual plan.

To be eligible for group insurance, you must normally join a group or association, such as a professional writers' organization. However, it is also possible to purchase group plan coverage for yourself and your family through the Foundation for the Community of Artists (FCA; see page 385 for details), the Small Business Service Bureau (see page 386), Support Services Alliance (see pages 385–86), or Co-Op America, 2100 M Street NW, Suite 310, Washington, DC 20063, (202) 872–5307. Each organization offers its own range of insurance plans.

Health Insurance

When comparing medical policies, be sure to note what each plan offers in each of these areas:

- Amount of deductible(s)
- Maximum lifetime benefits available ($1 million per person is reasonable)
- Covered charges
- Exclusions (items not covered)
- Maternity benefits
- Home health care
- Nursing home benefits (including the maximum daily benefit)
- Mental health benefits
- Alcoholism/chemical dependency treatment benefits
- Maximum daily benefit for hospital room
- Coverage for chiropractic care
- Coverage for organ transplants
- Coverage for cosmetic surgery
- Coverage for other family members

Three kinds of medical plans are available: hospitalization, major medical, and comprehensive. Everyone needs the protection provided by either comprehensive coverage or both major medical and hospitalization.

Make sure that any policy you purchase is guaranteed renewable. This means that the insurance company can't cancel your policy for any reason except nonpayment of premiums. Also make sure that your premiums cannot be raised in the event that you suffer a chronic illness, or a catastrophic illness or injury—or for any other reason. Be sure that your premiums can be raised *only* if they are raised equally and simultaneously for all policyholders in your age group and/or geographic area.

Rates, limitations of coverage, and deductibles vary widely, so you'll need to do some careful thinking on exactly what kind of coverage you need and how much you are willing to pay.

Under most plans your premiums will go up as you grow older. Be sure you know exactly what your premiums will be each year in the future before you begin coverage.

Health Maintenance Organizations

A health maintenance organization, or HMO, is not an insurance plan at all, but an organization that offers comprehensive medical coverage equivalent or superior to most comprehensive insurance plans, plus preventive health care, including check-ups, lab tests, classes, and so on. Many writers will want to consider HMO membership instead of health insurance.

Charges for HMO membership can vary as widely as the costs of standard comprehensive medical insurance. Compare benefits and costs closely, both between different HMOs and between HMOs and traditional comprehensive health plans. An HMO should offer most or all of the benefits of comprehensive health insurance, plus routine check-ups, X rays, lab tests, medications, well-baby checks, information and counseling, and many other preventive care services. HMO coverage normally carries no deductible.

Not all HMOs provide individual (as opposed to group) coverage. Of those that do, some may require you to submit a health history, and some may reserve the right to refuse partial or all coverage if your health has been poor or if you have a chronic illness. Other HMOs accept members regardless of their health histories.

Some HMOs have an *open enrollment* period of one month or longer each year, during which *anyone* may join, regardless of their health history. For more information on an HMO, on joining, and on open enrollment, contact the HMO's membership or marketing department. Be sure to ask specifically about the HMO's open enrollment period.

Special HMO plans are available in some areas for low-income and unemployed people; for dental care; and for those 55 and older. Many HMO plans accept Medicare payments from the U.S. government in lieu of part or all of their membership fees.

Life Insurance

Only buy term life insurance. Whole life and universal life plans are nothing more than term plans with restricted-access savings accounts added to them. You'll build larger savings by purchasing lower-priced term insurance and putting money into your own savings account, an IRA, or another investment of your choice.

Your premiums may go up as you grow older, and at a certain age coverage may cease. Before you purchase a life insurance policy, know exactly how much you must pay each year, and if and when the policy expires.

Disability Insurance

Disability insurance is sometimes considerably more difficult to buy on an individual basis than it is through a group plan. Individual disability plans *are* available, but you may have to meet certain guidelines concerning health, income, and/or self-employment. Both individual and group disability plans differ quite widely.

Here are some important things to consider when comparing and considering disability plans:

• Different plans pay benefits for different lengths of time. Benefits can run out after as few as six months, or they can continue all the way up to age 65. Two years of coverage is pretty standard. (This presumes that you are disabled indefinitely. Regardless of the maximum amount of coverage available, *any* plan ceases to pay benefits when you are able to return to your normal line of work.) The longer the duration of the coverage, the higher the premiums.

• Make sure that your policy entitles you to benefits if you are unable to perform your *normal* professional duties (that is, writing and/or editing), at least for the first year or two. Avoid policies that only pay benefits if you can't work *at all;* under such a policy, you're not entitled to benefits if you are still physically and mentally able to assemble widgets in a factory at the minimum wage.

• Some plans include coverage for disabilities caused by alcoholism, drug use, and/or mental or nervous disorders; some do not. Some provide smaller benefits for such disabilities, or provide them for a shorter period of time.

• Some plans offer a residual disability benefit, through which you can receive payments under certain circumstances if, as a result of a disability, you can no longer earn more than a certain percentage of the income you were earning before you became disabled.

• Some plans will waive premiums once a disability has existed for a certain length of time.

• Different plans set different waiting periods from the time a disability occurs to the time benefits begin to be paid. These can be as little as a week or as long as ninety days.

• Every disability plan has certain exclusions. Find out what all these are before buying any policy. Standard exclusions include disabilities caused by pregnancy or childbirth, war, or intentionally self-inflicted injury. Some plans do *not* provide *any* benefits if a disability is the result of an illness or injury incurred while you are at work! This opens an enormous can of worms, since it is very unclear what, for freelance writers, constitutes being "at work." Are you at work while flying to New York to interview someone for an article? Are you at work while getting informal tips on contract negotiation from another writer over drinks? A plan that pays full benefits for both on- and off-the-job disabilities provides far better coverage.

• The premiums for most disability policies will go up as you get older. Before you purchase a plan, find out exactly what your rates and coverage will be each year in the future.

• Under some plans, coverage will terminate or be reduced when you reach a certain age (often 65 or 70). Find out if and when such termination or reduction will occur before you buy. If benefits will be reduced, ascertain exactly how much they will be cut.

• Make sure any policy you buy is guaranteed renewable.

• Also make sure that your premiums cannot be raised for chronic illness, catastrophic illness or injury, or *any* other reason. Premiums for all persons in a certain age group and/or geographic area *may* be raised, but only if they are raised simultaneously and equally for all members of that group.

Sometimes disability insurance is available as an add-on option to life or health insurance plans.

Unemployment Insurance

Unemployment assistance is no longer available to full-time freelancers and other self-employed people. You *may* be eligible for unemployment, however, if you have been laid off from a part-time or full-time salaried job—even if you also have freelance income. Check with the Labor Department in your state to see if you qualify for benefits.

Social Security and Medicare

Freelancers and other self-employed people are eligible for the same social security and Medicare benefits as other persons.

AFDC, Food Stamps, Medicaid and Other Programs for Low-Income People

Both freelancers and salaried writers, as well as unemployed writers, are eligible for all forms of financial assistance provided by federal, state, local, and private programs. These include Aid to Families with Dependent Children (AFDC), Medicaid, general assistance, emergency assistance, food stamps, assistance with utility bills, and other forms of welfare and emergency aid. The primary qualification for these programs is a small, or very small, income. Contact your local welfare office to see which programs you are eligible for; call the Federal Information Center in your area for the appropriate phone number and/or address.

Certain programs (particularly those that help with utility bills) may be administered by non-governmental organizations such as utility companies or the Salvation Army. Check with your utility companies for details.

Inexpensive Medical Care

Physicians who are members of an organization called Doctors for Artists provide their services to artists and writers at a discount. Contact Doctors for Artists, 105 W. 78th Street, New York, NY 10024, (212) 496-5172, for more information or a referral to a member physician in your area.

13. ✎ _____

Taxes for Writers

WHAT THIS CHAPTER CAN DO FOR YOU

This chapter is a writer's guide to filing federal income and social security taxes. It has been written for two kinds of writers: (1) those who have earned (or will earn) small or moderate amounts of money from their writing during the current or previous year, and (2) those who have earned nothing at all from their writing but who have incurred writing-related expenses (for office supplies, postage, duplicating, and long-distance telephone calls, for example). For the first kind of writer, this chapter will outline what to do to keep your income taxes as low as possible; for the second, this chapter will explain how to use your writing-related expenses to lower your total tax bill. (Writers who earned, or will earn, $20,000 or more from their writing can also benefit from this chapter; however, I recommend to most of these writers that they hire a good professional tax preparer. Many writers who have earned less than this amount may also want (or need) to consult a tax professional, especially if they have items that require extra forms and calculations.)

Every suggestion and guideline for lowering and filing your taxes in this chapter is, to my best understanding, both legal and moral. Be honest in determining and filing your income taxes; it's the law.

WARNINGS AND WARRANTIES

I am not a professional tax preparer. I am not acting in an official capacity, or as a "tax expert." While I have taken pains to ensure that everything written here is accurate, I do not *guarantee* the accuracy of any statement. (The reasons for this will quickly become apparent.) I am simply one writer passing on his best understandings about taxes to other writers.

Information for this chapter was gathered from my own experience; discussions with IRS personnel, including Taxpayer Service Specialists and one auditor; IRS Tele-Tax tapes; and careful study of IRS publications.

All of the information in this chapter is current as of the 1987 tax year (for which returns were due on April 15, 1988). The information reflects the pertinent changes in tax law and IRS regulations resulting from the major tax reform bill passed by Congress in 1986, which began to take effect during the 1987 tax year. Some new IRS regulations and policies will doubtless go into effect beginning with the 1988 tax year, but few points of substance should change. My figures are as current as possible. Wherever I have stated a dollar amount or percentage that might change in a later year, I have noted the year for which that figure is accurate.

All deadlines listed are dates by which returns must be postmarked. When this date falls on a Saturday, Sunday, or national holiday, the deadline is extended through the next business day.

THE IRS AND ITS FALLIBILITY

The tax laws, and the IRS regulations that spring from them, are tremendously complicated and often difficult to follow. As a result, *many IRS employees themselves do not understand the tax laws and regulations fully (although they may think and insist they do)—including those employees whose job it is to answer your questions and assist you.* I cannot stress this strongly enough.

Also, tax laws and regulations are far more vague and open to interpretation than most taxpayers realize. What IRS employees may present as absolute fact may be no more than their best interpretations of a much more flexible regulation.

The result of all this is that when you call the IRS (or your state or local tax people) for information, you may be given inaccurate or even wholly erroneous information. *In fact, the IRS itself is not legally bound by any of the information given out by any of its information people, booklets, tapes, films, etc.*

How do you deal with this? If you have a question about your taxes, call your local IRS information number or (800) 424-1040. Request the name of the person who helps you. Ask your questions and get your answers. Then call the IRS again, making sure you get a different person on the phone. If two or three people give the identical information or response, the chances are pretty good that what they have to say is accurate. However, if the information is not identical, either (1) the item in question is open to interpretation, or (2) at least one of the people who gave you information is wrong. Obviously, simple questions like "Where do I send my tax form?" do not need double-checking.

IRS personnel will also answer questions in person at most (but not all) IRS offices. Certain offices may permit or require you to make an appointment in advance. However, service is usually available on a walk-in, first-come first-served basis.

IRS people may use words and phrases that are unfamiliar to you. Do not hesitate to ask for definitions, or for clarification of anything you do not understand—even if the person you are speaking with gets upset about it. Sometimes an IRS term will get defined with another IRS term, or an "explanation" will be circular. Continue to press for an explanation until you get one you genuinely understand. Never allow yourself to be intimidated.

The IRS has a staff of Taxpayer Service Specialists (sometimes simply called Technical, research, or backup people) who handle complicated or difficult tax questions. If the IRS person you are talking with is unsure of an answer, is having difficulty with your question, or is giving you a hard time—or if different IRS employees give you different answers to the same question—ask to speak to a Taxpayer Service Specialist or Technical person.

One useful alternative to dealing with fallible human beings is the IRS's Tele-Tax. This is a collection of short information tapes on a wide variety of tax topics. These tapes are quite clear, concise, and helpful, and they can answer many tax questions authoritatively. (The IRS, however, is not bound by any of the information on these tapes.) You can listen to as many of these tapes over the phone as you wish.

The phone number for Tele-Tax is different in each major city. If you do not live in a large metropolitan area, the number to use is (800) 554-4477. A complete list of available messages and of Tele-Tax access numbers around the country appears in the standard Form 1040 instruction booklet, which many taxpayers automatically receive, and which you may order from the IRS. Your local Tele-Tax access number may also be obtained from your local IRS office or by calling any IRS information number.

Tele-Tax does not provide any information on state or local taxes; some states may offer a similar service, however.

Answers to many (but not all) of your tax questions can also be found in IRS Publication 17, a fat book entitled *Your Federal Income Tax.* This is a fairly detailed (but *not* comprehensive) guide to federal income tax for individuals, which runs 150 pages or more. It's very helpful. Get a copy before you begin doing your taxes. Another large, useful, and highly recommended book is Publication 334, *Tax Guide for Small Businesses.* Two valuable new publications, Publication 920, *Individual Changes,* and Publication 921, *Business Changes,* cover recent changes in tax law and IRS policies.

GETTING STARTED

You will need the following forms and schedules to do your taxes: Form 1040 (you may *not* use the 1040-A or the 1040-EZ); Schedule C (Profit or Loss from Business or Profession); Schedule SE (Computation of Social Security Tax); and any appropriate state and local tax forms. You will also need the instructions for each of these forms and schedules. In many cases, the instructions are published separately from the forms themselves, and they will not always be sent automatically with the forms, so be sure to order (or otherwise obtain) both the forms and the instructions. Be sure to get at least two copies (preferably more) of each form that you will be using, so that you can practice and make mistakes.

Other forms some writers *may* need include Form 1040-ES (Estimated Tax Payments); Form 4562 (Depreciation); and W-2s from any employers who paid you salaries last year. It will also be helpful to gather all the 1099-MISC forms you received for the year; these will inform you of all the miscellaneous or freelance income paid to you during the year that was reported to the IRS. You do not need to file your copies of the 1099-MISC forms with your tax returns; however, they will be useful to you when you fill out Schedule C. You may of course also need other forms pertaining to income from nonwriting sources.

All federal tax forms, instructions to use those forms, and other tax publications can be ordered from the IRS by mail or phone (call 800-424-3676). They can be mailed to either your office or your home and usually take seven to twenty-one days to arrive. Most or all of these can also be picked up at any IRS office during business hours. Some of the tax forms and instructions listed above are available in banks, libraries, and post offices. You may photocopy any federal, state, or local tax form at your discretion. Most librarians have master copies of every federal and state form available for photocopying; some have local forms as well. Check with the reference librarian. Many libraries also have printed instructions for filling out the forms, and copies of most or all the IRS information publications. Some have cassette tapes which give instructions as well.

All IRS, state, and local forms, schedules, instructions, books, and other publications are free. They are available beginning January 1 for the previous tax year (for which returns are due by April 15 of the current year).

(For a complete list of IRS publications call the IRS, or order Publication 910; abridged lists appear in the back of the standard 1040 booklet, and in Publications 17, *Your Federal Income Tax,* and 334, *Tax Guide for Small Businesses.*)

Once you file a Form 1040 (not a 1040-A or a 1040-EZ), you will usually be sent a 1040 booklet in the mail in early January of the following year. This booklet contains multiple copies of the 1040, of Schedules C and SE, of Form 4562, and of other commonly used tax forms, as well as instructions for filling out each one. Form 1040 is the basic income tax form that determines your total tax owed or your total refund. Schedule SE is for computing your social security bill on your self-employment income. Schedule C is for your business expenses and income for the previous year. Schedule C is the form of greatest interest to writers, and the one I will discuss in most detail.

Schedule A should be used only if you choose to itemize your *personal* deductions, rather than take the standard deduction on your Form 1040. *Business* deductions (for office supplies, duplicating, etc.) are to be listed on Schedule C. Your writing is definitely a business, even if it isn't earning you any money yet. You may of course file both Schedules C and A in the same year.

Before you begin filling out any forms, gather all your financial records from the previous year. It is important to keep complete records of all income earned from your writing during the year, as well as records of all writing-related expenses. Generally, it is advisable to keep receipts. Theoretically, you're supposed to keep a receipt for every expense; but if your expenses aren't large, it is usually enough to keep a running account for each type of expense (for example, postage, professional services, or photocopying). You should, however, be sure to get, and save, a receipt for any business expense over $25.

Keeping complete, clear, and accurate records is quite important. If you are ever audited by the IRS, you have a better chance of coming out of the audit unharmed and unruffled if your records are complete. It is also important to save all your financial records for five years, and to save copies of all your income tax returns (federal, state, *and* local) indefinitely. This is for your own protection. The IRS has been known to question people's taxes years later; state and local tax officials may do the same.

The forms and schedules must be filled out in this order: Schedule C first, Schedule SE second, and Form 1040 third. After you have completed your federal forms, move on to your state and local taxes. Information from one completed form is needed to fill out the next form in this sequence.

You may round off all numbers on all tax forms (including state and local forms) to the nearest dollar. I recommend rounding, as it makes calculations easier.

SCHEDULE C

This is where you can give yourself the biggest legal and ethical tax break.

The beginning of Schedule C has some confusing and inapplicable questions. Here's how to handle them:

- For *Business name,* write "no name" if you write under your own name, your pseudonym if you regularly use one.
- Leave *Employer ID number* blank.
- For *Method(s) used to value closing inventory,* check the *Other* box, and add "No inventory."
- Answer *Did you "materially participate" in the operation of this business?* with *yes.*

Regarding your income: list all the money you made during the previous year from your *freelance* writing and writing-related activities (such as editing, lecturing, and giving readings) under "gross receipts or sales," and again under "gross profit" and "gross income." If you made no freelance income at all, enter a zero in all these spots. Do not list any income from a regular salaried job, or from any other activity for which you received a W-2 form (or from which taxes were withheld). No such income is listed on Schedule C; it is to be listed only on Form 1040 under "Wages, Salaries, Tips, Etc."

If you have more than one line of self-employed business activity, you will need to fill out a separate Schedule C for each general area of activity.

All writing-related income (including editing, lecturing, consulting, and freelance teaching of writing) can be lumped together on one Schedule C, however.

Regarding your deductions: here is where you get your tax break. You can deduct 100 percent of *all* your legitimate writing expenses (except for certain meal and entertainment expenses, as described below), even if your writing income for the previous year was small or zero. The lower your *net income* from writing (all your writing income minus all your writing expenses), the lower your taxes.

If your expenses exceed your earnings on Schedule C, you have officially taken a business loss. If you show a loss on Schedule C, the amount of your loss should be subtracted from your other (nonwriting) income on Form 1040—leaving you with a smaller total income for the year. Your total federal income tax is computed from this smaller total income, and your tax thus becomes smaller as well.

Several points must be mentioned here. First, in order to claim your writing expenses as legitimate business deductions, you must either: (1) make genuine attempts to make money from your writing during the year, or (2) be working on a piece of writing (say, a book or a full-length filmscript) that you intend to try to sell when it is completed. Making a profit (or any money at all) is not the only issue; whether you are genuinely writing *as a money-making activity* is what counts to the IRS. Thus, if you submit your work solely to magazines that do not pay their writers, you will not be eligible to use Schedule C. (Payment in copies of a publication does not count as payment in the IRS's view.) If, however, you sent at least one or two manuscripts to paying publications—whether or not those publications actually accepted any of your work—then you would be operating as a legitimate business. Or, if you submitted your work only to nonpaying markets, but the appearance of your work in those publications led to a paid reading tour or to your teaching a freelance workshop that earned you money, then the expenses you incurred in your writing would probably be deductible on Schedule C. (If you have no intention of making a penny from your writing, but somehow you do show a profit from it, the IRS will consider your writing a business, not a hobby, at least for that year, and you will have to pay income tax and social security on those earnings.)

There is another stipulation to all this: to operate as a genuine business according to the IRS definition, you must make a profit in at least three of the past five years in which you filed a Schedule C. This means that you can *normally* claim a loss no more than two years in a row, or no more than twice in any five-year period. Thereafter, you can for tax purposes reduce your writing income to as little as $1 per year by means of legitimate deductions, but you may not claim a loss and use that loss to lower your total yearly income. Exceptions have been made to this rule, however, and not infrequently: people who have been businesslike in their professional efforts and record-keeping are often permitted to show a loss more often.

Finally, you must use common sense in your deductions. If you made $50 last year from your writing, the IRS would probably allow you to deduct $200 in assorted business expenses. But if you also spent $1400 on tuition, room, and travel to attend a three-week writers' workshop in Vermont, the IRS would be less likely to allow the $1400 deduction (though in certain circumstances it might). Deductions for items that are extravagant or unnecessary will of course normally be disallowed.

As you can see by now, the IRS operates like a court of equity; it approves or disallows deductions on an individual basis—making its judgments based on the particular circumstances. The IRS regulations are often quite general or vague for the very purpose of allowing this flexibility.

Now to specific deductions. You can deduct the cost of any office supplies, postage, and repairs (say, typewriter or office furniture repairs) necessary for your writing. You can deduct the cost of any professional services used for your writing (attorneys, typists, manuscript critics); any relevant long-distance calls, including tax on those calls; any advertising (including flyers and business cards); paper and office supplies; and business use of your car (either the actual expenses or, if you prefer, a flat rate per mile traveled—see Publication 917, *Business Use of Your Car*, for details). You can deduct costs for photocopying, duplicating, and printing; dues for membership in professional organizations (Mystery Writers of America, the Writers Guild, etc.); and the costs of books, magazines, newsletters, and other information sources and research materials relevant to your writing. (Note: at least two writers' newsletters, including one published by a major writers' book club, have informed their readers that the cost of books and magazines is no longer deductible. This is *absolutely untrue;* they are 100 percent deductible.) Sales tax on any business-related expense is fully deductible as part of the cost of that item.

You can deduct the cost of a class, workshop, or conference if it helps you maintain or increase the skills you already use in your business (in this case writing, editing, and so forth). You can *not* deduct the cost of education which trains you to *become* a writer, editor, or whatever. The same course or workshop, then, could be tax deductible for one writer but not for another. Certain related expenses, including travel, lodging, and meals, may also be deductible. See Publication 508, *Educational Expenses,* for details.

The costs associated with seeking freelance writing jobs (the costs of duplicating and mailing out resumés, for example) are generally 100 percent deductible from your gross income. So are all costs you have incurred in promoting your book, play, or other project. (Again, certain meal and entertainment expenses are exceptions, and are limited to 80 percent. See below.)

You can deduct the cost of having a tax professional prepare your *business* tax forms—in your case, Schedules C and SE, and in some cases Form 4562—but *not* your personal taxes.

You can theoretically deduct any other expenses directly involved with your writing. If you are writing a piece on the Minnesota Vikings, for example, you can theoretically deduct the cost of tickets to two or three Vikings games. Deduction of the cost of a *season* ticket would be very iffy at best, however; and you could *not* deduct the cost of a guest's ticket. And I wouldn't suggest trying to deduct the cost of a new (or even a used) MG if you are writing a piece about sports cars. You *might* be able to deduct the cost of a one-day MG rental, though, provided the rental was genuinely used to research your piece.

There has been considerable outcry and debate over the deduction of expenses incurred entirely in the research and/or writing of a single work. The IRS looks at these expenses differently than it does at general expenses such as typewriter repairs, postage, and office supplies. As of this writing (July 1988), the IRS requires 50 percent of single-project expenses to be deducted in the year in which they are incurred, 25 percent in the following year, and 25 percent in the third year. General expenses may of course be deducted in the year in which they are incurred. So may expenses that apply to two or more different writing projects. And, in practice, so may *small* expenses incurred in preparing specific projects.

This is only an interim policy, however. The issue is in the process of being resolved by Congress, the courts, and the IRS. The probable resolution will be that expenses incurred in researching or preparing an individual writing project are fully deductible in the year in which they are incurred, just as other expenses are. Check with an IRS Taxpayer Service Specialist or a professional tax preparer for up-to-date details. [As we went to press in October 1988, Congress passed a measure allowing writers to deduct all legitimate expenses in the year when they were incurred.]

If an expense is incurred for both business and personal purposes, you must separate the business and personal parts as best you can, and you can deduct only the business part. For example, if you buy a new desk for $150 and use it two-thirds of the time for business, you can—and should—deduct $100 as a business expense.

The issue of deducting the rent and utilities paid for your workspace can be tricky. If you rent or own a physical space where you do your writing (such as an office or studio), then you can deduct the entire cost of maintaining that space, including rent, utilities, insurance, phone charges, repairs, and so on. If you use a portion of your home as your workspace, you can take a deduction for it, provided that it is used more or less exclusively for business purposes. Note: *workspace* or *workplace* can refer to a space of any size—including the corner of a kitchen or the back half of your garage or bedroom. You need not have a separate *room* for your writing—merely a separate area (of any size) devoted to business (in this case, writing) activities.

If you use an area for both business and nonbusiness purposes, however, you cannot take *any* deduction for it. This is an exception to the general IRS policy of allowing you to separate a single expense into business and personal parts. Once again common sense and judgment come into play here. If you use a room as a combination den and office, you cannot deduct any rent or utilities. But if you write an occasional personal letter and balance your checkbook in the room you otherwise use only as your place for writing, this would qualify as "exclusive" business use.

If you rent your home, you can deduct a percentage of your total rent and utilities equal to the percentage of square footage your workspace takes up in your home. For example, if your home totals 800 square feet and your office is 150 square feet, your office takes up 18.75 percent of your home. You can then deduct as a legitimate business expenses 18.75 percent of your year's rent and utility bills (*excluding* monthly phone charges). Alternatively, if all the rooms in your home are about the same size, you can compare the number of rooms used in your work to the total number in your home.

If you own your home, the calculations get considerably more complicated—too complicated to go into here. Call the IRS, tell them you own your own home, that you have your workspace in your home, that you wish to deduct the costs of this workspace on your Schedule C, and that you want to know how to go about doing this. Then be prepared for a long explanation. If you prefer a printed explanation, order Publication 587, *Business Use of Your Home,* from the IRS. A professional tax preparer's assistance may well be useful here.

The costs of repairs, maintenance, and insurance paid on your workspace, either as part of your home or otherwise, are deductible on Schedule C as well.

If you take a deduction for a workspace in your home, that deduction may not be used, after all your other business expenses have been deducted, to create or increase a loss on your Schedule C. For example, if you make $5000 from your writing this year and have $3000 in other business-related expenses, you may deduct no more than $2000 as a business expense for your home office during that year—even if your home office expenses equaled $3500. If you show a loss from your other business expenses, you cannot deduct the cost of your home workspace at all.

However, the amount of this expense that you incur but are not allowed to deduct may be carried over to one or more later calendar years and used as a deduction on future Schedule Cs. In the case above, only $2000 of a $3500 deduction was allowed; the remaining $1500 could be used as a Schedule C deduction the following year, along with all other business expenses (including 100 percent of the cost of your home office) for that year—again provided that the total deductions for your home office (including the carryover from the previous year) did not create a loss on that year's Schedule C. If you preferred, you could apply part of the $1500 as a loss on your Schedule C next year, and the remainder as a loss on your Schedule C the year after that—again subject to the stipulations set forth above.

None of this applies if your workspace is outside of your home, in which case 100 percent of all expenses for the workplace are deductible, even if they create or increase a loss on Schedule C.

If you have a separate phone line for your business or workspace, you can deduct the entire cost of phone service for that line. However, if you use a phone for both business and personal purposes, you may *not* deduct *any* portion of the cost of telephone service as a business expense, *even if* you have a separate workspace in your home. The cost of long-distance business calls (including tax) is fully deductible, though.

If you purchase a typewriter, a computer, or any other office machine for business use, you can either (1) deduct the entire cost of the item as a one-time business expense (called *first-year expensing*), or (2) deduct part of the cost of the item each year over a five-year period. You have the same options with office furniture and fixtures (such as filing cabinets), except that the long-term deductions should be spread over seven years instead of five. You may in the same year choose first-year expensing for some items and the long-term option for others. It all depends on how much you want to reduce your taxes this year as opposed to the years to come.

The five- or seven-year deduction method is called *depreciation* in IRS terminology. The total of all depreciation deductions gets listed on Schedule C; itemized depreciations must also be listed on Form 4562, Depreciation and Amortization. The regulations concerning depreciation are quite complicated; for details, see Publication 534, *Depreciation,* or call the IRS. Also note that the rules for depreciation are slightly different for items purchased before 1987.

If an item is used for both business and personal purposes, you can depreciate only the business part (that is, a percentage of the cost equal to the percentage of the item's use that is business-related).

There are two important stipulations regarding first-year expensing. First, the total deductions you may take in first-year expensing in any given year may not exceed $10,000. Secondly, the deductions are limited in any one year to the amount that, after all other deductions have been taken, reduces your Schedule C income to zero. You may not use first-year expensing to give yourself a loss, or increase one. You can, however, carry over the unused portion of the deduction and use it as an expense on your Schedule C during the year immediately following.

If you choose to depreciate an item over five or seven years, the depreciation deduction in any one year *may,* unlike first-year expensing, be used to create or increase a loss on your Schedule C for that year.

Any travel expenses directly connected with your business (for instance, the cost of your hotel, plane fare, taxis, and tips for a trip to New York to see your book publisher) are 100 percent deductible. (One exception: travel on a cruise ship qualifies for only a partial deduction. See Publication 463, *Travel, Entertainment, and Gift Expenses,* for details.) The cost of trips in your own car is also deductible in full, and you have the option of taking either a standard deduction per mile traveled or deducting the actual cost of gas, tolls, parking, and other related expenses, plus a depreciation allowance. If you do take a deduction for business use of your car, you must also fill out a part of Form 4562, *Depreciation and Amortization.* See Publication 917, *Business Use of Your Car,* for details.

The cost of commuting to and from a regular job is not deductible; the transportation costs associated with a local freelance assignment are. The cost of *meals* (including tips) while traveling is only 80 percent deductible, though costs of transportation to and from meals remain 100 percent deductible. The cost of any other legitimate business meals or entertainment (for example, when you discuss business with a colleague or agent over drinks and dinner and pick up part or all of the tab) is also 80 percent deductible. The option of a standard daily meal allowance, offered in previous years, is no longer available.

Travel and meal expenses are not deductible if you take a trip primarily for pleasure. If you take a trip for both business and pleasure reasons, you can deduct only the business part (the amount the trip would have cost if you had performed only the business activities). If you take a spouse, child, and/or friend with you on a business trip, only your own expenses are deductible.

It is important to remember that, if you are honest, the worst the IRS can do is claim that you owe them more than you have paid, or that you have taken larger or more deductions than you are entitled to. So if you honestly feel a deduction is legitimate, take it. If the IRS says no to all or part of it, you simply owe them the additional tax, plus a percentage of that additional money as penalty and interest. And if you feel the IRS's disallowance of your claim is incorrect or unjustified (or if anything the IRS does to you seems unfair or askew), you can appeal and argue the decision higher up within the IRS. The IRS has a Problem Resolution Office to deal with such cases; and you can go even higher than this, if necessary. People do sometimes win such appeals.

The fact is that there are a great many (deliberately) gray areas in federal tax laws, and in the IRS regulations that spring from them. As one midlevel IRS worker told me, "What one auditor will permit another one will disallow." So if you genuinely feel you're right and the IRS is wrong, don't hesitate to take the matter to the next level of decision-makers.

Your profit or loss listed on Schedule C should now be listed on Schedule SE and on your 1040 form. If you have filled out more than one Schedule C (for more than one general area of business activity), add up all your net profits and/or losses and put this total on the appropriate lines in the forms indicated above.

For more information on Schedule C in general, order IRS Publication 535, *Business Expenses*.

SCHEDULE SE

When you have properly filled out Schedule C and triple-checked it to make sure everything about it is correct, you are ready to move on to Schedule SE, Computation of Social Security Self-Employment Tax. This tax must be paid to the federal government in addition to your federal income tax.

If you are someone else's employee, social security (FICA) is automatically withheld from your paychecks. But if you are self-employed, either partly or entirely, you must pay social security tax on all your self-employment income. Schedule SE will determine exactly how much FICA you owe.

Schedule SE is fairly straightforward and simple, and the printed instructions should tell you everything you need to know. For most writers it is a simple matter of taking your total profit (net income) from Schedule C and multiplying it by the percentage the IRS gives you on Schedule SE. The result is your social security tax on your self-employment income.

Note: If your income from writing (after Schedule C deductions) is less than a certain amount ($400 in 1987), you do not have to pay any social security tax on this income or file Schedule SE. If you show a loss for your writing activity for the year, you of course pay no social security tax. However, although a loss on Schedule C can reduce your federal income tax on your nonwriting income, it *cannot* entitle you to a refund of any social security tax withheld from your salary during the previous year. That is, once any social security tax has been withheld from your salary, it is gone from your hands forever. The best Schedule SE can do for you is reduce your *additional* social security tax to zero.

However, in the case where you are making quarterly payments of estimated tax (see "Estimated Tax" below), you are entitled to a refund of any federal and/or social security tax you may have overpaid during the course of the year in estimated tax payments. This gets taken care of entirely on Form 1040.

FORM 1040

After you're done with Schedule SE, you come to Form 1040, which determines the final amount you owe the IRS (or the IRS owes you). It takes into account both federal income tax and social security tax.

You can very likely fill out the 1040 using only the IRS instructions as your guide. Don't forget to deduct the personal exemption for each dependent, including yourself, from your total income.

If you are wholly or partly self-employed, you may deduct on your 1040 up to 25 percent of the cost of health insurance (or membership in an HMO or group health plan) for you, your spouse, and dependents. However, this is subject to several complicated provisions. For example, you may not take this deduction if you were eligible to participate in any subsidized health plan maintained by your or your spouse's employer, even if you chose not to participate in the plan. Furthermore, your health insurance deduction may not exceed your net self-employment earnings for the year.

Note that this deduction gets taken on Form 1040, *not* on Schedule C. For details, see the 1040 instruction booklet or Publication 535, *Business Expenses.*

ESTIMATED TAX

If you work for someone else, federal income tax, social security, and state and local income taxes are normally withheld from your salary. If you are self-employed, however, and your self-employment earnings are more than minimal, then you must do your own withholding from this income. This is called estimated tax.

If you expect a significant portion of your total income for the *current* year to be earned through self-employment (either from your writing, from nonwriting sources, or both), then you may have to file and pay estimated tax. The matter of how much you must earn from self-employment before you are required to pay estimated tax is a tad tricky. The IRS says that you should pay estimated tax if such tax will total $500 or more, or if the amount of taxes (both federal and social security) withheld from your salary will equal less than 90 percent of your total federal and social security tax bill for that year.

When filing estimated tax, you estimate in advance what your total income for the year will be. Next you figure out approximately what your total federal taxes (both federal income tax and social security) will be on that income. Then you determine how much of your total tax, if any, will be withheld during the year by employers. The taxes you expect to owe, over and above those withheld by employers, should be paid as estimated tax. This amount gets split into four quarterly payments, which you must send in, along with form 1040-ES, by the following dates: April 15, June 15, September 15, and January 15 of the following year.

Fortunately, Form 1040-ES is very easy to fill out: you simply list the amount of money you are enclosing, and send it along with your check. (Remember to write your social security number and the words "1040-ES" on your check or money order.) You are supposed to go through a *very* complicated process to figure out how much to send—but because a freelancer's income depends largely on the unpredictable judgments of editors, you should simply make your best and most honest guess. If you make more or less money in any quarter than you expected, you can simply send in a larger or smaller estimated tax payment in the next quarter.

Most states expect you to estimate your state taxes the same way, and most have the same procedures and deadlines as the IRS. Most cities and counties that levy personal income taxes also have similar procedures and deadlines. Each state, city, and county will have its own estimated tax forms, which you are required to use.

If you make quarterly estimated tax payments with Form 1040-ES, you must still file a Form 1040 (including Schedules C and SE) between January 1 and April 15, just like everyone else. This means that between January 1 and April 15 of each year, you must file *three* sets of tax returns: the standard Form 1040, covering the previous tax year, plus Schedules C and SE; and two Form 1040-ESs, one by January 15, and one by April 15.

If you fail to pay all or part of the required estimated tax, you will be charged a penalty plus interest. However, these will not be levied against you if the total of all four estimated tax payments and all the taxes withheld by the federal government from your salary during the year equals 90 percent or more of your actual tax owed. Nor will they be levied if the total of all four estimated tax payments and all taxes withheld from your salary by the federal government during the year is equal to or more than the combined amount of federal income and social security taxes you paid during the *previous* tax year. If your underpayment is, in the IRS's judgment, due to negligence on your part, you may have to pay an additional penalty.

KEOGH PLANS AND IRAS

You may be able to reduce both your federal and state taxes (and, in fact, your total income on your 1040 form) by making payments to a Keogh

(HR-10) plan. This option is open only to people who are partly or entirely self-employed.

A Keogh is a retirement plan—you are in effect setting up your own pension plan for your later years. Some or all of your contributions to a Keogh plan are deductible from your *total income* on your 1040, *not* from your self-employment income on Schedule C. Certain limits and restrictions apply, and you cannot take any Keogh deductions if you show a net loss on Schedule C for the year (though of course you may still make payments to a Keogh plan).

You can also, if you wish, put money in an IRA, instead of *or in addition to* a Keogh. IRAs are open to both self-employed and nonself-employed people. IRA contributions are deductible from your total income on your 1040 *under certain circumstances,* even if you are also deducting Keogh contributions. However, there is also a limit to the amount you can deduct in any given year for IRA contributions.

The rules for both IRAs and Keoghs are rather complicated. Publication 560, *Self-Employed Retired Plans (Keoghs),* and Publication 590, *Individual Retirement Accounts (IRAs),* are helpful. However, if you are interested in either form of retirement plan, you should talk to a professional tax preparer and/or financial planner.

AWARDS

If you win a literary award, you must normally pay federal income tax— but not social security tax—on the award money. Most states and some localities also tax this income. Prizes and awards, including those of a literary nature, should *not* be listed on Schedule C or Schedule SE. Any award money should be listed only on Form 1040, under the heading "Other Income."

Awards of plaques, certificates, and other awards which have little or no monetary value are not taxable.

GRANTS, FELLOWSHIPS, AND SCHOLARSHIPS

Grants and fellowships may or may not be taxable. Some may be *partly* taxable. The IRS regulations on fellowships and grants are complicated and detailed; each grant or fellowship is examined individually, and a determination of taxability is made on a case-by-case basis. For more information call the IRS, or order its Publication 520, *Scholarships and Fellowships.* Tax regulations differ among the IRS, state tax bureaus, and local tax bureaus. A particular grant or fellowship may be partly or entirely taxable by one of these agencies but not by another.

TIPS FOR SALARIED WRITERS

If you are a part- or full-time salaried employee, and if (and only if) you choose to itemize your personal deductions on Schedule A rather than take the standard deduction, you may deduct certain expenses related to your job. In general, the same expenses that self-employed writers may deduct on Schedule C may be deducted on your Schedule A, and the same guidelines and limitations apply. You will need to file Form 2106, *Employee Business Expenses,* as well as Schedule A.

You may not deduct any amount for which you have been reimbursed by your employer; if you have been partially reimbursed for an expense, you may deduct only the unreimbursed portion.

Furthermore, deductions of unreimbursed business expenses are limited to the extent that they exceed 2 percent of your adjusted gross income for the year. For example, if your adjusted gross income is $19,000 and your unreimbursed business expenses total $670, you can deduct only $290 of those expenses.

Note that if you are both a freelancer and a salaried employee, you may file both schedules A and C and deduct allowable expenses on each (though of course you may not deduct the same expense more than once).

For details on deducting business expenses for a salaried job, order IRS Publication 463.

EXTENSIONS

If you feel you will not be able to file your taxes by April 15, get Form 4868 from the IRS, and file it—the sooner the better, but no later than April 15. Form 4868 is a simple form, and filling it out and sending it to the IRS by April 15 grants you an automatic four-month extension in filing your 1040 and other appropriate forms and schedules. (Note: you *must* file Form 4868 by April 15; forms filed after that date will not be honored, except in unusual circumstances.) You do not need any reason or excuse to file Form 4868, nor will you be asked for one. Remember that if you file Form 4868 with the IRS, you will still need to get separate extensions from your state and local agencies. Not all states and localities grant equivalent extensions, though many do.

Although filing Form 4868 grants you a four-month extension for *filing* your federal income and social security tax forms, it does not extend the April 15 deadline for *paying* your taxes without penalties. You must estimate your total federal income and social security taxes (over and above those withheld by employers and/or already paid through estimated tax) and, if you owe additional tax, you must enclose approximate payment of that additional tax when you file your Form 4868.

If you need an additional extension beyond August 15, contact your local IRS office; you will need to file Form 2688. Additional extensions are sometimes granted, but only for good reason, and normally no extension is granted beyond October 15.

If you file your taxes later than April 15, or later than the date specified in your extension, you will be penalized a percentage of the tax you owe (5 percent in 1987) for each month or portion of a month that you file late, with a maximum penalty of 25 percent of the tax due. If you file more than sixty days late, however, the minimum penalty will be $100, or 100 percent of the tax due, whichever is less. Therefore, it is always to your benefit to *file* by the deadline, even if you cannot pay all (or even any) of your tax on time.

If you pay part or all of your taxes late, you will be charged a penalty of ½ to 1 percent of the tax due for each month or portion of a month it is late (maximum penalty: 25 percent), plus interest on the late tax.

If both the late filing and the late payment penalties apply for any month, the combination of the two is limited to 5 percent of the unpaid tax for each month or portion of a month that filing and payment are late.

If you are a U.S. citizen or resident, or are in the U.S. military, and are out of the United States and Puerto Rico on April 15, you are automatically granted a two-month extension to file and pay your previous year's taxes. You need not file any form; however, you should attach a note to your return explaining that you were out of the country on April 15. You will not be charged a penalty for late filing or late payment, but you *will* be charged interest on any tax paid later than April 15. You can get an additional two-month extension to *file* (but not to pay) your taxes by filing Form 4868 by June 15.

PAYMENTS TO OTHERS FOR SERVICES
OR PUBLICATION RIGHTS

If you have made payments to any one person or firm of $600 (this figure may change from year to year; it is current for 1987) or more during the previous calendar year, you must report these payments to the IRS.

Payments made, for example, to editors, writers, critics, attorneys, illustrators, and photographers for their services should be reported; so should payments totalling $600 or more made to any one person or firm for the right to publish written or visual work in a project of your own. If you collaborate with someone on a project, accept full payment from the publisher for it, and in turn pay your collaborator his or her share, you must also report these payments if they total $600 or more during the calendar year. (You will of course also deduct these payments as business expenses on your Schedule C.)

To report these payments, send the IRS a copy of form 1099-MISC for each person or firm involved *by the last day of February* following the year for which you are reporting. Send a copy of this same form to the person or firm, *by January 31.*

All the 1099-MISC forms that you send to the IRS should be sent together, in the same envelope. One copy of another form, Form 1096, must accompany the IRS copies of the 1099s; no 1096s need be sent to your payees.

Both Form 1099-MISC and Form 1096 are quite brief, and easy to fill out. The 1099-MISC requires the social security number (or employer identification number) of the payee, so be sure to get this information when you make the original deal.

When ordering these forms from the IRS, also order the unnumbered publication *Instructions to Filers of Forms 1099, 1098, 5498, 1096, and W-2G.*

SOME FINAL WORDS

For the most part, your state and local taxes are determined by the figures on your federal income tax forms, particularly Form 1040.

However, each state and locality has its own unique tax regulations, forms, deadlines, and procedures. Some of the states and localities tax certain kinds of income that the IRS does not, and vice versa; some states' and localities' rules regarding deductions (both business and personal) and extensions differ from those of the federal government.

The best of luck next April.

Index

About the Author

A successful freelance writer, Scott Edelstein has also worked as an editor for two book imprints, several magazines, and a newspaper. He has been a writing tutor, freelance editor, ghostwriter, literary agent, instructor of writing at several colleges and universities, and writer-in-residence in public schools. In addition, he has been a literary consultant since 1980— privately, for a university, and in association with The Loft, one of the largest writers' centers in the world.

His previous books include *Surviving Freshman Composition, College: A User's Manual, Putting Your Kids Through College, Future Pastimes,* and four ghostwritten titles. Over eighty of his articles and short stories have appeared in magazines, including *Writer's Yearbook, Glamour, The Artist's Magazine, Essence,* and *Ellery Queen's Mystery Magazine.* He has written a monthly column for *Writer's Digest* magazine since 1985.

He lives in Minneapolis, Minnesota, where he continues to do freelance writing, editing, and consulting.